Tales From My Life

Ignaz Bing

Tales From My Life

Memoirs of a merchant
and cave explorer
in Germany
1840-1918

Translated from German by
Carolin Sommer

Every effort has been made to ensure that any reproduction of copyrighted materials has been done so with the permission of the original creator or publisher, and I am especially grateful to Horst and Heidrun Wagner as well as the municipal archive of Gunzenhausen and the city archive of Nuremberg for granting permission to reprint some of their photographs. In some cases it has not been possible to contact the original creator or publisher prior to publication. However, the editor will be glad to rectify any errors or omissions at the earliest opportunity.

ISBN 978-0-9563370-1-6

First Edition published 2013 by Inspiring Young Minds Publishing.

Edited and translated from German by Carolin Sommer.

Contents

Foreword, Or: A Note From The Translator

When Ignaz Bing sat down at the beginning of the 20th century to record his memoirs (although he would probably never have called them anything as grand as that), he did it for his children and grandchildren. Little did he know then that a hundred years on, his descendants would still be just as interested in his life and experiences, nor that they would no longer be speaking German and instead need the services of a translator to understand them. It has therefore been an enormous privilege and joy to be entrusted with the task of making Ignaz Bing's story available for his great-, great-great- and great-great-great-grandchildren.

Ignaz Bing's story is that of a life lived to the full. Without the benefit of an academic education, he became one of Bavaria's most successful businessmen, employing thousands of people and selling his products all over the world. He was extremely well-read, and his interest in natural history led him to discover one of Germany's most beautiful and impressive dripstone caves, still named after him today. Ignaz Bing loved to travel and explore treasures of art and nature, but nothing surpassed his love for "his" Streitberg. He was a very generous and charitable man, donating large amounts of money to the local natural history society and any friend in need. He led his life according to the great poet Goethe's words "Let man be a noble creature, helpful and good." His personal credo makes an inspiring read that would be refreshing to find in the mission statements of companies today. Reading Ignaz's words, one cannot help but be touched by his unshaken belief in the good in people and his unwaveringly hopeful outlook. His fierce patriotism is heart-breaking, knowing what we know of the future that lay ahead for his family, his fellow Jews and the country that he loved.

Throughout these pages, Ignaz Bing insists that his writing has no literary value; he dictated his thoughts directly to his secretary who subsequently typed them up. Apart from the odd scribble in the margins of the manuscripts, there was little revision, and the style is very much "from the horse's mouth". In this translated edition, I have endeavoured to follow this style as much as readability allowed in order to let the author's voice be heard through the English text, although his often page-long sentences benefitted from being broken up in places. I have also left intact all references to "today", such as in "a shoe shop that is now Moritz Fay's". Whenever I did comment on the current time, I did so in a footnote, never in the text. Furthermore, I have used footnotes widely to comment on references to places, historical events or literary works that might not be obvious to readers less familiar with German geography, history or literature than Ignaz's originally intended audience. For this reason, I have also included several maps, photographs and some historical background in this edition to further explain the context.

Carolin Sommer, February 2013

Timeline

1840	Ignaz Bing is born in Memmelsdorf.
1847	His mother, Babette Tuchmann, dies.
ca. 1850	His father marries Henriette Birgstein.
1853	The family moves to Gunzenhausen.
1854	Ignaz Bing moves to Ansbach to attend a vocational college.
1855	Graduates as a "commis" and spends several weeks travelling, looking for an apprenticeship.
1855/6	Begins apprenticeship at J. Em. Wertheimber's Bank in Fürth (unpaid).
1856-8	Works as commis (clerk) for B. Berneis' haberdashery business in Fürth.
1858-9	Spends six months working for a former rabbi in Aschaffenburg.
1859	Returns to Fürth to a position of a clerk.
ca. 1860	Begins working as a travelling salesman in Wallerstein in the Ries.
1862	Resigns due to ill health. Travels to the spa town of Streitberg for the first time to recover. Returns to Gunzenhausen to work in his father's hop business.
1863	Ignaz founds a wholesale hardware business in his own name; official owner is his father, Salomon Bing.
1864	Along with his brother Adolf, Ignaz establishes the *Gebrüder Bing* company.
1865	Ignaz moves to Nuremberg and rents a small shop in Karolinenstrasse 14; facilitated by a relaxation of trade regulations, they soon expand into new sectors.

1866 Austro-Prussian war; as an ally of Austria, Bavaria is on the losing side. Nuremberg is invaded by Prussian troops.

1867 Marries Rosa Schloss, who dies five weeks later.

1869 Marries Ida Ottenstein.

1870 Birth of Fritz Bing.

1870/1 Franco-Prussian war. King of Prussia, Wilhelm I, is proclaimed Emperor ("Kaiser") of the newly formed German Reich; Otto von Bismarck becomes the new Chancellor. Laws are introduced stipulating the uniform use of metric weights and measures across the newly formed Germany. With clever foresight, the *Gebrüder Bing* company introduces a product line of weights and measures and experiences a vast upturn due to the subsequent surge in demand.

1872 Birth of Max Bing, who dies 4 months later.
Bavaria enacts the Federal Law granting Jews full emancipation, one of the last German state to do so.

1873 Birth of Bertha Bing. Financial Crash in Munich. Ignaz travels to Paris.

1875 Birth of Frieda Bing.

1876 Fritz Bing, Ignaz's eldest son, dies aged 6 years.

1877 Birth of Anna Bing.

1878 Purchase of the large site in Marienstrasse, including a warehouse. Beginning of tin toy production.

1879 Birth of Siegmund Bing.

1880 Birth of Stefan Bing. The company starts manufacturing in their own name.

1882 First Bavarian National Exhibition; the company's attendance is a great success.

1883 Ignaz Bing takes over sole leadership of the company.

1885 The company has 500 employees.

1886 Birth of Marie Bing.

1891 25th anniversary of the *Gebrüder Bing* Company; they now have 800 employees.

	Ignaz Bing is awarded the title of "Kommerzienrat", receives the Silver Citizen's Medal from the city of Nuremberg and is made honorary citizen of Streitberg and Grünhain.
1895	The company is turned into a joint-stock company, its new name is *Nuremberg Metal and Lacquer Wares Manufacturers, previously Gebrüder Bing* Company *plc.*
	Ignaz is awarded the title of "Königlich Bayerischer Kommerzienrat" and the medal of St. Michael by the King of Bavaria.
1896	Ignaz travels to Venice with his daughters Anna and Frieda as well as his niece Lina.
1899	Buys *Villa Marie* in Streitberg.
1900	Donates a well to the town and people of Streitberg.
1903	Finances the electrification of Streitberg.
1905	Discovers the *Bing-Höhle.*
1906	The company has 3000 employees.
	Ignaz travels to Sylt for the first time with his sons Stefan and Siegmund.
ca. 1907	Travels to the Adriatic Sea with daughters Anna and Marie.
	The *Bing-Höhle* is fitted with lights.
ca. 1908	Ignaz returns to Sylt with Herr Dr Sommer.
1908	Hosts Prince Ludwig of Bavaria and his entourage at *Villa Marie* in Streitberg.
	Travels to Italy with his nieces Olga and Aennie Hirsch around this time.
ca. 1909	Travels to Nice and Italy.
1914	World War I breaks out. The company change production over to strategic war-related goods.
1915	Ignaz writes *Tales From A Merchant's Life.*
1916	Writes *My Family and Friends.*
1917	Writes *My Travels.*
1918	Ignaz dies at home in Nuremberg, aged 78.

Kings Of Bavaria

Throughout his memoirs, Ignaz Bing frequently mentions the various Kings and Princes of Bavaria, either in reference to some historical detail or when relating his personal encounters with some of them. The table below shows the different Kings and Princes ruling Bavaria during Bing's lifetime. It is included here to give context to and clarify those references.

Ludwig I	1825-1848	Abdicated in the Revolutions of 1848. *(See: Bad Brückenau)*
Maximilian II	1848-1864	Son of Ludwig I
Ludwig II	1864-1886	Son of Maximilian II. Often referred to as *Mad King Ludwig* of Neuschwanstein fame.
Otto I	1886-1913	Son of Maximilian II. He was mentally ill throughout his reign, and his functions were carried out by the following princes regent: * Luitpold of Bavaria 1886–1912 *(see: Bavarian Exhibition in 1896)* * Ludwig of Bavaria 1912–1913
Ludwig III	1913-1918	Son of Prince Luitpold. Last King of Bavaria. *(See: Lunch at Villa Marie.)*

Currency Conversion

During the 19th century, a number of different coins were in use in Bavaria, ranging from the small kreutzer to the valuable gold mark. They converted as follows:

60 kreutzers = 1 (Bavarian) gulden

1¾ guldens = 1 (Prussian) thaler

2 thalers = 3½ guldens = 6 marks

1 thaler = 3 marks

In 1873, after German unification, decimalisation was introduced across the country. Between 1873 and 1914,

35 kreutzers = 1 (German gold) mark

In 1881, 1 gold mark was the equivalent of around €16, £12 or $20 in 2012.

In 1910, 1 gold mark was the equivalent of around €13, £10 or $16 in 2012.[1]

---

[1] Conversions to recent currencies based on http://privatschule-eberhard.de/interessant/Preisindex.htm.

Maps

The German Confederation 1815-1866, incorporating amongst others the Kingdom of Prussia, the Kingdom of Bavaria and a large part of the Austrian Empire.

The German Reich 1871-1918

The City of Nuremberg, 1882

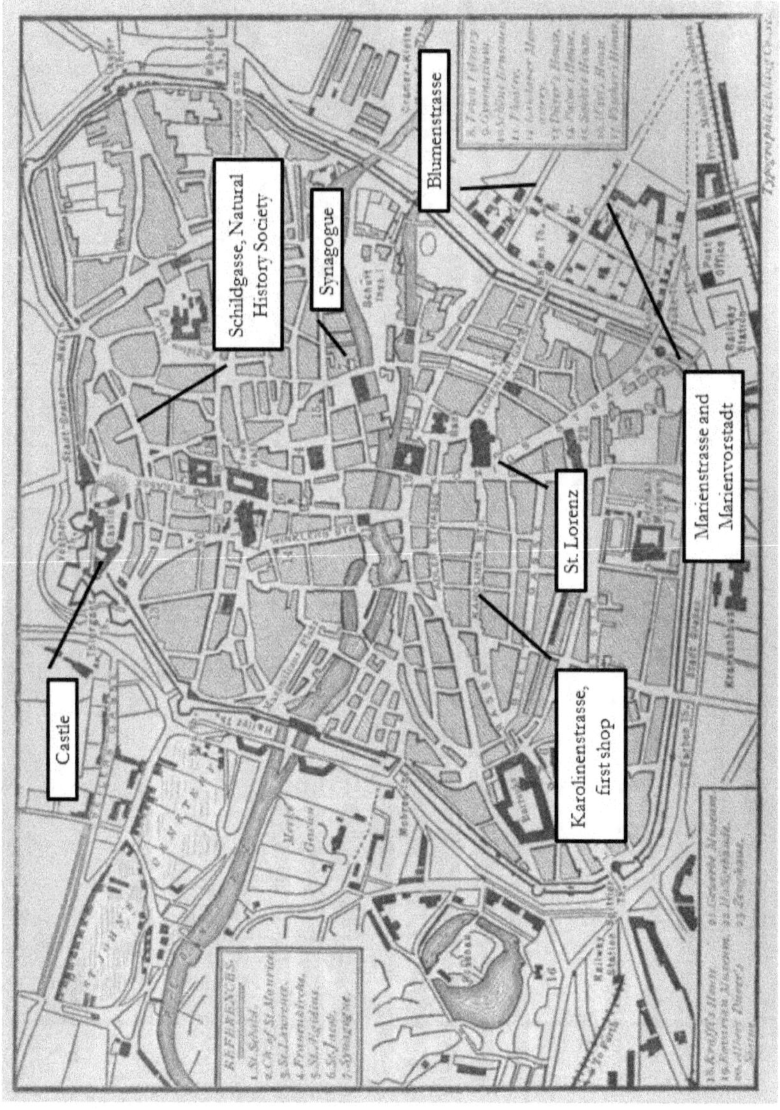

Important Cities and Places in Ignaz Bing's life
(Germany shown with post-1990 borders)

Family Tree

Babette Tuchmann b. 1814 d. 1847
m.
Salomon Bing b. 1816 d. 1878
m.
Henriette Birgstein b. 1822
Heinrich Ottenstein
m.
Ida b. 1838 d. 1882
Ignaz Bing b. 1840 d. 1918
Adolf b. 1842 d. 1915
Berthold b. 1844 d. 1910
Heinrich
Oscar
Edmund
Antonia
Seppi
Marie
m. Max Hirsch
Olga
Aenny b. 1888 d. 1970
m. Dr. Elkan
Annemarie
Ruth
Robert
Rosa Schloss d. 1867
m.
m.
Ida Ottenstein b. 1844 d. 1919
Max b. 1860 d. 1947
Karl b. 1864 d. 1886
Babette b. 1866
Anna b. 1871 d. 1892
Fritz b. 1870 d. 1876
Max b. 1872 d. 1872
Bertha b. 1873
Frieda b. 1875
Anna b. 1877 d. 1925
Siegmund b. 1879 d. 1961
Stefan b. 1880 d. 1940
Marie b. 1886
m. Heinrich Hirschmann
Ernst
Paul
Trude
m. Ludwig Bruell
Dora
Otto
m. Sigo Kuhn
m. Lotte Pickard
Marianne
m. Ida Jung
Franz
Lilli
m. Leo Benario
Irene

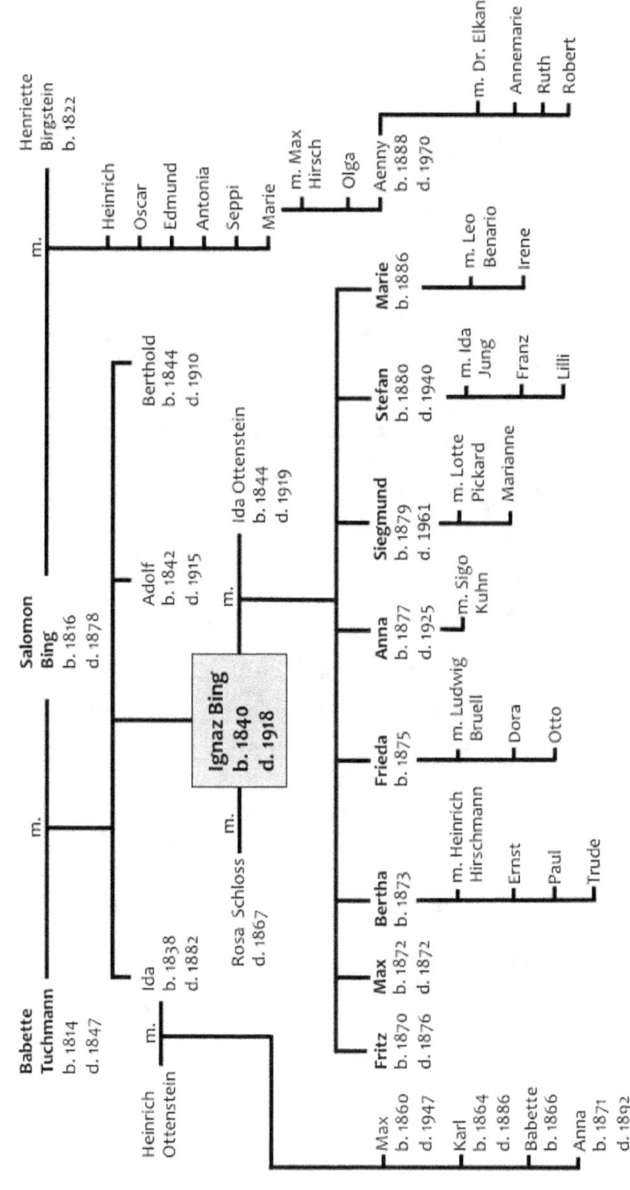

Edel sei der Mensch, hilfreich und gut.

Let Man be a noble creature, helpful and good.

J. W. von Goethe

Tales From A Merchant's Life

I came into this world on 29th January 1840 as the second child of Salomon Bing, a master-dyer in Memmelsdorf in the Itz valley. My sister Ida had been born two years earlier, on 18th February 1838. My brother Adolf followed on 18th February 1842 and my brother Berthold on 4th February 1844. My father, who was born into a large and well-respected family in Scheinfeld, a small town in the picturesque foothills of the Steiger Forest, was just 20 years old when he purchased a dyer's workshop in 1837 and married my mother Babette Tuchmann, two years his senior, from Ülfeld.

It must have been pretty hard times for the young couple to support themselves, even more so since my father's job required my mother to take an active part in the business, and over and above this, the children arrived soon and in quick succession. They dyed mainly heavy, home-made linen, light or dark blue according to the farmers' tastes, and then added simple patterns in white or yellow by hand. The soaked cloths were heavy and had to be pulled out of the troughs with the use of a pulley several times a day. When the dyeing process was finished, the cloths had to be taken off the iron hooks and dried in the air. During this process, it was my mother – I remember this very well – who carried the heavy, wet cloths, and this was not her only task.

This may well have been the root cause of the serious lung disease that befell the delicate woman, the early signs of which became apparent after the birth of my brother Berthold, and which led to her death just three years later. She died on 21st June 1847. Despite the fact that we children had very little personal contact with our mother because of her long and difficult illness, I will always remember how her cry for air rang so dreadfully from her bedroom to us children in the adjacent living room. I will also never forget how, after she passed away and our father came into our miserable bedroom calling, "Children, get up, your mother has died!", a sharp pain flashed through me. I was gripped by a deep sorrow and the need to see our dead mother once more. In the evening, I crept into the chamber where the body had been laid on the floor, and an old Jewish woman was sitting Shiva, as it is the custom. I begged her to let me see my mother's face one last time, but the woman sent me out with harsh words. For as long as I continued to live in Memmelsdorf, I harboured a deep, bitter hatred towards her.

Fig. 1 Babette Bing's tombstone © Horst und Heidrun Wagner

The next day, we four children and our father followed the coffin, which was covered with a black cloth on a cart drawn by oxen, to the cemetery, which was a long way from Memmelsdorf, where it was committed to the earth.

It goes without saying that our father, too, was deeply moved. I can still feel today how hard my mother's death was for me, even though a seven-and-a-half-year old would not usually comprehend such a situation fully. The house seemed barren to me, I stayed away from my games, and every morning and every evening I cried bitter tears during the Kaddish prayers, which were held at synagogue and which I would not have missed for the world.

After some time, the pain, which my father had always respected compassionately, lessened. I enjoyed school again and wholeheartedly rejoined the games which the youth in the country enjoy playing. But even more than these games I enjoyed reading books, any books I could get my hands on, and that included the Bible. I remember how I spent a lot of my time with a day-labourer who helped out in my father's workshop and who had a small flat in our house; the main reason being that his grown-up daughter had entrusted me with the first part of a story about a knight. I remember the name to this day, it was the brave knight "Haspa a Spada", whose wife had been kidnapped by monks and whom, with the help of his friends and mates, he tried his hardest to free. I read this book – a forgotten loan from a library - numerous times, and I would have given my little finger to find out if the noble knight eventually found his wife and punished the bold robbers. I would like to mention here that many years later I managed to find "Haspa a Spada" in the catalogue of a library and was therefore able to satisfy my curiosity.

My sister Ida, who was by now about ten years old, had to run the household with the help of a farmer's maid, and my brother Adolf and I were also called to carry out jobs in the dyer's workshop when we were not at school. We enjoyed the work, especially when our father trusted us to prepare the precious blue dye – it was indigo – in the special way. We used a copper kettle, and four or five large or small iron marbles. By rotating the kettle, the marbles would grind the violet iridescent material until all the grains had been broken up. We also derived great pleasure from taking the dyed cloths that had been rolled onto wooden pins, into the press, which was weighed down with stones, and then moving the press by ourselves.

We children benefited from the simple food and the hard work, and I don't remember ever seeing a doctor coming to the house. In spite of the hard work, my father could be very caring, and this story shows how: On a school trip, while walking from Memmelsdorf to Banz castle, my brother Adolf was carving a stick and caught me in the left eye with the tip of his knife. Nevertheless, I continued on the long walk in bright sunshine, but the eye got worse; my vision was badly impeded and showed no improvement. My father took me to a see an eye specialist in the neighbouring Coburg, and following the doctor's advice he had the largest room in our house, the living room, painted green in order to be easy on my eyes, yet at considerable personal expense.

Let me talk about my father now: He was a very handsome, charismatic gentleman with extraordinary talents, always led by his desire to educate and better himself. Every week he would bring back from his business trips to Coburg several volumes of *Meyer's Groschen-Bibliothek*[2], and then he would explain them to us

---

2 A series of cheap books, like a "Penny Library".

Fig. 2 Salomon Bernhard Bing

children in the winter evenings. This was how we developed a love of reading, and combined with attending a pretty good elementary school, it ensured that our general education was certainly not far behind what nowadays the better schools in the towns and cities are aiming for.

It was almost impossible for my father to keep the household running without the help of a woman, and so the day came when he announced that we would soon be getting a new mother. We were happy about it as we were too young to know what a new marriage meant (especially one into which the husband brings four young children). One day our father went on a trip and said that after a few days he would return, bringing our new mother[3] with him. We were just about to start preparing for the arrival of the new mother when someone came running in and shouted: "Your father is arriving with the new mother, the carriage is already on the Merzacher Hill!" We started crying with the dreadful news for we were nowhere near ready, but thankfully we managed to get ready in time and stood on the forecourt, beaming with anticipation, to greet the parents.

---

3 Henriette Birgstein.

First came the young woman, youthful, pretty and with a friendly smile. She shook each of our hands. Then came our father, who told us - after the young wife had left - to stay on the forecourt until he called us and that we must not call the young woman 'mother' straight away. He added that with time it would happen naturally that we would call her so, and that he would explain to us later why he had asked us not to. My eyes welled up with tears. I must have been the shyest of all of us when we were finally called into the room and each had to say our name. At last the mother spoke, saying that their stay in Erlangen, the place of the wedding, had been so short that she had not been able to buy us a present as she had intended. All she had to that effect were pretzels, and we were now allowed to retire. When we children were together again, my somewhat sentimental mood changed and, caused by the pretzels, I started to laugh almost happily. "Children", I said, "from now on we'll be having salted bread!"

It did not turn out quite like that, but we did experience some unwelcome limitations to our hitherto very loving relationship with our father! My father was understandably very much in love with his new wife, who was not only young and pretty but also excellent at managing the household, and it seemed as if he always wanted to apologise to her that there were already four children causing her a lot of work. In addition, the low income from the business was forcing him to make savings everywhere, something to which little attention had been paid during the motherless times.

The busy and capable housewife sometimes had to punish us for one thing or another, which did not hurt as much as when Father came back from a short trip and his first question was whether we had been good, and our mother did not answer or broke down in tears. Our father would punish us then, which was usually painful, but our anger was always directed at our new mother.

I certainly do not want to make any accusations on these pages; it was a normal relationship between a mother and her children, where mistakes were made on both sides. Our mother was really a good and hard-working woman whose life we made difficult at times, especially when we cold-heartedly, albeit unintentionally so, accused her of being cruel or thrifty when she was merely being economical because she had to. This situation declined further when a new brother arrived, and it became necessary to stretch the small income even further. I want to mention here that the relationship soon improved because we children grew up, and mother got used to us. Because of her kind words and friendliness we even grew to like her after a few years.

The dyeing business became less and less profitable, and my father tried to create some extra income by selling hops, which grew in the area. One of the reasons behind this was that my first mother came from a family where several members were highly successful in the hop trade, who today still own the most important companies in the industry and who have amassed great fortunes through their businesses. My father, too, seemed to be successful in this field, if however not to the same extent. Our household was less scanty, and our parents took the decision to sell the dyer's workshop and resettle in Gunzenhausen on the Altmühl. There were two main reasons for choosing this place: it bordered an important hop-growing region, and a teacher and family friend of my mother, had moved from her birth town to

Gunzenhausen and become an elementary teacher in the Jewish community. It is to the daughter of this teacher and Cantor Simon Ottenstein, Ida, that I have been happily married for 46 years.

It was thanks to the help of my then future father-in-law that we overcame the significant difficulties associated with the move to Gunzenhausen due to the former *Heimatrecht*[4]. Therefore one day at school we were proud to announce that we would leave Memmelsdorf shortly and move to Gunzenhausen. I was almost 13 years old then and wanted to stay in Memmelsdorf until I had celebrated my bar mitzvah and graduated from school. To enable the latter, I had to sit a solitary exam, which was to be taken in the vicarage of Memmelsdorf, supervised by pastor Pabst, who had always been very kindly disposed towards me. The subject of the essay was to express my thoughts about leaving Memmelsdorf. I have to say that the task really moved me and that I carried it out in such a way that the vicar, a dear old fellow, was moved to tears. I wrote that the town of my birth was especially dear to me because my mother's grave, up there in the quiet forest cemetery, would always remind me to never forget my *heimat*, my home. I was awarded an excellent school leaving report, which I have given to my grandson Ernst Hirschmann together with some other papers. I have often returned to Memmelsdorf to visit my birthplace and to reminisce in melancholy.

[4] Lit. "right to stay and make a home". In the days before a united Germany (1871), each community determined who was allowed to settle there. In order to move to a different town, it would have been necessary to prove that one had the means to support oneself and one's family. Having "Heimatrecht" meant that one was entitled to the same social benefits as any other citizen of that community.

The Jewish cemetery is situated on a high hill jutting out of the middle of a timber forest, surrounded by an eternal peace. Little spruces were planted in the cemetery when I was five years old, and in the many years that have passed since then they have grown into tall, magnificent trees. My descendants will piously protect the lonely grave!

Fig. 3 Jewish cemetery in Memmelsdorf
© Horst und Heidrun Wagner

My bar mitzvah[5] was a more cheerful event: My late mother's parents, who were still living in Ülfeld, permitted me to choose a present for the reception, and my paternal grandmother said she would do the same. In my childish fantasies, and also in order to impress my new hometown Gunzenhausen, I thought to ask for material for a new suit. A black velveteen coat and trousers, a

[5] Note that Ignaz writes "my confirmation" in German.

scarlet velveteen waistcoat and a light blue velvet cap. My wish was granted, and what was more my grandparents gave my younger brother Adolf the same. A not entirely untalented tailor transformed the material into the clothes I had designed, and I also had him add black borders to the velveteen coat. The cap-maker delivered the light blue headgear to my greatest satisfaction.

When we arrived in Gunzenhausen we were greeted at the station by the teacher's family, the Ottensteins, and many other curious people. Our arrival in these unusual uniforms had exactly the effect my brother and I had hoped for. In Gunzenhausen we moved into quite a magnificent flat compared to how we had lived in Memmelsdorf, and after my parents' financial situation improved, the black velveteen coat and red waistcoat suited our changed situation nicely. In Gunzenhausen we were deemed aristocrats. For a few months I attended my future father-in-law's Jewish elementary school, and I have to say that I thought him a great pedagogue. Apart from the elementary subjects, he taught us *Fröbel*[6] games outside, which not only gave us children enormous pleasure, but whose educational importance is obvious to me even today. Furthermore, it was here, during school hours and at these games, that I met my wife and learned to love and appreciate her. She was a little doll, and one of the things that made her so interesting to me was that she would spend hours sitting cross-legged on the piano in the classroom, bent over a book, reading with her slightly short-sighted eyes. Despite her

---

[6] Friedrich W. A. Fröbel (1782 –1852); a German pedagogue, a student of Pestalozzi's, who laid the foundation for modern education based on the recognition that children have unique needs and capabilities. He developed the concept of the "kindergarten". *(source: Wikipedia)*

smallness she was the cleverest pupil in the whole school, and to me the most attractive amongst all of my female classmates. We would often have quite precocious discussions, and I asked her advice in all things where I was unsure how to tackle them. As a reward for her benevolence I later took her as my wife.

When I was 14 years old, I continued my education at a vocational college in the neighbouring Ansbach. The value of this institute lay mainly in the fact that the principal also had a small business, i.e. a plain little shop with an even plainer stock of linen goods. The trick was that by attending the college one was automatically apprenticed to the company and therefore graduated from the institute one year later as a "Commis", an office clerk. The quality of the theoretical commercial training was questionable, as was the prematurely hatched status of Commis. The owner and director of the institute was a spirited and clever man, and I could think of nothing more interesting than him lecturing about one thing or another at the table. He often talked about contemporary literature, and he soon found out that not only was I the pupil who best understood him, but he could also talk with me about some of the things I had read. This was because in Ansbach I had plenty of opportunity to feed my greed for books, so I had become some sort of favourite of his. When one day my fellow pupils, who were mostly sons of Jewish cattle dealers from the neighbouring villages, accused me of not keeping the religious laws, he called me to his private office. He told me that while I was staying in his house I had to follow the house rules, which included, of course, the religious customs; on the other hand he kindly made me understand that he too believed that these customs were mere formalities, but that I wasn't to vex my fellow pupils.

Fig. 4 Gunzenhausen Synagogue and Hebrew School.
© Stadtarchiv Gunzenhausen.

The school itself did not benefit from the director's splendid qualities. Herr X was also the teacher of modern languages at the grammar school, and his work there, together maybe with his honour and concern regarding his relationship with the professors, did not seem to allow him to spend any time with the pupils at his own institution. The leadership of said institution was left to his son Feis and some other meaningless teaching assistants. This Herr Feis was a very strange man: kind to the point of weakness, soon foaming with rage, scolding and hissing like mad. Not really a bad-looking man, but at the same time with such an unkempt appearance that was frightening, he probably knew his subjects fairly well, but he did not have the means to share this knowledge with his pupils in a useful or pleasurable way. He therefore lacked any of the respect required by a teacher who wants to advance his pupils. We were naughty and laughed in his face when he was fuming and wanted to call his father for help, or when he threatened to attack one of us with clenched fists. How little respect he enjoyed can be demonstrated by the following case, in which I myself played a role: He asked who could recite a poem; I said I knew one, one by Gellert. I did know such a poem by heart and remember to this day that the first line began with "A feisty monkey". I started to recite, but I didn't say "a feisty monkey" but "a feis-ty monkey[7]". The whole school laughed, and even he grimaced a smile before he fell into a raging fit during which I deservedly had my ears boxed. We knew that due to the institution's financial situation they could ill afford to lose us so we took quite some liberties, which I regret today because the director's family was - with the one exception -

---

[7] The German title of the poem is "Ein feister Affe", where the German "feist" really means "fat" or "stout" and is rather derogative.

a kind one, and this was especially true for their four pretty daughters.

After my year-long stay in Ansbach I passed the public exam at the town council and was awarded a certificate stating that I was a fully qualified clerk, so I returned home and started looking for a suitable job. I soon lowered my expectations as I realised that my newly awarded, shining certificate was not exactly a fair representation of my newly acquired skills. After a long endeavour I was therefore happy enough to accept a voluntary placement with the respected J. Em. Wertheimber Bank of Fürth and Frankfurt. The principal, Herr Emmanuel Wertheimber, was a most extraordinary businessman, but at the same time very odd, and I had to pay for the privilege of living in his house and eating at his table with some serious inconveniences.

Herr Wertheimber was a bachelor, and a timid brother of his and I shared his flat and table with him. A pretty decent cook, who was close friends to varying degrees with almost all the "better clerks" at the office, managed his household. Her friendship proved useful to me, albeit in a totally innocent manner. When I remarked that we were being served such delicious soups, she solved the riddle by confiding in me that the good and robust taste of the broth stemmed from ingredients that might not be served, but would make good stock. These ingredients were lungs, liver and other offal. I asked if I could not be served some of these delicacies with my breakfast; a request which she most willingly granted. This is how I came to experience culinary pleasures in Wertheimber's house which far exceeded, in quality and quantity, anything I had ever sampled in my simple life before.

My principal was usually quite strict and inconsiderate, and one of his characteristics was that he tended to work until eleven o'clock or later, requiring me to be present, but I endeared myself to him with my musical skills. I could play a few popular and light pieces from opera, various dances or sentimental pieces such as "A maiden's prayer" etc., and my touching performances delighted my principal, who had no ear for music at all. This went so far that he wanted to introduce me to his sister-in-law, whom I knew to be highly musical indeed and who would only mock or smile pitifully at my performances. Week after week I knew to save myself from this danger by claiming that I still wanted to broaden my repertoire, and the poor sister-in-law never did have the pleasure of listening to my playing before I left my position shortly afterwards.

My reasoning was this: staying in this industry where I would never be able to establish myself due to my parents' modest circumstances would be highly impractical; whereas in another area I might progress more quickly as a commis or travelling salesman, and it would not be impossible that one day I might start up my own business. Herr Wertheimber was quite indignant about my leaving; less so because he was losing my services but more so because he regarded it as a disdain of my position in his house, which was quite unpaid, and also as a breach of trust, which certainly had not been my intention. He did not give me a reference either, but that was of little consequence as, after weeks of negotiations, I had already secured an interesting position with B. Berneis in Fürth.

I will add something here that happened after I had left Wertheimber's. Despite the bank's size with regard to its funds and its revenues, certain business arrangements were rather primitive. There were in Fürth a substantial number of companies in the cloth and textiles industry that often asked for so-called "wild notes". That was the name for the banknotes from Thuringia and other small countries which were always a quarter or a third of a percent cheaper than the Prussian notes. Sometimes the bank had large amounts of these to use up, and it was one of my jobs to personally call at the merchants to ask if they needed any such notes. Usually I had the relevant amount with me to hand over immediately. When I came back from these rounds I gave the accountant a little note explaining which company I had given the notes to, and the amount was then debited to that company. In my opinion the bank's mistake was that no receipt was requested from the company when their account was debited.

One day I was called back to Wertheimber's and was told that a sizeable company in Fürth was claiming a sum of 370 thalers was missing in their accounts because apparently they had never received it. The blame fell indirectly on me, suggesting that I had never delivered the notes or had embezzled them. I was obviously very embarrassed and could only state the truth, which was that whatever I had reported as delivered to the accountant I had actually delivered to that particular company.

There followed a court case, which found that the company in question did not even keep a proper cashbook, and that anyone, whether they were entitled to do so or not, would sometimes make notes in their so-called cashbook in pencil. Then I was asked to give evidence. I did so according to the truth in the presence of two barristers and one very distinguished judge. Afterwards, the crafty wholesale dealer stepped forward and asked permission to ask me a question. It was of course his right, and so he asked me to explain why I was no longer at Wertheimber's and why I had been let go. At first I felt awkward about the question, but I wanted to answer it right away and quickly asked the judge if I might be permitted to ask the interrogator a question in return. Permission was granted. I then said that I had not been let got but that I had left Wertheimber's on my own accord and explained the reasons why. When this was done I posed my counter-question by asking the wholesale dealer for information as to why his cashbook was kept in such an improper and unclear manner and why the entries were not made by a certified commis but by anyone, and in pencil. The judge and the barristers laughed heartily, and even the Public Prosecutor said literally and with a smile on his face, "The boy is quite right". The textiles magnate was not only shown up but lost the case too.

Many years later, Wertheimber and I both enjoyed the memory of this event from my youth when I referred to it in a reply to his letter congratulating me on the 25th anniversary of our company and my coinciding appointment as Kommerzienrat[8], in which he also highlighted the important connection between my company and his bank.

So to the horror of my friends, I resigned from the respected bank and started offering my services to B. Berneis, Co. The haberdashery business was located in Helmgasse in Fürth, in an ugly building, and the office and the shop were no bigger than a

---

[8] Pronounced "Comm-AIR-tsee-yen-RAHT", roughly: Councillor of Commerce. A rare title, and a great honour, conferred by the Prince Regent of Bavaria during the German Reich, usually awarded to important personalities of industry to recognise their substantial contribution to the common good.

large living-room. In the front room, i.e. the shop, Frau Berneis sat enthroned on a large chair, and, as long as there were no patrons in the shop, usually knitting; I have to say that we had as much discipline and respect for her as we had for our principal. When I say "we", I mean an apprentice and one or two sons of the Berneis family. The business was a pretty good one, and the items for sale were collectively known as "mercery goods". We stocked all types of knitting yarns, sewing threads, strings, tapes etc and sold them at a good price to resellers, usually peddlers.

Herr Berneis was an exquisitely educated businessman of high rank. He had married Frau Berneis, a widow who brought four children, three sons amongst them, into the marriage, and he was very particular about their upbringing. Their marriage brought forth three more children, two sons and a daughter. I would like to point out that even after I left their business I stayed close friends with all of the sons, and still am to this day, with all those who are still alive. Herr Berneis, who had been an accountant for a large company in Fürth did not understand the industry as well as his wife did, so that sometimes they had small differences of opinion, but due to Frau Berneis' loving and understanding manner they never got serious. Herr Berneis also used to take long strolls during opening times; he often stayed away from the shop for hours because he knew that his clever, business-minded wife complemented him extremely well in practical things, especially sales. I soon found my way and must say that despite the simple and almost petty manner that resides in the industry I enjoyed working there, especially since the business moved to much bigger premises in a good location a year later.

While looking through some old papers I chanced upon my reference from Herr Berneis, which I have copied here:

> *"Herr Ignaz BING from Gunzenhausen held the position of commis in my business from August 1856 until August 1858, leaves said business today in order to further educate himself in foreign parts. I had every cause to be very satisfied with his commercial and practical performance, and I am no less happy to confirm that he distinguished himself in the main virtues, namely being loyal, hard-working and honest, in the truest sense of the word. Wishing him all the best for a prosperous future I am glad to certify the above, verify the present with my seal and confirm it with my own signature."*
>
> *Fürth, 23rd August 1858 – signed B. Berneis*

After I had been with Berneis for almost two years, I was overcome by a great yearning to leave the town and my position. Life in Fürth, i.e. life as it was lived by most of the young clerks, traders and shopkeepers, did not satisfy me. True, I did have some good friends, and among them were some whom I did not just have true affection for but whom I also held in the highest regard. What revolted me were habits that came with being a merchant, even though in general the merchants of Fürth could indeed be deemed sophisticated, this was mainly due to their mastery of modern languages. Among those habits, however, was spending long hours sitting in coffee-houses and the habitual playing of card games. Rarely did a group come together to strive for a higher purpose such as education, and it was only after I returned to Fürth later on that I was able to initiate such endeavours in a group.

I was looking for a new position and found such a one in Aschaffenburg. My experiences there were original in so many respects that I shall describe them here in quite some detail. The owner of the shop – which, according to the list sent me after my engagement in the company, traded in mercery goods and cheap jewellery amongst other wares, a fact which made the position very attractive to me since I had the necessary factual knowledge – was a former rabbi. I shall not delve here into the reasons as to why he had given up his holy office and opened up a shop; I will only state as much that his divorced wife was living with a brother of hers in Gelnhausen. This brother was a hunchback and received, in spite of the preceding events, goods from his brother-in-law to sell on commission. After he had come to Aschaffenburg once to purchase goods in person, I maliciously named him the "leaning shareholder of Gelnhausen", which raised a cheer from my only colleague, a young clerk from the Westerwald[9] mountains.

My new position came with a salary of 100 guilders per annum and free board and lodgings. Upon my arrival in Aschaffenburg, I was greeted by my new principal with friendly words, and I found him a truly spirited and original individual. He introduced me to his son and successor, a young gentleman who, I soon discovered, very much enjoyed stimulating his intellect, which he expressed by writing theatre reviews for an Aschaffenburg newspaper, amongst other things. The young man, however, had a slovenly appearance and other properties which, if one did not know him very well, had to lead one to misjudge his character. He talked very loudly and in the so-called "Aschaffenburg

[9] A low mountain range on the right bank of the River Rhine.

dialect", and when he came to see me in Nuremberg later on and I introduced him to my circle of friends, he caused me some embarrassment. Yet on the whole, the young man was, as mentioned before, well educated, not uninteresting and of honest character.

There was also a daughter, who - given how old she was - could have been the one appointed to manage this entirely leaderless household. She really was quite a clever girl, who had read much, but who, having grown up without a sensible mother's support, was totally incapable of thinking her way into womanly duties. She preferred to spend hours on the shop floor, yawning, without carrying out any tasks relating to the business. Sometimes she would hold a book, next, attempt a drawing, but really she preferred to yawn and do nothing at all. It was no help either when her father sarcastically praised her for arriving at the shop at eleven o'clock in the morning. She paid no heed to her father's reproach and could not care less about the tasks of the business or the household. For my part, I had earned the right, and I don't know how, to give her a piece of my mind. Not exactly to her face, but by telling her, in the presence of her brother and my colleague, how in my previous employments the young ladies embraced their tasks, and how the family members treated each other with love and kindness. In my conversations I even referred to her cleanliness, her hair, how she cared for her hands, in short anything I considered in need of reform with the young lady. She understood me well and would laugh, saying that I should not lecture her; she would not change, and it was none of my business anyway. My colleague from the Westerwald, a blond, shy young man from a respected family whose parents had sent him for an apprenticeship to our principal - a business connection of theirs- enjoyed these things immensely, but he would only express his joy with a little smile. Later in the evenings, when we would spend an hour together, he would laugh out loud at my courage for making these indirect, foolish remarks to the principal's daughter, and he would love it when the next opportunity for these arose. There was no shortage of such opportunities.

On one side, the house bordered – quite tellingly – the road named "Duck pond", and sadly the name befitted the whole of the interior of the house, too: dark rooms that had not seen a painter or a paper-hanger for twenty years or more; the disgusting conditions in the kitchen and other rooms filled one with such revulsion that one could not appreciate the meals properly – had there been anything to appreciate. No cook stayed for more than a fortnight, and it was not due to their treatment since all the cooks, no matter how great or little their skills, were quite supreme. It was because no order-loving girl could get used to such an abandoned and greasy household. Alas, for us the constant change was of great significance and benefit since during the first few days at least the new cook would always try especially hard to prepare a nice meal. How unwillingly I ate the otherwise plentiful food may be explained with the following example: I used to line my pockets with cardboard and would often stash some of the repulsive dishes in them until I had an opportunity to get rid of them somewhere. The only things I could eat with any appetite were my 10 o'clock sandwich and the afternoon tea.

Similar conditions dominated the room that had been made available for me and my colleague from the Westerwald to share.

One could not imagine anything more unreal or, in fact, more horrible. The beds were of poor quality and dirty; as soon as it got warm, bugs arrived in abundance. Furthermore, in the room there was a barrel of matches that were no longer useable, and every night in the darkness there rose from the barrel a blue-ish, glowing smoke, which, heavy and stinging, settled on the lungs. They were too thrifty to remove the stuff and somehow had lived in the hope that one day the tinder would, all by itself, become usable again. Every time my colleague and I stood by the window we looked longingly at the flat in the house opposite where a poor tailor lived, with a clean room and crisp white sheets at his disposal. We had a burning desire for such comforts, and we would have loved to swap lodgings with the tailor!

The shop business was novel; we only served retailers, and it was mostly people from the rural Spessart[10] population that were amongst our preferred and best customers. We had coined a greeting for these kind of customers, and every time a farmer from the Spessart entered the shop, the person nearest to him, i.e. the principal, the principal's son, the Westerwalder or me, approached him with the words "How can I help you, man of God?" We repeated this phrase several times each day. When there were no customers, we had absolutely nothing to do, never a letter to write or a pen to dip into ink. Instead, once the old Herr had left for his regular daily stroll with his constant companion, a pipe that reached to the ground, Neuburger Jr drilled us as soldiers. He enjoyed nothing more than to watch us, each

---

[10] A low mountain range in north-western Bavaria and southern Hesse.

shouldering a walking stick, marching in step through the shop until another customer would interrupt the military exercise.

In the summer, the shop was open continuously – except for the short lunch break - from six o'clock in the morning until nine o'clock in the evening, and in the winter from eight in the morning until nine in the evening. The only distraction from this boring and unregulated work was the occasional attempt at cleaning some equipment that was covered with ten years' worth of dust and grime. During opening hours, no-one was allowed to leave the premises even for a quarter of an hour, even when the business was dead quiet and most yawningly boring. Furthermore, going out after nine o'clock was only allowed on two evenings a week. We were most upset by the arrangement for Sundays, the free use of which could have been a source of great pleasure in the wonderful surroundings of Aschaffenburg. The shop opened at eleven o'clock in the morning, so there was hardly time for a long walk. By this time, twenty or more Spessart farmers were waiting for the shop to open, and the arrangement was, despite many fierce arguments, never changed.

Then one day I received a letter from Fürth, which I missed terribly and to which I still felt very connected through vivid correspondence with my many old friends. In this letter I was offered an annual salary of 250 guilders with free cost and lodgings. The company in question was not a large one, but their inadequate financial means had increased thanks to a substantial lottery win, and the owner, thus supported, intended to modernise his enterprise accordingly.

It was thanks to the owner's son, who was a friend of mine, that I had been approached. I met with my principal and urged him to release me from our agreement which bound me to his business for another six months or so, and to allow me to accept the, in my circumstances, excellent offer. However, he stubbornly insisted on the contract; I would have to stay the remainder of the term and I could not for the life of me convince him that he was doing me an injustice. Then, like a sign from above, I received a letter from my brother Adolf who was working in our parents' business in Gunzenhausen and who was yearning to come out and see the world. I have to add here that my parents' financial situation had improved significantly in the meantime and that my brother usually accompanied my father on his business travels. Therefore he did not want to stay away from home for longer than the beginning of the hop season, and it would be in his and my interest if my principal permitted my brother to take on my outstanding duties, like some form of bail as celebrated by Schiller. I presented this plan most animatedly and was able to convince my principal that the forced relationship which he was asking of me would neither be in his nor my own interest, and that my proposal was the best solution for all involved. I did feel guilty that, even though it was for a limited time only, I was causing my brother to take up a position, the strange circumstances of which were indescribable. I had accepted those circumstances with a sense of humour, I saw things in the most positive light, I often spoke my mind with sarcasm, and strangely I had not lost the good will of my principal and his family for one moment. My brother arrived and was accepted, and I moved happily on towards my beloved Fürth.

My clothes were in a miserable state. I was proud of not needing my parents' support, but, with an annual salary of 100 guilders, this was only achieved by making great sacrifices. I would not and could not ask my parents for anything. Their family had grown, and there were now no less than ten children to look after, and I was the only one of them who did not need any support. This, however, did have some drastic consequences. For example, when I accepted the position in Aschaffenburg in November, I did not have an overcoat. I was forced to send to my parents for such a piece of clothing, and I intended to repay the relevant amount later. My mother found a solution. She had a tailor make a so-called Raglan coat from an old, light-green coat of hers. I regarded the siskin-green object that was sent me with some mistrust, as my penchant for brightly coloured clothes had faded considerably since the days of my confirmation. My fear that my new Raglan coat might cause an unwanted stir was not unfounded. We were given Christmas Day off, and my colleague Hugo, the Westerwalder, and I had arranged to travel to the neighbouring Darmstadt, where we had not been before. The "siskin-green one" would be worn for the first time. We had not even reached Aschaffenburg station before my colleague and I noticed that people were looking at us, laughing. I immediately sensed that my Raglan was the cause of their amusement. I took it off straight away as I did not want to cause a sensation in Darmstadt either. Consequently I was miserably cold and from then on had to make do without the Raglan as well as I could on those occasions, rare though they were, when we ventured out into the wintry cold.

When the initial joy of returning to my friends, and under such favourable circumstances, had subsided, I began to worry about how I was to present myself there. I had been paid half of the 100 guilders, and there was hardly enough left of it to pay for the journey to Fürth and to purchase a few absolute necessities. But a youth does not ponder these things for long, and I thought that I was sure to find a solution once I was in Fürth. And that is exactly what happened. A friend of mine had credit with a busy tailor there and promised to introduce me to him. My first outing in Fürth was to see this helpful clothes-artist, accompanied by my friend. I truthfully explained my circumstances; he trusted me and gave me credit for a suit and a summer overcoat. In my gushing gratitude I gave him free choice as to which material to use. For the overcoat he decided that I should have material that resembled a zebra skin. I feared that with a coat from this cloth I would steer towards a new Raglan-astrophe. It was not quite that bad, though, partly because, if the worst comes to the worst a summer overcoat can always be carried over the arm, but I did indeed have to put up with the odd remark concerning my original overcoat. I hasten to add that I did pay my debts on time and that I was so grateful that I kept in touch with the good master tailor as long as I was in Fürth and long after that. After many, many years, when we had both grown old, we once met again and were delighted to talk about the old times and about the striped, zebra-like summer coat.

So I was back in Fürth. I carried out the tasks assigned to me in my new employment with ease and relative success. The principal, an extremely kind gentleman who used to be some kind of teacher and studied the Talmud, lacked all initiative. The intention to improve the business, which was urgently needed, was fulfilled merely by moving to bigger premises. The company stuck to the same field, which was a badly performing retail and small wholesale business selling cleaning and fashion goods to milliners. Therefore they also employed a travelling salesman, an elegant young man whose popularity with the light-hearted milliners, however, resulted more in personal friendships than substantial orders. Nevertheless, the principal did not dare reprimand him since he, despite being lazy, still managed to use his personal influence to introduce a good connection or two when he chose to do so. The principal's wife - and it was the custom in Fürth that the lady of the house also worked or was at least present in the business - was a good woman who never uttered a harsh or unkind word, and she was very fond of me. Sometimes I wished she had shown her kindness in different ways; for example when we had sauerkraut for our meals, she used to give me a small glass of blueberry schnapps so that I would not suffer from the "heavy food" when instead I would have preferred it much more if she had given me another plateful of sauerkraut instead of the spirits.

In addition there were two unmarried sisters of the principal's wife working in the business. These two ladies, who were quite advanced in years, also were quite fond of me and took pleasure from the knightly manner in which I treated them. They were both exceptionally ugly, and I would spend a long time watching them to decide which one deserved the prize. There was nothing in it, nor was there any difference in the wonderful beauty and kindness of their eyes. I accompanied the elder one when visiting the Nuremberg trade fairs. We did not have a booth as such, but a small shop with Herr Leuzinger on the Schütt[11]. We would both wait there for customers, but also had plenty of free time to

---

[11] An island in the river Pegnitz that runs through Nuremberg.

chat. I shared my youthful hopes and dreams with the old lady, but more interesting was the fact that at lunch time I was snatched from the boring repetitiveness of my existence and given twelve kreutzers which I would spend on a sumptuous meal at the *Herzle* or at *Freudenberger's.* My main task, however, was to do the accounting, and apart from this formal work I used my time to look after the business' interests that went beyond mere book-keeping. I pointed out to my principal that, for example, where a milliner has owed the business 400 guilders since the beginning of the year, I did not think it appropriate to extend her credit until the outstanding amount had been paid off, or at the very least until it was ascertained, by thorough investigation, that granting further credit would not incur a risk of loss. My principal, who mainly focused on packing the goods ready to be shipped, could not disagree with my objections, but alas, he did not have the energy to let go of the "pretty commission" if the answer was unfavourable. The elegant travelling salesman wrote that everything was in order and that the accountant's grousing was inappropriate. When I subsequently proved to my principal in minute detail that it was out of the question that the business would prosper under such circumstances, and when I further explained to him the losses which had already occurred during my relatively short employment in the business due to thoughtlessly granted credits, he said nothing; I seemed awkward to him, and the sales went through regardless. I let it go and accepted things as they were, especially considering that his son, who was working in a relative's company, also ignored my warnings.

Otherwise I enjoyed life in Fürth. Moreover, since my most ardent wish -to form a circle of young people who were striving for ideals to meet each day in order to advance themselves- was unexpectedly realised very soon. The circumstances surrounding its conception were strange and peculiar enough: Apart from being able to express myself quite well in speech and in writing, a skill which was further developed by reading many books, I was also quite good at writing poems for special occasions. Some years ago I had already supplied an award-winning poem for the choral society in Gunzenhausen, and equally I was awarded an honorary prize by the Fürth Gymnasts' Association for a song I composed for them. The little poem, which caused me no headache, went like this:

Bright, Pious, Cheerful, Free![12]

Brightly strengthen body and mind,
Brightly be with all good deeds,
Bright in the fight for the Fatherland,
Bright be, too, your love of art.

Piously honour your fathers' traditions,
Piously turn your hearts to them,
Pious words and pious deeds,
Pious be on all life's paths.

Cheerfully fulfil your duty,
Cheerfully dry your neighbour's tears,
Cheerful in drunken revelry,
Cheerful, too, on dreadful days.

Freely speak your mother tongue,
Freely break the bondage of the mind,

---

[12] "Frisch, Fromm, Fröhlich, Frei", the motto of the 19th century German gymnastic movement.

Free and united in the fight against danger,
Freely protect the right to be free.

Then the German Oak may strengthen,
May strongly protect the German land.
So make them true, you gymnasts all,
Those words "Bright and Pious and Cheerful and Free".

This harmless product of my muse is certainly not the only one I could list here. Every young lady I admired – and there were many – received, when the opportunity arose, a rhyming token, and at the famous Arnstein Institute for Girls I was already renowned as a great poet and an interesting personality.

This supplement to the external part of me was much needed: I was short, unattractive, had curly black hair, and my lofty thoughts always stood in some contrast to my external appearance; something many a young lady had me understand. As a consequence she would be punished with a poem. I was also at that young age of *weltschmerz*, that world-weary disillusionment, fed by Heine's[13] *Book of art songs* which I was reading at the time, and quite often in a lady's company I sought to be satirical rather than kind, on the premise that it made me more interesting.

This approach caused me to confront a young elegant clerk with excellent manners, who had come to Fürth from Hanover, in a very provoking way. Let's say we both admired a very pretty but coquettish girl; I from afar, he sure of victory and as closely as possible, which meant that every night he promenaded in front of

13 Heinrich Heine (1797–1856); one of the most significant German poets of the 19th century. Born Jewish, he converted to Christianity for political reasons. His radical political views led to many of his works being banned by German authorities.

the beautiful girl's window. I watched these promenades, accompanied by my friend, with internal wrath, and one evening I saw him, lost in a glance towards the window where the idol of his heart was standing, stumble in some ridiculous fashion, right under said window. This prompted me to publish the following verses, as far as I remember them, in the *Fürther Tageblatt*[14]:

> When in the evening I steer my steps
> towards you, o beautiful Königsstrasse,
> I'm filled with the highest joy, since in your middle
> lives she, the queen of my heart.
> My loyal deeds are not unrewarded,
> Smiling kindly, she casts me gracious looks,
> Oh may this smile never grow cold,
> I look up – I dare – and return the smile.
> Tonight she even laughed out gaily,
> Standing at the last window on the first floor,
> But I blush to admit what made her laugh so,
> Since it was my pure humiliation.
> Naughty pavement! Cursed be you!
> A stone of yours lies at my feet.
> The amazing power of my oh so pretty foot
> pulled it out as I stumbled and fell.

The poem was signed "A poet from Hanover".

It was an open secret that I was the author behind this bold poem, even for the person it was aimed at. The next day the following notice was published in the same paper: "If Herr B. should ever again dare to take his Pegasus for a walk in limping

---

[14] The local daily newspaper.

iambs[15], he will receive a reply that will painfully remind him of the Hanoverian colours" (green and yellow).

This was the end of the story, and for a few days I was the hero of the Arnstein Institute again. But another event followed this episode, which was not of little consequence for my life: I received a note from a friend stating that he had been asked to introduce me to a very well-educated and intelligent lady who had enjoyed my poem very much. When I asked who the lady in question was I was told that he was not in a position to say. He added that I would probably be disappointed by certain superficial aspects if he were to divulge any more, and I was to follow him without any preconceptions if I agreed to his introduction. I accepted these secretive allusions and he led me to the *Zur Stadt Würzburg* inn, across the river Regnitz far out of town. I could not imagine that this third-class inn, frequented mainly by country folk and messengers, had anything to do with his romantic message, and he just informed me that this inn offered very good and cheap fare; the rest would manifest itself soon enough. And that is exactly what happened. My friend introduced me to a very pretty young lady who brought us our small meal, and who entered into a short conversation with us with tact and grace. My friend then pointed out that she still was not the one. And so at last the Fräulein who wanted to meet me arrived. I was disappointed by her appearance; thin and tall, at least four to five years older than me, awkward and a little shy, she tried to apologise for having the audacity to invite me. She said the invitation did not have to be personal, I could not have known whether there might be a business interest as well, and the whole

[15] In ancient Greece, a *iamb* or *iambus* was mainly a satirical poem.

conversation made it clear that she was a highly intelligent person.

Despite her lack of external advantages, Johanna Bischoff was the most interesting woman I had ever met. Through reading and her own thinking she had achieved a high level of education, coupled with an unparalleled kindness; no mean thought would cross one's mind when she was near. "And behind her, in shadowy outline, lay the vulgar, which we all, alas, obey!"[16] Her kind-heartedness was even stranger since the environment in which she had grown up was a downright repulsive one. Her father, the landlord, impoverished and troubled by the worst money worries, was rough, loud and abusive. The patrons, usually drunk and abusive too, were of the lowest kind, and the daughters of the house had to spend their days amongst this – and we can call it thus - "garbage", far from any noble-minded company. Eventually it was the eldest sister who created a temple in this chaos, where she found shelter and protection from the roughness surrounding herself and her two sisters. Attracted by her intellect, a small community of distinguished and noble young men began to grow and thus formed a phalanx against those guests and foul elements which usually frequented the inn.

I ended up renting a small garden cabin from the inn-keeper so that I could enjoy the magic of this company, since her two sisters were, like her, not only intelligent but also pretty and kind. At the same time I encouraged my like-minded friends to join this new club I was planning. This cabin, which was located in a

[16] Adapted quotation from Goethe's Epilogue to Schiller's "Song of the Bell".

meadow belonging to the inn, was to serve us as a club-house; a piano was purchased, and so I was able, within a short space of time, to form a sociable circle with the aim of serving the noble goals in life and binding us all in loyal friendship for life. It goes without saying that not all of these aims were fulfilled as some members soon left us to pursue coarser pleasures. The majority, however, found an even greater pleasure in the regular social gatherings in the cottage, since very often we were joined by one or the other of the sisters who became a regular part of these cosy conversations. I may well say that these meetings stopped me and my friends from embracing those pleasures normally pursued by the carefree youth, especially in the towns and cities where many young clerks and shopkeepers come together. Lifelong friendships were made and kept.

And yet, I had a feeling that Fürth was not the right place for me. It was an idle business which led me to overestimate my small talents, including especially my ability to express myself poetically. I was sometimes overcome by a *weltschmerz*, unjustifiable really, that being a clerk was not what I should be. That feeling was reinforced by the oversized appreciation my friend Johanna had for my talent. I wished for an occupation which would cure me of my reveries and my *weltschmerz*, imagined and real, and which would lead me to healthy professional work. My wish became reality; I was offered a new position. The club was dissolved; however, we could not afford to pay the outstanding sum for the piano hire and other little debts relating to the founding of the club. I was terribly embarrassed to admit this to my lady friend and to ask for leniency. Nevertheless, within the space of a year I paid off the debt along with another friend of mine. If Johanna had had it her way I would not have paid anything at all, since she always pretended that I had already paid the outstanding amount at an earlier occasion. I cannot describe here what a deep and lasting impression this impermissible magnanimity made on me, or how gratefully I often thought of it. I can only say that many years later I was able to save my friend and her good mother from shame and destitution.

The new job was with a young company in Wallerstein in the Ries and involved travelling duties. I was accepted subject to a personal interview. I agreed to the interview but on my journey I was filled with dread that my personality would not please the new master, that I might be too dull. Contrary to what I had expected this was not the case, and I left with a contract in my pocket that, under the circumstances, was not unfavourable.

There was just one clause that I felt uneasy about, namely that during my stay in Wallerstein when I was not travelling I was to take my meals in the house of the older partner one week, and in the house of the younger partner the next, instead of being able to take my meals in the only, and rather modest, guesthouse as I would have preferred. During my first stay I also met the wives of the two principals, and I was immediately fascinated by one of them; her kindness and her certain dark beauty. I entered the business in early October and was due to start my travels in early November. There was therefore only very limited time to prepare myself, but I knew a part of their industry and the other part I hoped to cope with. That I had taken on a difficult task became self-evident after I had worked in the business for just a few days. The company, which was only two years old, had quite insufficient means, and therefore any outstanding debts had to be collected as quickly as possible. A customer had hardly unpacked the goods when we were already asking for the money, and that made it even more difficult for the travelling salesman, already battling against the superior competition. Another extraordinary custom further complicated the matter as follows:

I was to be on the road the whole year long, and initially the partners took it in turns to accompany me on my visits to the customers. Since the pecuniary situation of the company did not allow for the purchase of sufficient goods, the agent was given an almost complete list of all the goods in store at the beginning of his travelling activity. This meant that every evening he had to not only mark his own sales off the inventory but he was also sent the sales lists of the other representatives (or principal) and had to mark their sales off, too, in order to know the accurate availability of the stock. The purpose of this huge task, which did not allow even the thought of a free evening but which had to be carried out each night, after a hard day's work and often until the early hours, was to prevent the agents from selling more of an item than was available back in the warehouse. When an item was no longer in stock according to the inventory lists, it was obviously not possible to sell it any more.

The principals interacted with each other and with the few, insufficient staff in a disrespectful manner, and I did not care for it very much. One day, when the partner in whose house I was dining that week was travelling, I took the opportunity to be honest and, encouraged by the kind tone of my principal's pretty and interesting wife, told her that I was afraid I would not stay long in the business. She tried to console me with kind and sensible words by telling me that she counted herself amongst those who had to suffer much from her husband's moods, or business worries. She thus apologised for the modest fare, and I can say that the encouragement given by this fine and tactful woman did indeed comfort me, and that I bore the difficulties burdened upon me by this new job with new courage.

At last I was to take off. It was already quite wintry, and my principal asked whether I had a proper fur coat for the road. I was horrified; I had not thought about it at all, but even if I had, I would not have been in a position to afford one. As I mentioned before, I had already left Fürth with debts, and it was only owing to my brave and sensible sister Ida, who in the meantime had married a certain Herr Ottenstein, that I had been able to pay them off. Given my brother-in-law's modest financial situation I did not dare to ask for a new loan, and I was too proud to ask my parents. My principal, however, told me categorically that if I had no coat there was no question of starting off on the journey, he would not be held responsible if I was to return home ill in the first few days. My reply that I might be able to get by with a horse-blanket fell on deaf ears. So I wrote quite a heart-rending letter to my parents, asking for a fur coat and reassuring them with a solemn promise, which I truly intended to keep, that I would pay back the debt shortly after I was to receive my first salary. I received no reply, so I sent a desperate telegram explaining that if the coat did not come I would not know what to do under these "shameful circumstances". At last I received a fantastic racoon fur coat, purchased even before the arrival of my telegram, and as a consequence I was not only eternally grateful but also the expression "shameful circumstances" became a catchphrase in the family and still is with some members today.

Now we could set off. There is not much to say about the rest of my employment with this company. I was incredibly busy and worked hard, and I became friendly with honest weavers, small tradesmen, shopkeepers, haberdashers etc., and some of them I remembered fondly for a long time, even after I left Wallerstein. Much later I was able to save some of these families who were facing serious difficulties by giving them good and helpful advice, or at least to lessen the impact of looming troubles. I did enjoy the travelling, but my tender body was not up to such exerting tasks. Even if my father had not requested that I join him in his business, I would not have been able to carry on with this hard work without seriously harming my health. After two years in Wallerstein I resigned from my position, in harmonious agreement with my two principals and their families and with a splendid reference.

It goes without saying that there was many an evening during my engagement with the Wallerstein company when I thought of Fürth with tender sadness – especially when my travels had taken me to some small, lonely place. Sometimes I received a letter from my lady friend asking how I was, always in poetic format. Here is one example:

Lives he still, the loyal friend;
So close to me, so far away?
No word from him to brighten my day
has come from him for a long, long while.

What could it be that has him captured
That holds him back with such a force?
That leaves my desires unfulfilled
That has him not remember me.

Such a tribute made the prose of life all the more vivid again for me, and my rhyming answer to Johanna demonstrates quite accurately my melancholic mood at the time (except for the final verse which I added out of a certain chivalry):

Indeed he lives, your loyal friend
His life a lonely, dark existence,
And every day he thinks anew
Of that dear place so far away.

Thinks how his life is like the valley
Where the sunlight never shines,
Where neither star nor ray of hope
Glimmer in the dark of night.

Woefully he thinks of those sweet hours
Gladly spent in her sweet presence,
And how he may never convalesce
Now that this joy has been withdrawn.

Just one thing could undo the spell
Which has ensnared his soul.
This broken heart will only heal
When he can be with her again.

When once again his ears can hear
Her sweet angelic words.
Then through the heart's wide open gate
Come peace, joy and reconciliation.

Reconciliation then with you, oh world,
Being in which I have often lamented,
Which only a fool thinks wonderful
When it withholds the most wonderful from me.

It is a funny thing, this *weltschmerz*, a feeling that in my opinion is often entirely made up or is at least born out of an immodest desire, which will never be fulfilled, to lay claim on everything beautiful, good and desirable. As long as I was more than sufficiently busy and working hard in my position with the Wallerstein company, I was rarely affected by melancholic moods and was quite happy with myself and the world. Only when I was gently prompted to write once again, and usually it had to be in poetic format, was I overcome by a longing for the circle of friends I had left behind. A longing which I then expressed in a much exaggerated poetic reply. I remember, for example, one time when I was on a business tour staying in Pfaffenhofen on the Ilm that I received such a request from my friends to write something, especially about my youth. So I sent the following sonnet to Fürth:

Of the years of my youth you want me to speak?
It was a happy, joyful time.
But everything, everything, I've since seen disappear
Except the ugly ills of life.

When will the tired one find peace at last,
when will Death, so often mocked, get his revenge
and break the chains, already brittle,
that tie me to this barren life?

It's not selfishness that causes me this pain,
nor is it lust for fame that hacks at me and scratches
a thousand wounds that may never heal.
I am condemned to watch humanity's woes,
Its blinding misery fills my heart with sadness
and a deep longing to run away, far, and soon.

It goes without saying that this was a colossal exaggeration of my gloomy feelings, and I remember exactly how that evening, after I had posted the poem, I went straight to dinner and enjoyed a most delicious meal of a quarter duck à la Lower Bavaria with quite a number of handsome potato dumplings, and that amongst the travelling brothers I was the merriest. It is possible that some people may experience such emotions for real, but I believe that they must always be predisposed in such a way. Heine, I am sure, enjoyed getting drunk on his *weltschmerz* out of a certain coquetry. He was very intent on ensuring that his poetry had the same effect on its readership, who would then feel sad and gloomy, or who would eat themselves up with loneliness, condemned to a life of feeling misunderstood. While other geniuses such as Lord Byron, Lenau, Kleist etc. may express their melancholy and *welt-schmerz* without affection, these sentiments are still unhealthy and usually the result of an abnormal mental predisposition.

When I was back at home with my parents, the doctor recommended that I spend a little while in clean and fresh air, in the conviction that my health would soon be fully restored. My good sister Ida, who had consulted her family doctor in this matter, suggested for this purpose a famous sanatorium in Streitberg in Franconia, led by Herr Dr. Weber, where instead of spa water patients were given whey to drink. So it was in the May of 1862 that I visited Streitberg for the first time. I was delighted by the lovely valley, the simple yet nourishing fare seemed to me the best I ever tasted, and it was busy with people, amongst them many northern Germans, whose gregariousness had a very stimulating effect on me. I particularly noticed two ladies from Nuremberg – daughters, I heard, of a well-respected clergy-man. They were two sisters who strangely complemented each other.

The younger one was taking the whey to strengthen her weak lungs. Her appearance slender and attractive, she was intelligent, sprightly and exceedingly musical. The other one, a few years older, cared for her younger sister in a very touching manner, almost motherly. Both girls, kind and modest, kept their distance from the other guests so that I, too, only exchanged a few words with them. And yet I was filled with a great desire to get to know them better, and so I gathered my courage and had an anonymous poem delivered by the chambermaid, who happened to be Frau Nützel, future mayor of Streitberg, who is still alive today. This is the poem, as usual in my preferred format, the sonnet, but made even more original by being an acrostic[17]:

Reminiscences of Streitberg

Ah, search not for the author of these words,
Nor be angry with the donor of this modest gift
Not long now, and the dream will come to an end
And I shall have to leave your presence, sadly.

Laugh not, mock not, the magic is gone,
I depart, and you will not shake my hands.
Look, do you care if I send a thousand greetings,
If I take your image with me in my heart.

But like the man who in the deep, dark night
Looks up at the soft and golden stars
That travel brightly beyond reach,
I, too, may be allowed to think of you
And may immerse myself with longing
in the memory of those days I spent close to you.

---

[17] A poem where certain letters spell out another word; here the first letters of each line spell out the names Anna and Lili.

Fig. 5 Streitberg, ca. 1879.

In the evening I was able to watch the effect of my audacity. The older sister, Anna, came down to dinner all pale and showed the mysterious find to her sister Lili, who was already in the dining hall. The latter read the lines quietly and said simply and without emotion, "Well, that is very nicely written." I did my best to pretend that the incident had nothing to do with me, but my heart was beating wildly with excitement. The following day was the day of my departure, and both sisters came up to me when I was already in the carriage, shook my hand affectionately and bid me farewell. That was their reply, I thought.

I returned to my parents' home in the knowledge that my restored health really obliged me to make myself useful again. However, I found that the tasks I was meant to take on in the parental business did not give me sufficient opportunity to do so.

My father's main business, the selling of hops to resellers and breweries, was not significant. There were many reasons for this, but the main one, I believe, was that in contrast to other companies' practices, my father was too honest to follow the dishonourable paths that would have led to greater success. He was extremely frugal with himself and expected the same of his children. The fewer expenses one incurred while on the road, the more efficient he considered one to be, even if the commercial success was only small. If instead we had followed the competition and offered large and plentiful gifts to the brewery masters, directors etc, we would not only have made up for these expenses easily, but we would also have significantly increased our sales.

Outside the hop season my father added to his income by running a small business with some rather well-to-do relatives in which they bought large estates and resold them in smaller lots. The public felt a certain hatred towards this kind of business, which is expressed quite tellingly in the odious name they had for it: "estate wreckers". From my own observations, however, I can say that no other commercial business was conducted more honourably or more fairly than this very land trade, at least as far as I was involved. I enjoyed taking over the management of one large estate, purchased by the consortium, in the vicinity of Bobingen near Augsburg. I led the whole transaction by myself from beginning to end, for the duration of six months, and despite the probably not unjustified prejudice – since quite often this type of business is not conducted very honourably – I earned the respect of the whole population. Bobingen is a very large village of about 2000 inhabitants, and to this day I count my time there amongst my fondest memories. After a day's work I would play cards with my host's 85-year-old father - an old hunter who had had to emigrate from Garmisch because he had shot several poachers when he was royal forester - and with the Catholic priest, whose remarkable feature was his enormous Adam's apple, but who was a highly educated, benevolent and kind clergy-man who lived and let live. When some time later a small antisemitic movement formed, incited by an inn-keeper who had lost out a little in my business deal, the Right Reverend preached emphatically against it from the pulpit, noting that one must not begrudge the honest businessman his earnings, and that included the land consortium and its representatives.

Another episode that I want to relate here is the following: One evening, when I arrived for the card game, there was a third man in a grey jacket. So now there were four of us playing, and since we were on such informal terms he was not properly introduced. In the course of the evening, the gentleman was addressed as "Herr Fürst", and when I asked the hunter the next day who this Herr Fürst actually was, he told me, "Well, that was Fürst (=Prince) Fugger". I scolded him for not allowing me the joy to address the Prince with "Your Highness", which he thought was very funny and entirely unnecessary. The priest went on to become a member of the chapter at Augsburg cathedral and died at an old age; I stayed in touch with him for many more years.

When the business in Bobingen was finished it was time to set off on the road and sell as many hops as possible. I was to concentrate my activities on Bavaria, a country that was already inundated not only by professional hop traders but also by those who made a living from selling other products such as hare skins and cattle as well as hops. From the first days onwards, I was repulsed by this kind of travelling business, and while I may have done the odd deal here or there with the help of various friends I still had from my previous travels, I thought the whole environment insufferable, and I would get nervous as soon as I arrived in a small town in the country and saw the signs of the public houses such as *The Black Horse* or *Farmer George's*. I met my father, who was also travelling and selling hops, in Passau and told him – with a certainty that he knew meant I had considered it well and that I would not change my mind – that I did not have the skills required to be a travelling hop salesman and that I would depart for Gunzenhausen the same day. At the same time I asked him to provide me with the financial means to start up a wholesale hardware business, assuring him that this would provide him with, if not a better, but at least a more secure income than his other business dealings. I said this because recently a new business model had emerged, which involved a kind of loan for second mortgages, which were brokered by middle-men and usually finalised in coffee-houses. It was in blossoming Munich where this kind of business was developing particularly well. This kind of trade, too, was free of reproach as far as business honour was concerned, but while the relatively large and easy profits compared to other lines of business was very tempting, in a sudden financial crisis the business risked heavy losses which could even threaten its mere survival. I mention this here because my father replied that he was already making a lot more money than he would by investing a substantial sum in the manner suggested by me. At last my father agreed to my request in principle after I declared that if he had no confidence in my proposal I would find another employment.

Let me say here now that the risk of heavy losses incurred by these mortgages described above eventually became true in a most dreadful manner. In the year 1873 Munich experienced a total crash, and no-one had the enormous means required to pay off the new loans. The mortgage debts were therefore simply written off, and it goes without saying what dreadful losses my father and his partners incurred in that disastrous year.

I returned to my beloved Streitberg, mostly for health reasons. Again I found some good company and a number of lovely ladies from Saxony with whom I had been sociable in earlier years, yet I was missing the kind sisters from Nuremberg, of whom I had heard and seen nothing. Time and again I had to content myself thinking of their parting words from the previous year, especially when I was in Streitberg. I assumed that the sisters had not told their parents about this little episode, and I could not rest until I had sent the older sister, Anna, the following poetic words, again anonymously of course:

He who has cast away his day-work's worries
And found true happiness just once,
And found a quiet valley on his wanderings
Where he is safe from the daily grind,
He will think with woe of the morrow
When woods, mountains and valleys are in the past
And he, tightly bound to difficult duties,
Must obey the daily work.

I found the woods, the fields, the deep dark valley,
I found it all just as before,
And as before I listened to the birds' sweet songs.
But how strange, today I feel the urge to leave,
A sweet image came gliding through my soul which

I sought in the woods and fields, without success.

Despite the fact that I lived in Nuremberg later on, I never actually saw the sisters again. The younger sister Lili went to Gotha and found work in Perthes' famous publishing house where she translated English and French novels into German; she died relatively young. The elder sister Anna stayed in Nuremberg, though, and for many years she was employed in a highly esteemed house to support the education of a motherless girl. She was still employed there when she died at a very old age far away from Nuremberg, in Merano, which she visited every year. She had even requested to be buried there.

After this digression I return to the establishment of my business, which I instigated most energetically upon my arrival in Gunzenhausen. I estimated how much money would be needed to establish a viable business in the ribbons, yarns and haberdashery industry; the line I knew best. It appeared that a sum of no less than 18,000 guilders was required, but my father, who had grown to like the idea, did not balk at the amount. I have to make clear that this was not my business in the strictest sense, but that I was only to establish and lead the business in my name for my father. Once the financial arrangements had been made and the question of location had been decided – my father offered me some of the downstairs rooms in our house – I continued making preparations, which meant at first that I had to be granted a license. Trading regulations had recently been relaxed, and the extreme difficulties one used to face when attempting to establish and run a business, often resulting in year-long struggles, had lessened significantly. This was especially true for businesses that would not compete with the town's residents, particularly retailers, in other words, for the wholesale businesses. The wholesalers' license was granted on the condition that the applicant passed a public exam. If the pupil passed the exam with top grades, no magistrate could deny him the right to trade wholesale. I passed the exam with magistrate Ansbach, and, I must say, with flying colours. I received my license, and in no time at all the necessary storage rooms were furnished accordingly. A beautiful sign in sealing-wax red, fashioned by an artist from Nuremberg, announced to the astonished residents of Gunzenhausen, and in golden letters no less, that I was the proprietor of a ribbons, yarns and haberdashery wholesale business, and when, time and again the good citizens of Gunzenhausen came to visit my shop, they were amazed by the tidy stashes of goods in store. Despite being busy with the many tasks associated with the establishment of the business, I did not overlook the fact that opposite the shop there lived a simple, unpretentious and pretty girl that frolicked about her relatives' house all day, singing and chattering like a cheerful little bird. I must not devote too much space to these little interludes and will only say that we were brought together for a short time in a pure relationship which over the course of time, and without any heartbreak on either side, developed into a loyal friendship which still lasts today. We both treasure the memories, which are unsullied by incidents, but which on the contrary have strengthened our selfless friendship.

A similar story happened during my next stay in Streitberg in 1865, and again I was the benefactor insofar as, when my girlfriend encountered great difficulties, I, grateful for our harmless exchange of letters in our youth, parted with a very large sum of money for her.

The business did not do too badly, but the effects of being located in a small town soon became evident. Customers rightly assume that they are better off dealing with wholesalers based in larger towns and cities since larger manufacturers and traders would not frequent the smaller places, and also because the wholesalers in the large towns have more means and opportunities to stock the latest products and to keep up with the competition. The business was also suffering from lack of a decent sales representative, and from difficulties in finding a few people, apprentices really, to help me out. So I hired my third brother, Berthold, as my travelling sales rep, whose commercial training was quite insufficient but who had a great talent for ingratiating himself with other people. However, this apparent advantage, which under certain circumstances could have been extremely useful for a sales rep, turned out to be a disaster in the case of my brother and his weak character, and eventually it wrecked my entire business, still then in its infancy. My brother sent orders from people, often his friends, which far exceeded their needs. Years later I would still have to accept returns of two-thirds of the goods after the customers claimed that my brother had sold them on a sale-or-return basis. In other cases he recklessly gave credit to bad debtors. Then there were invoices of several hundred marks for rarities he had apparently bought, sometimes antiques, sometimes thorough-bred dogs. In short, with all his popularity he would have risked the survival of the young business had I not kicked him out in time. His recklessness was indescribable, and even his worst experiences would not make him change his ways. Shortly after he left my business he went to America because of some stupid pranks, only to be followed by his future wife a year later. I myself had to direct him from

Vienna to Hamburg because Father did not want to see him again, and I had to make sure that he really did board the ship. He seemed to me like a man condemned to death, and instead of being angry with him in Hamburg I treated him in a very brotherly manner, giving him as much money and food for the journey as I could afford on my little means. I bought his ticket which allowed him to travel second class to England and from there on to America as a steerage-passenger. He spent many years over there and held many different jobs such as bottle-cleaner, comedian, etc. He married his lover, and I think he often hit hard times. He always wrote letters full of longing, begging us to forgive him and to send him the money he needed to return home with his family. It was my sister Ida again who took pity on him and who collected enough money from within the family to allow him to come home. He returned to Bremen with his wife and many children, and when he arrived in Nuremberg, where my parents now lived, he was received with open arms. He was provided with all he needed, including a large amount of cash, to set up his own cigar shop in Gunzenhausen. After a short while, however, all this had gone to the devil – the money, the shop and his honour. Several times the family and I made heavy sacrifices to keep his head above water but I cannot relate in detail all the events following his return from America that led to a succession of troubles for himself and for us. I will only say so much that in the last 15 years of his life he was hard-working and honest in a difficult job, and that he strove, successfully, to be independent of any support and to lead an honourable life. He died in the 64th year of his life, and I was truly saddened by the loss.

My brother Adolf was the total opposite: thrifty to excess, yet industrious and not lacking in the characteristics that support dealings with customers. What stopped him from being a visionary entrepreneur did not come to light until much later when the business' activities grew more and more significant; this shall be explained later.

I suggested to my father that he leave the business to my brother and me, obviously not to the total value, but I would draw up a balance sheet that would show how much income had been generated in the first two years after its creation. He could then let us have as big or small a portion as he considered appropriate for our dowry. We would simply owe him with interest a part of the capital invested in the business, and would then pay back the remainder when we got married. My parents, who were growing impatient with the unrest in the house, especially since, with the exception of my sister Ida, all their sons and daughters were still unmarried, liked the idea. So I started to take an inventory and to add up how much profit we had made in the last two years from the initial investment of 18,000 guilders.

I had absolutely no doubt that no profit whatsoever could have been made. While the turnover had been low, the losses incurred by my brother Berthold had been comparatively significant. In addition to that, there had been considerable costs for the establishment and the furnishing of the new business. In short, I knew myself that any talk of a profit was out of the question. Instead we should be relieved that we had not suffered any losses against the originally invested capital. And so it was. Nevertheless, I knew only too well why there had not been any profits, nor did I doubt that if I ran the business, not for my father, but instead was free to act as I thought fit, I could hope for good results in the future. On the other hand, I did not want to disappoint my father, and so I told him that the business had increased in value by 7,500 guilders and that it was now worth 25,500 guilders. Even so, my father was not very satisfied with this result, and he signed the business over to my brother Adolf and me. We had to pledge to pay back his investment of 18,000 guilders in agreed instalments. The profit I had invented of 7,500 guilders was to be my brother's and my dowry. There was nothing to say against my father's actions since a dowry of nearly 4,000 guilders for each child was quite generous.

The new company *Gebrüder Bing* then moved to the building next door. My brother and I took turns in visiting customers, at least for the first three years. My sister in Nuremberg sent us a cook, who was as ugly as she was economical; we employed two young men who paid for their apprenticeship, and we managed the business as carefully and industriously as possible. Naturally, I told my brother that, having thought the matter over well, and with the conviction that it would lead to a healthy and successful business, I had paid our father a certain premium and thus had given him the warm feeling that providing for his sons had not actually cost him that much.

In Gunzenhausen I kept quite interesting company; a large percentage of the townspeople was made up of more than enough so-called railway and postal assistants. Most were students who for some reason had not taken their final exams, but were otherwise friendly and talented people, and I often found their company stimulating. There was even some form of casino in Gunzenhausen, which was dominated by the small town's civil servants and which was inaccessible for members of the Israelite conviction. The postal workers, with whom I was very popular, often teased me gently that this temple was closed to me and suggested that I protest against it. They were all members of the casino but had no vote. I myself had no doubt that I would fail with flying colours in any attempt to be accepted as a member. It was merely a question of principle, though, and since my acceptance as a citizen of Nuremberg, which shall be discussed in more detail later on, had already been confirmed, and my move to the city was imminent, I applied to join the casino. I received a visit from a very benevolent gentleman – a government official in Gunzenhausen as well as a member of the board of the casino – who pointed out that it might be better if I withdrew my application since I was not really serious about it and that it was just for protest's sake. I insisted, however, that the application be dealt with properly. As was to be expected, my application was rejected, with seven votes to six. I was informed about the entire process, and I was also told that once the rejection was confirmed, all members agreed that I, with my character and position, would have fitted in very well at the casino, only that what they would grant me today would be demanded tomorrow by people who entirely lacked the characteristics required for acceptance into the corporation.

The greatest voice against my acceptance was that of the provincial judge, who I knew to be a grandson of Jean Paul's[18]. I also knew that he would often show his thrift and pettiness by advertising books by Jean Paul, books he had inherited and were now

---

[18] Jean Paul (1763 – 1825); German Romantic writer, best known for his humorous novels and stories.

at his disposal, in his official gazette. I wanted to punish him, and so I published a number of epigrams under the heading "New wisdoms by Democritus[19]" in this his own gazette. My intention was to name and shame in a similar fashion all those who had voted against me.

I still remember to this day the epigram I dedicated to Jean Paul's grandson:

> He does well who seeks to sell
> That which he does not need, which he cannot grasp.
> You want to buy Jean Paul's master works?
> Indeed, I know just the man.
> He will sell them to you, and very cheaply, too.
> What does he, who cannot think himself, want with a thinker's goods?

The whole town laughed, the printers of the paper lost their contract to print the gazette, but apart from that the men, to each one of whom I had dedicated an epigram, did what was probably the best thing to do under the circumstances – they remained silent.

After a while, as I mentioned above, we began to consider leaving the small town for the reasons explained, and moving to a bigger place instead, where it would be easier for us to buy and sell, and where it might be useful for our products to have a city clientele. My father wished us to move to Munich because he went there often and because he thought that we would be able to further his business interests if and when necessary while we were there.

---

19 Democritus (ca. 460 BCE – ca. 370 BCE); ancient Greek philosopher and influential pre-Socratic philosopher.

We let ourselves be talked into applying for acceptance into Munich, and we were more than just a little proud when, after some time, the certificate arrived granting us citizenship of the Royal Residency and Capital City of Munich.

However, I had some concerns; in Munich all we could do was continue with our existing product line. I had the impression that being the middle-man for these products was no longer very profitable since the larger companies were selling them much more cheaply, had a much bigger range, and we were left with only third-class customers, in other words the leftovers from the rich men's tables. I raised the following point to consider: should we familiarise ourselves with the Nuremberg industry, on the premise that we would be able to sell many of the articles there that were currently being manufactured by cottage industry in Nuremberg, alongside ours and without having to keep a large warehouse stock? This logical consideration proved to be very useful and we decided to reject the idea of Munich and start our business in Nuremberg instead. We moved in 1865, and I rented a small shop in Karolinenstrasse, which is now occupied by Friedrich Kaul's shoe shop. We paid 450 guilders for it, and I had to do a lot of flattering, bowing and scraping until the owner agreed to a five-year contract with us. He asked me what would happen if we were to go bankrupt etc., but I knew how to dispel his concerns, and I was supported in this by his very pretty daughter, a widow, who seemed embarrassed by her father's tactless remark.

Fig. 6 Company logo 1880-1902

The move to Nuremberg did not take long, nor did the furnishing of the premises, and we were proud to own a shop that could be seen from St. Lorenz all the way along Karolinen-strasse. This is where the business developed in a new direction. Along-side our usual products, we began the sale of metal goods and fashion accessories, and what really helped us here was that the recently introduced freedom of trade had caused many shop-keepers to expand their previously restricted line of business and to offer a variety of related articles. This allowed us to give our company a broad base because almost any business was now open to receive merchandise. The turner acquired walking sticks, the shoemaker bought his hemp-yarn, the rope-maker his manufactured whipcords, the comb-maker rubber combs, the book-binder portfolios, the pewterer tablespoons; teaspoons and serving spoons made of Britannia metal, but above all it was the plumbers who bought many items that we had had manufactured by cottage industry in Nuremberg.

It would be too much to explain all these circumstances in detail; all I can say is that there was hardly a craft business that we did not deal with in one way or another, and that gave our business a base that continued to grow, and profitably so. Soon our business outgrew our premises and we had to look for a new location.

In the meantime we had to cope with a major crisis, namely the Austro-Prussian War of 1866. The horrors of this war, however, were much less severe than had been feared initially, and after just a few months the victorious Prussians, or rather the Brunswick and Mecklenburg troops, marched into Nuremberg. It was astonishing how well informed these troops were, who had been welcomed in the name of the city by the mayor at Heroldsberg. It was impressive to see the Mecklenburg cuirassiers take the town hall, the station, in short all the strategically important places and immediately announce on posters that from now on the inhabitants had to follow the orders of the Commander of the occupied city of Nuremberg. When it was certain that the enemy's troops would march into town, my anxious brother wanted to hide all those goods that might tempt the soldiers and attract their attention. I, however, was of the opinion that all items that the soldiers might consider as a souvenir, such as cigarette tips, pocket knives and other fancy goods, should be displayed openly in the windows, which is what we did. The expectation that this would ensure plenty of sales to the soldiers was fulfilled entirely, and we achieved a tidy sum of sales during the occupation of Nuremberg. There were, however, some costs, too, especially associated with having to quarter eight men in our flat. The troops' behaviour in general was outstanding, and soon we were all so cosy with one another that men from both sides, giving quarters and receiving quarters, would sit together in inns and coffee shops almost on a daily basis and late into the night, having a good time. The ladies of Nuremberg were not unjustly accused of surrendering to the enemy despite the fact that the enemy never requested such a thing, and one can say that those were merry times.

The main reason for moving in 1868 into the larger premises in Weizenstrasse (in Philipp Rosenbaum's house) was that we wanted to focus entirely on metal wares. We gave up haberdashery altogether. We were quite busy, increased our staff in the shop as well as on the road and were full of confidence for the future.

Our own financial means were still too small for the growing business. I asked my brother Adolf to start looking for a wife amongst the daughters of the land since, due to his handsome looks I supposed that he would bring more money into the business via a marriage than me, the older and physically disadvantaged one. A good match was indeed found[20]; not only a good one but in my opinion an excellent one. She was the daughter of a well-respected businessman in Fürth, and the inquiries made, mostly by me, resulted in reports that the young lady had all the necessary characteristics of the heart and of the spirit to make a man happy. The dowry, too, was adequate, and I urged my brother to consider the issue. A place was chosen for the young people and the two sets of parents to meet, and the pre-negotiations suggested that the proceedings would be favourable. I was excluded from them, and the remarkable circumstance that I as the elder was not marrying first was explained by the fact that I had chosen to remain a bachelor for a while out of regard for my various other interests. In the following days the father of the bride-to-be, Herr Bierer from Fürth, came to meet me and really, he said, if it was possible, to check the state of the business. He offered this quite shyly, but my feigned confidence, in contrast to my brother's, who was also

[20] Fanny Bierer.

present at the meeting, obviously impressed him. Amongst other things I pointed out that it would please me very much if Herr Bierer, having checked the books, wanted to check everything in more detail because I would take the result of the careful audit required by him as a full guarantee that he himself would pay the promised dowry in full and on time. I, or my brother, would not, I added, require any additional guarantees for said payment either. He laughed heartily about my words, and we had the most enjoyable time so that the audit was never mentioned again. Back at home he related the way I had negotiated with him, saying that he was delighted to have found someone in me who, in a light conversational tone, had quickly found all the answers needed and who was quite happy to have him eventually give up on the idea of an audit altogether. These stories made his family imagine me as a very interesting personality, especially his daughter, and I probably did not meet their high expectations during later visits. After some difficulties, not with my brother but with the daughter, we celebrated the engagement at last, and I met my future sister-in-law and found her to be a kind and highly intelligent young lady. The rest of the family was also very likeable, and when my brother was on the road, as was almost always the case, I was accepted not as a deputy husband but as a welcome guest into the Bierer home. The wedding took place a short time later. I won not only a lovely new relative in my sister-in-law but also a true friend and a good companion. She was also an exquisite pianist, who introduced me to the world of music.

I was feeling quite lonely, though, and thought about making my choice amongst the daughters of the land, too. That was easier said than done. Many of these daughters were out of the question simply because of my modest looks and my even more modest wealth, and others whom I could have approached with confidence did not appeal to me. It seemed unthinkable to me to enter a marriage without true affection, and I often and rightfully mocked the way some couples are introduced to each other.

And then I found a pretty and lively girl whom I had met before in the Franconian Switzerland, where her parents resided. The family now lived in Nuremberg, and I often found myself in the company of the young lady. And while I enjoyed her youth and her pretty looks for a time, I sometimes worried about the affected manner in which she tried to imitate the language and countenance of the educated townspeople in an effort to sound like them, an effort that always failed simply because she was lacking the preliminary condition of a good education. There was something about her character, too, that smelled of a peasant's slyness. Yet time and again I was drawn to the beautiful girl, and also her parents seemed very encouraging and benevolent to me, but when at last I had decided to ask for the girl's hand I spotted their intrigue: the family were going to lower the already very small dowry even further. I left the arena and was made richer by the experience.

My sister Ida was an excellent counsel to me in all things, and I cannot praise this unique woman often enough for always knowing the right thing to say, and to anyone. Even I, who was pretty self-reliant and on an intellectual par with her, could not extricate myself from her spell, and her influence and recommendation had me soon engaged to a girl[21] who was merely a few years younger than me and who was staying with some relatives

---

[21] Rosa Schloss.

in Nuremberg who were friends of mine. She was the daughter of a teacher couple from Speyer who were blessed with many children and few earthly goods. We met with the intention of getting to know each other better. That, however, was quite a difficult task, at least for me. The girl could be called a beauty, and her general knowledge, too, was as broad as was to be expected with her solid middle-class education. She lacked just one thing that I noticed: she was not interested in anything that went above and beyond her narrow middle-class horizon and her tender affection for me. To use a common expression, she could not care less about art, literature, music etc.; she wanted to love and be loved, to manage her simple household, to have good relations with her relatives, maybe even share in her husband's worries – a lovely creature who stirred in me an unreserved feeling of very tender affection. I often asked myself if these characteristics described above were sufficient for a wife of mine to fill a whole life. Since I had developed a real liking for her right at our first meeting, however, I construed the issue in such a way that I convinced myself that I had always favoured this kind of homely nature in a girl, and that I had always disliked the well-educated, so-called "better daughters" of the upper class, especially the bluestockings, with their superficial airs.

We got engaged, and she stayed in Nuremberg for four weeks, where we usually met in the house of her relatives. My family, too, accepted her as my bride with open arms. Once she returned to Speyer, we started a correspondence where my bride showed a passion that sometimes frightened me. If a letter from me arrived per chance an hour late, she would be so alarmed that she would not sleep for days. If she had a simple cold, she told me once in a letter, she would move my picture so that I would not catch it. In short, her letters had little content, none whatsoever of things of general interest, only ever expressions of her passionate love, which was fully requited by me but without ever going beyond what was the reasonable temperance of the emotions. We were engaged in November 1866. One request she repeated over and over in her letters was for me to come and visit her in Speyer. That was certainly no unreasonable request, only I was already extremely busy at work, and I will also admit that I shied away from the expense that such a journey would entail, especially since my financial situation, as mentioned several times already, was extremely weak and that my bride's dowry did not change that situation much either. My bride's burning desire for me to visit her was like a red thread that wound its way through all of our correspondence, and one time she even suggested that her girlfriends must think my physical appearance was such that it was inhibiting me from presenting myself in Speyer. This appeal did the trick, and that May, two days before we were to be married in Aschaffenburg, I arrived in Speyer. For my little bride's sake, I made numerous visits to the families that were friendly with her parents, and I tried hard to fulfil this task with the appropriate eagerness and joy, even though I really did not enjoy the prospect of it at all. I did win the hearts of all my bride's girlfriends, which filled her with happiness. The wedding, too, was a very jolly affair, and I suggested to my new wife that we spend our honeymoon in my favourite Streitberg. This was in May 1867. We arrived in Streitberg, and this is when the tragedy began; one that I believed would shatter my life's happiness. My young wife was suddenly struck by a severe mental illness. I called my sister and my sister-in-law, and together we travelled to Nuremberg, but we could not move into the flat I had prepared for us. My wife, who regained her senses periodically, was cared for most lovingly by my sister. We were able to ease her symptoms temporarily, and after a week we could even move into our little home.

A trustworthy physician, who was also a friend of both families, believed that there were blockages in the veins which would disappear by themselves after a while, by which time my wife would then recover. It was not to be, however, and five weeks after our wedding the dreadful thing happened; my wife suddenly passed away.

I returned the small dowry to my wife's relatives, and I have stayed in touch with them to this day. Later on, when I had come into wealth and the company was expanding, I was able to help and support several members of this family.

So I was on my own again. I was gripped by a deep melancholy, and it was only through hard work and regular contact with my trusted friends, including two cousins of my late wife's, that I was able, after some time, to find peace again. Like I said, I was engrossed in the business more than ever, I worked from the early hours until late at night, and I soon exchanged our flat, which held such difficult and sad memories for me, for a very friendly bachelor's home, with the intention that it would serve my friends as a cosy spot for merry get-togethers.

I would like to mention here that until I was struck by this terrible tragedy I had been a religious man. My thinking was that everyone, no matter which religion they belonged to, would have to be deeply moved in a religious, but not confessional, way by the wonders that surround us. From that tragic moment on I began to lose my religious feelings more and more, and I became indifferent to religion, both the confessional and the spiritual aspect of it. In fact, I did not think about it much, but I had a vague feeling that one could not count on the existence of a god.

Then came the time when a new synagogue was being built in Nuremberg. The idea was to build a temple for the fast growing community with the intention not only of deepening religious significance but also of making visits to this house of God more attractive, with the support of external means. These included first and foremost organ music, unusual for a Jewish place of worship, and solemn singing by a mixed, selected choir. I was indifferent to this project, and yet, many years later, when the synagogue was being consecrated, I attended the opening ceremony, but more out of curiosity than out of religious interests. The dedication speech was delivered by the new rabbi, Dr. Levin, who had been called from Berlin, and I found him to be a mesmerising speaker

Fig. 7 Nuremberg Synagogue, completed in 1874.

who, free of any zeal or any confessional overtones, had deeply inspired me with his wonderful, enthusiastic speech. I was converted in so far as that I decided to believe again in Providence and in God, whatever Being or Power was to be understood by that phrase.

The following sonnet, which I sent the rabbi anonymously together with a silver cup, expressed my mood at that time. It was not until a few years later that it became known, by chance, that I was the author of the poem and the donor of the trophy. The donation brought me belated recognition and a lasting friendship with the man, who was, just like his very pretty wife, really of a very jolly nature. The poem went as follows:

> Condemned to watch humanity's endless woes,
> And myself hurt by the harshest blow,
> The faith of my youth was floating away
> And with it Hope and Love and Trust in God.
> Time passed on, and I saw the people building,
> Saw a temple rising to the sky.
>
> It meant nothing to me, it did not move me,
> To me it was a house for women, children and the old.
> The gates are opened, gleaming in golden light,
> Full of harmony, the temple is radiating in its splendour
> Like red sky in the morning, and slowly sinks the night.
> And when your voice rang out, so strong, so true, so mild,
> When you, like a seer, unrolled the image of the future
> A heart rejoiced, and converted to you.

I would like to point out that I usually had the urge to write poems about events that moved me deeply. It was my way of dealing with these things, and sometimes it seemed as if it allowed me to free myself from the thoughts that tormented me. Of course, most of the numerous products of my muse have been lost over the course of many years; only very few have survived, which, if they have not been included in these memoirs, I may give a new but only short life in a separate appendix[22], in other words none of them will make it to posterity, and rightly so.

For many years I was also a permanent contributor to the once very popular puzzle pages of the esteemed newspaper *Korrespondent von und für Deutschland*[23], which has since been sold to a new owner. My speciality were homonyms (words that are spelled the same but have two different meanings), whereby I took special pride in creating puzzles of a more exact form than was usually the case with puzzles. Again, only a few of these survived, which are included in the appendix. It was remarkable that my dear wife Ida, née Ottenstein, whom I married in May 1869, had a certain fondness for these puzzles of mine; she did not know that I was the creator, but her inkling that it might be me proved to be correct. If, with a better education and more time for aesthetic things, I might have found fame in poetry, I do not know. I found writing very easy. For example, I once dictated a poem to my daughter Berta - which served as a prologue to a comedy shown at the *Phoenix* theatre and which was received with great applause - as easily as if I had expressed myself in prose. The originality of the thoughts and the poetic form, however, lose out, of course, where the hard job of earning money plays such an important part.

---

22 This appendix does not appear to have been written.

23 Roughly: Correspondent from and for Germany

What did become a real oasis in my everyday life was my love of nature combined with my energetic endeavours to gain an insight into human prehistory. I will return later to the topic of my own experiences and experiments to understand the said subject better.

I have previously mentioned that in the meantime, namely in 1869, I married my second wife, and I will describe this event that brought me such happiness in more detail:

After nearly two years had passed since the death of my first wife, my sister Ida, who was very close to me and who had been my loyal counsel in so many important issues, urged me to remarry. She had chosen for this purpose her niece, i.e. the daughter of the previously mentioned teacher Simon Ottenstein, who by now had moved his family from Gunzenhausen to Bamberg. It was the same girl whose good-heartedness and intellect I had noticed and liked back in Gunzenhausen, and who I had met several times, now a young woman, when I visited my sister in recent times. My sister, and a wise and favourite aunt of mine who also lived in Bamberg, were both right in saying that I would not find another woman who would bring me more happiness or fulfilment. No praise was necessary in this respect though, since I knew my future wife very well. Moreover, I knew that for a long time she had been quietly very fond of me, and that she and her parents would be truly delighted if the union proposed by my sister materialised. After what had happened in the past, I myself would never be able again to play the jolly, loving suitor. I could see for myself that this union might bring me a happiness and peacefulness that I had no longer hoped for, and on 11th May 1869 we were happy to be married. Our marriage was so harmonious and the days passed with such tranquillity that we were both extremely happy in our modest home. I enjoyed my work more because I knew that after a hard day's work in the business I could look forward to peace and cosiness at home. The marriage had also slightly improved my financial situation, though not enough to completely solve the question of finances necessary for the further development of the business. It was just enough to pay back the debt owed by us brothers to our dear father and to keep the business afloat and out of trouble. I knew that my commercial knowledge and abilities would guarantee that this development would be significant and materially successful, if only there was the prospect of the fertilising element, i.e. more credit. I had to accept that one day the future would hold more promise for my intention to take the company to greater heights than seemed possible today.

Soon a new trial lay ahead like a dark storm-cloud gathering on the horizon, and this time it was one that could affect the whole world. The year 1870 started well for business concerns, things were moving forwards. Our customer-base grew, and the security of our revenue improved by the day. Even the recently extended premises were no longer sufficient and we had to rent additional space. However, a terrible thunderstorm broke soon, and by mid-July Germany found herself in a just and powerful fight against France. The German army marched from victory to victory, and just a few weeks after the war began the French army was pretty much defeated so that Germany went confidently back to business as usual. Our company had sought hard and righteously to fulfil its obligations wherever and as far as possible during the previous, difficult weeks; a commitment that turned out to be like a seed, sunk deep into the ground, the shoot of which was an unshakable confidence shown by our associates after the war, which in return proved to have a significant impact on the future creditworthiness of the company. I will show just one example of this: A large, old company in Augsburg that did not really run a banking business but looked after the delivery of our goods, granted us a small credit to the limit of about 3,000 guilders. Just before the start of the war we drew up a banker's draft for 1,500 guilders and discounted the draft with a banker who liked me personally but who did not normally give credit. When the war broke out, the company in Augsburg wired us the demand to immediately return the draft, i.e. they would not honour it since the war would not allow them to carry out such transactions. I was horrified, if only with regard to the possible effect on the Nuremberg banker. I gathered all the money I could find and departed early the next morning at 3 o'clock with 1,500 guilders for Augsburg to deposit the money with the company there in order to have them accept the bill of exchange. The senior director of the company was so delighted about my honourable response to this business affair that he sent me straight back home with the money and said that he would accept the bill of exchange without the deposit of a security. We had a similar experience with a banker from Paris where we also had a credit of several thousand francs and where we returned the value of the bill of exchange before its due date as soon as the war broke out. The Paris banker, a relative of the Bierer family, supported us during the course of our business association by granting us a very large credit because we had gained his implicit trust through our actions as described above.

As mentioned before, after the battle of Wörth, business continued as usual, and we did particularly well with what is nowadays called "Liebesgaben"; gifts given as a symbol of love. The year 1870 marked the point in time when the company began its continuous growth in importance, expansion and confidence.

In those days, just before the start of the war, my wife and I were blessed with the birth of our son Fritz, whose arrival delighted both of us and which gave our lives a new direction. I regard it as the hardest trial of my life when this child, whose physical and intellectual development had been so extremely promising, was snatched away from us by Death when he was only six and half years old. When our second son, Max, died at the age of 20 weeks we were in despair and wondered whether we would ever experience the joys of parenthood again. And yet we were to be blessed with many children, namely two sons and four daughters who are with us today in good health, and with numerous grandsons and granddaughters.

In late December 1870, the outcome of the Franco-Prussian War was as good as decided. The only resistance the Prussian army met were a few troops in the South, scrambled together and led by the generals of what is now the French Republic, who battled on bravely but without being able to affect the outcome of the situation in any way. Paris was being hemmed in more and more closely from all sides, and when at last the large siege-artillery was moved in and applied, all further resistance became futile. In mid-February 1872 an armistice was agreed upon which already included the conditions for peace to be signed by the republican government, which at the time was convening in Bordeaux.

In the months that followed the truce, the German economy experienced an immense upturn. The French retributions included amongst others five billion francs in gold plus an enormous territory on their Western borders with the imposing castles of Strasbourg and Metz. Seeing that France was now weakened to such an extent, it seemed humanly impossible to imagine that there would ever be another war between the two nations.

The election of the Prussian King as German Emperor meant that Germany now had a mighty and externally representative organisation, and in the interest of complete unification certain laws were introduced that governed the use of unified weights and measures. I recognised that someone who understood the importance of the new law early enough would benefit from significant commercial success for many years to come. I put all my efforts into establishing a cottage industry in Nuremberg that would enable our company to supply the new weights and measures quickly. I was absolutely convinced that vast quantities would be needed since almost every household and every commercial business would need to get hold of these new weights and measures. We informed our customers in good time that we would be in a position to supply these new important items, and we received more orders than we were able to fulfil. By relying more and more on the cottage industry we were able to respond even to the increasing demand, and soon we were supplying these items not only to Bavaria but all over Southern Germany too, in significant quantities.

Over time other companies started to compete with us of course, but there was always enough business to be had for us, and it took several years for the first level of demand to be fulfilled. Weights and measures form part of our range of products to this day.

Using the same, but much enlarged, cottage industry - and Nuremberg was the right place for this - we also used to distribute a large number of home and kitchen utensils; even if they were slightly more primitive versions they were still better and cheaper than those made by the tin-smiths. There were only very few manufacturing businesses that made these products, however, there was an ancient, important cottage industry in the Saxon Ore Mountains. I went to inspect the situation and found that they offered a great opportunity to expand on a very large scale the production facilities of home and kitchen utensils, which were still quite limited in Nuremberg.

There were, in the Ore Mountains, a number of companies who delivered half-finished products to their workers and then paid them for the finished goods. The finished products were then sold to plumbers and ironmongers, usually at the Leipzig Fair, but I saw immediately that there was no real organisation to properly develop this industry of ever growing importance. Since the war, plumbers had a lot of construction work and the work-shops of the old tradesmen, with their little or totally insufficient equipment, could not keep up with technical developments, and people were glad that they could buy the goods required in their shops from us. To illustrate how important this range of products was for our business, I can only say that it was more difficult getting hold of the goods than selling them.

In 1872, I visited Grünhain in Saxony for the first time. It is now the location of our factories for enamelled goods, and from one of those companies, the one with the largest production facilities, I bought common kitchen utensils made of tin-plate for no less than 36,000 thalers. We sold them easily within a year and at a good profit, and demand for them kept rising. The positive effect this new speciality had on our business became clear on the balance sheet for 1873. It showed a net profit of around 24,000 guilders, 12,000 for each partner. My wife mentioned this in a letter to her parents in Bamberg. Strangely they did not reply to this. During a later visit to Bamberg I brought this up, and they were embarrassed to admit that they could not believe that we had achieved such returns. My wife was a little upset that they had thought her husband capable of such a boastful lie.

Compared to what the tin-smiths were able to make, the goods produced in the Saxon Ore Mountains were little pieces of art, yet there came a time when they were no longer sufficient either. Far away in the Northeast, in Elbing, a young, diligent merchant set up shop, a certain Herr Neufeldt, who beforehand, if I remember correctly, had also spent some time working in a tin-smith's shop. Everyone was praising his qualities as a manufacturer who turned the famous tin into remarkable products, such that Neufeldt's goods were an adornment to any shop. We procured some samples and found they absolutely deserved this unreserved praise. The good thing about these products was that Neufeldt employed skilled mechanics, and that through the use of mechanical equipment and tin-working machines from England, he was able to achieve not only consistently high quality but also relatively low manufacturing costs. We contacted the company with the proposition that we become their sole agent for Southern Germany and guaranteed annual purchases of at least around 100,000 marks.

After some time a letter arrived from Neufeldt in which he explained quite patronisingly that he would certainly not grant our request to be his sole agent for Southern Germany; however, he would consider entering into an agreement for Bavaria. He had obviously sought information about our company and had received a very good response. He then invited us to visit an exhibition in Kassel which he was attending so that we could discuss everything else in person. Even then, such exhibitions were organised by the German Association of Tin-workers and held in a different town in Germany each year, and they marked the beginning of the great development of the hardware industry, which previously was situated, quite modestly, mainly in Ludwigsburg.

My brother and I travelled to Kassel and found Herr Neufeldt to be a very eloquent yet fanciful and flashy man. We let him say all he had to say and did not seek to rein in what must have been some kind of megalomania. I then started to explain to him the benefits of a liaison with us and clearly proved to him that enormous freight costs would make it prohibitive for a small trader from the far South to purchase his relatively cheap goods from the East of Germany. He would therefore gain immensely from having us as his representatives, and he liked to hear especially that he would be the bigger winner since we would import his exceptional products to Bavaria. Of course, we presumed that he would sell us the products at better rates than the retailers were able to buy them since we had to stock much larger quantities of all the products we were going to import. Yet in his pride he could not bring himself to agree to that, so in the end all we achieved was the sole agency for a few years for Bavaria. In the end, we agreed because we told ourselves that the products were so good and relatively cheap that we could easily charge 20 to 25% more than his usual price, and even more so since we did not have to worry about competing against him in Bavaria.

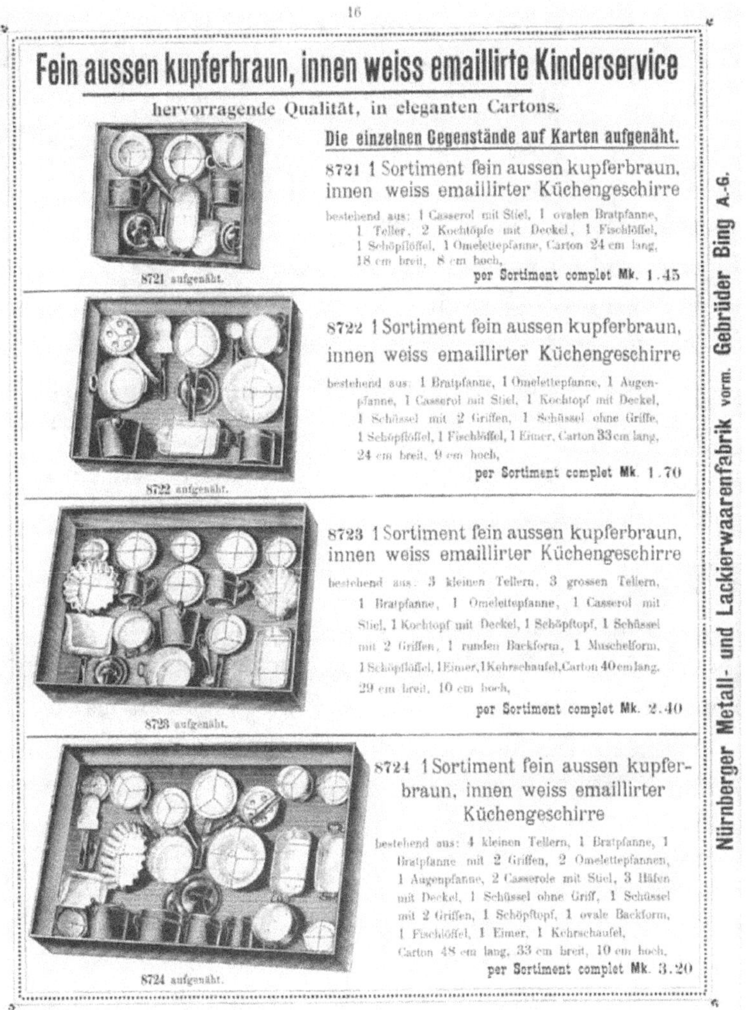

16

Fein aussen kupferbraun, innen weiss emaillirte Kinderservice

hervorragende Qualität, in eleganten Cartons.

Die einzelnen Gegenstände auf Karten aufgenäht.

8721 1 Sortiment fein aussen kupferbraun, innen weiss emaillirter Küchengeschirre

bestehend aus: 1 Casserol mit Stiel, 1 ovalen Bratpfanne, 1 Teller, 2 Kochtöpfe mit Deckel, 1 Fischlöffel, 1 Schöpflöffel, 1 Omelettepfanne, Carton 24 cm lang, 18 cm breit, 8 cm hoch,

per Sortiment complet Mk. 1.45

8721 aufgenäht.

8722 1 Sortiment fein aussen kupferbraun, innen weiss emaillirter Küchengeschirre

bestehend aus: 1 Bratpfanne, 1 Omelettepfanne, 1 Augenpfanne, 1 Casserol mit Stiel, 1 Kochtopf mit Deckel, 1 Schüssel mit 2 Griffen, 1 Schüssel ohne Griffe, 1 Schöpflöffel, 1 Fischlöffel, 1 Eimer, Carton 33 cm lang, 24 cm breit, 9 cm hoch,

per Sortiment complet Mk. 1.70

8722 aufgenäht.

8723 1 Sortiment fein aussen kupferbraun, innen weiss emaillirter Küchengeschirre

bestehend aus: 3 kleinen Tellern, 3 grossen Tellern, 1 Bratpfanne, 1 Omelettepfanne, 1 Casserol mit Stiel, 1 Kochtopf mit Deckel, 1 Schöpftopf, 1 Schüssel mit 2 Griffen, 1 runden Backform, 1 Muschelform, 1 Schöpflöffel, 1 Eimer, 1 Kehrschaufel, Carton 40 cm lang, 29 cm breit, 10 cm hoch,

per Sortiment complet Mk. 2.40

8723 aufgenäht.

8724 1 Sortiment fein aussen kupferbraun, innen weiss emaillirter Küchengeschirre

bestehend aus: 4 kleinen Tellern, 1 Bratpfanne, 1 Bratpfanne mit 2 Griffen, 2 Omelettepfannen, 1 Augenpfanne, 2 Casserole mit Stiel, 3 Häfen mit Deckel, 1 Schüssel ohne Griff, 1 Schüssel mit 2 Griffen, 1 Schöpftopf, 1 ovale Backform, 1 Fischlöffel, 1 Eimer, 1 Kehrschaufel, Carton 48 cm lang, 33 cm breit, 10 cm hoch,

per Sortiment complet Mk. 3.20

8724 aufgenäht.

Nürnberger Metall- und Lackierwaarenfabrik vorm. Gebrüder Bing A.-G.

Fig. 8 Doll's kitchen utensils. Catalogue 1898.

Neufeldt was a very strange man: handsome, experienced, almost a cavalier, while at the same time he could not hide the fact that he possessed a certain slyness, which he wanted you to see just as much as his cavalier-like demeanour. He was vain and incessantly talked about how he would travel the world to distribute his products so widely that everyone would have to pay tribute to him. I quite enjoyed listening to his exaggerations, and I took good care not to contradict him; quite the opposite in fact: I spurred him on in his ambition by pointing out to him that I had further ideas for where I absolutely needed his help as a manufacturer. That was indeed the case. We needed significant quantities of very basic tin crockery for doll's houses, and we were certain that if manufactured to Neufeldt's usual high quality we could expect to bring in even bigger sales. In time we agreed on this, too, and so the business relationship developed along nicely without any further problems.

Everything went well until 1878; however, by then our business had grown so much that we could no longer restrict our sales of Neufeldt's goods to Bavaria only, and we requested to buy the right to sell wherever we liked. At first Neufeldt had no objections since it was all about selling increased quantities of his own products, but he was weak enough to set great store by the objections of his own sales reps. They told him that we used the Neufeldt products as advertising for our own, less well-made goods and thus indirectly damaged Neufeldt significantly. They claimed it was easier for our customers to buy from us than from Elbing, and it would be much more in Neufeldt's interest if Bing was no longer able to offer Neufeldt's products. All of this had to be taken with a pinch of salt seeing that Neufeldt's reps were paid on commission and that they would not have liked losing out on commission to our sales. It could not have amounted to much, though, because their sales area was restricted by the cost of freight, and his natural area was really in the North and in the East where we did not venture at that time. Neufeldt, however, was not enough of a businessman to separate truth from fiction, and the thought that we could have a negative impact on his reputation made him act against all common sense. He broke his solemnly made promise to keep our affiliation discreet by telling his sales reps to clarify the relationship between us and his company with their customers. He was obviously determined to break the relationship between our companies, but he was tied to the contract with us until 1880.

In 1879 the Association of German Tin workers held a large and important exhibition in Nuremberg. It took place in the gymnasium, and even though we were the owners of what was already regarded as the most important dealership in Germany, and I was a member of the committee, we were not allowed to exhibit our goods. It was a ruling that was to serve us well.

In the meantime we had rented larger premises in the Deutsche Haus in Pfannenschmiedgasse, now Wittelsbacher Hof, but after we had been there for eight years they were becoming insufficient for the expanding business, so in 1878 we purchased the house at 15, Marienstrasse and built a - for those days - comparatively large warehouse. Since we had been excluded from the actual exhibition hall, we used the new warehouse to host our own exhibition, which had been designed very impressively and which many of our business associates visited more attentively than the exhibition in the gymnasium.

Fig. 9 Marienstrasse 15

Our sales figures, including the Neufeldt products, and especially the cooking sets made to our specifications, were impressive, and this was of course noted and discussed among the experts. Neufeldt, who had attended the exhibition in Nuremberg, was so upset about this that he told everyone he knew in confidence that our success was due to the products that he supplied to us. The fact that Neufeldt broke his word was even more reprehensible since there was no truth to his boastfulness. True, we sold his products alongside our own ranges, but our efficiency had increased so much due to the development of the Saxon industry, which was mostly owing to our involvement, that we could easily predict that a break in relations with Neufeldt would not result in our business suffering the slightest loss in sales.

In the meantime we had made great progress in the tin-toy industry, and we had contracts with the large and rapidly growing Baumann company in Amberg, for whose enamelled products we had sole selling rights in certain areas. Furthermore, we had introduced cheap petroleum lamps, which were growing in demand by the population in both the towns and the countryside, and which we had made by the hundreds of thousands in dozens of different types, by a very efficient and well-trained cottage industry in Nuremberg.

We were relatively calmly looking toward the dissolution of our business relationship with Neufeldt in 1880, yet we had to start preparing for the event now. Neufeldt was sending his reps to Bavaria, though not with goods, since our contract stopped him from selling there, but with the news that from 1880 onwards Neufeldt's products would only be available through Neufeldt's reps. He grossly underestimated the progress made by the Saxon industry in the meantime, and he was deluded to think that when he started offering his products in Bavaria he would be greeted like the Messiah. Our customers, too, understood the existing relationship quite well and regarded the boastfulness and exaggerations displayed by Neufeldt's reps as nothing more than a prologue to the massive disappointment waiting for Neufeldt. Alas, it was now time for us to think about how to efficiently ward off Neufeldt's attack.

At around that time the Bavarian Trade Museum announced that in 1882 they would host the first Bavarian Exhibition for Trade and Industry in Nuremberg, and immediately the preparations began. It was a generous plan, supported by all factors, and the venue was going to be what is now called the *Max Field*[24]. I might as well mention here that for more than 20 years I was a member of the administrative council of the Bavarian Trade Museum – now called the Bavarian National Trade Institution - and I may be allowed to say, without being immodest, that my activity within this corporation was useful and constructive. Today I am still a member of the national committee of this highly-regarded institute that has been such a blessing for Bavarian trade and industry.

In view of the upcoming exhibition, it was the right time to set up a factory for the manufacture of such products as we had previously obtained from Neufeldt etc, and to prepare ourselves to display these products for viewing at the national exhibition. After long discussions with my brother, who as I could have predicted had little inclination to carry out this plan since he considered the risk of a factory too great, I was able to convince him that there was no other option and that there were ways to avoid or lessen the risk so feared by him. At last we reached an agreement, but unfortunately I had to promise that for the next six years I would not undertake anything beyond the modest factory building for which the plans had already been drawn up. I also had to promise to find someone who would take on the

[24] It ceased to be called that in 1882; Ignaz Bing probably means "what was then called the Max Field". It is now the main park of the city.

actual risk of the manufacture and who would sell us their products at certain prices.

I asked a young owner of a factory from Saxony, who had been supporting our company for a good few years, to take on the production for us in Nuremberg. In 1880 a neat new factory building stood proud in Scheuerlstrasse, not extremely big, but sufficient for several hundred workers. The new factory manager, Herr Heckler, who was really the owner and who rented the premises from us, brought with him a large number of Saxon workers so that the factory looked in order and had a certain capacity. We hired good workers from the various manufacturing sites to paint items made from brass, nickel, black plate and other metals, and our company, including the large workshops which we contractually maintained all through the year for the cottage industry, soon employed 200-300 workers. That was quite a respectable number striving for a considerable revenue with the many products in our range, and as far as I remember we turned over our first million as early as 1880.

So we were well prepared for Neufeldt's debut, and indeed this debut was a harsh disappointment for Neufeldt and his company. The reps used the same tactics everywhere, for example, they threw tea trays to the floor to prove that the paint would not come off and other such antics and they insulted our company (often receiving quite complimentary replies from the customers). In short, it was a miserable defeat that our big-headed adversary could have avoided, and it was one from which he never recovered.

The year 1882, the time of the first Bavarian Exhibition, was a triumph for our company. A massive display cupboard, 24 meters long, showed a magnificent array of the items that we manufactured, and we often had to answer the question as to how it was possible that in such a short time we had been able to achieve such high quality and variety in our production. The question was indeed justified, but we did not need to explain to everyone that it was entirely legal to procure "raw goods" for our painted products and to resell them as "painted goods" so to speak. This was explicitly permitted in the statutes for the finishing trade, and of course this enabled us to display an almost excessive number of shapes and colours.

Finally I want to relate a meeting with Neufeldt which brought me much joy. In his wisdom, Neufeldt had applied for the design patent to the little dolls' kitchen utensils which he had been manufacturing to our specifications. I knew perfectly well that such protection for items like these small dolls' utensils as a copy of the large adults' versions was worthless, only Neufeldt thought he was being very clever when he picked one item – it was a children's teapot – and sued us for patent infringement. This was just before the start of the exhibition. The case was simple, and in response to our factual objections the Nuremberg court declared the design patent as null and void, a fact that Neufeldt was unaware of before the opening of the exhibition.

I happened to see Neufeldt one day pacing to and fro along the front of our exhibition display, carefully reviewing our wares. He then came to the compartment where "his intellectual property" was represented, tastefully arranged: they were no longer his products, but the designs were like the ones he used for these items. He did not notice me, and I was able to observe him smile mischievously. I could not deny myself the pleasure of striding towards him, even though the relations between our two companies had ceased completely and Neufeldt's hostile and dishonourable behaviour really should have prohibited me from interacting with him. After the greeting, which he returned in a very friendly manner since he had really always respected me, I commented that he had not acted very nicely and said that given that it had been our idea to make the small kitchen utensils, and it had not been us who wanted to break off the business relationship, that now he was suing *us* for infringement of his design patent, and successfully so, I lied, for we had been fined a very large sum and ordered to cease production. He laughed heartily, shook my hand and said I should not take the matter to heart because I should prepare myself to hear the same judgement a hundred more times since he was going to take us to court over every single infringement. After the teapot, every single item was to follow one by one.

I pretended that this hellish news made me shake all over and begged him for leniency. I invited him humbly and woefully to have a glass of wine with me in the exhibition's very *gemütlich* wine tavern. He welcomed the invitation for he sought to gloat over my anguish. As we were sitting together over the wine in the company of my colleague Herr Dietz, who was a brilliant sales representative and who saw through the joke, I repeated my request to drop the matter, which would be of no use to him and only trouble for us. It was useless; he even wanted to gloat over the wording of the judgement. He laughed even more about my objection that it wasn't a very Christian thing to do, and so I asked Herr Dietz to fetch the letter with the judge's actual decision in the case *Neufeldt v. Gebrüder Bing* from our office. Herr Dietz returned, gave me the document, and I still played undecided as to whether I should hand it to Neufeldt. I was afraid of the colossal rejection, and really I did not want to fall out with this man with whom I had spent many a happy hour. Then he read the decision. His face fell, and all colour drained from it. Without a word he handed the document back to me, and I looked at him very reproachfully which really seemed to hit him hard. He became very quiet, said nothing more about the matter and then excused himself, saying he had to catch the next train to Munich. When I reminded him of how good we had been to him and how we could have worked together happily for many years to come, he was able to swallow his pride and admit that he was sorry too, but that he had become a victim of his sales reps, and he apologised for apparently breaking his word, since most customers knew anyway that we were selling his goods. He bid us a quick farewell and left, headed for - I might as well pre-empt it - an unhappy future.

The exhibition was a huge success for our company. Even though we already had a good name in the industry, the original novelties we exhibited were much admired and purchased in great quantities. The exhibition increased our annual sales by 100,000 marks. What was even more valuable, however, was the fact that our company became known all over Germany, after the exhibition was described as most extraordinary by the industry's journals and regarded as a great success in all areas.

The silent battle with my partner, however, remained the same. The restriction placed upon me to not expand the factory for a further six years was in itself incredibly hindering. Another obstacle was the fact that we did not manufacture ourselves but had employed a middleman instead. My brother's apprehension was further fuelled by the fact that, at the end of the exhibition year 1882, despite an increase in turnover of 100,000 marks, our net profits were no higher than in the previous year. This was obviously explained by the enormous expenditure of 30,000 marks for the exhibition. He did not count the immaterial profit, the great moral success; the outstanding reputation we had gained, the high regard in which the exhibition was held by the experts or the fact that we, a young company, had been awarded the highest honour, the Gold State Medal, at our first exhibition.

Fig. 10 Gold State Medal 1882

These differences of opinion between my brother and myself posed a danger and a hindrance for the development of the business which I no longer wanted to accept. Though entrepreneurial, I was conservative, too, and I went no further than making the most of the given circumstances and only as far as the existing means allowed, and that included, of course, any available credit from the banks. On the other hand, I could not bear the thought that the business would come to a dead-end or even a decline because of my partner's small-mindedness and lack of courage. My brother abhorred it when we introduced products that he could not sell to his customers in Augsburg or Munich. He overlooked the fact that we were no longer limited to the province of Bavaria, but that we had to strive to expand our sales area further and further, which would even include, in due course, overseas territories.

I could continue in this respect, for example how his opinions were directly opposed to mine in all such matters regarding the company's interest, something that was made worse by his friends harassing him and telling him that it was not practical to let a business become so large, saying that it was much better to follow the local saying "small fish, good fish". All things considered I could not really hold his narrow-mindedness in such things against him. His constricted view of the business was so intertwined with his nature that he could not act any differently than he did, and always at the cost of the company's development. I had to bring about a change, which meant I either had to separate from him or take the directive responsibility of the business entirely into my own hands. Some of his relatives, hard-working merchants, took part in these discussions and, having checked the facts, totally agreed with me. In the end we changed the agreement of the partnership to the extent that from 1883 onwards I was to be solely responsible for the leadership of the business.

Furthermore, I was granted the right to transform the partnership into a company with either private or public limited liability, whenever I considered the time right for such a move. He maintained all the other rights of a partner in the company, and I avoided everything that could have humiliated him.

The success of this agreement - which gave me free reign to add to our product range, to expand the cottage industry, to increase the sales areas, to create elegant and clear price-lists, which was something new at the time, to set up new branches and warehouses for samples in the main trade centres - can be judged by the fact that in the same year I took over the leadership of the company, we increased our net income by 60,000 marks.

How detrimental my brother's stipulation that we must not take on the risk of production ourselves turned out to be, shall be shown by the following:

The artful Saxon, who for five years acted in the fictitious position as our factory director, had, even while still under contract with us, cleverly manoeuvred things underhandedly and had supplied products manufactured in our factory to a company in Nuremberg in his own name. After five years he returned to Saxony, having amassed a fortune of in my opinion, around 200,000 marks, and continued to produce exactly the same items which he had made for us in Nuremberg. With his low selling prices he harmed us as much as he could, and that was quite a lot. Nonetheless, his devious actions and the way he abused our trust did not earn him many rewards, since once he had turned his business into a joint-stock company there was little left for him, and as far as I know he died a poor man.

In Elbing, too, things were rapidly deteriorating. Our former friend Neufeldt, who against his best intentions had done so much to aid the stellar rise of our company, entered into projects for which he did not have the necessary funds. He built a large factory for enamelled goods, in itself quite a good idea, but it cannot be overlooked that the location of Elbing is a highly unfavourable one for any factory that is not based on sea shipments.

In addition, Neufeldt had a tragic idea that finally put the nail in the coffin of his business. Apart from the fact that the annually issued pricelists always contained the same old typographical errors, i.e. it was obvious that they were never revised or recalculated, he also had quite a peculiar view of how to conduct his business affairs. I had heard from his first master, who by then had joined our company, that Neufeldt thought the principle applied by the post office – the cheaper the price of a postage stamp, the more letters are being sent and thus the more revenue is created – would be even more effective when applied to the shipment of goods. In his pricelist updates he wrote that for orders worth 60 marks or more he would deliver to the whole of Germany, Austria etc. freight prepaid. Now, we tried this several times ourselves; to ship a crate with a value of around 60 marks, provided the contents does not consist of heavy items, from Elbing to Nuremberg costs 15 marks, in other words 25% of the value of the goods. It is easy to imagine the losses the business suffered from these freight costs, since the only times they could have achieved a small profit was when they shipped to places in the vicinity of Elbing. Furthermore, Neufeldt expected his customers to return the empty crates to Elbing at their expense, something no customer would agree to, and so this new idea that Neufeldt had thought so promising really was the beginning of the end. Neufeldt's problem was that he displayed a great arrogance and a lack of business know-how in all things. When no more investors or lenders could be found who were willing to part with their money, the company was turned into a joint-stock company and the shares were mostly used to pay off his debts with the banks. At first, Neufeldt stayed on as director, but the pitiful results declined year on year, and the situation in Elbing grew entirely untenable. There were differences between the banks and Neufeldt which eventually led to him giving up his post as director, and, as far as we know, making some of his shares available to the banks too. Later he founded a bicycle factory in Freiburg in Baden, again with someone else's money, which he had to close down again after a while due to heavy losses. In Elbing itself, business has been in decline ever since, for many years no dividends have been paid, and there is little hope that it will ever pick up again. Until recently the banks have been offering us the whole company for a merger with our business, but we have, very wisely, declined the offer.

Given that I have talked about our relationship with Neufeldt in such great detail, I shall not miss the opportunity to relate what else I have heard from and about him. One day, after his business in Freiburg had come to a tragic end, I received a long letter from him addressed to me. He began by telling me that amongst all his competitors I had been the most generous and kind-hearted towards him, despite all the injustice he had committed against my company. He added that he still had many useful ideas and plans which would prove to be incredibly successful for the tin goods industry. He asked if I would like to allow him to join our company for that purpose, in exchange of course for providing the necessary equipment and means as well as a fixed salary. Any returns from his work would be our company's, while all he asked for was that the items produced by him should always be described as "Made by Neufeldt". This ludicrous request just went to show that he was still the same old megalomaniac, and I politely turned down the project. I heard no more from him until one day a bookshop in Elbing sent me a little volume of poems stating Neufeldt as the author. The book is entitled "Young dreams of an old man". It contains mediocre poems, and one single poem entitled "Elegant packaging" is reminiscent of the industrial past of the poet who had travelled the world on his "steed of steel".

In 1891 our company celebrated its 25th anniversary in a very memorable and appropriate manner. This is what the *Fränkische Kurier* said at the time about this important celebration:

25th Anniversary of the *Gebrüder Bing* Company in Nuremberg

> *The celebrations to mark the 25th anniversary of the* Gebrüder Bing *company held in the halls of the Maxfield Restaurant on the 5th day of this month for their clerical staff and factory workers was a great success that all who took part will never forget. It will probably be of interest to a few of our readers to hear more about this event, and since we know that it would not find favour with the modest hosts if we were on this occasion to relate in great detail the enthusiastic ovations delivered by members of the clerical staff, the factory management and the workers, we will instead limit ourselves to a rough outline of the dazzling festivities:*
>
> *The office staff had agreed, together with the factory management, that the 25th anniversary of the* Gebrüder Bing *company was to be celebrated in a solemn act, and they had kept the secret so well that the two brothers were more than a little surprised and astonished when, on the morning of New Year's day, they were invited by a deputation to go to their offices to receive the congratulations. The entire office staff -*

counting well over a hundred people - the factory management and the master craftsmen, also large in numbers, were already gathered there in festive order. Junior partner Strubell, who had been with the company for 18 years, delivered a loyal and heartfelt address, a copy of which had been signed by the entire office staff, the factory management, the master craftsmen and the fore workers. The truly artistic address, put to paper by Herr Luckmeyer in his usual masterful calligraphy, rested in a magnificent cover, which had been donated by a foreign business associate of the company. A deputation then presented a very splendid album, which had been produced in J. G. Kugler's factory with the most solid workmanship and in the most tasteful manner, and which contained pictures of those men from the office and factory staff who were in a way considered to be the generals of the company. On the outside of the album was an artistic silver cast, masterfully made by the sculptor Hasenstab (the cast itself was made in Rome), depicting the emblems of trade and industry, crowned by genies, and a medal with the relief portraits of the owners of the company. The assiduous young artist can only be congratulated on his exquisite work. The album itself will in due course be displayed for general viewing at the exhibition of Nuremberg artists, which is now open.

The presentation of the album was followed by more congratulations, led by junior partner Kohn in the name of all the staff, on the occasion of Ignaz Bing, part-owner of the company, being awarded the title of Kommerzienrat by the Prince Regent of Bavaria. The speaker stressed that it was to be considered a fortunate omen for the company that the 25th anniversary coincided with such an award, and that all the personnel, the factory and all those who had played their part in the past, present and future of the company were honoured by it. The two partners were very moved and thanked everyone and then proposed to round off this most solemn occasion with a celebration for the entire workforce from the offices and the factory and for those master craftsmen who had been working for the company, independently yet consistently from the beginning. This celebration took place, as mentioned above, on Monday evening.

It was an imposing sight to see more than 500 people in festive attire rising from their seats to welcome the two brothers and their families when they arrived in the beautifully decorated hall at around half past seven, to the sounds of a celebratory march. When the music had died down, an employee of the company stepped onto the podium and delivered a witty prologue in verse that he had written himself and which expressed the sentiments of all those present. Soon after that, Herr Kommerzienrat Ignaz Bing took the floor to welcome the guests and to give a short but precise review of the past and preview of the future of the business. He said:

'Dear guests! Please allow me to extend a very warm welcome to you all who are here today to celebrate the 25th anniversary of the Gebrüder Bing *company. This is indeed a significant moment, and to review how the company developed from its very modest beginnings to its current role on the global stage would be an interesting task. I will, however, limit myself to simply hint at the number of battles we had to fight against unfavourable circumstances, despite the fact that God has evidently given the enterprise his blessing. One thing that I may*

emphasise with satisfaction, however, is that the unshakable principles of strict integrity, diligence and vigour have always been the company's guiding lights, and the shield of our business honour has remained spotlessly clean to this day and shall remain so, God willing. Of all the important activities the company engaged in over the years, I will only mention the foundation of the factory about ten years ago, which was very soon after rewarded for its products with the highest honour, the Gold State Medal, at the Bavarian Exhibition in 1882. We are overjoyed that a considerable number of independent master craftsmen, some with large workshops of their own, have been loyally working for us, solely and continuously, side by side with the factory, and that we can welcome some of them here with us today. I will leave it to my brother and business partner to give credit to the loyal and trustworthy employees we have found in our clerical staff, in our two trustworthy and dutiful junior partners, in our keen and hardworking travelling representatives, in our cautious directors of the various areas of the business, in everyone. I myself will only use the beautiful words of the poet[25] *to describe the programme for the future:*

> *Work adorns the burgher greatly,*
> *Blessing is our labour's prize;*
> *Honoured crowns make princes stately,*
> *But in work our honour lies.*[26]

The absolute proof that honour lies in these hands' work is in the award that I have been granted in recent days from the highest order. I accepted the award for you all in the

[25] Friedrich von Schiller in *The Song of the Bell.*
[26] Translation by Margarete Muensterberg on www.bartleby.com.

understanding that honest work and ambition will not be in vain, and I am sure you will all join me happily in a toast to our noble regent of Bavaria, the high protector and supporter of art and commerce, of trade and industry, His Royal Highness Prince Luitpold, long may he live!"
The toast was followed by a standing ovation while the orchestra played the royal hymn.

Next, Herr Adolf Bing took to the podium to describe the difficulties experienced at the formation and throughout the growth of the company in a humorous manner, and he used the closing remarks of his warmly received speech to express his heartfelt thanks to all who had helped the company to grow and bloom, especially the management team. Amongst the many and always warmly received toasts that followed were several noteworthy ones, namely one delivered by one of the Bing brothers' little daughters in honour of Johann Eberhard, a packer who had been with the business in loyal duty for almost 20 years; a poetic one by factory manager Scharlach in honour of the commercial staff; a thank you from junior partner Kohn to the factory management and last but not least a heartfelt toast from long-serving junior partner Strubell, who received from his boss, Herr Kommerzienrat Ignaz Bing, a very special thank you and the assurance of unfaltering loyalty.

With that, the official part of the evening was over, and what followed was a succession of quite exquisite songs performed by some friends of the firm who had beautiful voices, and some uplifting singing by a double quartet made up of staff members, a performance that was received with thundering applause. The fact that there was no shortage of light-hearted numbers and funny or dramatic performances may well be explained by the large number of young and joyous clerks who are in the service of the company.

The highlight of the celebration was certainly the living picture displayed by several employees with the help from the sculptor, Herr Hasenstab, and special thanks is due to factory manager Scharlach who put a lot of effort in to make it happen. After a speech which outlined the history and the statistics of the business from its beginnings to its current role on the global stage, the curtains parted and the audience was surprised to view an allegoric scene depicting trade and industry, under the wings of Noris[27]*, surrounded by the emblems for technology and merchants. The brilliant and attractive image, which unleashed a rapturous, unending applause, was preserved for eternity by the photographer.*

It is impossible to describe all the details of this uniquely beautiful celebration. Suffice to say that it was early morning when, after much merry dancing, the last guests left the Maxfield in the highest spirits. There is no doubt that kitchen and cellar had their part to play in this, and we are discreet enough not to mention the quantities in which offerings were made to Gambrinus and Bacchus[28]*. It was a celebration worthy of the importance of the company, worthy of the animated zeal displayed by the employees in the interest of the company, and worthy of the harmony with which all factors usually come together and which are called upon for the future*

---

[27] The female personification of the city of Nuremberg.
[28] Patron saints of beer and wine.

to ensure the realisation of all the good wishes expressed on the occasion of the company's 25th anniversary.

It was by pure chance that the anniversary coincided with my award of the "Kommerzienrat" title. I want to stress at this point that I was never striving for titles or decorations, and that if that had been my aim I could have achieved ten times more. The manner in which titles and decorations are usually awarded today was at that time completely out of the question, and awards, at least where trade and industry were concerned, were granted merely on merit.

Wherever the many and difficult tasks of my business activities allowed it, I enjoyed taking part in all charitable endeavours. Twice I was called upon to act as counsel to the Bavarian government in the negotiations of commercial treaties, or corporations asked me to be their expert adviser on important questions regarding trade and commerce.

At around the same time, a large association was formed in Leipzig. Its aim was to represent the commercial interests of the various branches of the metal working industries. There were about 100 companies present, and I was immediately elected, by acclamation, to preside over the proceedings of the formation. When it came to elect the chairman of the board, again, I received all of the votes.

The joint-stock company *Vereinigte Eschebach'sche Werke* from Dresden was considered to be the most significant member of the new union. Herr Geheimrat[29] Eschebach returned from his

---

[29] Title which equates roughly to "Member of the Privy Council".

holiday in Italy especially to attend the formation of the association in Leipzig. He entered the room when the negotiations were in full swing; I interrupted the proceedings and announced that Herr Geheimrat Eschebach, "the Eiffel tower of the German tin goods industry" had just arrived, and I permitted myself to invite him to take a seat at the board of directors' table. There were shouts of "Bravo!" and "Hear! Hear!", and my intentions were thus wholly fulfilled. It was very important to me that this company from Dresden join the association, and I knew that after my comment Herr Eschebach would be keen to support our endeavours. I had been serious about the comparison with the Eiffel tower: Despite our excellent growth it seemed impossible to me that our company might come even close to the results achieved by his company, which was so much more significant in revenues etc. And yet, not only was this exactly what happened just a few years later, but indeed Nuremberg turned over several million more per year than Dresden.

At a later personal encounter with Eschebach in Nice, where he greeted me with his usual cordiality, he asked if it was now me or him who was the Eiffel tower of the tin goods industry. I replied that now there were two Eiffel towers; however, he was the taller one, since indeed compared to me he was a giant. Today, a long time after Eschebach's death, the company is still highly regarded, though somewhat stinted in its commercial development.

Our own development, however, continued upwards. New buildings for manufacturing purposes were bought, and the commercial premises were also expanded over the years as our financial situation allowed. This was made possible by the purchase of a large place in Blumenstrasse, where our main office is now located. Additionally, expecting that the factory works would also need to be enlarged accordingly, we purchased a large piece of land which was very well suited to the company's purposes and where the very extensive factories that were build over the years are now found. The value of land and properties there, too, will increase over time.

Fig. 11 Blumenstrasse 14, Nuremberg.

Apart from worrying about furnishing the warehouse and the manufacturing premises necessary for the growing business in Nuremberg, we were also dealing with new undertakings that were to become a new support in our long-lasting relations with the Saxon Ore Mountains. Neufeldt's factory in Elbing, which was the first to introduce enamelled toys for children and which was soon attracting a large customer base, partly burned down, but the company did not pick up the production of those products again. This prompted us to set up our own manufacturing branch in Grünhain, for enamelled toys to start with, which over time and together with the production of other items, developed into a large and productive business.

At first we wanted to set up a factory for enamelled goods in Nuremberg, which was becoming indispensable for our industry. However, once the manifold needs of the company, which required constantly expanding manufacturing facilities, were met, we clearly knew that we did not have the significant means necessary left over, nor did we want to take out any more credit than was absolutely necessary, so instead I came up with a plan to involve a number of capitalists in the establishment of a factory for enamelled goods in Nuremberg. My idea was bolstered by the fact that I wanted to help a cousin, Siegmund Hopf, who had been a friend of mine since our youth, by taking a great worry off his mind. It was like this:

A poor cousin of Hopf's had married a mechanic called Carette in Paris. The man died, leaving behind a son. He was a handsome, intelligent boy, who, sponsored by my cousin, received his commercial education in Nuremberg and then started in our company as an apprentice. In this position he proved himself to be hard-working and intelligent, and he had a certain charm that was quite bewitching for anyone who had dealings with him. After he had been with the company for about six years he went to England. His adopted parents, however, wanted him to come home and furthermore, his mother had moved back from Paris to Nuremberg in the meantime. That was why my cousin was nagging me to find the young Carette a job; he would in turn ensure that the youngster was supported with sufficient financial means.

Therefore, I was thinking of proposing Carette for the role of director of the new factory. The consortium formed for the pre-negotiations, however, proved itself, during the actual negotiations, to be completely unsuitable for the formation of a business in the manner intended by me. Right from the beginning of the pre-negotiations I was put off by their petty views, their requests for guarantees of immediate high returns etc, and one day, when another more than narrow-minded opinion prevented the purchase of a cheap property, I declared my departure from the consortium, and that was the end of the story.

But what was to happen to Herr Carette, who had only just returned from England? I suggested to my cousin that Carette should set up a factory to supplement our toy industry, the products of which would be sold to the general export customers and to us. It was a promising proposal, and I was convinced that Carette would be well-suited for this job. The agreement was finalised, and a new factory was built in Kobergerstrasse, far away from our own properties. That was the reason why we could not be part owners of the freehold, but instead we agreed on a rent which guaranteed my cousin, who was the owner of the building, a pretty high return.

It goes without saying that our company faced many difficulties with the development of Carette's business. For many years we were the new company's only customer. Naturally, the goods were often of inadequate quality and caused us great inconvenience, which could only be overcome thanks to the reputation of our company. We were partners in this company, and yet we were unable to have any influence on important matters concerning the factory. It was down to Carette's strange behaviour, who manipulated his already suspicious adopted father and protector in such a way that correspondences were being sent to and fro, which seemed unprofessional and bitter. A proviso made by us most considerately was blown out of all proportion and talked about in the factory and, especially, in Hopf's home so that I had only one name for this whole tittle-tattle: Koberger Gossip.

I do not want to go on about this too long since the older employees who are still working for the company today know the story only too well. I shall only say this much, namely that once the business started to grow and return a profit, Carette and my cousin did all they could to try and take the business into their own hands. After ten years of partnership we parted, and even the loose connection we still kept with the company did not survive the separation for long. Only later did we learn how unfairly Carette had treated us behind our backs, while he was still in partnership with us and we had full confidence in his personal integrity; but he too would have to pay retribution. Today our former partner lives abroad with no chance of ever returning to Germany. He always remained a Frenchman on the inside, his sons are serving in the French army, and eventually it was the vox populi that accused him of serving France to Germany's disadvantage, which caused him to flee from Nuremberg.

Apart from that, the years were filled with toil and trouble as well as with satisfaction regarding the growth and success of all the company's endeavours.

Despite my numerous tasks I still sometimes found the time to follow my own interests. I remember, for example, my attendance at an excellent meeting of the German Association of Anthropologists which had convened in Nuremberg under the chairmanship of Professor Rudolf Virchow from Berlin. I was also a member of the press committee, and one of my jobs was to compose a few sing-able songs for the choir that were to be performed during the social gatherings of the anthropologists' conference. I earned much respect for a parody in one of those songs, especially from Professor Virchow who came up to me after the performance, shook my hand and then took every opportunity he had during his stay in Nuremberg to talk with me (which was very unusual for him). This is the song:

Sung to the melody of "I don't know what it may signify"[30].

> A tower, so grey and weathered,
> From the rock it looks down below.
> It has trembled with many a sigh,
> Hit by many a lightning strike.
>
> Shrouded by many dark tales
> It proudly looks all around,
> The ancient walls lamenting
> In the middle of the night.

---

[30] *Ich weiss nicht, was soll es bedeuten*; famous poem written by Heinrich Heine about the beautiful maiden Lorelei, the siren who sits on a high cliff overlooking the river Rhine, and who with her singing causes the ships below to crash into the treacherous rocks.

A proud young maiden lives there,
All lonely and unmarried.
He who comes looking for a bride
will be met by a ghastly fate.

With her oh so powerful arms
She will press him close to her heart,
Until the warm blood of *his* heart
Washes the love into the earth.

And whoever kisses her mouth,
Will see his lips go pale.
Should he dare to take little sips,
He'll find the eternal dark'.

And ask you where lives this maiden,
Who behaves in such a cruel manner?
She's up there in the old castle,
Kept there by the magistrate.

Gone may well be these old days
When the iron maiden's might
Could cause a man's bitter demise
Deep down in the tower's pit.

The beautiful women of Noris
Have learned their lesson though:
When they look a man in the eye,
Their hearts begin to ache.

At the *Merkur* association, I delivered speeches on the commercial apprentice system and other things; they were well attended and received with much applause. It goes without saying that I supported all humanitarian or charitable projects, and not just with numerous significant monetary donations, but in individual cases I also made my modest poetic talent available. Here follows a sonnet that was published in an advertising pamphlet for a holiday colony, put together with input from the most excellent artists and poetically gifted personalities of Nuremberg:

Goethe

A prince of poets, he wants to take his people
To dizzy heights in eternal pure beauty;
Magic sounds ring from his works
Creating a new world inside us.

His gaze lost in unmeasured distances,
So that posterity may crown the scientist in him too,
So that his people may get used to deep thought,
That's how we see him striding through the century.

But let us consider these words still higher
Which, free of dogma and dark delusions,
Let through the light of philanthropy's ardour.
The poet sinks these words into the gates of our hearts
and creates a new path for the poet's words:
"Let Man be a noble creature, helpful and good".

This poem of mine also expresses my own sentiments, which were quite appropriate at the time when the beast of antisemitism, caused by bigotry, started to stir in Germany.

I also held a modest office at the town council for more than 25 years. On the occasion of this anniversary the magistrate gave a worthy speech, and I was awarded the Great Silver Citizen's Medal, a rare honour.

Further honours were bestowed upon me when I was awarded the freedom of the towns of Grünhain and Streitberg, and I would like to point out the curiosity that my predecessor as honorary citizen in Grünhain was no other than Count Bismarck.

I never had much to do with politics. Of course I belonged to a party, the National Liberals, and after their formation in Nuremberg they asked me to join them on the board. I always refused though to do any more than my duties as a citizen, and I stayed away from politics as much as I could.

My social credo is, briefly summarised, as follows:

I believe that every good human being has to have a social conscience, i.e. he must understand that, even though incredibly important and significant things have been achieved over the years by social legislation, the work cannot be done yet. I believe that the workers' demands for better quality of life, whether in this area or that, are justified; the working classes have bettered themselves over the years, and one finds among them not just a few parents who are desperate to give their children a better education and thereby a better future. Even though the wages paid currently may be more than sufficient for the young, unmarried worker, when it comes to families where there are concerns for accommodation, children's education and needs etc, the conditions are far less favourable. The working classes are still suffering from a certain social hardship, and whatever has been done over the past years to improve the situation was merely the undeniable duty of the employers aimed at making up for the sins committed in times of less social empathy. One has to ensure order and discipline, all the while treating the workers with true, not diplomatic, benevolence, and to make sure that the officers and supervisors are in line with these sentiments. This may not smooth away all differences and solve all the issues that employers justifiably complain about, but a real sense of goodwill running through the board will at least be conducive to the formation of a certain number of reliable and loyal workers.

I am proud to say that I have always been guided by these principles, and that I have again and again obliged my colleagues to abide by them, too. The proof that these seeds were not sown in vain lies in the fact that whenever difficulties arose in the factory, discussions with the workers, and several times even speeches delivered to the entire factory staff, always led to a resolution of the differences, and that since the establishment of the factories, i.e. between 1880 and today, we have not had one day of strike or any serious unrest in our company. Long may this continue!

It would be interesting to find out what has become of the many thousands of young clerks whom I introduced to the commercial world, and who left the business sooner or later after they had finished their apprenticeship with us. Naturally I stayed in touch with several hundred of them after they had left. In several places, I know for example in New York, they formed associations for ex-employees of the *Gebrüder Bing* company. I have often been able to enjoy signs of loyal affection, such as greeting cards or in person, and many young people who were apprenticed in our company achieved commercial success and became very wealthy.

Of course, the profits we earned each year were not sufficient to fund the appropriate development and modernisation of the company; much higher sums were required for that. Furthermore, I was concerned that my brother had a number of sons who he naturally wanted to employ in the business, and who would evidently become my associates. I sincerely wished that my brother's sons, as well as my own children, would have the talent and the love for the business that would enable me to find them a position in our own company, and to grant them all the things that I myself took advantage of. However, as far I could see at the time, my brother's sons did not have the qualities to take on a leading role in the business. They were good, decent boys, and at this point I shall only say that today three of them are working for the company, and they are trying very hard to meet the demands placed upon them.

Fig. 12 Gold State Medal 1896

Employing my nephews, however, was only possible because in 1895 I exercised my right to turn the *Gebrüder Bing* company into a joint-stock company. It was this solution that laid the path for the development of the company into a large-scale manufacturing business and that eventually allowed me to give my brother's sons the opportunity to prove themselves in their employment, not just with me but also within the joint-stock company.

Furthermore, I had the opportunity to bring about marriages between my daughters and such young men who had been working in the business for quite some years and whose character and abilities were sufficient guarantees that these unions were also in the company's best interest.

Let me talk a bit about my employees. My brother was pretty much excluded; he had long since stopped being a travelling salesman, and the statistics he liked to produce were meaningless, but they kept him busy in a way. On the other hand, early on when the company was still a partnership, I had promoted my especially reliable and conscientious colleagues into positions which allowed them to refrain from setting up their own businesses, and I hinted at the prospect of increased responsibilities and increased remuneration in line with the further development of the company which included the formation of the joint-stock company. These employees were also junior partners. They were: My son-in-law, Herr Hirschmann, Herr Ferdinand Kohn, Herr Martin and Herr Strubell; loyal employees who at the time had been with the company for over 25 years and whom I granted the right to invest up to 50,000 marks and to share a percentage in the company's profits accordingly.

It proved an additional benefit for the gentlemen mentioned above that when the business was turned into a joint-stock company, they received 50 shares for their investment of 50,000 marks without having to pay any premiums.

The opening balance sheet was audited and found to be in good order. I appointed the following people to the board of directors:

Herr Justizrat[31] Josephthal as director for legal affairs, Herr Josef Schmidt to represent the Dresdner Bank and my old friend Karl Böck. I was going to be President and my brother Adolf Vice-President of the board of directors.

It is now 20 years since the formation of the joint-stock company, and it has grown quite substantially in those years. Describing this development in detail would be going too far. It was possible thanks to the proficiency of its directors, external finance and the fact that all opportunities were grasped which allowed the sale of the company's thousand-fold products within Germany, Europe and overseas, as well as the continuous growth of those sales. While in 1895 the opening balance sheet showed 1,600,000 marks of capital, it now stands at 6,700,000 marks with liabilities of 3 million and a reserve fund of 2,850,000 marks. The value of the factories, warehouses and the land totals nearly 5 million alone, and still the company is compelled to rent premises at a cost of 50,000 marks per annum. No fewer than 15 sample stores have been established throughout Europe and beyond, and it may also serve to assess the company if I add that between 1895 and 1915 machinery and premises depreciated by nearly 5,500,000 marks.

Fig. 13 Company logo 1912

[31] Pronounced: yoos-TEETS-raht; similar to the English title of "King's Counsel".

As to my own role as President of the Board, I continued to work as usual during the first five years after the change. Since the joint-stock company was formed by the family, the founding members were prohibited from selling their shares during the first five years. It goes without saying that I was on hand with help and advice in the organisation and also with all large projects once they were at the stage of execution. My greatest service to the company lay in my extensive experience and in the unusually great confidence I enjoyed everywhere as a merchant and also personally. This also enabled me to arrange the often rather substantial sums of money that were needed. The building of large factories and warehouses in Nuremberg as well as the main office in Grünhain in Saxony was only possible partly because the relevant construction companies proved the immense trust they had in me and in the company by agreeing to building projects worth millions of marks and accepting longer payment terms.

Fig. 14 Factory in Grünhain in Saxony.

How little man can understand whether the buildings he has constructed with joy and success tell if his life's work is good or if it is threatened by great danger is testimony to the times in which I am writing these memoirs of my life as a merchant. A world war has broken out, which has rained down over industry with a paralysing and eradicating force, and it is as yet unforeseeable what terrible consequences it is going to entail for all people, including for Germany and her allies. Russia, France, England, Italy and other exotic people are opposing Germany and her ally Austria. It is simple envy, hate and angry jealousy of Germany's success, united in the aim to obliterate our fatherland; yet after ten months of war our enemies have not achieved this; the successes are on our side and, God willing, we will continue to wrestle down our enemies, or at the very least keep them at bay.

The evening of my life could have been quite a quiet one, spent together with my lovely wife in the lovely Streitberg, in my simple country house in its charming location, which has often served my relatives as a retreat too, if only we had been spared this terrible war. During the last few years that I spent in Streitberg, since the directors took away more and more of my commercial responsibilities, I have been able to dedicate more and more time to my deep love for nature and the natural sciences. I have achieved quite a few things in the area of research, which I enjoyed all the more since I did not neglect my commercial tasks either. The *Bing-Höhle*, a cave discovered and developed by myself, is the most extraordinary natural wonder in Franconia, and every year thousands of people come here to enjoy it and to be uplifted by it. The property of the cave is unalienable and in some ways everlasting. It will carry my name forward through the generations even when all that I have achieved in material things will long be gone and forgotten.

It took me only a few days to write down these memoirs, with the aim of giving my children and grandchildren a simple impression of their father and grandfather. They do not claim to be exhaustive or original in any way, they have been typed up from my dictation, uncontrived and without striving for a certain style. Furthermore, I have avoided the inclusion of any words of warning, admonition or advice, since I am convinced that those members of my family who are called upon to lead and assist in the leadership of the business will work to keep within limits that will guarantee a solid future for the company and will not do anything that would endanger what we have built. The current war is a lesson on how even the best and most carefully led businesses are threatened by sudden, unforeseen dangers, and that under certain circumstances, years of successful work can be followed by a quick and tragic decline.

Let us hope for the future that world war will soon be followed by world peace, and that what the war has destroyed will soon be rebuilt on the trusted principles of the *Gebrüder Bing* company, i.e. untiring drive and vision combined with commercial prudence and harmonious cooperation.

Amen!

Streitberg, 12th June 1915

Ignaz Bing
Geheimer Kommerzienrat

Fig. 15 Ida Bing, Ignaz's wife, with their children Stefan, Frieda, Berta, Siegmund, Anna and Marie (in chair)

My Family And Friends

In 1915, at a time of war and in a gloomy, anxious mood, I felt the urge to write down my memoirs under the preface of *Tales From A Merchant's Life*. Primarily, I wanted to create a legacy for my grandchildren; to paint a picture of their grandfather before it was too late - given that by then I was already over 75 years old.

Those memoirs described my life in detail only up to the beginning of my adulthood; from then on I sought to finish them in chronological order without regard to which other happy or sad event from my commercial activities or from the circle of our family and friends I could also have related. I felt a duty - rather than an inner urge - to talk about my youth, leading up to the part which I played in the development of the *Gebrüder Bing* company from its rather modest beginnings to its prominence in the industrial world today.

Because of this unfortunate war I found no pleasure in this work, and I tried to get over it as quickly as I could. This now presents me with the task of adding certain things that might be of interest and concern to the younger members of the family, even in the future. What I am beginning to write today is more of a chronicle than an autobiography. I will start from the time when the *Gebrüder Bing* company, whose founder I was, moved its place of business from Gunzenhausen to Nuremberg.

In Nuremberg I found the ground well-prepared to give me plenty of opportunities to socialise after a busy and hard day's work in the business from early morning till late in the evening. I was especially pleased to find a number of old friends from my time in Fürth, who welcomed me with open arms. There would be no point in mentioning any names; I can and will only relate those events that I remember most vividly and as far as is suitable for this context.

Fig. 16 View of Nuremberg in the late 1800s.
© William Vaughn Tupper

What is more, at that time (1865) a large number of my, mostly maternal, relatives were living in Nuremberg. Here, too, I will refrain from explaining who they all were in great detail. I mixed with all members of both families – some of my paternal relatives had moved to Nuremberg in the meantime, too – on very friendly terms. I especially enjoyed being in my uncle Salomon

Tuchmann's house; he was a senior partner in one of the largest hop companies in Bavaria. Since my time in Fürth I had been close friends with his son, my cousin Fritz, who was several years younger than me, and our friendship, never broken or interrupted, lasted all our lives. There will be several more mentions of this kind, loyal and trusty friend in these pages. I was also attracted to the only daughter of the family, a very bright and kind, if not exactly pretty girl, but I was very aware that according to the song "Each other they could not possess"[32] a union was out of the question – not because the water was too deep but rather because the dowry was far too great. When one day I mentioned to my uncle that should choose me as a husband for his little girl, and that he would be in for a good deal since I would be happy to accept a quarter of the dowry he intended for his daughter (I was joking of course), he replied in his Ülfeld dialect "Schlemiel, she knows better". I had to agree.

At the time, the city of Nuremberg had about 50,000 inhabitants and was considered the Bavarian stronghold for liberal views regarding all aspects of public life. Its good and honest citizens were free from any anti-Semitism. I mixed more with well-educated Christian people, including even young ladies, than with those of the Jewish confession. In brief, we all lived together in a cosy, friendly manner without my ever feeling that I was only tolerated in those circles.

Apart from the performances at the municipal theatre, and especially the excellent operas there, the other main events for recreation after a day's work were the simpler, instrumental

[32] Tragic German song *Zwei Königskinder* about a prince and a princess in love who were separated by a large body of water.

concerts in the Adler hall. They took place on Saturday evenings, where, without much ceremony, one simply joined the young ladies sitting at the tables with their parents. One was always made very welcome.

The character of the city can be summed up in a few words like this: an eagerness to work amongst all professional classes, a simple and undemanding lifestyle, easy and jovial intercourse without any confessional division amongst the citizens; in short, one felt completely at home in Nuremberg, wherever one went. There were numerous small but cosy and reputable public houses where one could meet with one's friends and acquaintances for an evening drink and a simple but well-prepared meal. It was especially in the plain, smoky rooms of the inns *Zum Bärleinhuter*, *Zum Göckerla*, *Zum Jammertal*, *Zum Leistlein*, *Zum Essigbrätlein*, *Zum Einhorn*, *Zur Wolfschlucht* etc. where one would always happen upon a number of familiar faces. I only mention a few individual inns because their names have a certain originality.

In contrast to the many public houses, the café lifestyle was only little developed. When I arrived in Nuremberg, the city boasted only one such place (that is not counting the many coffee bars where the farmers' wives took their breakfast and lunch when they came to market), namely *Café Maestrami* on Kaiserstrasse. It was established by an Italian, was very well managed, but despite the good service and the very cosy ambience in the admittedly very small premises, it was not very well patronised at all. Frau Maestrami passed away just a few years ago, at the age of 81. When the *Café Panorama* opened much later on the Plärrer[33], it

[33] Large town square in the south-west of Nuremberg.

was considered an amazing, big city creation. Those who know Nuremberg today will hardly be able to imagine the contrast between then and now.

Fig. 17 Plärrer Square with café in the background, 1891.

Once the *Gebrüder Bing* company had moved to Nuremberg, my brother and I continued to run our own household, if only because the company was obliged to continue to board and lodge the two apprentices who had been working for the company in Gunzenhausen. We rented cheap but suitable rooms on Vordere Ledergasse in the front house, facing Josefplatz, that belonged to Frau von Stadler and is now owned by Ellern. The entrance was on Josefplatz, and we therefore benefited quite nicely from the noble glamour of the simple but elegant house.

The amicable relationship with our cook, whom we had brought with us from Gunzenhausen, experienced a number of disruptions in Nuremberg, caused mostly by the masters. In Gunzenhausen everything had been very cheap, and therefore our already very economical cook managed to get by on very few expenses indeed. I remember that the weekly expenditure for a household of four, sometimes five people was never more than five to six guilders. In Nuremberg those costs increased to double that amount, to around 12 to 15 guilders, and my somewhat suspicious brother could only find one explanation, namely that cook was dishonest. In addition, one of his suits went missing one day. The situation escalated to the point that he and the cook had a row, which eventually led to her dismissal.

But for me, this event had tragic consequences, despite the fact that I would normally side with the cook who was usually clever and, in my opinion, honest and prudent. The suit, by the way, was later found and its apparent disappearance explained naturally.

That same day I had invited some friends for the evening whom I wanted to treat to roasted pigeon, which our cook knew how to prepare most deliciously. The friends arrived, as did the roasted birds, but I missed the usual appealing and appetising smell of a good roast. Also, the pigeons seemed remarkably large. When the birds were being carved - oy vey - it became apparent that in the confusion and excitement the unjustly accused girl had forgotten to remove the giblets from the pigeons, and that therefore the whole meal - normally so delicious - was now of course very unappetising and ruined. The guests laughed at the ghastly discovery, and I myself comforted the poor girl, who had served up such a disappointment for me and my friends, as well as I could.

In 1866, my parents and their large family – they had three adolescent daughters and three sons by now - resettled to Nuremberg. The following goes to show how mean-spirited even the liberal Nuremberg was at that time when it came to granting the right of citizenship. My father's application, which I had personally supported at the town council, was rejected on the grounds that their declared assets of 40,000 guilders were insufficient, claiming that there was the danger that - in the case of impoverishment - the six children would become a burden to the city's poor box. Upon appeal to the government, the councillor received a reprimand and my father his letter of citizenship. Considering that nowadays almost every resident, even from the working classes, is made a compulsory citizen, this event sounds like a fable.

While I am on the subject I will add that previously, in 1860, my brother-in-law Ottenstein, who was married to my favourite sister Ida and who certainly was not without means, had also been refused the right to citizenship, and that when he took up residence in Nuremberg it was merely as an occupant who could be expelled at any time.

I saw my sister almost daily; we had a very close relationship that is rare amongst brothers and sisters, right up until her far-too-early death. We shared joy and sorrow, and it gave me immense pleasure when I could delight her – and I did this quite often – by sending her a delicacy from the *Dorner* wine tavern near her flat - now the *Rotes Oechslein* in Brunnengasse, which was then the best-reputed kitchen in Nuremberg.

The year 1866 brought the war of brothers between Prussia and Austria, where Bavaria and the other Southern states joined Austria as allies. I will not go into cause, events, purpose and consequences of the war here. These things are history now; however, I will always remember the day when the victorious Prussians marched into Nuremberg. That day, my uncle Bernhard Bing, a brother of my father's who had died relatively young, was laid to rest in the newly established cemetery near Fürther Strasse. On the way home, there suddenly appeared immensely splendid, mounted soldiers (Mecklenburg cuirassiers) who seemed over-sized to me on their mighty horses. All main roads, public places, the gates, the station, the town hall etc. were occupied by the enemy. It was a striking, imposing picture. Bavaria was conquered, and until the peace agreement Nuremberg was under Prussian rule.

The military image that Nuremberg displayed at the time, and especially the wonderful horses of the Mecklenburg cuirassiers, reminded me of how I used to ride horses for pleasure in Gunzenhausen, which only offered a very dull social life. I had always had a penchant for this noble sport, and during the time when I was managing a large estate in Bobingen (see *Tales From A Merchant's Life*) and had access to a large stock of horses, I was offered some lessons to find out if I had what it takes to make a good rider. That was indeed the case, according to a chief farm hand who had served with the Cheveaulegers. It only took a few riding lessons, which were given by a local former staff sergeant in the neighbouring Ansbach. With my instruction completed, all I needed was a horse for riding, and I felt like calling out with

King Richard III: "A kingdom for a horse!"[34] Where to find the kingdom, however, was a different question altogether. And yet, help was at hand in the shape of some young clerks - former students now working for the postal and railway services - who knew how to ride, and the keeper of an inn in Gunzenhausen which I regularly frequented and whom I talked into buying a horse. We explained to him that he would earn good money by renting the horse out to us. He followed our temptation, after all there was no great risk involved for him. For very little money he bought a good, well broken-in horse, which had seen its best years a long, long time ago. The horse also had the habit of immediately breaking into a gallop whenever we were riding it on grass. Now, my brother Adolf also wanted to have a go at riding the horse, which I of course agreed to. I told him to mount the horse on the road and then to direct it into the adjoining meadow. Once on the grass, the animal automatically – and for my brother, unexpectedly - broke into a gallop, and my brother found himself on the ground, albeit unhurt. He was a little offended by my wicked little act and never got on a horse again.

The horse-renting business was such a success that the inn-keeper soon bought a second horse to rent out for riding.

In Nuremberg I had no time to think about such knightly pleasures and no money either for such luxurious expenses. Nonetheless, I was lucky enough to talk much and often about horses and the art of horse-riding in general with my barber in Spitalgasse. This was not very surprising since the barbershop

---

[34] Shakespeare's Richard III's famous words "*My* kingdom for a horse!" are often misquoted in German as "*A* kingdom for a horse!", hence the question where to get *a* kingdom from.

was right next door to Kastenhuber's, the horse-butcher. The barber, whom I had previously told that I had been a passionate rider in Gunzenhausen, claimed that his neighbour Kastenhuber, for one reason or another, sometimes slaughtered horses which even a general would be proud to ride. We agreed that next time this happened he would inform me; I really wanted to try out such a general's nag before it was slaughtered.

Such a case presented itself, and sooner than I had dared to hope. The honest horse-butcher informed me that a noble *Rocinante* was ready for me, but I had to arrange for the riding gear myself. In Frau von Stadler's house there lived a certain Major von Deufenbach, a fine gentleman, who always returned my respectful greetings most affably. His stable boy, too, had taken a liking to me since I always gave him a little present, which I could obtain cheaply or for free from the *Gebrüder Bing* company, for the little errands he would sometimes run for me. I asked him to politely ask the Major if I could borrow a saddle so that I could show myself high on horseback once again. My wish was granted willingly. The stable boy went to the horse-butcher to fetch and saddle the Arabian horse for me; naturally not before I had instructed him not to tell anyone who the owner of the horse was that had been offered to me.

It was indeed a lovely little horse which he brought, slender and in good condition. It had come directly from a real major into the hands of the butcher. When I mounted the steed in the courtyard of von Stadler's house, all the windows facing the courtyard were busy with people curious to see how the event was unfolding. Everything went according to plan. The horse stood to attention in an almost coquettish manner, performed elegant courbette hops, and I thought it was strange that it had even been considered to turn this fine animal into sausages so soon.

The two of us, I mean the horse and I, started our "ride to the land of old Romance[35]" in good posture. My aim was the Marien Gate[36]. From there I intended to go to the Dutzend pond, but not before I had completed some extravagant riding exercises on the parade ground. Everything seemed to go very smoothly. A few ladies whom I knew looked at me in awe. Now I was getting closer to the Marien Gate (it was still standing at the time). Once we were within sight of the same, however, the horse would go no further - in spite of many good words and much flattery, despite whip and boot heel it tried to turn around - and since I expertly stopped him from doing so, the horse soon went to the right, then to the left, and finally mounted the pavement and painfully pushed my legs against the wall of a house. A crowd gathered, many people gave me tips on what to do, others wanted to lead the horse on by its reins, in short, it was an embarrassing and ridiculous situation from which I eventually freed myself by turning around quickly and following my steed's will. Soon we were happily trotting along, without any incidents, through the King's Gate, around the ring to the Plärrer, along Ludwig Strasse and back to my flat at Josefsplatz. I told the Major's servant who led the horse back that everything had gone well, and of course I did not mention the adventure at the Marien Gate. But I never went on a horse again. I did hear later that the horse had been sold by his military owner purely because it had become

[35] Quoting a poem by Christoph Martin Wieland.
[36] Marientor; city gate to the south of the city, knocked down in 1891 to make space for the increasing traffic.

impossible to take it through the Marien Gate. That way led to the parade ground, the joys and sorrows of which the noble steed probably wished no longer to take part in.

Fig. 18 King's Gate, 1891.

By now my brother Adolf had married, our household had been dissolved and I had moved into a lovely bachelor's pad on Josefsplatz with a certain tailor called Muschler (now Moritz Fay's). One evening of the week was devoted to the friends who would come for tea, and the hours would pass very enjoyably with cheerful and serious conversations. This was partly because my landlords had two very pretty daughters who often joined us at these tea evenings and who took a lively part in the conversation. It may have been a merit of that time that despite the evident courtesy of the gentlemen, no unseemly words were ever spoken, although the daughters of the house were very accommodating, and their mother appeared to have a propensity for match-making. The older sister, who through a hapless love had messed up her life in some way, later married an older, aristocratic forester; the younger one married a seriously ill man of the law who through his early death made her a "merry widow". As far as I know she is still alive today.

A Herr Schlesinger from Breslau was one of the frequent guests at my tea soirées. He had come to Nuremberg many years ago and had found a position in *Schmidt's* well-renowned music shop. He was looking after the musical part of the business, and above all he was independently in charge of the loaning of musical instruments. It was well known that he was excellent in his field, which was also proven by the fact that he worked in his profession at *Schmidt's* for 15 years. His extraordinary versatility was further supported by an exceptionally beautiful tenor voice. He was considered the "star" of the male choral society which he was a member of, and he usually sang the solo parts. It needs no further explanation that such a gift made him seem a valuable acquisition for our tea soirees, and that in turn we happily accepted his many weaknesses. One of these weaknesses, which had a certain impact on our enjoyment of his artful singing, was the languishing manner in which he would roll his eyes while singing. I certainly do not believe that he was putting on a pose, but that his eyes were merely reflecting how moved he was by the performance of an especially sentimental song.

It was because he had met the company of so many young and ambitious clerks and merchants at my flat that the desire stirred in him to move on from his respected employment which left him time for his artistic activities but was badly paid, to another industry which was not about music any more but about great, clinking earnings. My friend Adolf Dünkelsbühler, about whom I will talk more later, offered him a helping hand. To the shock and horror of all music-loving ladies who had met him,

Schlesinger entered into a very prosaic business, the sphere of influence of which introduced him to the ramified world of ribbons, strings and tapes etc, and it was only through the personal friendship with the principals that he was able to keep his spirits up and endure the boredom of a mundane commercial business as best as possible. Nevertheless, it did not last long. The situation grew intolerable for him, and one day he declared that he would stay no longer, but that instead he would pursue his craving for an artistic activity and try his luck as an opera singer. I should add here that Schlesinger had indeed a good commercial knowledge which could have been put to good use to his and others' advantage had it not been for his eccentricity, at least at that time, which impacted his work in business.

I liked Schlesinger very much, and to have him and his singing just to myself I once asked him to accompany me on an excursion to Streitberg, which I would of course pay for. Schlesinger, however, was so sensitive in certain areas that I could only get him to agree to this if I made up a reason why I it was necessary for me to have him, or rather his voice, with me in Streitberg. I said we would overnight in a brewery where I was hoping the owner would place an order for hops with my parents' business. Schlesinger could support me in this with his beautiful singing, I said, and therefore it was only right that I paid for the costs of our joint journey to Franconia. He accepted that. I am mentioning this event here because it later became the cause for a falling-out between Schlesinger and me.

So, Fedor Schlesinger took to the stage, and as far as I remember his first performance was in Augsburg. I sometimes read a review about him in the Augsburg evening news. He sang the

"Lorenzos" and "Alfonsos", and the reviews always stressed that he possessed a magnificent voice, but that his acting performance was beneath criticism. Let me add here that even off the stage he had a rather unfavourable appearance; he was short and fat – one could just about put up with the configuration of his face – but apart from being short he also had bandy legs, and he waddled. That he was being praised for his singing performance on stage despite his most unfavourable personal appearance may go to prove just how lovely this voice was that a very kind Mother Nature had bestowed upon him.

He (Schlesinger) once confided in me casually that his first director in Augsburg used to express reservations about his lack of confidence on stage, which he thought had an immense impact on the effect his splendid voice and singing had on the audience. In order to improve his posture and movements he demanded that Schlesinger took on small roles in comedies or plays. So it happened that one day he was to play a knight in the comedy *Count Waldemar* and say the words "Or would you prefer to play with pistols?" Schlesinger entered the stage, but before his cue, then suddenly realised that he had appeared too soon, but despite his confusion he started his line anyway, but ended up saying it like this "Or would you prefer to play with pi-pi-pistols?" Resounding laughter followed the involuntary comic effect, and the director greeted him off-stage with the words, "You should become a clown in the circus. You'd be successful."

For many years Schlesinger did not return to Nuremberg, but during a time of ten years he performed in Magdeburg, Gdansk and finally for two years at the Thalia Theatre in Hamburg. Sometimes his work must have been an ordeal for him; actors and singers tend to tease and bully a colleague who is perceived by the audience as odd and funny simply because of his lack of acting talent and a certain shyness that stems from his inadequate physical properties.

Anyway, one fine day Schlesinger reappeared in Nuremberg. I met him unexpectedly in the beer hall I sometimes patronised opposite my flat in Pfannenschmiedsgasse. When I saw him I greeted him affectionately, but I avoided mentioning his past since I feared that it might embarrass him, so I started a conversation by asking if he remembered our joint trip to Streitberg. He replied almost venomously, yes he did remember the time, and in particular he remembered the fact very well that I had dragged him to Streitberg for nothing because I only wanted to sell hops using his voice. I was annoyed about his tactless and spiteful remark, even more so since strangers were present, and I replied "You know very well that the hops sale was a story I made up with the intention to alleviate you of the humiliation that I was paying for the trip. The fact that you see the matter as you do simply goes to show the lack of gratitude and consideration that you have got accustomed to in your singing career, and I can see why, since you obviously haven't earned many laurels, or otherwise you wouldn't be here now." The end. We said nothing else.

Schlesinger continued his search for some kind of employment, but wherever he applied he was turned away. However, he often had to hear people suggest that he come to me since, so they thought, he was a friend of mine and the company *Gebrüder Bing* was such a large one that surely it would be easy enough to find him a suitable position there. With all his pride, he saw the truth in it and he overcame his pride, visited me in the office and asked for an appointment. I have never made it difficult for anyone who approached me in this manner. I engaged Schlesinger as a correspondent since I knew that his good general knowledge and his beautiful handwriting – we had no typewriters back then – made him suitable for that role. But alas, my wish and my hope did not come true. His eccentric and arrogant nature, his presumption that he was more educated than everyone else did not allow him to express himself with the necessary clarity and calmness in his correspondences as is required in business. When, for example, a customer complained that a certain item was missing from a box, and after an investigation into the event he was to write a reply, he ended up making the most ridiculous remarks and accusations. In one such case he wrote something like this: "You clearly have no idea of how things are organised in our diverse business. Everything is regulated here. The goods ready for dispatch are treated like shrines, and once they have been checked no-one is allowed to touch them except the packer who is sworn to the strictest order and is reminded of this on a daily basis. How could it be possible under such circumstances that a letterbox goes missing? Is it not the case that at your locality a piece might easily be unpacked and stored in a place with your other goods? Have you not got children who could have made a game of removing such a piece, etc, etc." This is not exaggerated. Schlesinger was incapable of dealing with such a matter in plain and simple words, even though I reminded him a thousand times, and the worst thing was that he took no offense at all when he was admonished – he simply laughed; but he was no longer allowed to write letters independently.

Thus his career with us was over in a way, since in his role as accountant, which he excelled at, he hardly earned more than 1,800 marks at the time. That was too little, especially since the small business run by his wife did not make much money either. I therefore grabbed the opportunity to move him to my brothers-in-law, the Justin & Albert Ottenstein company, a very large hop business, who were looking for a cashier and accountant. I had a clear conscience when I recommended him as an honest and very trustworthy gentleman, and even his other characteristics, including the one that he was not sensitive to criticism, made him especially suitable to working in a business where people did not mince their words. The owners, who sometimes had laughed about his strange idea of business affairs, were practical enough not to be taken aback by it, and so Schlesinger achieved a good reputation and a good income thanks to his exact book-keeping and his reliable services as a cashier; he became a junior partner, and when he left the company several years ago he was even honoured with a large, life-long pension. He died at a very old age. I just cannot believe that he would ever have forgotten his years as a travelling singer, and sometimes he may well have thought about what his life might have been under happier circumstances.

I have talked about these events, which range from my time as a young man up into my old age, since it would be difficult to fit these episodes in chronological order into some form of timeline.

One of my closest friends in my youth was Adolf Dünkelsbühler. We were both apprentices in his parents' company Berneis in Fürth. He soon moved to America to be taught how to be a proper Yankee by his uncle, a job made much easier by his knowledge of the English language. After a short while, however, he returned home, having spent some time in Paris, too, and our close friendship picked up from where we had left it. Dünkelsbühler suggested that I apply for a subscription to lunch at the *Goldene Adler* restaurant at the *Schlenk Hotel,* where he himself, along with some other young acquaintances of ours, partook of the table d'hôte. The relationship between the owner of the hotel, which was frequented mostly by travelling salesmen, and his subscribers was a strange one. In order to offer lunch day after day, as was expected in a hotel of rank, a certain number of guests were required, and that was why subscribers were needed. Nonetheless, the innkeeper did not make any money from those guests. On the contrary, the owner had to subsidise them. The "needs must" guests paid the small amount of 24 kreutzers – 70 pfennigs, and what was more, the obligation to have wine with the meal, which was really just an expectation, was ignored by most. It is easy to see that the innkeeper will accept only as many subscribers as are absolutely necessary to make the table d'hôte viable, and it is thanks to my friend that I was not rejected. Sometimes, guests would inconsiderately heap comparatively large portions of the expensive delicacies from the always abundant succession of dishes onto their plates, and they would find a "pink slip" on their place asking them politely to leave the lunch table at the *Adler*.

The wonderful food was delicious, yet I could not shake the humiliating feeling that I enjoyed my meals at the innkeeper's expense and that we were only regarded as a necessary evil by him. After a few months, when I was better known, well, I can even say much liked, by my eating companions, I proposed that with regard to the completely insufficient price that we were paying for such fine food we voluntarily suggested an appropriate increase to the hotel owner. My proposal was not received with unanimous agreement. A sharp and cynical member of our group, just as witty as he was selfish, called me an über-noble dreamer and said that he could not care less if the owner was going bankrupt as long as the quality of the food did not suffer until then. However, I had some who were thinking like me on my side, and the price was increased to 36 kreutzers – 1 mark.

My expectations, however, that from now on I might be eating less guiltily at the *Adler*, not merely as a tolerated guest but as an appreciated one, were sadly not fulfilled. There were still pink slips for guests who were considered too greedy. Several times the head waiter hinted that despite the - offered and accepted – voluntary increase the restaurant still had to consider us as loss-making "parasites". I may well assume that that did not include me since not only did I meet the expectation to have wine abundantly, but I also often had dinner at the hotel in the evenings. Nonetheless, I was lacking the thick skin required to accept a service which left the innkeeper with a loss, and so I left, and with me four or five other gentlemen.

With our help we enabled Frau Schultheiss, a remarkable cook who was known all over town, to take over a small restaurant. There we had lunch and dinner, simple, but exquisitely prepared, and guests and owner could be very satisfied with each other. Soon there were more guests than the small premises could handle.

I have described this really quite unimportant story in such detail to show that every good deed hurts when it is delivered with the spoken or unspoken reproach that one is doing merely a charitable act.

Even in my later life I often had this feeling. I have always been extremely grateful for even the smallest favours, but I cannot bear to accept a service when it is offered unwillingly. I have a clear conscience when I say that thousands of times I have helped people with word and deed, even those whom I hardly knew, as much as and wherever possible. I never asked for thanks, and even numerous disappointments and base ingratitude did not sway me from my creed, which is summarised so wonderfully in Goethe's words "Let man be a noble creature, helpful and good". Whoever lives by these words can dispense with any religion.

Amongst my friends was one whom I particularly cared for, who came from a respected family of teachers and who had achieved quite extraordinary results at school. As soon as I arrived in Nuremberg, I immediately rekindled the amicable friendship he and I had enjoyed during our time in Fürth. He was a junior partner in a very large wholesale business, and one of the owners was a relative of his. Furthermore, we had a number of mutual friends in Nuremberg, and so the old circle of friends was soon socialising again. On Sundays we always went on joint excursions into the surroundings of Nuremberg. It was always my friend who proposed where to go. Yet regularly, after we had sat down together for a while, my friend would leave us to join the table of an elderly gentleman and a young lady. It was clear to me that the suggestion of where to go was somehow correlated to the old gentleman and the young lady. Still, I thought it odd that we were totally excluded from the company of these people and that we played a role that seemed ridiculous to me. I mentioned this to the other sufferers and was told that this behaviour was in accordance with my friend's expressed wishes.

One Sunday we happened to sit very near to the table which the old gentleman had taken with his daughter, and where our friend appeared once again as the only admirer. I took a closer look at the girl and realised that I had met her less than a year ago in Streitberg; I even remembered her dress, in large black and white check. Her parents lived in Heiligenstadt then, near Streitberg, and had moved to Nuremberg in the meantime. Having set up in Nuremberg, their son played a big part in the expansion of the business, and my friend was rendering the company a good service with his excellent business acumen.

I could assume that my friend perhaps harboured the hope to marry the principal's sister. Nonetheless, I did not see why I, and maybe the other friends too, had to be kept away, and I therefore freely approached the forbidden table to greet the young lady as an old acquaintance. She obviously enjoyed this and even told me on the way home how embarrassing it always had been and still was for her that my friend's selfish desire to be on his own with her was preventing other gentlemen from introducing themselves to her. She expressed her indignation in a rough and rustic manner, and the old man grinned shrewdly and winked at me as if to suggest that I knew what his daughter meant. The girl was pretty, too pretty perhaps for my friend who was not blessed with physical assets, and she did indeed suffer by his courtship which, as described above, discouraged other men from approaching her.

I met the young lady at other occasions at families we both knew, without forgetting in her company the restraint I owed to my friend or his hope. And still it came to a falling out with this friend, which kept us apart for 25 years, and this is how it happened.

When I once happened to meet the young lady, she asked me to come and visit her in her parental home. I replied that I had certain reasons not to. She then said almost passionately that she knew the reasons, but that I should know that my friend had robbed her of any joy of her Sunday excursions with his constant harassment and his attempts to keep other young people away from her. Finally she asked me most agitatedly to inform my friend of her dislike of him, a feeling that could never be changed into anything else. Obviously I replied that I would never put myself in that position and we said goodbye, maybe at bit more warmly and definitely more excitedly than usual. I had the feeling that, in making this revelation, she had a certain intention to flatter me.

In this mood I entered the café where we usually met and found, as I had expected, my friend. He was accompanied by one of his close North German acquaintances, a man I had always disliked because of his blunt and presumptuous Prussian-ness. When I wanted to join them at the table the two men did not respond to my greeting, and when I asked what the matter was the Prussian said something along the lines of "With your intrusion into S.'s family you have destroyed the hopes of our friend, which would have been fulfilled if it had not been for your intervention. We therefore have to break off socialising with you." I looked at the two with astonishment and thought about what to reply. One voice inside my head said "Spare the friend.", another said "Don't take this grave and baseless insult without punishment." I chose the middle way. "If my friend", I began, "suspects me of enticing his sweetheart away by socialising in the most harmless manner with a lady I knew long before him, then I can understand that, as jealousy sees dangers even where there are none. He could have talked openly to me about it, and it would not have been difficult to convince him that I neither crossed his paths nor wanted to cross them. However, now that he has so deeply and intentionally offended me I absolve myself from any moral obligation for the future, and I don't know what it will hold. Nonetheless, as a friend I will do him one last turn by telling him that the hopes he might have cherished would never have been fulfilled. He surely knows that best himself, and I think it extremely unfair to be held responsible for something when the cause for this unhappy situation was within his own person. He is free to have this confirmed by the proper sources."

I left, and it was 25 years until we met again. The house, in which my then happily married friend lived and worked, suddenly collapsed; he lost much, reputation and wealth, and he was enmeshed in worries that no-one could help him with. Yet I could! I invited him, welcomed him with open arms which wiped away any self-consciousness, and backed by my company's considerable development I was able to find him a highly regarded, independent position which he held until he was an old man, free from worries about how to feed his family and easily meeting the obligations that arise from having his two hard-working sons at university. We remained true and cordial friends until he sadly passed away a few years ago.

If I was in any way to blame in this episode I cannot say today. It has been a long, long time. In any case we were pleased that the long time of separation and estrangement between us was over and forgotten.

Then came the year 1868, in the November of which I became engaged to Ida Ottenstein, a friend of my youth and daughter of the teachers Simon and Babette Ottenstein in Bamberg. A sister of my late mother lived there, one of my favourite aunts, and she suggested it to me. Her letter to me began with the words "If you want to be so stupid and get married, then come and get Ida Ottenstein". I came, and we married on 7th May 1869. We moved into a very simple but charming flat on the third floor in the house of Lotter, the coppersmith on Josefsplatz. The house does not exist anymore, in its place is now the *Café Bristol.*

It cost no more than 700 guilders to furnish and decorate the entire flat to our taste; the rent was 250 guilders per year. Besides, we were given a number of practical wedding presents by my relatives, which helped to complete the homely comfort. The pièce de résistance was considered to be a rug donated by my sister Ida which covered the floor of a rather large bedroom. Sadly, the "real" Persian was woven from cotton and hence not very durable. In fact, we thought our home was too elegant for us. In contrast, the following episode will show how thrifty we really had to be given my financial situation.

Amongst the impractical wedding gifts that served as showpieces was one that stood out: a silver breadbasket, given by my rich uncle Salomon Tuchmann. Shortly after the wedding, I sold this treasure for the price of 20 guilders since I wanted to invest the value of the basket. We were comfortable without such jewels and happy in our home, and so were our friends, one or another of which would usually share our more than simple Sunday dinners with us.

A veritable ghost story, however, threatened to ruin our honeymoon. This is what happened: My wife brought a stout cook with her from Bamberg who was not afraid of ghosts or people. I found this very comforting since I had to spend the whole day in the company, apart from the short break for lunch and the evenings. In the meantime, our shop in Karolinenstrasse, now Kaul's shoe shop, had been closed, and the business moved to premises in Weizenstrasse, which were larger but also further away from my flat.

When I came home one evening, my wife told me – and the maid confirmed this – that during the day, and in the evening too, the doorbell had been rung, but when the door was opened there was no-one there. I did not think much of it when suddenly the bell at the front door shrilled loudly. I ran the few steps to the door, opened it, but no-one could be seen or heard. I could not explain what had happened. Outside our flat was a very long corridor which led to the attic rooms, and it was impossible that someone could have rung the bell and run off given how quickly I had come to open the door. On the other side was the staircase which was in plain view all the way down to the second floor. Where was the culprit? This happened day after day, and when I came home I heard again and again about the ghostly bell-ringing while the ghost itself remained uncaught. There was no explanation for the spooky happenings.

My wife, our maid and I myself remained calm when several times a day or late in the evening, and even at night, the eerie sound of the bell rang again. The maid often spent hours lying in ambush by the door to open it as soon as the bell started ringing, but nothing suspicious was ever seen.

Now things were stirring in the house, and people, especially the servants, started whispering stories to each other. The housekeeper, perturbed by the worries of the other tenants, was becoming nervous and unfriendly towards us, as if we had something to do with it and wanted to tease the others. There was even talk of one tenant wanting to stop paying rent because of these events. At last we, too, felt uneasy with this silly story, since the mischief did not want to end.

One Sunday morning – we had given the maid the day off – my wife and I were going for a visit. Having reached the courtyard I wanted to lock the door when we both had a fright at the sudden and shrill sound of the bell inside. How to explain it? So it was a ghost after all! But then it dawned on me. I examined the bell pull, which was made of brass wire, and found the solution to the riddle: on the back of the bell pull there was, at a certain height, a half-moon shaped dent. If someone pulled the brass pole slowly downwards, then it was caught in that dent until being pulled back with force about five minutes later by the spring at the top, thus explaining the extremely shrill ringing of the bell. Evidently one or more of the other maids knew the secret of the house; they slowly pulled the bell when passing and then had several minutes to get away before the ominous and spooky ringing started. That was the end of the romantic ghost story, and everyone in the house laughed, but none more so than us!

Our flat was opposite my parents' one, so it went without saying that we saw them regularly, even more so now that the sisters and brothers were growing up and there was already talk of dancing lessons for the girls. The daughters were, in age order, Antonia, Josephine (Seppi) and Marie. The sons were Heinrich, Oscar and Edmund.

Of the girls, I favoured the funny and naive Seppi, a good, lovely and agreeable girl, and this preference for her has lasted to this day.

Of the brothers, it was the youngest, Edmund, who started to display a certain originality combined with an unusually keen perception when he was still at school, and not just in commercial affairs but especially in music, too. By saying this I certainly do not want to slight my brothers Heinrich and Oscar, whose great and successful commercial talents, of such importance for the whole family, were combined with a good general education.

With my brother Edmund, I have had the most versatile relationship over the years, all the way into my old age. We used to write numerous letters to each other, trying to outdo each other with originality, not out of vanity or because we wanted to impress, but because we really enjoyed the exchange of our different opinions. He will come into his own later on in these pages.

I took an active interest in the marriages and negotiations of all my siblings, especially in those of my youngest sister Marie, who was highly educated and greatly valued by me, but who sadly passed away much too soon. She was deeply mourned by me, and I had a deep and congenial understanding with her right until her very sad death. To Olga and Aennie, the two daughters she left behind, I was always a true and faithful uncle and mentor. There will be more to say about this later on.

I always sought to have good relations with the brothers and sisters-in-law whenever my married siblings introduced them to me, and I do not recall any troublesome incidents that might have disturbed these relationships.

When I think of times gone by, "all the fullness of my doing"[37] rushes forward in my mind, yet I cannot relate it in its entirety within the confines of this volume, which is dedicated to all the members of my closest family. The events that marked the lives of the closest members of my family - and they are my children, my sisters and brothers and those of my wife - will remain with me forever. From the lofty look-out of my 77 years I look down on joyful events as well as on grave and solemn ones. But where to begin, where to end? I must limit myself to talk essentially about those events that my grown children, who have obviously walked a long part of the journey of my life with me, have also experienced. After all there is quite a lot that will be new and interesting for them. Nonetheless, it is to my grandchildren that this book is dedicated most of all, and from this viewpoint, covering certain unimportant occasions in detail which my own children know already cannot be avoided.

I am writing these memoirs without any preparations; I have not gone through any old material, have not made a plan, just one guideline exists: In order to find my way through the labyrinth of a lifetime of memories in some chronological order, I will draw on the times and places where, after a day's hard work, I would

[37] Quoting from Goethe's *Faust*.

meet with my good companions and loyal friends of an evening. By the way, with regard to such memories, one should start in the early days of one's adulthood to keep a diary of all events that might be of interest to one's descendants.

I have always held the delight of quiet domesticity in high regard and have taken pleasure from it, but one should not, and must not, become a hermit. Instead remodel Schiller's famous words "Man must go out into hostile life"[38] into "Man must go out into hospitable life"! He who works hard and fast during the day, who meets worries and struggles in his everyday life, should every now and then take refuge among his cheerful friends to rest and enjoy hearty food and good wine so that he may gather new strength for the difficult struggles in his work. And that is what I did! Even if my wife sometimes wanted to tie me to the house – and that is understandable, and no man wants to miss out on such an attempt to keep the husband at home – I explained to her that going out was for me in some sense a capital investment, since looking forward to such a natural pleasure always invigorated me for work, even more so since I was only talking about modest delights of the table, namely dishes that I loved and which only rarely or even never appeared on the menu of our domestic kitchen. Think for example of the magic words "roast suckling pig", so common and popular in Nuremberg.

The first venue where we friends used to meet and where we formed an alliance which is still in existence today, i.e. more than 40 years later, was the wine tavern *Zum Roten Oechslein*, then the most famous one in Nuremberg, run by Herr Dorner, the well-

---

[38] Quoting from Schiller's *Song of the Bell.*

known champion shot, and owned by Herr Segitz, the owner of the coffee house *Zur Sonne.*

The landlord, whom we knew from our days at the coffee house, was exceptionally well educated for someone in his profession (previously, he had been the manager of an elegant hotel in Dresden); but he may have piqued a guest or two when, with his cool lordliness, he refused to be treated in too familiar terms by his guests.

In the early years, the club formed at Segitz's was really just my intimate friends Fritz Tuchmann, Josef Merzbacher and Karl Böck. Josef Merzbacher lives in Munich today, and my closest friend and cousin Fritz Tuchmann died in May 1916 aged over 74 years. Our dear friend Böck passed away 18 years ago.

How many evenings did we sit together cheek by jowl, how much cheer and banter enlivened the fast-flowing hours! Soon the circle grew, and each member brought something to the table: There was Samuel Bloch, the music-loving financier who could contribute well, and much, to any conversation; then his friend, a fine man of the law, Herr Dr. Obermeyer, a very wealthy but also very careful and frugal man. With the support of Herr Bloch I always tried to talk him into transferring a large sum of money as a loan to the *Gebrüder Bing* company. Of course, this was just a joke. He agreed and said that he would make available a sum of 500,000 marks to the *Gebrüder Bing* company, and he would only ask for a modest interest rate. In return he claimed an undoubtedly safe guarantor, a first mortgage and a bill of exchange on the account of Herr Bloch. He wanted to be safe in all things!

Herr Bloch and I had been socialising for years at the *Café Sonne,* where we met several times a week. I enjoyed talking with the knowledgeable gentleman, and I had heard from other guests that he thought the same about me. Apparently he thought that I was a very clever man, and that he would not be surprised if I achieved great importance in the commercial world. I am only saying this because a later incident proved to me that he would not put his money where his mouth was when I had to negotiate with him. When certain circumstances forced our company to look for new banking arrangements, I went to him to see if his bank might be inclined to open an account for us. He received me with his usual suave politeness and offered me a cigar, which by the way I did not like. I brought up my request; not as a supplicant but with the knowledge that my company had made very good progress and that we would easily be given credit somewhere else.

Herr Bloch grew a touch more buttoned up and asked how much credit I was asking for. I replied that I would leave it up to him to evaluate the credit-worthiness of our company, there was no urgency to the matter, and politely asked for a written reply on the issue. A few days later a letter arrived from the bank, informing us that they were agreeable to entering into an agreement with us, provided that a loan of 3-4,000 marks was sufficient for our needs.

I was very surprised about this offer, which suggested a very low esteem of the credit-worthiness of our company. So this was the meagre fruit that had ripened from the (in his words) respect and high regard that Herr Bloch had formed of my education and commercial knowledge after knowing me for many years. And yet our business had expanded vastly, our means had grown considerably, and there were few people in the commercial world that did not know about this. The very presentable business premises were at the time located at the *Deutscher Hof*, now *Wittelsbacher Hof*, in Pfannenschmiedgasse. We employed around 100 staff, and apart from the sale of merchandise, we were profiting from a significant cottage industry which we had established and grown.

Herr Strubell, our proven junior partner who kept a close eye on all business affairs, read Bloch's letter with a disparaging expression, which was obviously directed at the bank, and then looked at me as if we had both been slapped in the face. I laughed, and his surprise grew when I explained that I considered the offer made by Bloch's company acceptable. I can still see today how the face of my loyal colleague darkened. Then I ordered that a loan of 3,000 marks was to be taken up with Bloch & Co., and that simultaneously – and now Herr Strubell's face brightened up again – the amount was to be covered in notes receivable. Then I added "In a few days, my dear Herr Strubell, you will write to Bloch's bank that we would prefer not to have an account with them, i.e. that we will not make use of the granted overdraft facility." That is what we did. Strangely enough, whenever I met with Herr Bloch afterwards, he never raised the subject, and of course I did not mention it either. We were at ease with each other as usual.

A few months later, Herr Bloch appeared in our offices out of the blue. A rare visitor, whom I welcomed with all honours. He wanted to speak with me in private in my office; however, I explained that I did not have one and that he could speak freely in the presence of Herr Strubell, our junior partner, assuming it was concerning a business affair.

He explained then that he had come to make good an injustice committed by him, or rather his company. He had had no idea, he said, how significantly our business had grown, but now he knew, and he invited us to make use of a loan of 30,000 marks, gladly offered by his company, the sooner the better.

It was tempting to point out to Herr Bloch that he could have found out several months ago, i.e. after my visit to him, that which had had him come to see us now. Nevertheless, I restrained myself and thanked him for his offer.

It was several years until our company began to deal with his bank, and it had grown considerably by then. My personal relationship with Bloch also developed most cordially; he joined our circle of friends and remained one of the most frequent attendants at the scheduled meetings at Segitz's.

Another member of our "Free Society" – that was the name we later gave our sociable circle – was a Herr Seibert who spent almost every evening at Segitz's and therefore became closer to us over time. He was the same artist who had once made the showy company nameplate for me in Gunzenhausen and who actually considered himself some sort of artist in his profession – company painter and template maker. What he made was indeed very good and tasteful. In his small workshop he was always seen wearing a brown velvet jacket with a red, Turkish Fez pulled over his balding head. In the street, however, he always wore a black frock and a meticulously ironed top hat. But what really distinguished him was his baritone voice, which was just as beautiful as it was powerful. He enjoyed being admired, and therefore he often volunteered one song or another at Segitz's. The choice of songs was certainly narrow; I remember that he never progressed beyond *On the green banks of the River Rhine*, *The young boy with the curly hair* or the aria of Count di Luna from *Il trovatore.*

I must add some more detail on the subject of the performances by our friend with the powerful voice and the poor memory - he sometimes got stuck with the words even when singing the few songs that he knew well musically: For a short time Seibert had been married to a very pretty woman; however, the household was being led in the most gypsy-like manner. His wife was not faithful. In his quixotic manner and with bombast, which may have stemmed from him being a member of the Nuremberg society *Forty Knights*, namely as *Hans von Liebenau*, he "bade the hag leave". She did leave, and as it seemed, not unwillingly. Some days later, however, when he returned late at night from the beer house, the "hag" sat waiting for him by the door. After all sorts of talk he took her back in, yet a fortnight later the repentant sinner fled with her lover, this time to the other side of the ocean. The motto of our little club, "Wine, Women and Song" was limited for a while to "Wine and Song".

In fact, Seibert was a true and loyal friend, whose personality at times appeared a bit strange. He ought to have lived in much more romantic times, where his bombastic style and his assumed role of a noble troubadour would have been more at home. We shall meet him several times more in the course of this testimony.

Amongst the guests who sometimes joined our convivial evening circle at Segitz's was the French Vice-Consul, Herr Léon

Duplessis. His mother was German, and therefore his command of our mother tongue was excellent. His father, a general in the French Army, had died a long time ago. Duplessis had seen much of the world and had served as consul in Lima for many years. Subsequently, he went to Gdańsk and Helsingfors until he finally came to Nuremberg. His main task seemed to be to understand the industrial situation as much as possible and to report back to his government everything that might be useful for the French industry. I think I can assume that that was the reason why he introduced himself to me in the first place, and why he tried to find out certain things from me. He was clever enough not to show it, and I was careful enough not to fulfil his intentions.

Duplessis was a kind, intelligent man who had even written plays in German, and it seemed to me that he acquired his diligence and determination as well as his extraordinary knowledge from his German mother, while his explosive, impulsive and sometimes wild manner stemmed from his Latin father. Here is an example: Duplessis must have been over 40 years old, and despite his many years in this official service he was only a vice consul. Most certainly he was awaiting his appointment as consul in Nuremberg one coming New Year's Day. When we were all sitting together comfortably for our New Year's Eve dinner, Duplessis was among us, and in what seemed to be a terribly irritable mood that alarmed me. One of our friends was careless enough to ask what had caused Herr Consul to be in such a bad mood. A storm broke loose like none of us had ever thought possible. He clenched his fists, rolled his eyes, his face contorted in an almost animalistic rage and he shouted so loudly that people in the road could hear him: "My name is Leo the Lion, I will tear the miserable wretches apart! I, the cruel, enraged lion, I spit on these scoundrels!" We stood as if frozen before this eruption of raving madness of this usually so sophisticated and reserved gentleman. At last his outburst subsided; his voice became whining, and he explained that the incredible tension and disappointment of not being appointed consul had made him senseless. Please would we forgive and forget.

The following day the decree of his appointment arrived, and Duplessis insisted on treating us to a fine dinner at Segitz's accompanied by the best brand of exquisite French champagne in order to help us forget that awkward New Year's Eve.

A short time later by the way, we had a rather entertaining and enjoyable evening in our local pub thanks to him: The renowned humorist Stettenheim from Berlin was to give a reading in Nuremberg. Duplessis was a great fan of his, and on friendly terms with the "master" as he called him. He asked us to appear in full numbers at Segitz's since he wanted to introduce the "master" to our circle after the reading. I still have to laugh when I remember that hilarious evening. Much wine was drunk that night........... Everyone did their best to contribute to the lively conversation, and so the famous humorist was outdone because the funniest jokes were made by us. He could not stop laughing. Long after midnight we started to go home. In front of the church of St. Lorenz another funny episode happened. Friend Böck had had his share of the wine and its spirits held him in their clasp so that suddenly he threw his arms around the "master" and called out "Herr Doctor, our St. Lorenz!" again and again. His intention was to talk about the church, the landmark of Nuremberg, of its past and present; however, all he managed to get out was "Herr Doctor, our St. Lorenz!" He must have repeated it ten times!

Fig. 19 The church of St. Lorenz in the 1800s.

Stettenheim cried with laughter, and all of us with him. One did well not to mention this episode to our friend lest he become upset and loud, even though he was not usually sensitive and was able to see a joke.

As far as I know Duplessis is still alive, at a ripe old age, living in Versailles, as consul general, ret.; at least that was where his last letter came from.

A dear companion of mine, and of everybody else's, was Herr Gugler, owner of a not insignificant glove factory, a simple and honest citizen, loyal and reliable, and who liked me. I called him "brother-in-law" since he was indeed the brother-in-law of my dear friend Böck's, and the two of us liked to share "all good things".

Now I have introduced all the friends associated with the "Free Society" – though some were merely welcome guests – and I can now return to that which is connected to the development of the *Gebrüder Bing* company.

The business premises in the *Deutsche Hof* had grown far too small for us. Our means permitted us to consider the purchase of our own property. When the opportunity to buy a suitable house at 15 Marienstrasse came up we jumped to it, and immediately after the sale went through we started to build a rather imposing warehouse for the time. The purchase of the property, the setting up and fitting of the warehouse obviously stretched our finances to their limits; however, over the past years we had secured confidence and relevant credit with my friend Bloch as well as with the large bank L & E Wertheimber, Nuremberg and Frankfurt.

Herr Josef Schmidt was regarded as the chief director of the Nuremberg branch of Wertheimber's. I had known this gentleman for a long time, and he had always been an interesting personality for me, maybe because it was so difficult to get close to him. With regard to his inapproachability, he was known in some circles as the "stony guest". When he made an unannounced visit to a business with connections to the bank, it usually ended in wailing and gnashing of teeth for the afflicted party.

The bank did not need to tout for business, since anyone who needed money had to go to Wertheimber's – unlike today there were not a number of large banks in Nuremberg. A personal visit from Herr Schmidt therefore usually meant that an existing credit agreement was either going to be cancelled or curtailed. For that well-known fact alone we had always been careful in our company not to exceed our credit limit, even though especially at that time our financial situation was somewhat tight due to the purchase and extension of the property in Marienstrasse.

I therefore had an uncomfortable feeling when one day I saw Herr Schmidt cross the whole breadth of Marienstrasse in large strides and with a dark face, heading straight towards me. Without the slightest hesitation – I remember the words exactly - he said, "You are deep in the red". To my question as to what he meant, even though I knew exactly what was meant by those words, he replied, "You have significantly exceeded your credit limit with us. We cannot allow that to happen because the local management is bound by Frankfurt in determining credit limits." I knew that that was not the case since the decision on credits lay fully in his own hands. Nonetheless, given my brief and our junior partner Strubell's strict reliability I was pretty certain that the credit limit had not been exceeded, or if it had, only by an insignificant amount. I told Herr Schmidt that I would investigate his claim, and he left without barely saying goodbye. When I went into my office, my assumption proved to be correct. The limit had not been exceeded, on the contrary, we still had more than 20,000 marks available to us.

I did not want to deny myself the satisfaction of personally informing Wertheimber's, or even its director, Herr Schmidt, of this fact, and so I did what I only very rarely did and made my way to the "Lion's den" as I used to call it in jest to Herr R, the second junior partner at Wertheimber's whom I often met at the Phoenix club. Of course, he, too, had been informed about the situation, even though he pretended that he did not know what I had come for.

Herr Schmidt had not yet arrived at his office. Now, I have to mention this first: As I was leaving my office I had had the sudden idea that it could do no harm to show the decision-making gentlemen at the bank our company's secret book. This document, normally kept out of reach of anyone but me and my brother, showed clearly, and for a long number of years, how our revenues had grown continuously and how the profit had increased year on year. So I considered myself well-armed for the coming argument with the gentlemen from the bank. Soon Herr Schmidt arrived, and the discussion began. I explained that I was surprised at the dressing-down. I had presumed that given our company's solidity and its continuously growing size, exceeding our credit limit would not frighten the bank. Yet, I did not want to talk about that, since the mere expression that our company was "deep in the red" with the bank was factually not true, unless the bank's account had logged our account in the wrong colour ink. On the contrary, we still had 20,000 marks to play with within the limit of the agreed credit. I handed Herr Schmidt a copy of our books, and he was quickly convinced that I was completely right and that there had been a gross mistake on the side of the bank's accountants. He admitted this magnanimously.

Now I thought it was time to prove to the gentlemen what good results our company had to show for itself by producing the secret book. Surprised faces, congratulations, hand pressing, all followed by a personal, respectful escort to the front door of Pluto's temple.

On the way home I felt as if I had grown wings, since the fact that a usually stiff and cool banker had turned polite and friendly held great promise for the future.

A few days later, Herr Schmidt came to our offices, which was unusual in itself, and asked again to excuse his mistake and informed me that our credit with his bank had been increased by quite a substantial amount. Such was the impact of the secret book!

I could say much about the good things and the bad that I received at the hands of various bankers. I specifically remember one epigram about an onion, which ended with the words "One cries, yet eats it anyway".

I will close this story, which I probably told with a little too much detail, by saying that in the end I saw that justice was done to Herr Schmidt. He had achieved a high level of education, he had an excellent commercial and financial knowledge, and he possessed a rare understanding of the specific issues of every type of business, even if it was outside the banking industry. For years he was an influential director at the Nuremberg branch of the Dresdner Bank, which had affiliated Wertheimber's at the time. When the *Gebrüder Bing* company was converted to a share-holding company, he joined its board of directors. He held this office for 20 years, and I deeply deplored his departure when he retired at an old age. He was a precious, extraordinarily wise and experienced advisor, who despite having to represent his bank's interests of course, never contravened anything that I considered necessary for the prosperity of the business. If it did happen once or twice, it was exactly for that reason, namely that he had to put his bank's interests above those that he was representing for our company. Herr Schmidt, who is the same age as me, is still alive today; he is retired and lives, mentally and physically fit, in Munich.

I always kept close ties to my parents. My late father worried about my boldness, which he considered to be recklessness, and a phrase he uttered often was "As long as my Ignaz won't think of buying St. Lorenz!" His fear, thus expressed, that I might go beyond our means totally disappeared over time. He was proud of the success of the company, proud of what he heard other people say about it, and of course he was most pleased that our financial situation was no longer a cause of fatherly concern for him.

My sisters had grown up, and my parents, following the old adage of "Marry young, never regret", wanted to marry them off one by one. It was natural that I was asked for advice and took part in these negotiations, since I, along with my long-since married sister Ida, was quite adept at such things. My sister Antonia married a man from Bamberg, Seppi moved to Fürth. It would go too far here to go into more detail about their marriages. My sisters married decent men. No need to explain that fate rarely spares a marriage. My brother-in-law Kommerzienrat Mohrenwitz in Bamberg, a respected, successful industrialist, sadly died too soon, in 1911.

My brothers Heinrich and Oscar married sisters from an esteemed family and lived in married bliss with their companions, who brought with them all those qualities that are required for the establishment of a nice and homely household. My brother Heinrich's wife sadly died when she was still very young.

My sister Marie, whom I held in especially high esteem and who distinguished herself by her all-round education, followed her husband to Heidelberg. Whereas my favourite brother Edmund, of whom I could tell many an amusing prank, all of which were kind in nature, had – true to his character – many sweethearts before he finally settled with his first true and lasting love. He married a tall, beautiful, good girl, and they had a harmonious marriage which was even blessed with two pretty and talented daughters.

I would like to share a humorous interlude that happened at my brother Edmund's wedding: The cleric who performed the marriage ceremony dropped a few comments in his speech which I, even though they appeared to be made in all innocence, considered somewhat spiteful. The text itself upon which his speech was based and which dealt mostly with dying and burying was, in my opinion, not appropriate for such a joyful occasion either. Once the holy act was over and we were all standing merrily together, I expressed my surprise and displeasure in the text to him. He sought to enlighten me in a few short words, and I forgot about the whole affair. To my great disconcertment, however, the respectable man later arose to deliver a toast at the table in which he mentioned that sometimes even respected industrialists and Kommerzienräte criticised things they did not understand. He implied that I had in some way rebuked him with regard to the text of his sermon and went on to explain said text as a deeply religious one and one suitable for the holy ceremony of a marriage. I obviously could not leave this public dressing down unchallenged.

I answered the holy Herr Doctor that I fully agreed with his point of view, I had to accept his reprimand. However, I could verify with pleasure that Herr Doctor himself was not only a worthy, sharp-thinking minister, but I was confident that he was also very talented in my own field – namely the processing of tin[39]! My words earned general laughter, the rebuttal had spoken straight from the guests' hearts.

For years now my brother Edmund has been a partner in a large manufacturing business in Bamberg, which was co-founded there by my brother-in-law Kommerzienrat Mohrenwitz. Using his deep understanding, coupled with a great aptitude for business, he has contributed much to raise the company to its current esteemed position. His current business partner is the only son of my late brother-in-law.

Of course, I would not find it difficult to go on talking about the many interesting incidents, of a serious or light nature, that happened within the family circle; however, I have to consider that the "master knows to stay within the limits". (My brother Edmund might say that he "knows he has his limits"!) I will only say this much, that with a very few exceptions I have been bound together most harmoniously in brotherly love with my siblings, right up to my old age, and even where this harmony was not always possible I am not aware of ever being even partly to blame.

I enjoyed a closeness of the most profound kind with my sister Ida. She was the oldest of the four children from my father's first marriage, which was followed by six children from a second marriage. What distinguished my sister was her impressive and interesting nature combined with an active mind and her warm compassion for human misfortune. This meant that quite often

---

39 Pun based on the expression "Blech reden" (literally "to talk tin") for "to talk nonsense", and on the fact that Bing produced tin toys.

this compassion was directed towards those people who did not really want for anything serious but who enjoyed revelling in a certain *weltschmerz* which seemed more or less affected to me. I often urged her not to crowd so many people around her person whose plaintive features, which she often noticed where I saw nothing, gave them the licence to bother my sister with their real or imagined sorrows and dissatisfactions.

I will not deny that her marriage to a handsome, simple and good man, who, however, had no intellectual interests whatsoever, did little to satisfy her natural aptitude, which was geared at a higher intellectual activity and the company of educated people. I do not blame here either for inviting into her house people for whose concerns and experiences she felt a deep sympathy, especially when they were the types that always felt misunderstood. My sister was always expected to see more in them than the rest of the unfeeling world. It goes without saying that this position of guardian angel entailed some bitter disappointments for the angel herself.

Another trait that distinguished my sister, one which I never again found in another woman to the same extent, was how easily she made her simple home feel cosy and snug. She kept cool in any situation, for example when someone in the family was worried or facing misfortune, my sister brought order, calm and solace even to such cases where everyone else had lost their head. Sadly she died at only 44 years of age, in 1882, during the time of the First Bavarian Exhibition, and she died from a disease that nowadays, by today's state of science, could easily have been cured. I can still see her clearly before my eyes, with her beautiful, thick hair, which had turned snow-white when she was in her early 30s, how pleased she was, then already severely ill, about our company's exhibition, and how we often sat together in the uniquely beautiful exhibition grounds in those days when she seemed to forget her suffering for hours. She never complained, yet her features betrayed the harrowing truth that I would soon lose my beloved sister. In the long night of her passing, my wife and I sat by her bedside until the end. Even death could not mar her looks; her features were ennobled and wraithlike, and when she was dead one had the impression of looking at the wonderful marble statue of some great artist.

How many stories I could tell of the things my sister and I experienced and worried about together, and how many cheerful times, too, we had to thank each other for. We shared the same interests, and without wanting to boast, it can be said that we were both always first on the scene whenever help was needed, and without expecting gratitude in return.

Her bereaved husband was a half-brother of my father-in-law, the teacher Herr Ottenstein in Bamberg, in other words an uncle of my wife's. His task was now not only to raise his four children – two sons and two daughters – but also to continue to manage his difficult business without the irreplaceable aid of my sister, who had been his successful advisor and loyal friend.

Let me describe here the circumstances under which the marriage of my too soon departed sister came about, and in retrospect dedicate a few words and thoughts to this marital union. I was a witness to the engagement; the place of the event was a long corridor in the *Württemberger Hof Hotel* in Nuremberg. The prospective groom and I stood alone by a window in said corridor, and in conversation I sought to get an insight into my future brother-in-law's thoughts and feelings. That proved not to be too difficult: A kind, honest outdoors-man of good stature and bursting with health. I had no reason not to believe him when he told me that in his job he had wrestled down many a stubborn bullock and thrown them into a roadside ditch.

He did not have a steady job at the time. Previously, he had been buying hops for a friend's hop company in Fürth. He possessed no personal wealth because, since his father's death, he had had to care for his mother and sister, which he had done in the self-sacrificing manner of a well-behaved child. When I asked him how he was going to support his future wife and family, he replied in his innocent and truly touching manner, "You know (he had offered me the informal "Du" straight away), no girl is lost with me. Should I have no job at all, I'll take to the country and buy a silver pipe bowl off a farmer, and that would earn me at least 36 kreutzers". I was seriously concerned about this idea of his future career and decided, for this reason and others, to talk with my sister in earnest about her plans before the engagement was final. When I raised the issue with her, my sister replied that she knew the virtues and weaknesses of the man whom fate had determined for her husband quite well; what she liked about him was his healthy masculinity, his pure and honest character, and she respected the hard work he had carried out for his nearest and dearest from a young age, with devotion and joy. She was confident that it would be a good marriage. She said – in roughly these words – that she would guide, lead and educate the "pure fool" as required for him and his future tasks in the home and the family, and that she much preferred it this way rather than having a strict master who would not listen to her. I was not to worry, she added, given her modest dowry she could not too be too choosy anyway.

In these philosophical words I could hear my sister's idea of wanting to "reign supreme". This seemed to be an inherited trait in the line of the Tuchmann daughters, who generally exerted a great influence on their husbands and their businesses all the while being exemplary housewives. The engagement was announced, and I began to seriously worry about how I would obtain, and pay for, a worthy wedding gift.

My future brother-in-law had his residence in Pares – please don't think I made a mistake and meant PARIS! This tiny village was in the vicinity of Neustadt-on-Aisch. His business, and his journey to see his bride, often brought him to Fürth, where I was in service at the time. On one of those journeys to Gunzenhausen he showed me some material for a dress which he had bought as a present for my sister. From his choice of material I gathered some information as to my sister's taste in these things since she had chosen the material. I asked him not to give this present to my sister, pretending that her taste was quite peculiar, and, kind as he was, he gave in to my request.

I also taught my future brother-in-law some fine lessons on how to ensure that his appearance when visiting my sister was appropriate to his new situation, for his clothes, his manner of speech and other habits unmistakably showed him as the provincial man, or rather the simple peasant, that he was. He did not take the slightest offence at even these kind of remarks!

One day he brought his sister along, a good ten years his senior, who poured a torrent of words over me, her new relative, from which I gathered to my horror that she expected me to show her how to have a good time in Fürth; in Pares, she had no life. I can still see the lady before my eyes, advanced in years, in an outrageous yellow dress with black polka-dots, which were about the size of ten-pence pieces. What was I to do? Apart from the fact that there was nothing to see in Fürth, something had to happen that could be regarded as a personal honour for the siblings. Luckily, I had an idea. I promised to collect my brother-in-law and his sister from their guesthouse *The Three Kings* in the evening after work and to take them to meet some cheerful company. Their visit had come at a time when my circle of friends and acquaintances was in full bloom. Everyone was asked to come to *Bischoff's* beer hall, to be on time and in their best dress, stating that we had a festive occasion to celebrate, which was to be followed by a dance.

As promised, I collected my guests in the evening. Once arrived, I confided in my intelligent and always understanding friend Johanna Bischoff and asked her to be especially kind to my visitors from the country, and to ask her sisters to do the same, and this kindness was not to be sporadic but should be constant throughout the whole evening. Of course, my wish was granted willingly and heartily. I then left my brother-in-law and his sister in the care of my friend to meet with my friends already gathered at the restaurant in order to discuss how I thought they could best help me out of this situation. I certainly did not omit to remind them that these were very simple people whom we were to greet and entertain as best as we could, but all offensive banter was strictly forbidden and any such remarks would be considered by myself as spiteful and severe indiscretion.

The restaurant was more brightly lit than usual, and the large gathering of young guests in festive attire looked sufficiently impressive. Then I led in my guests. My friend Steinhardt was already sitting at the piano playing the *Entrance March of the Guests* from *Tannhäuser.* The reception and the presentation were very festive, and every single person there summoned up all their charm to impress. My brother-in-law adjusted to the situation quickly and well as he was blessed with a very good ear especially for music and song, and in his very agreeable tenor voice he performed upper-Bavarian *Schnadahüpferln*[40] in particular quite well. So he, too, contributed to the general merriment.

His sister was simply drunk with delight from the attention she was receiving from the gentlemen and their amiable manner. She had to dance with all of them, clink glasses with them, accept their flatteries and compliments; in short, it was a heavenly evening for these two country folk. Their hearts filled with gratitude, they both left very late at night, and I have to add that my friends themselves took pleasure in how harmoniously the humorous evening had passed.

I will not omit to mention here and now that my sister's marriage came to meet her expectations. True, my brother-in-law remained the simple man who did not think much of the finer joys of life and living, but his thoroughly honest character, his naive manner, his untiring diligence and his kindness to everyone made him many friends, and his business prospered.

---

[40] Improvised epigram-like poems, usually humorous and daring; especially popular among the population of the Alps.

My sister was like a kind spirit to him, who in the true sense of the word, led him through life like a big child without upsetting his sensitivity as a hard-working man. Whatever my sister wanted, this was his law. He was of the unwavering conviction that whatever she said was right, no matter if it was regarding business matters or family concerns.

In the meantime, my sister's children had grown up. The two sons were looking to support their father in his business and thought that Italy could be developed as an important and promising sales territory. This assumption was based mainly on the experience of several years spent abroad by the eldest son, my nephew Max. For this purpose, Karl, the second - and sadly sickly – son, also later went to Italy to obtain knowledge of the language and the place. In his head, my brother-in-law already pictured the upturn his company would experience once his sons applied all their strength to the business. Sadly, those hopes were not met. The younger son returned home, desperately ill, and his suffering soon found an end.

My nephew Max, a sporty, strong, active and handsome boy, tried to improve his father's business by accompanying his father when visiting existing customers in Bavaria and strove for an increase in sales in Saxony, Thuringia, etc. Those efforts were not very successful either. I must mention here that I was not the least bit surprised about this, and that I did not think that my nephew was lacking diligence or good will. The sale of hops, which is what their business was, could not strictly speaking be considered a normal commercial business activity. If one is not able to remain undisturbed in the face of humiliation and rough treatment, or if one does not make use of copious amounts of beer and wine as selling aids from the start, or if one does not know how to make efficient use of palm grease in a discreet manner, then one has not got what it takes to become a successful hop trader. In any case, even these things have changed in our lifetime, at least this is what the situation used to be, I saw it with my own eyes (see *Tales From A Merchant's Life*). Knowing this, I did not cast a stone at my nephew, of whom I will have much to tell later on.

In the meantime, my brother-in-law's daughters married. I had always had a liking towards Babette, the eldest, who had inherited many of her mother's features, not necessarily in her physical appearance but in her character; today she lives happily and contentedly with her husband. They married after having been in love for a long time; a romance which is rare in other marriages. And now, a grown daughter of theirs, a bright and pretty girl, is married to one of our company's junior partners, who holds a respectable position. No need to point out that, reminiscent of my sister Ida, I played "Cupid" to bring about this union.

My sister's second daughter, Anna, was a beauty and distinguished by her grace. Her happy marriage did not last long. The birth of their first child was paid for by her young life, and this child himself, a healthy, handsome boy, incredibly capable and popular with everyone because of his intellect and excellent character, grew up only to die for the Fatherland, to give his life on the battlefields, at the tender age of 24; an officer decorated with the Iron Cross[41]. The tragedies of life!

---

[41] Robert Ottensooser.

Fig. 20 War memorial commemorating Jewish soldiers who died in WWI. Robert Ottensooser is listed on the reverse of the memorial. © Israel Schwierz

Now let me talk about those other members of the Ottenstein family, who through my marriage became close in-laws and dear relatives. Apart from the daughter who was to join me in my life, the Otten-steins, a family of teachers, had four sons. They were well brought-up, equipped with rich skills and know-ledge, and apart from Albert, the youngest, they had all been prepared for a commercial vocation and were working as such. In order of their ages the sons were called Justin,

Luitpold, Theodor and Albert. I actually went to school with my brother-in-law Justin, in Gunzenhausen, and we remained friends throughout our lives.

When I got married, Justin, my oldest brother-in-law, was working in his uncle Wassermann's hop business in Fürth, and so successfully so that, despite his youth, he received a share of the earnings. Shortly after our wedding, he and his uncle's son took over the business. My brother-in-law was a first-class member of staff for the company, and in addition to his convivial and endearing manner, it was his distinct musical talents which were sometimes behind his business successes. Many a time he won over a new customer with his excellent piano playing and his good, steady voice, and combined with his youthful vigour and health he had no issue playing the part of a "drink-able" man without coming to any harm. I have to add this funny story here:

My brother-in-law was visiting a business associate who was staying in a hotel in Nuremberg. It goes without saying that the occasion was celebrated with one – or rather several – bottles of strong wine. At the time, he was already married to his childhood sweetheart, a very beautiful girl from a respected family from Bamberg. The meeting went on until midnight, and for the short journey back to Fürth, Justin took a fast train. The next morning we received a note from Fürth asking if my brother-in-law had spent the night with us, since had not arrived home yet. We grew concerned as they could not explain what had happened. Distressed as we were, we were thinking about going to the police when we heard the news that a telegram had arrived from the town of Hof[42] in which my brother-in-law informed us about his arrival in Fürth that evening. No word of explanation. What had happened? Our dear Justin, overcome by the effects of so much wine, had fallen into such a deep sleep on the short journey to Fürth that he not only missed his stop, but what was more, he could only be roused and made to leave the compartment - with some difficulty! – once the train had reached its destination in Hof.

My other two brothers-in-law, Luitpold and Theodor, were striking lads in their early 20s. Hard working, ambitious and well-educated merchants. The fateful visit of an uncle thought lost in America was to blame for the fact that the two brave boys were to meet a tragic fate.

This uncle, whom I knew personally, was beyond doubt an honest and good man in his nature who had only the best intentions for his nephews. His intellectual aptitude, however, seemed to me somewhat below average. He himself had gone to America at a very early age and set up a store in the South, in the town of Mobil, without, however, making any great fortune from it. He talked my parents-in-law into entrusting him with my brother-in-law Luitpold at first. He would set up another branch somewhere, and Luitpold was to manage it. The plan was that his brother Theodor would follow him once the store was up and running. I am certain that he assumed that that would enable the two young men to set themselves up and make their fortune. Luitpold and his uncle went "across the water". The "somewhere", where the branch was to be set up, was deep

---

42 80 miles northeast of Nuremberg, near the border with what is now the Czech Republic.

inland where the woods had to be cleared first before a new settlement could be built. The accommodation facilities that were already available in this newly established town were shacks of various sizes made from corrugated iron. In one of those shacks was the new store which my brother-in-law took on all by himself. Behind the shop was a small room which served as his bed and sitting room. A hostile climate, an apparently growing population with a majority of dangerous elements and inadequate provisions all undermined the health of the poor boy. In his letters home he cried for help, and Theodor did find his way to him, but both returned home mortally ill only to die from an irrecoverable exhaustion in their parents' home. And the uncle? I was absolutely convinced that he was to blame for this tragedy, and it seems that he too recognised that he was guilty. The family never heard from him again.

My parents-in-law's youngest son, Albert, was just about to take his final Abitur exams when his sister and I were married. He attended a grammar school specialising in Classics and had already been enrolled in the university of Würzburg for the coming semester. Albert was very talented, and he had reason to be especially proud of his excellent knowledge of mathematics. I suggested - maybe because he excelled at this science and because I also found him to be free from any revelries or youthful romantics; on the contrary, he looked at all things in a very level-headed manner - that he take up a commercial career. This coincided very much with his own desires, and I employed him in our company. In a short time he had learned the ropes; he preferred almost exclusively the practical side of the business, working in the shop and in the warehouse. He did not care much for paperwork at all, and given his classical training I did not consider it absolutely necessary to introduce him to the written formalities of the business world. When he was still very young for this kind of work, the company sent him on the road, and despite his youth, his success exceeded that of his much older and much more experienced colleagues.

I will return to what happened to my brothers-in-law and their families later on; now is the time to return to my circle of friends. Despite the landlord's increasingly difficult peculiarities we continued to meet at Segitz's and even expanded the conviviality by introducing an annual celebration of our society's anniversary to which our wives were invited too. This went on for ten years or so until a great crisis came about. What happened was this: our hard-drinking friend Seibert was a great hugger of the bar. When we went home at a suitable hour, he would ask for another glass of his usual cheap wine, fall asleep over it and often snoozed for hours as the last guest in the restaurant. Our by now wealthy landlord was thereby prevented from closing up and going to bed. He started to resent this situation and explained this curtly to our friend, which not only insulted him but also piqued all of us. In truth, our landlord had every right not to engage in our friend's late-night sessions. Yet we thought the form and manner in which he expressed his displeasure were insulting. He could have had a word with one of us beforehand; then we would have found ways and means of sorting the issue gently.

So, we needed a new meeting place for the "Free Society". It was not without a certain melancholy that we left the old one. The person responsible for this "exodus" in the first place was ordered to find a wine house that would welcome us with all our faults and benefits. The question was answered quickly, but not particularly happily. A small wine tavern in Heldengässchen took us in. The landlords were a young couple and very obliging; moreover, we were not bothered by many other guests. The wines were average, and the food, which for us had really always been the most important thing, was below average.

The guests were far and few between, but amongst them was one tall, handsome young man who evidently wanted to be included in our group. Something he often spoke about, and this was mainly of interest to our music and song-loving friend Herr Bloch, was his beautiful, well-trained tenor and how he played a big part as the soloist in the "Sängerklause", a highly esteemed choral society. Since a guitar hung on one of the tavern walls for the purpose of accompanying any singing, it was only natural that occasionally we asked him for a sample of his talent. Then he would sing lively or melancholy tunes in his beautiful, bright tenor voice, and Herr Bloch noted that this young man did indeed have a great understanding of music. Over time, the artist became ever friendlier, and finally he suggested that we put our money where our mouth was and support his great talent financially; he would then be able to take singing lessons with a famous teacher and repay our thus incurred expenses with gratitude and interest.

There seemed little interest to embark on this business, even if we made no pretence of the fact that he probably deserved such support. His name was Kraus, he was a poorly paid clerk, already married, employed with a small company (lithographic shop and art printers), and, as he intimated, not very well educated.

In the meantime, our new landlords, who did not profit enough from us to keep them afloat even though we were used to live and let live, gave up the lease of the tavern, and we were homeless once again. Our friend Seibert had to go out again to spy out a place where we would be welcome and in good hands. This time he resolved his task most splendidly. We found a hospitable reception in Hoffmann's wine tavern, located most suitably for all of us in Lorenzer Strasse. Friendly hosts, a cosy lounge with a separate room for special occasions, exquisite food and attentive service by, amongst others, a pretty adolescent daughter, who was well brought up and of a modest demureness. I always called her "Elise, the girl as she ought to be", after the title of a book on the education of children I had read, and she deserved the praise not only because her name was identical to the "model Elise". Her younger sister who still went to school, a charming child, was the favourite of the family, and of the guests, too. I will mention here now that when her husband died after a long illness, Frau Hoffmann sold the house and the business, and that a little while later the sisters joined our company. They still work there today and are recognised for being clever and appreciated employees of the company. The younger sister will go down in history for once again taking on the task of taking dictation of these sheets and reproducing and multiplying them on the typewriter (a task which she had fulfilled already so skilfully and reliably with the production of my memoirs in *Tales From A Merchant's Life*). An excellent secretary, she has always served me extremely well while being friendly and untiring at all times, and it is not only I who owe her heart-felt gratitude but also all those for whom I am writing down these recollections.

We were convening regularly at Hoffmann's now, usually in the general dining room, which was often frequented by other friends and acquaintances, too. Only for special occasions did we use the private room where the piano was. One day, Herr Bloch asked us to reserve the private room for the evening, he said he had good reasons and would come a bit later. Accordingly, all of us were present that evening. When Herr Bloch arrived, he brought a guest with him, someone most of us knew and appreciated from the past. It was the famous Kammersänger[43] Vogl from Munich. With his magnificent voice and his accomplished dramatics he must have been recognised and revered at the time as *the* best singer of Wagner's works. Vogl had connections to Bloch's bank. He had a passion for agriculture and bought the large Deixlfurt manor near Tutzing. The development and maintenance of the estate as well as the improvement of the soil devoured huge sums of money, for which the artist had to sing not only in Germany but also abroad, mainly in America. These circumstances gave birth to the connection between art and finance. Vogl's love for farming was mocked with a well-known rhyme:

> One day he's at home, mucking out dung
> The next, on stage singing the Nibelung.

We welcomed Herr Vogl with open arms. As usual, he enjoyed our company and the conversation was merry. The artist held me in particularly high regard, which I can say here without boasting.

---

[43] Literally "chamber singer", an honorary title for distinguished singers, often bestowed by kings or princes.

Then another visitor arrived, our singer Kraus from Heldengässchen. He was accompanied by a pianist whom I had met before and who was carrying a stash of sheet music. Astonished faces all round! We had not seen or heard from our singer for a while, but it appeared that Herr Bloch had kept in touch. Herr Bloch turned to Herr Vogl, introduced his protégé Kraus as someone who had delighted us many times with the performance of a song, and then asked him to assess if Herr Kraus' musical talent was such that by developing it further he could be ensured a career in music.

Herr Vogl looked somewhat surprised but happily accepted the request, adding that there was no need for the pianist brought in by Kraus, he himself would accompany the voice of his future colleague. Then the assessment began. Kraus appeared very anxious and shy; when Vogl asked him what he wanted to sing he did not know what to say. We called out the title of a meaningless song, which he had performed for us many times. He sang it, but it made no great impression, and so Vogl asked if Kraus wanted to sing something else, something more difficult that went beyond the character of a much-performed song. By now Kraus had regained his composure and answered defiantly, "Yes, Herr

Fig. 21 Heinrich Vogl (1845-1900)

Kammersänger, I have practised the *Narration of the Grail* from *Lohengrin*". A little sarcastically, Herr Vogl asked if he did not want to stick to something lighter, but at the same time he began to play the piano, masterfully, to back the voice.

Kraus then sang with such harmony and musical confidence that I still believe today that I have never before or since heard this exquisite tenor part from *Lohengrin* performed so strikingly and with such an effect on me. The other members of the audience all felt the same. The Kammersänger appeared moved and pensive. He shook Kraus' hand and said, "Your vocal power is much greater than mine was at the beginning of my career. You have what it takes to become a great artist, but you have to practise most diligently. You have a wonderful voice but lack a number of other things."

Kraus was happy, and we set up the "United Pinhead Factories", as I would later call our scheme facetiously, when our plans to support Kraus and enable him to have a musical career did not work. Kraus went to Munich to take lessons from the famous Italian master singer Gallieri, for which at first we made sufficient funds available to him. We did not hear much from him. The money we had collected was almost used up. Bloch was the spiritual father of the "Kraus Protection Association", and he suggested that Kraus come back to Nuremberg; we wanted to see for ourselves if the sacrifices made for his training as a singer were justified and fruitful. Rumour had it that Kraus was spending his time and our money playing pool and cards, accompanied by plenty of beer and cigarettes, rather than employing it for the purpose of his being sent there in the first place.

Kraus returned - and displeased us. He had lost his fresh physical appearance, he looked unkempt and unhealthy. His singing had lost its former harmony, and it was only with great difficulty that he achieved those splendid highs which had delighted us so when he sang the *Grail Narration* from *Lohengrin.* He sensed how severely he had disappointed us. He explained that he had not been feeling very well; his appearance and his difficulty singing seemed to confirm this. But we could not excuse that he himself, or his way of life in Munich, had undermined his health, and we decided, for the time being, not to support Kraus any longer. Even Kraus' attempts to obtain money from any "united pinheads" remained fruitless. As far as I remember, when we sent for Herr Kammersänger Vogl's opinion from Munich, his reply confirmed our decision.

Now Kraus was left to his own devices, but eventually luck was on his side. In order to earn some money he performed as a concert-hall singer, and during one such occasion he was spotted by the director of the renowned Grand-Ducal Theatre in Mannheim. He was hired as first tenor by this theatre, and after a few years, and at a time when his voice was at its most splendid, he joined the Royal Opera House in Berlin in the same role. He has been there now for many years, and he has built on his fame through guest performances, especially as a singer of Wagner roles in Bayreuth and Munich.

To his credit, I have to say that he never held it against us that we no longer wanted to support him financially at that time. He remained grateful that the help we did offer at first allowed him to pursue a musical career and that our refusal to continue with that support, which he had brought on himself, had forced him to change his ways, which had been beneficial for his advancement. Many years later, Kraus once came to Nuremberg, where he excelled as the main entertainment at a musical evening at Bloch's; it was his way of showing his gratitude to Herr Bloch's suggestion that we supported his endeavours.

I have spun out "the story of the singer Ernst Kraus" more than it may deserve; but given the fame that he achieved even far beyond Germany's borders, this elaborateness seemed justified.

An important factor for Nuremberg's social life was to be the establishment of the *Phoenix* club[44]. The idea originated in Marienstrasse, where at the time the notables, or rather the aristocrats of the fast growing Jewish community lived. Of course, the purpose was not to create a confessional association, and indeed some of my friends, namely Herr Karl Böck and Rudolf Neidhardt, joined as members and remained loyally so, much appreciated and respected, for the rest of their lives. The more democratic Jews had settled in the city centre, beyond the Plärrer Square, as opposed to the Marienvorstadt[45]. Not long after the association was established, a certain dichotomy became evident between the two factions. The first board consisted only of members from Marienvorstadt, i.e. no democrats. In addition, at the foundation stage the board took the view that the association was to be for gentlemen only, and that it should remain as such. The democrats, quite justifiably, saw this policy as an expression of arrogance and an effort to keep the wives and daughters of Marienvorstadt from having to socialise with the plebs. They were to remain a class apart. Personally I did not

[44] In 1873.
[45] Literally: the suburb of St. Mary's.

share this view completely, yet I did have my doubts and felt more attracted to the democrats. After the first election the picture was completely changed; not a single member from Marienvorstadt was elected to the board.

The first decision enforced by the new board was to change the statutes to the extent that when a new member joined the association, their membership obviously included their wife, too. The decision had a deep impact on the kind of association we were. Gentlemen only means nothing other than card games in all their variations! Now we had to think about organising social entertainments such as concerts, dances and plays, since the young people, sons and daughters, wanted to dance and have a good time as was the custom in the larger clubs. Over time, my small talent was to be appreciated too, which was mostly expressed in being able to quickly supply what I believe were appropriate songs, prologues etc. It was my task to compose a couplet for a "Social Soirée", which was to be performed by a young man blessed with a good singing voice. The lyrics were to consist of some sort of homage to the individual members of the board. At the time, these were:

Moritz Frauenfeld,	1st Chairman
S. Geyershöfe,	2nd Chairman
Julius Silbermann,	Secretary
Charles Haas,	Treasurer
Ignaz Lang,	Administrator (Owner of a margarine factory)

I am including this couplet merely because it had certain consequences for me which I had of course not intended, and which were completely independent of the great applause it earned for the singer and the poet on the night. It was sung to an effective and at the time very popular tune.

Couplet dedicated to the members of the board

What I am singing in scantily clad verses,
This song, it's dedicated to the few brave men
Who saved you from exile, my dear ladies,
Like knights riding through the Mother of all storms.
It's thanks to them that we have the joy
Of looking into your beautiful eyes today.
And what I want to describe in this song
Is the board of directors in whom we trust.

It's not easy to steer this ship
When storm and wind make the going tough;
But the Phoenix steers with steady hands;
He has stood the test of time again and again.
As you know, we're paying dearly;
The house, of course, out on the Rosenau,
The chairman's paid for it with our fees.
He won't like to hear it, but we all know it too well.

Every office has its difficult duties, and some
Who are highly honoured to accept one,
Later wish they could return it.
Only, resigning is not an option.
There is just one office that I know of
That honours the bearer without much effort.
And if one day I might turn out to be someone,
Then I wish that it might be second chairman.

A man who offers up his time and peace so willingly
Soon gains the gratitude of his peers;
The man who is always in the highest of spirits

Even when taking the longest minutes with precision.
Once we have our own handsome home
For the club we hold so dear to our hearts,
Our secretary will no longer have to wander about,
He'll have the first floor at the *Phoenix*.

Finding a reliable treasurer nowadays
Surely must be the rich man's greatest concern,
But we are relieved of such a pain,
Since our Haas has "reliable" as his watchword.
He does not like to help himself,
And what he gives is counted well.
As it should be! He who scrimps a little here and there,
Will always be re-elected by us as treasurer.

I must not forget the brave man,
The administrator, who takes care of so many things.
Food and drink and many others,
He even lends us money to play Tarock.
To him this ode shall sing the highest praises,
And hot gratitude shall burst from our chests,
But please, Heaven spare us
The products of his factory out there!

The wish that I had expressed in the third verse was to be fulfilled. At the next election I was elected second chairman. It was not something I particularly enjoyed.

I was very popular in the club, and I owe the club many a happy hour which I was grateful for, given the hard work in the business. My main task on the board was directed at the social events where my poetic talent could be of assistance. I do not know what happened to all the casual poems I wrote for the various occasions. I only want to mention one of my poems, which was saved by chance in a printed book. It was a prologue to the farce *In the Land of Cockaigne*, written by my two cousins, Fritz Tuchmann and Heinrich Iglauer, and me. The aim of the poem was to portray the difference between prose and verse and to urge people not to forget or disdain verse in this time of technology and profit-making. The verses, which I dictated to my daughter Berta, the most poetic amongst her siblings, in the course of half an hour went like this:

In the Land of Cockaigne

Who I am? It is not without apprehension
that I step in front of the festive, expecting crowd,
And I am right to feel anxious
Since I tend to stay clear of the crowds.
I am the fairy tale that likes to hide her face from you,
I live in the quiet of the woods, in gullies and in valleys,
But oh, the people call it superstition
And want to steal our last refuge.

What I want? It's not easily said,
For it is humans who endanger us,
And yet it's hard to bring a charge,
When I look at all their great works.
The magic, which used to live in legends,
The human spirit seeks to overtake it.
But these new times swiftly mint the fruit
Of my golden imagination into wicked gold.

What I am presenting here to you in jest,
Even if clad in banter and in wit,
It still reflects our fate to come,
Of our holy realm swaying menacingly,
And how mankind, harsh and spiteful,

Wants to destroy the dying fable.
It is their wish to let nothing survive
That has no use in their daily lives.

What I ask of you? That in your midst you offer
Protection and cover to this poor child of poetry,
The most beautiful gift of your youth,
who shyly stands before you now.
Even if I find it hard in these new times,
Nothing stops me from this grave step,
I share the humans' joys in jest and pleasure,
and aptly serious I share their sufferings.

What we bring? You shall feast on the sight
Of the joyful goings-on in our fairy wonderland.
No matter how mad or wild they are,
There is some wise meaning in all our games.
Oh, protect the fable, hear its sincere begging,
Don't let it be destroyed by human hand,
Just like we comfort you with fragrant flowers,
Care for us with grace and with indulgence.

It was evident that this poem, the purpose of which was to prepare the club members for the following play, made a deep impression on the audience, and the reader and I were both rewarded with loud applause.

It goes without saying that for families with many children the *Phoenix* also served the not unimportant purpose of introducing the adolescent sons and daughters to each other. Concerts, evening entertainment, plays, balls, later even five o'clock teas offered a variety of opportunities for young and old to put to good use any existing talents at the *Phoenix*, and the young ladies especially were able to show off their particular advantages at these occasions. A small chamber orchestra was formed, led by my previously mentioned very musical brother-in-law Justin Ottenstein, which yielded some surprisingly good results. Above all, however, the young generation came into their own, and my own daughters, too, enjoyed following the call of the *Phoenix* and certainly did not come off badly in the process.

I shall quote a verse from a prologue I had composed for a social evening entertainment at the *Phoenix*. I will let it speak for itself, which will then relieve me of having to say any more about the most important impact the association had.

> The youth find their joy, if not their highest bliss,
> In the ball, that's really what their hearts long for,
> And the old ones, too, enjoy looking back,
> To a time when we thought we were gods,
> Some pretty eyes looked at us with gratitude
> When we extended the rights of the dance somewhat.
> Many a union of the hearts may well have been sown
> At a time when dances were held in these rooms.

The time when my participation in life at the club was most animated was when I took over the post of Secretary many years later. It was not that I was particularly inclined to do it, but I did it in order to support my dear and esteemed friend Salomon Forchheimer, who at the time was heading up the club as first chairman, and as a proof of my loyal allegiance to him.

It was not always easy to keep an inner harmony between the members of the board. Salomon Forchheimer stubbornly stuck to what he considered right and was very sensitive to any opposition. In addition, two other members of the board, Karl Heim and Ignaz Schnebel, had their own funny ways, and several times

I was called upon to smooth over the threat of an argument between the board members. Generally speaking, however, every individual did their best to serve the club as best they could, and looking back to those days brings back lovely memories.

The purpose of the following verse was also to serve as some kind of programme for the club members that would lay out the ambitions the board had for the further development of the club.

May in the course of these changing times
Be fulfilled what we are striving for so honestly,
And may the passing of each year see how
The *Phoenix* rises high and higher!

And more and more the message shall be spread
That glee and harmony surrounds it,
And everyone call out as one:
We strive for all things "true and good and beautiful!"

Until his sad, untimely death, Salomon Forchheimer and I remained loyal and faithful friends. I was glad to be allowed the joy, in his lifetime, of asking on behalf of my nephew Julius Ottenstein for his charming daughter's hand in marriage. After they were married, my friend was able to spend many years with me enjoying how successful and harmonious the marriage of the young couple that had come forth from our friendship turned out to be.

I could say so much more about what I remember of life at the *Phoenix*. I could talk about many interesting events of personal or general nature, only the participants have long passed away, and much of it would seem odd or incomprehensible to the coming generation for whom I am writing these pages. I already have the feeling that I lose myself in rambling stories and descriptions of things and events that cannot be so interesting for my descendants.

I will therefore only add briefly that these days, when winter sends me home from Streitberg, I still spend a couple of hours of an afternoon at the *Phoenix*, and that I properly enjoy myself there. I am a constant and welcome kibitzer at the table where the better Skat[46] players sit. I have practised this "Chess amongst the card games" mostly in Streitberg and have grown to like it. Like no other game it helps, especially the old, to forget whimsies and sombre moods.

Another institution to which I owe much enjoyment and education as well as the acquaintance of men of science who, free of any arrogance, had a stimulating effect on me, is the Natural History Society. I also urged my friend Fritz Tuchmann to join them as a member, and we both remained, I think I may say so, helpful supporters of this honourable, hundred-year-old society which was often struggling with financial difficulties. One reason why I held this society in particularly high regard was that any political or confessional discussion had to be left behind at the doorstep. Every Wednesday evening, unless we were prevented from doing so by some unforeseen events, my friend and I hiked to "Rose House"[47] in Schildgasse. This historically interesting building belonged to the Natural History Society and included the auditorium and smaller rooms where the associated sections, such as the ones for anthropology, geology, botany, geography etc. held their meetings, as well as the insufficient, cramped rooms for

---

[46] A very popular German card game.
[47] It was actually called "Haus Zur Blume", or "Flower House".

the collections. Many valuable items that had been donated by supporters of the society were unable to be displayed for lack of space. We had to make do as best we could, and there was little hope that these unfortunate circumstances would ever change.

The members paid a small annual fee, the total income of which was barely enough to cover the costs of lighting, the caretaker's salary and the interest on the rather large mortgage on the building.

Fig. 22 Haus Zur Blume

As mentioned before, Wednesdays were dedicated to plenary sessions. Usually, a subject was chosen by the learned members of the society from amongst the manifold areas of the natural history sciences, and after the presentation the subject matter would be discussed freely. Sometimes, however, a naive and unbidden speaker came to abuse the easily reached platform. I remember for example one young man, a clerk, who climbed onto the platform and announced that he was going to give a talk about West Africa. The subject seemed well-chosen, since Germany's new colony there had aroused general interest in the matter. The young man then opened his speech by saying that he had never actually ventured much beyond Würzburg, but that he had read a lot about Africa. Then he began, literally, with the words "When travelling along the West African coast, you notice huge sand-dunes." Hilarious laughter interrupted the promising speech, and Herr Professor Spiess, the excellent director of the society who was distinguished by his dry sense of humour, asked the astonished speaker in his typical humoristic manner "if he believed that the members had paid their school fees for nothing?"

The general hilarity that ensued told the young man that he best retreat immediately. Professor Spiess, an incredibly popular teacher with his students at the local grammar school, generally had a gracious way of conducting himself as chairman of the society, no matter if he were dealing with men of science or with zealous laymen. He was also exceedingly amiable when he needed a small amount of money for the society, say for the acquisition of a necessary book, and there was no money available for such things. He would then say how very desirable this acquisition would be for the society, only this excellent book costs six marks. He impishly went on to say "that there are men amongst us who could easily help. I won't mention their names, but will only look at them." His gaze was then fastened on me and my friend Tuchmann, and he achieved amid general applause exactly what he had intended with his hypnotising look.

Apart from the Wednesday sessions of the mother society, I rarely missed the monthly meetings of the anthropology section in whose aims and purposes I was especially interested. This section was tasked with overseeing the society's most extensive and relatively well-ordered collection, with discussing what had been unearthed in some place, and with personally helping out to raise the treasures embedded in the earth. The extent of what could be done in this area, however, again depended on the modest means available, to which I made quite a few contributions, but at least something was actually done with this money.

The president of this section, Herr Dr. von Forster, knew how to make these meetings quite interesting. By the way, Dr. von Forster still holds this post today, after a good 30 years, with the same freshness, and who is in a way now regarded as the leader in Northern Bavaria of the current anthropological societies set up to study Bavaria's prehistory. His only flaw was that he always arrived for the meetings much too late, which very much restricted the members' sleep those nights.

Fig. 23 Dr. Sigmund von Forster source: Natural History Society, Nuremberg

I furiously learned as much about anthropology as I could, and I used every opportunity available to do so, and in particular I rarely missed any opportunities to be physically involved in the excavations. It would make me really sad when that tyrant called "business" prevented me from doing so. It is really something quite delightful to witness the opening of a prehistoric burial mound under expert guidance somewhere in the woods and meadows –

usually it was in the woods. The main task is to exhume the remains of the person who has been resting there for thousands of years and to search for artefacts that may have been placed with him in the grave by his family or friends. I must say that in this respect I was impressed by the piety of our ancestors. When nowadays a rich person is consigned to their grave, all their jewellery including any tight rings etc will be saved for the "mourning heirs". Even the teeth have to give up the gold that the dental technician once used to preserve them.

How different things were with the humans who lived 4-500 years BC and even longer ago! They adorned their dead with clasps, pins, belts, rings and weapons! What rich and for the time relatively luxurious bronze items were buried! I was often a witness at such rich grave finds where splendid pieces were brought to light, pieces which today form part of the collections of the Natural History Society. That those graves were almost always found in scenic locations is probably no accident. It seemed that prehistoric humans had a keen sense for the beauty in nature when selecting burial sites.

The fact that ladies were present at these excavations also seemed a merit to me. Apart from the fact that bringing in the beautiful sex is never wrong, the ladies sometimes provided food and drink for us. I remember for example that in the wooded areas on the Glatzenstein hill, where there was an entire necropolis of a prehistoric settlement, we collected lots of mushrooms which were turned there and then into an improvised, luxurious, tasty lunch for us. Only the intelligent, kind and very learned Frau von Forster actually joined the men in their work, and I often watched her digging through the earth of an exposed burial mound with her beautiful white hands, searching for grave artefacts, or "tutenbala" as they say in Nuremberg.

Of course, not all the excavations I took part in were successful, but the organisers and participants were extremely good at making the very best of the situation. The provisions brought from home were merrily shared round, and there was no shortage of good and bad jokes.

I will have more to say about the Natural History Society and its development later on.

Amongst the things I did when I needed a little rest and relaxation to keep me fresh for the hard work of the business and its related tasks were of course my occasional excursions to Streitberg. When I sometimes felt tired and exhausted from the day's worries and burdens, our trusted family doctor – Hofrat[48] Dr. Maas, who died a few years ago at an old age – would always suggest that I spend a few days in Streitberg. Usually, and mainly in the autumn, I would choose Herr Dietz to accompany me; he had been with the company for many years as sales representative for Upper Bavaria and Austria. My favourite journey to Streitberg was via Pegnitz. In order not to miss anything in the office, we would normally take the train to Pegnitz on a Saturday evening and spend the night there. The next morning we would then start our hike to Streitberg as early as possible. The hike was quite a long one, and we wanted to arrive in Streitberg early enough to make it back to work on time on Monday.

[48] An official title for deserved civil servants.

My companion was a handsome and bright young man, whose success in business was due largely to his winning manner when dealing with customers. His business knowledge was negligible, and his interest in general knowledge was non-existent. His blond beard and the lovely way in which he pronounced the Austrian "Hob die Ehre, gnädige Frau"[49] won him the hearts of the women, who after all really played the lead amongst our customers, since they were the sales people. Our conversation on the long walk was adjusted to my companion, too. I asked him to describe the different places which he visited on his business travels; in particular I wanted to know about the inns and what they were like, and so we could talk for hours about these things. I really did take a vivid interest in these descriptions of the country and its people. In these conversations, the issue of whether the food at the inns in question was very good, good, indifferent or bad played a distinct role; in other words, my companion knew of no greater offence committed by his fellow man than the disgrace of serving his food late or, even worse, badly prepared. Even the memory of it would make him go wild.

On one of these walks we came across the Altenhof, near the Schütter mill. The Altenhof lodge sits in a secluded location, surrounded by wonderful woods and run by a forester and his wife. I had called on them several times before, but my companion did not know the route via the Altenhof. The forester was a character. Being the son of the famous teacher Grasser, who had a memorial erected in his honour in Bayreuth, he knew a lot of things which he would drop into the conversation whenever he felt like it and he was in a good mood. However, that was always

[49] Roughly equates to "The honour is all mine, ma'am."

the exception. In general he had an incredibly rude and loud manner, even towards his intelligent and hard-working wife and in the presence of guests. Over the course of several stays with them I came to find his favour by way of my diplomatic behaviour, and it came about like this:

The forester's lodge had the licence to offer tired ramblers a drink for money. Whether food was served with the drink was down to the goodwill of the owner. Most ramblers were misinformed about the optional part and asserted certain claims, the consequence of which was usually the request to leave the house. When I came to the Altenhof, I would first ask modestly if per chance they had a spare bottle of wine, especially one of that same excellent quality I remembered from previous visits. I knew that the forester held such guests in particularly high esteem, and I also knew that it would open the door to a nice bite to eat.

A few kilometres before our arrival at the Altenhof, where we wanted to take our lunch, my companion complained about being tormented by hunger and thirst, and I could not stop him from running ahead to, as he put it, order the food. I could have advised him to be careful, since he did not know the situation, only I thought there was no harm in him being taught a wholesome lesson for his hurried greed. And that is exactly what happened!

I was nearing the Altenhof when I saw him coming back towards me; he looked hurt and humiliated. Things had gone badly in the forester's lodge. In reply to his first question, namely what was for lunch, the "wild boar" - as the good forester was often called – grunted that he should go to hell, adding that this was "no inn where any boor could demand whatever he liked", and other such things. I laughed heartily and promised that we could still count on a substantial lunch, and my prediction came true. Upon arrival at the inn I first apologised for my companion, who was waiting outside, for misunderstanding the hospitality of the house and then asked modestly if we could possibly have a bottle of wine. Now the forester turned very agreeable and asked his wife, who was quite favourably disposed towards me, if there was even some food available for the hungry ramblers. A few minutes later we were tucking into a sumptuous and savoury meat platter. Furthermore, we were served by a very pretty and lovely young lady who happened to be staying at the lodge. This fact, combined with the wonderful food, helped my companion to quickly forget about his humiliation.

I will just add that the forester was to find a peculiar death. One day he did not return from a hunting trip, and he was found, with the rifle in his hand, dead on the ground. He had died of a heart attack. His capable wife subsequently bought the inn in the Schütter mill, and through her talent in the kitchen and her lovely way of being she managed to make some success of it.

We arrived in Streitberg in the evening. As I mentioned before, these outings usually happened in the late autumn, at a time when the Hotel *Zur Post*, where we were to spend the night, did not usually accommodate guests. I always made the same joke upon arrival, namely I asked if they had a room to spare, and they always returned the reply that they had “a whole floor available”.

This good old house with its honest owners almost seemed to me like a place where I was welcomed like a king and where I felt looked after like one, too. In the evening, we would play a cosy game of cards with the huge and very good-natured sons of the landlord. Early in the morning we would return to Nuremberg.

Of course there were plenty of other occasions where I visited, on a more direct route, my beloved Streitberg. I have recruited many friends and followers for the delightful little town in its pretty location and with its many other merits, be it through my enthusiastic descriptions or, even more so, by inviting certain employees of the company as my guests.

I will come back to Streitberg later on, this town which still provides me with a blissful place to stay, even in my old age, and it is especially now at this old age, much more so than in my youth, that I have realised how an inner connection with Nature can be regarded as the only true pleasure, when one is no longer attracted to the superficial and fleeting joys of this world.

In *Tales From A Merchant's Life* I have already explained the important effect the Bavarian National Exhibition of 1882 had on our company. As is commonly known, the Bavarian Museum for Trade and Industry was in charge of planning and organising the three successive Bavarian National Exhibitions, namely for the years 1882, 1896 and 1906. During the first exhibition, Herr Director Stegmann was president; for the second and third it was Herr Director von Kramer, who had been entrusted with organising and managing the artistic part.

At the time I was a member of the administrative board of this respected institute and obviously took an active part in the discussions regarding this exhibition. Before I talk about my memories of the splendid exhibition of 1896, however, I would like to give an account of my relationship with the president of the Museum for Trade and Industry, Herr Dr von Kramer. We were a lot closer and I thought him a lot more agreeable than any of the other members of the board. I do not need to elaborate about Herr von Kramer's artistic talent, especially in his profession as an architect. The buildings constructed to his plans in Nuremberg, such as the home of the Culture Association or the Faber castle[50], speak for themselves.

He also rendered a great service to the institute where he was a competent teacher, and to his numerous subordinates he was a benevolent boss who was always striving for their advancement. His fault was, at least according to his opponents on the administrative board, that he was too independent in all his

Fig. 24 Home of the Culture Association.

50 Art nouveau-style home of the famous Faber-Castell pencil makers.

doings and that he did not show enough compliance in areas where he had to act contrary to his own beliefs. This resulted in many heated arguments, where I always attempted to find a balance between the polar opposites.

Once, when von Kramer had barely recovered from a severe episode of typhus and had gone to the South for rehabilitation purposes, his absence was used to dig up anything that could be used against him. In the main he was supposed to have significantly exceeded the allocated budget for the rebuilding of the museum. His opponents were full of venom, which embarrassed me, and even more so since the accusations against Herr von Kramer were partly exaggerated or blown out of all proportion. Some other objective men who respected the undeniable merits of the director and I, took on the defence of the absent man. Upon his return Herr von Kramer learned what had been planned against him and what had been prevented by his friends and followers. From that moment on he was loyally devoted to me, a sentiment that I returned sincerely. We are still friends today, even though I left the administrative board 20 years ago, and our wives are good friends, too.

The 1896 exhibition was opened by Prince Luitpold. The centre-piece of our large stand was a very pretty children's play kitchen, which we had made even more attractive for young and old by adding some funny details. A very capable sculptor had supplied the necessary figurines. There was a plump cook who was giving her sweetheart, a strapping soldier, a tasty dish from the master's kitchen. Both, the cook and the soldier, were being caught by the lady of the house, and the whole genre picture appeared quite comical to the crowds.

When the Prince Regent came to our booth I gave him a tour, and when we arrived at the kitchen, I drew his attention to the humorous scene which illustrated quite a common occurrence. He stared at it blankly. Only when I explained it to His Royal Highness, did he laugh heartily and called his entourage over to share the joke with them.

Fig. 25 Luitpold, Prince Regent of Bavaria

At that time the new building of the Museum of Trade and Industry was pretty much completed, at least externally. The internal decorating, however, had not progressed much. The Prince Regent was due to inspect the new building where possible, and the entire board came out in all their finery to welcome His Highness.

The location for the gathering was a bare room which did not even have a proper floor covering. The Regent appeared in dress uniform and listened to the 20-minute long speech delivered by the chairman of our board. This speech was full of all things concerning the building, the costs, etc, but it was not very powerful. I felt sorry for His Highness, if only out of respect for his advanced age, that he had to listen to such a boring speech for such a long time in an unheated room. I admired the patience and resignation with which he endured this trial. When the speaker was finished, His Royal Highness noticeably sighed with relief, shook the chairman's hand and said "You really have a very good memory."

Before I move on from the Museum of Trade and Industry I will just mention that apart from eagerly carrying out my duties as a member of the board, I also donated significant amounts of money to the development fund of the institute and its charitable institutions. I donated the means for the purchase of a material testing machine, as well as significant sums for other purposes, and finally I transferred 20,000 marks into the newly established pension fund, which was an extremely important institution for the welfare of the employees. Roughly calculated, the monies I donated over the course of the years may well add up to 50,000 marks.

While writing down these events I have no documents to support me, I have to rely solely on my memory. Having said that, they are not really important events that I want to describe, but they are more like pictures of my dealings with thousands of people over the course of my long life and which I am now reviving. But how much remains unsaid, which in itself is no less or more important than what I considered worth retelling! This also explains why the things that I am reporting are not always strung together harmoniously. Goethe's words, "The best you cannot tell", also oblige me to a certain reservation, even if not in the same sense as Goethe. I mean thereby that I do not want to say anything that might hurt anyone who is still alive, even if these events might be of a funny nature.

Let's return to my friends. We could stay no longer at *Hoffmann's* as the restaurant closed down. We departed reluctantly and moved over to the *Strauss* hotel where we found a cosy place to stay in the elegant wine tavern, even more so since other close acquaintances of ours had been convening there for a while.

There were two men in particular who joined our circle and whom I will always remember as loyal, reliable friends. They were the Royal District Magistrate and councillor Herr Gareis, and the rentier Heinrich Berolzheimer, who was later honoured with the title *Kommerzienrat*. It fills me with a certain melancholy that I have to speak for them, for now I am all alone! All the friends I made and had over the years have passed away, with one single exception.

I first met Kommerzienrat Berolzheimer at the *Phoenix*; I did not think that I would ever be friends with him. I was prejudiced against him because I knew that he owed his great fortune to the founding of a large pencil factory in New York[51] and that he had done a disservice to the German industry by setting it up in America. Neither could I understand why he was awarded the title of a Bavarian Kommerzienrat and shortly afterwards the medal of the Bavarian order, or why he received an invitation to the royal dinner which was hosted at the castle to celebrate the opening of the Bavarian national trade exhibition in the year 1896. Even in Berolzheimer's presence I made no attempt to disguise the fact that I thought these awards were unmerited. I often mocked the "silver bullets" that must have played a part in this. Strangely enough he was quite unperturbed by such sarcastic comments from me. It was as if he felt that there was not much to say in his defence.

---

[51] The Eagle Pencil Company, later renamed Berol Ltd.

Fig. 26 Heinrich Berolzheimer

Furthermore, I held it against him that he, as rumour had it, did not pay the appropriate amount of tax on his large fortune. One day when numerous friends and acquaintances were gathered at the *Strauss,* the subject of the frequently occurring tax evasions came up, and I declared that even amongst us was one who, if visited by an able tax inspector, would suffer a serious blood-letting. I named no names, but everyone knew whom I was talking about.

The next day Berolzheimer came to see me; we had a long talk which convinced me that my indirect accusation was unjustified and that the man had more and better qualities than I had at first assumed. Especially his descriptions of how at the beginning of his business activities he hit very hard times which had him fight for his survival, and how it was only thanks to his iron diligence and with a feeling of emotional isolation in an alien land that he had been able to work his way up. What he said reminded me vividly of my own past, and we parted as friends.

This budding friendship was to be of more significance than I imagined at the time. Berolzheimer had transferred his

American-style, business to his two sons Philipp and Emil in New York. Another son was a philosopher of law in Munich, and his only daughter was married to a highly-regarded lawyer in Munich. I have met all the members of the family and hold them in high esteem. Soon after I became friends with Berolzheimer, his wife died.

Berolzheimer himself was a stately man, highly educated and with very good business knowledge, too. I often went to his house, and we always had a good time when we met up with our other friends. Berolzheimer then always appeared much younger, and it seemed as if he had found something in this circle of friends that he had either missed in the past or had not known how to create it. I was allowed to make fun of some of his particularities without him taking any offence; for example, on our walk to the *Phoenix* he would regularly remind us that they charged 20 pfennigs for a cup of tea, but 30 pfennigs for a pot. He suggested that we share a pot in order to save 10 pfennigs!

At another occasion he complained that his barber was impolite; this barber happened to be the one I had visited for years, and I had never noticed even a hint of rudeness. I knew, however, that Berolzheimer always wanted to be served quickly and preferentially before others, but that he did not leave any tips for the assistant. It did not take much ingenuity to guess what the reason was for this lack of courtesy. I told him openly that he should, like me, offer a small tip to the assistant, and then he would be sure to have nothing to complain about. I did not accept his objection that in Fürth, where he used to live, he had never been asked for more than 20 pfennigs and that here he had to pay 25 pfennigs and therefore no special tip was necessary. He was intelligent enough to follow my advice eventually, and from then on he never again had reason to complain about impropriety of any kind.

On our trips to Streitberg he always suggested that we travel third class, and I could list many other occasions where his drive to save was almost petty and where he must have given any outsiders the impression that he was either forced to save or a Scrooge. I soon realised, however, that it was just his habitual way of working things out meticulously, and that his in fact very generous nature only needed to be stirred and inspired in order to emerge. I will talk more about this later on.

Just how selfless he was and I had to acknowledge him to be even when his very own interests were at stake shall be explained by the following case:

He owned a sizeable number of shares in my company and increased them steadily. It was only natural that I should discuss with him, in his capacity as major shareholder, the development and other important questions regarding the company. This gave me an insight into his clear views and his business acumen, and I do not deny in any way that in many cases I followed his advice. I seriously invited him to join the company as a member of the supervisory board as this seemed to me to be in the interests of the company, and I really wished for him to have the modest share in profits that came with the job, too, but he declined with thanks and with determination.

At every year-end when the accounts were drawn up and before the dividends were agreed, he urged us to increase the depreciation and to reduce the dividends considerably. His advice was made in earnest, despite the fact that he, as a major shareholder, would have to accept the negative consequences in form of a loss of interest payments as well as a decrease in the value of the shares themselves.

Moreover, I will use this occasion to point out that Berolzheimer, despite all his funny quirks, was not only a great merchant but also a magnanimous human being who simply did not talk much about what he considered worthy causes to support. Further evidence for the trust my friend had in me personally is this account: one economically difficult year he granted our company an irrevocable seven-year credit of 650,000 marks at a very reasonable interest rate, secured merely by an IOU.

Another equally esteemed friend, who through me also befriended Berolzheimer, was the senior councillor Gareis. For many years, this senior civil servant held the post of district magistrate and Royal commissioner for the city of Nuremberg. We met when one day when he came to our offices to ask if our company would consider manufacturing collection boxes to his design for his charitable institution – a children's nursery in Stein. I had often heard about the charitable work this good man was doing, so I accepted the order and offered to pay for the production costs myself. It was the beginning of a friendship that was guarded by us both like a treasure, and where we were both willing to make the greatest sacrifices for each other. He got on very well with my other friends, too, and the more time we spent with this unpretentious, noble man, who was so wise and easy-going, without any arrogance or prejudice, the more affection we felt for him. It seemed to all of us as if he had been one of us for many, many years.

I often accompanied him to the various towns in his sprawling district to visit one or another of the humanitarian or charitable institutions he had founded. I was very interested in learning from the nature of these institutions, which all stemmed from his practical, experienced mind or from his warm compassion for human welfare. I learned many things that had been alien to me: fish and fruit farming, bee-keeping, agricultural winter schools, children's nurseries, hospitals, the cultivation of fields and forests, and later on, when I usually spent my summers in Streitberg, I would often astonish the farmers when I expertly talked with them about agricultural questions and could even tell them something inspiring or instructive.

My friend also joyfully accepted my invitations to accompany me to Streitberg, the setting and qualities of which he enjoyed very much. There he found a country inn, just to his taste and the free use of an extensive trout-fishing lake, which he loved passionately; and the long walks through the woods which we undertook together were incredibly instructive for me since his forestry knowledge was just as profound as that of any practical forester. He also introduced me to the "bread of the forest", i.e. the world of mushrooms. How gentle and sensitive he could be can be shown with this example: During one of those excursions to Streitberg I shared with him, over lunch at the inn, that my son Siegmund was probably feeling a little uncomfortable at this time, seeing that he was then sitting his legal practitioner exam in Würzburg. In any case he must have noticed that I was not feeling too comfortable either. I retreated to my villa for an hour's nap, and I knew that my friend also appreciated his usual nap very much. Not even an hour later the door bell was rung vigorously. When I looked to see who was seeking entry so boisterously I saw councillor Gareis outside the door, shouting excitedly, "Congratulations, your son has passed his exam with flying colours!" My true friend has sacrificed his nap to keep watch by the post office until the expected telegram from Würzburg arrived. The post expeditor did not hesitate to share its contents with this gentleman, whom he knew personally. Thus he was able to be the first to bring me the happy news.

I could describe many more such examples of this subtle friendship, but I will limit myself to one case, which actually was not quite so simple. My nephew Max Ottenstein, whom I will talk about much more later on, had leased some hunting grounds near Nuremberg, within the district of Nuremberg. He himself did not know the exact borders of the grounds, so in the beginning he would take an attendant with him who knew the area well. Nevertheless, it happened that at one such occasion he shot two partridges while on someone else's grounds. After the event, his companion informed him about the transgression. Obviously, my nephew had no interest in poaching, yet the accident could not be undone. To this misfortune was added another because my nephew did not immediately go to the offended owner of the hunting grounds and hand over the wrongfully killed birds and offer his apologies as would have been the right thing to do. Instead he merely sent his attendant, an awkward lad, with an appropriate amount of money to pay the owner for the kill. He was charged with poaching at the district court in Altdorf, which belonged to the district of Nuremberg. The situation looked bad. Having consulted a lawyer and discussed it with an expert, it seemed that we would be lucky if my nephew was not sentenced to prison but only fined, and it was taken as given that the rifle and the dog would be confiscated.

I told councillor Gareis, who knew my nephew superficially, the misfortunate story and asked him what to do. He thought that in his opinion it did not look as if my nephew was to blame, even if he had been careless in all aspects of the event. He then went on to explain that he could not interfere in an existing case, but he would see what he could do. Several days - followed no doubt by sleepless nights for my nephew - went by,. Then we received a note from the councillor saying that he had heard from the presiding judge at the court in Altdorf that the Ottenstein case had been pre-examined, and Herr Ottenstein did not need to make a personal appearance at the hearing or indeed have a lawyer represent him. The circumstances under which the poaching offence had been carried out where mitigating to such a degree that the accused poacher was expected to be acquitted. And that is exactly what happened!

Herr Gareis, this able district magistrate from Nuremberg, was equally well respected in government circles, especially in the ministry. His way of managing the district, of knowing its needs and its peculiarities, was exemplary. The people, and I often witnessed this, loved and honoured him for being a man who used his great knowledge and ability for their benefit and who avoided everything that smacked of red tape. Once for example, in the town of Lauf, I witnessed a constable submit several cases of transgressions of legal regulations by the population - I cannot remember what they were exactly – and saw him being ungraciously rebuffed. The judge said that it was not the constabulary's job to press charges for every insignificant misdemeanour, unless there was evidence of malicious intent. Where this was not the case, a warning was appropriate, but not a charge.

My revered friend was equally objective with regard to confessional concerns. He was a Catholic, but he could not care less which faith his friends belonged to. He judged people only by their qualities and by their deeds, and in all the years that I have known him, I never heard him utter a word for or against any religious group. On the other hand I know that the only reason he rejected the high office of president of the district of Lower Bavaria was because it would have been impossible for him, as a free thinker, to officially participate in the Corpus Christi procession.

A strong and simple son of the Upper Palatinate, he had a dislike for titles and courtly demeanour, and he loathed any form of hypocrisy. Prince Ludwig, now the King of Bavaria, held Gareis in particularly high regard, and he particularly appreciated his candour, his practical views and his deep understanding of agricultural situations.

During one visit to Nuremberg, the Prince wished to visit several industrial enterprises. Our sample warehouse was to be one of them, and this may well have been due to a suggestion by my benevolent friend. His Royal Highness spent rather a long time in our premises and listened with great interest to my remarks about the needs and wishes of the industrial sector. Having assured myself with the present Herr Gareis that it would not be considered a breach of etiquette, I asked the Prince for permission to send a prettily decorated doll's kitchen to his princess daughters in Munich, who were still of an age to take great pleasure from such a gift. I was granted the favour happily with a hearty handshake.

Fig. 27 Ludwig III, the last King of Bavaria.
Source: www.Billerantik.de

Now, I had ordered that all the office staff of the company – and there were hundreds of them, even then – assemble in the anteroom to welcome the Prince upon his entrance with a small homage. A usually very intelligent young man, Herr Meisl, a Saxon reserve officer who I thought was well suited for this job, was instructed to pay the proper homage to the prince with the words "His Royal Highness, Prince Ludwig of Bavaria, noble supporter of agriculture, trade, industry and business. Long live the Prince!" as soon as the noble visitor appeared. The speaker had had days to prepare for this moment. When the moment came to say those few words, however, he failed completely. He stuttered "His Majesty" or something, mixed everything up so that it made no sense, and only because a colleague whispered in his ear was he finally able to proclaim "Long live the Prince!" The Prince saw the funny side of the affair, nodded affably towards the misfortunate speaker and asked him if he was Bavarian. That was the end of the homage. As he was passing, I was able to assure the Prince that the speaker, who was normally our best, had failed because of an easily-explained shyness. The Prince laughed again and stressed that he knew exactly how well-intended it all was and that in his experience even the most eloquent speakers sometimes have accidents.

I would like to point out now that, based on my many encounters with the Prince, and some were still to follow this one, I am sure he would have been regarded as a wise and well-versed man even had he not been born a prince.

But now I must take a giant step backwards in time to focus on my family, and first of all on my nephew Max Ottenstein, the son of my unforgettable sister. I have mentioned before that he was ill-suited to expanding his father's hop business and making it profitable. My nephew had now married the daughter[52] of a colleague of his, i.e. another hop dealer; she was a sentimental girl, wealthy, and blessed with many female virtues. His father-in-law, with whom I was conducting the prenuptial negotiations, was regarded as a man of honour who had gained much respect and amassed a fortune. I must admit that this responsibility weighed heavily on me, since I had no doubt that my nephew had no sense for the hop business, and that he would never develop any. I thought, however, that this marriage together with the challenges and the improved financial situation it entailed for my nephew would at least allow him to earn enough to keep a family living a simple lifestyle, decently fed and clothed. Furthermore, his future father-in-law was well aware of the circumstances under which he was going to look after his daughter, and this lessened my responsibility to a degree.

---

52 Adele Sahlmann.

What was bound to happen, happened. The hop business, in which my brother-in-law was also involved, became less and less profitable year upon year, until at last the losses were so great that some serious thinking had to be done as to how the untenable situation could be improved. My nephew and I had some frank discussions about it, and he completely agreed with me that a change had to be brought about.

Now I had mentioned previously how talented my nephew was at sports. When the first bicycles were being manufactured, my nephew was the first to demonstrate such a dangerous-looking penny-farthing to the astonished people of Nuremberg. This "mammoth" of a bike was followed by the safety bicycle. My nephew developed such mastery at cycling that he won a valuable first prize, presented to him by a royal princess, on the Munich race-track. Given this mastery, which I presumed went hand in hand with a certain technical understanding of the bike, and given his general love of sport and, most importantly, the bright prospects of the bicycle industry, I thought it would be best if my nephew took a share in such a company or set one up himself. Indeed he liked the sound of my proposal, especially since he was an even better judge of how, for years to come, the bicycle would guarantee the local industry a constant growth, by serving not only as a sport but also for practical and economic purposes.

That was all fair enough, but how to overcome the existing difficulties, and in particular the financial situation? A solution was found more quickly than anticipated. I found a partner for my nephew in Herr Max Frankenburger, a private scholar and man of private means, who lived in Munich. His brother, a lawyer working in Nuremberg at the time, conducted the prenegotiations. My nephew and Frankenburger, who did not have a significant fortune either, got on like a house on fire; even more so since their individual strengths complemented each other perfectly. My nephew was and always will be a technician at heart, while Frankenburger was a shrewd, hard-working businessman who was to represent the company as a travelling salesman with much success later on.

It would go too far to follow the development of the new company, which came into existence bearing the proud name *Victoria-Werke*[53], in much detail. Suffice to say that all beginnings are difficult, and the two business owners had their fair share of pressing worries, not least caused by the lack of finances. However, it was not long until the company was able to exchange its much too small, rented premises for a respectably large factory that was their own property. A very wealthy industrialist and property developer, whom the two owners and I knew very well, committed himself to not only sell the land at a reasonable price, but also to assume the construction costs for the new factory building and to agree to a contractual repayment schedule that was easy and comfortable for the company. This agreement was very favourable and could be regarded as a stroke of luck, even if the noble helper was undoubtedly counting on a significant profit for himself, too.

Now the company moved steadily onwards, and within a relatively short time they achieved a high rank amongst the

---

53 The company, founded in 1886, was actually first called "Frankenburger und Ottenstein, Nürnberg". It was not until 1899, when the company moved into the production of motorcycles, that they renamed it after the brand of their bicycles, Victoria. *source: www.Victoria-oldtimer.de.*

constantly growing competition. To my joy and satisfaction, the two intelligent and ambitious gentlemen were earning a lot of money. Their products were considered first-class, and they were able to command a high price for them. The company was also reaping the fruits of their labour, not only while it was in the hands of the original two owners, but those fruits increased even further when, a relatively short period of time after its establishment, the company was turned into a joint-stock company under very favourable conditions. I did not think it right that in the process the two original owners, young men in their 30s, did not hold on to their positions as directors but were happy to act merely as members of the supervisory board. I was happy to see, however, that the times when my advice was needed were over. The two gentlemen had become very wealthy, and this gave them the confidence to know what to do or not to do. By no means do I want to suggest that they forgot how I had been able to help them with the establishment and later the development of the *Victoria-Werke* company. On the contrary, they always remembered it gratefully, and I remember many proofs of their gratitude. Their acquired wealth was also demonstrated by the fact that both men built grand mansions for themselves in Pirckheimerstrasse.

My nephew's enviable gift for making his life nice and comfortable emerged as soon as his successes allowed him to do so. And that happened relatively quickly. To his credit I have to add that even as a rich man he respectfully offered his father everything that would enhance his retirement years, and I will give just one example. My brother-in-law's love of music, at which I have hinted previously, led him, in his advanced age, to a passion for emulating the opera *The Trumpeter of Säkkingen,* albeit not very melodiously. My nephew therefore brought him a silver cornet back from Paris once, which caused his father endless delight.

His brother-in-law Kohn, who could be described as a hard-working and dutiful businessman, was appointed director of the *Victoria-Werke* company, which really pleased me very much since I had a great fondness for the Kohns and a keen interest in their lives. And I will also add that I have cause to be grateful to my nephew as I hold dear memories of many happy hours spent in his company.

Like me, my nephew dearly enjoyed spending time in the great outdoors, and he had plenty of opportunity for doing so. With some friends he jointly owned an extensive fishery by the canal at Bach, adjoining the abundant hunting grounds he had leased. He frequently organised cycling tours to which ladies were also invited, and those tours had a certain reputation amongst sports-people. Sadly I was not able to join in on those fun events, since even though I had a real interest in cycling, my age prevented me from actually practising it. I did enjoy fishing though, and I loved to give in to temptation and sit by the banks of the canal reading my newspaper, the *Frankfurter Zeitung*[54], on not-so-busy afternoons. My friend Gareis sometimes joined me, but of course he was a learned, experienced angler. In the early evening we would then wander peacefully over to Leyh, where the

[54] The leading liberal newspaper in Germany at the time, whose readers included professionals, businessmen, academics and independent-minded people whom Bismarck riduled as "pillars of public stupidity". (source: Amos Elon, *The Pity Of It All*, p. 196f.)

wonderful, spit-roasted chickens we had pre-ordered were already waiting for us.

I will add one more thing, namely an outcome that resulted from my personal relationship with the fishery society. My nephew had asked me to join this highly respected enterprise, after all it incurred only a small annual membership fee. Of course I could and would not refuse. Not long afterwards, I was sent a very nice carp to my home address with the note that it was my share of the large catch which was hauled in the canal. Nothing much happened then until a few months later when I received a bill asking for a contribution of 109 marks towards small fry to be added to the fishing waters. A subsequent exchange of letters between me and my nephew did not alter the ending of the sad affair for me. It seemed a pretty expensive pleasure to be reading the *Frankfurter Zeitung* by the Ludwig Canal!

In that way the hunt was more beneficial. I could not hurt a hare or anything else with a shotgun, and it was not really possible to send me a separate bill for quietly following the huntsman around. An afternoon spent in such a way in the countryside was always some kind of fountain of youth for me. Later we would sometimes take the quadricycle, which I had dubbed the "sea cow", to get to the hunting grounds. I purchased the "sea cow" later at a very high price. I could only actually use the monster if my nephew or some other exceptionally strong driver set the thing in motion for me. Twice, however, I had a little mishap despite having a safe driver. Once I came off near Erlenstegen, thinking that since the machine was going uphill I could come to no harm; alas, I was sent sprawling. Aching limbs and wobbly teeth were the result.

Nevertheless, a different tour with the “sea cow” was very enjoyable. It was an excursion to the Fichtelgebirge[55] with Herr Frankenburger. Once we arrived in Redwitz, our bike was loaded off the train, and we rode it to Alexanderbad-Wunsiedel. The quadricycle was a kind of tandem; the two riders sat behind each other and each had a set of pedals. The person at the back was in charge of steering and braking. The unique model had been created to find out if any fans could be found for it who might not normally be able to ride a bicycle. It took an enormous effort, however, to get up to speed, and only under the right conditions. These conditions were: a well-maintained road and strong legs. Uphill one had to double up one’s efforts in order to climb the hill at a snail’s pace. On the other hand it was very agreeable indeed to ride downhill along the soft slope of a long stretch of road, as was the case during the romantic ride from Wunsiedel to Bernock via Silberhaus and Bischofsgrün. If, however, a steep hill was to be descended, braking and steering

Fig. 28 The "sea cow" probably looked like this.

[55] A range of low mountains to the northeast of Nuremberg; near what is now the Czech-German border.

had to be in reliable hands. In one such case I thought to assist the brakes by back-pedalling; yet before I knew it the heel of my boot had come right off, and I had to be glad that it was only the boot and not the foot itself that was injured. That was the second mishap!

Part of the enjoyment for my nephew seemed to be the fact that he had burdened me with this monstrosity for a serious amount of money, although I must add that eventually his company bought it back, albeit at a loss for me. Anyhow, it died as the first and last of its kind.

By contrast, more hopeful times began when the first papers were bringing news of the invention and use of the motorcycle and the motorcar. They alluded to the expected change in traffic conditions and to the profound importance the automobile was estimated to have on the movement of goods and people.

My nephew and I shared a keen interest in this new invention. We discussed the impact it would have on our joined trips in the future; we made and rejected plans, but we were unwavering in our intention that the destination of our first trip had to be Streitberg. These wild ideas were realised sooner

Fig. 29 Benz Patent-Motorcar, 1885.

than we had both assumed. The *Victoria-Werke* received from Benz in Mannheim a type of tricycle which, equipped with a petrol engine, was able to achieve 20km/h[56] in top gear. It was a strange-looking thing. I am not enough of a technician to describe it properly. Build, form and design were almost completely unrelated to the modern car of our times. If one were to compare the two, one might as well look at the differences between a prehistoric dug-out and a steamboat such as those which sail on Lake Starnberg today. And yet we were strangely proud, my nephew and I, when we cautiously introduced ourselves as the first motorists of Bavaria, to the amazement of the people of Nuremberg and its surroundings, who gaped at us as if we were mythical animals, before we dared, after a while, to extend our journey as far as Streitberg. When on one of those journeys we arrived in Erlangen and stopped to have lunch at the *Walfisch* hotel, the entire square in front of the inn was teeming with a marvelling crowd, and so many more people were pushing in that the landlord had to lock the gate. Our first successful trip to Streitberg had all the makings of a victory parade. This is what it must have been like for the captain of the submarine *Deutschland,* when, after a dangerous journey, he steered his ship jubilantly back into the harbour.

It goes without saying that the nature of our vehicle meant that it had its whimsies, which we were not always able to understand or explain. Sometimes the thing just stopped, and it was impossible to get it moving again. I remember once, for example, we got stuck in Thon, in the close vicinity of Nuremberg, and we asked a pub landlord if we could park our vehicle in his coach house. He

---

[56] Equates to 12.5 mph.

refused point-blank, saying he thought it was too dangerous, and so we had no other choice than to return the car to Nuremberg using animal power, i.e. with a yoke of oxen, accompanied by the shouting and halloing of the great crowd that had gathered.

Often the trips passed swimmingly and without any upsets; other times we could not even take the car beyond the city limits of Nuremberg. And yet these experiments were a wonderful time for us, and this hybrid thing, which despite its flaws was regarded by the lay audience as a modern marvel, represented the first seed for the fantastic development of the automobile industry.

The technology progressed rapidly, and soon this prototype, or rather this caricature of a motorcar, which had given us so much pleasure, was overtaken by the perfected automobile. Nevertheless, the first generation of cars was not very reliable either and cannot stand comparison with the modern car of today, with all its luxuries and equipment. I remember how the first cars built at the *Victoria-Werke* had their engines and parts completely exposed to dust and dirt and that their ignition and carburettors often failed; and yet they were pieces of art compared to our old Benz, which today, just like the first German train engines, has been laid to rest.

We, i.e. always my nephew and I and a close friend of his, took a car built by the *Victoria-Werke* and seemingly suitable on a trial run to Streitberg with the crazy idea of returning to Nuremberg via the Trubachtal valley and Gräfenberg. The spirited attempt was a great success, apart from one little incident. This incident was actually quite funny: At the height of Gräfenberg the ignition failed; our car – which in my first delight I had baptised

Thunderbolt – came to a halt, and with all the will in the world we could not get her started again. Just ahead of us was the inviting Gräfenberg. A snap decision later we were pushing our *Thunderbolt* along a short stretch of road until it descended towards the town. The car started to roll again by itself, and its living power carried us even without the use of petrol to the doorstep of the inn where we were going to have lunch.

No-one knew by what magic we had arrived "on land"; and the reason why our *Thunderbolt* had not sparked as it becomes a proper thunderbolt was soon discovered. The battery which feeds the electrical ignition had gone flat and needed to be recharged. Luckily, this could be done at our inn, the *Gräfenberger Mühle*. As we were preparing for our departure for Nuremberg, I was overcome by the worry that on the way back any number of further incidents might happen. I had a compelling reason to arrive home on time that day. Apart from the fact that my wife worried anyway as she severely disliked seeing me exposed to such a risk, which is what she considered a journey in a car, but on that day we were also celebrating the engagement of my nephew Max Ottenstein, the son of my brother-in-law Kommerzienrat Ottenstein[57], and Fräulein Lina Gutmann. The reason why I absolutely had to be present at the affair was that I had promised to propose a toast to the two families. To ensure my presence at the top table of the engagement party and to guarantee that I would be able to enjoy the good food and shine as a speaker, I engaged a coachman from Gräfenberg to follow the car in a carriage and pair all the way to Herrnhütte. Once

---

[57] Justin Ottenstein also had a son called Max, so Ignaz Bing had two nephews of the same name.

arrived there, he was free to turn back. Had we had another accident en route, the coachman could then have taken me home. This costly prudence, however, was unnecessary. Our *Thunderbolt* rattled uninterrupted through the countryside, and we felt very proud to see the people working in the fields running up to the road and looking after us with amazement.

A description of this outing was published in the *Kurier*, and it was only recently that I gave it to my nephew as a "keepsake for posterity".

Over time, cars built by the *Victoria-Werke* were becoming more and more reliable and elegant. My nephew - whose circumstances in terms of time and money allowed him much earlier than me to purchase a motorcar - and I went on many several-day long outings, especially from Streitberg, which were made even more comfortable by my nephew's confidence and safety behind the wheel.

A Victoria car that I later bought together with my sons and sons-in-law is today, after more than seven years, still in perfect working order and is awaiting its resurrection after the war.

When I said previously that I am grateful to my nephew's penchant and skill for all things to do with sport, I hope that the preceding and other anecdotes help the reader understand that this feeling of gratitude in remembrance of times gone by is justified. My nephew later sold his magnificent mansion and moved to Munich. Yet, we still met regularly in Streitberg, where he and his friends and family came to holiday in the late summer. We called them the "Munich Circle" and came to appreciate the various members, e.g. Herr and Frau Rickoff and Dr. Picard and his wife, very much. I will always remember in particular Frau Rickoff, with her masterful singing voice which she had trained at the academy of music, and the kindness with which she would always grant my wish to hear the melodious sound of her voice.

My nephew Max, who I believe had always treated me with a certain amount of devotion, had, as long as I can remember, only very little contact with the relatives on his father's side, i.e. with the Ottensteins, and I cannot really explain why that was the case. My brother-in-law, Kommerzienrat Ottenstein, was the eldest of his siblings, a well-meaning, warm-hearted and self-sacrificing character who knew no greater pleasure than bringing joy to others.

His brother, my brother-in-law Albert, a very wise, calculating man of great honesty and with a love of truth that was not affected by his eager commercial spirit, lived more for his family, while his older brother and business partner, with his sociable nature and supported by his great musical talents (he was chairman of the *Phoenix* club for many years), made many friends. Both brothers were, each in their way, great businessmen who accumulated a fortune thanks to their diligence, expert knowledge and respectability, as well as the trust of their customers. But just as on the battlefield many soldiers either languish in disease or die the hero's death, the two brothers both caught a disease on the battlefield of business, or at least that of the hop business which in its very nature is plagued by certain occupational illnesses, which led to their much lamented, early death. Without a doubt, the children were grown up and the estate was more than enough to secure their future. Nevertheless, the loyal togetherness between husbands and wives, between sons and fathers was interrupted, and the grown sons, especially those of my brother-in-law Justin, were left with a heavy burden for an inheritance; they were to continue and grow what their fathers had built with much hard work and knowledge. That was a difficult task, since in the hop business the relationship between seller and buyer is purely a personal one and is key to its success.

It was Justin's eldest son Max whose job it was to maintain the personal relationships with all the company's clients, even though he only knew a very few of them, and to bring about the same results as his father and uncle had done together so successfully. My nephew was a cheerful soul, winning and lovable; he had subdued manners but also stamina when he had to stand up for the company's interests. He was surprisingly quick to secure the existing customers' trust and to make new connections. Sadly his young and active life was cut tragically short by a malicious disease. He died in his early thirties, deeply mourned by his inconsolable wife and two young daughters. It was a sad loss that was deeply felt by many people; by his many friends and relatives, and by everyone who had known him personally. With his death, the large and respected company lost its third loyal and incredibly successful partner.

It is worth pointing out that my nephew Max, like his brother Julius, received their first commercial education as apprentices in our company, and my efforts to introduce them to the theory and practice of commercial affairs were amply rewarded.

The monumental task of maintaining that which had been built up and brought to flourish over a long period of time fell to Julius. Up until his brother's death he had co-managed the business, and with extraordinary skill, too. Even when he was an apprentice, I could see that he never worked mechanically, but that he always carried out his tasks thoughtfully and reliably. I was therefore very confident that with his gumption, clear thinking and the knowledge of what was at stake, he would in time come to fulfil his new, enormous responsibility and that he would be able to preserve his inheritance for himself and his off-spring. Two still very young sons of my late brother-in-law Albert were on hand to lend their support, but because of their young age alone they were unable to contribute any more than the keen will to serve the business interests. Today, both are junior partners in the firm.

With indefatigable enthusiasm and overcoming all difficulties, my nephew managed to develop the most important part of the business, namely the travelling part, so successfully that not only did the company not lose any significant customers, but he was also able to make new and important connections within no time at all.

As I mentioned before, circumstances forced my circle of friends to leave our much-loved inn at *Hoffmann's* and move to *Strauss'* instead. Just around that time an incident happened which deeply moved all of us. It involved our friend Seibert. We knew that he lacked the means to develop his business and that the earnings from his small company did not leave him anything to save up for a rainy day once his daily expenses were covered. Based on these considerations we volunteered to arrange a loan for him. This would allow him to expand the manufacturing capacity for his much sought-after products and as a consequence achieve a greater revenue, which would leave more profit than just covering his very modest living expenses. He accepted our offer very gratefully.

It seemed that the first effect of the loan was his immediate engagement. Seibert was nearly 60 years old, he was short and fat and adorned with a boldly twisted moustache which he had dyed jet black. His whole appearance could be called "ceremoniously grotesque". And who was the lucky bride-to-be? None less than the first dramatic alto singer at the local town theatre, who had often wowed me with her weighty, melodious voice during performances of heroic roles, especially of Ortrud (Lohengrin). And yet she was a posh Viennese lady, who despite being past her prime still looked noble and attractive. Her reputation and family were also beyond reproach. What had brought about the engagement to the aging man was a chance meeting at a family's with whom they were both friends, and that our friend impressed her, an eminent professional singer, with his mighty baritone voice. More than that, however, it later emerged that the deciding factor was that the lady thought our friend to be a rich and important industrialist who would be able to lead her across the stage to a plush, middle-class life.

We were surprised about this love-marriage but too discreet to make our concerns heard. Our fears, however, that neither party was bound to find happiness in it, were sadly to come true.

As the day of the wedding approached, it sometimes seemed that our usually so cheerful friend had become thoughtful and self-conscious. We wanted to give a special wedding present and asked him what he would like for the new household. His replies were non-descript and unsure, and they gave the impression that everything was not quite in order.

Then one day Seibert went missing. No-one knew where he had gone, and yet it was obvious to us that it could only be the fear of the marriage, for which he had neither the courage nor the means, that made him take to his heels. This opinion was shared by his deserted bride, whose embarrassing situation we felt very sorry for.

Now, quite some time after this incident, we heard by chance that our friend had been seen and approached on his way from Munich to Salzburg by a fellow man from Nuremberg. We learnt from this man that Seibert appeared very absent-minded and shy and that he was obviously keen to get rid of his compatriot. He told him shortly that he was going on a trip to the Königssee[58]. Now we were without a doubt that our poor friend had gone on his last journey and that he had ended his life in the waves of the Königssee.

We were deeply moved by the tragedy of this case. In the meantime we had also asked the bank to which extent our guarantee for Seibert's loan had been made use of. He had withdrawn just over half. This seemed new evidence to us that Seibert had met his death, since he would surely have taken the rest of the money to prop up his means had he wanted to merely run away.

Our sincere grief over the tragic passing of our friend was a little impaired, however, since we had to cough up a relatively large sum [to repay the loan]. My friend Böck and I did not think

58 A lake in the southeast of Germany, near the Austrian border.

much about the pecuniary loss we had incurred, but some of our "guarantee-friends" took the loss they suffered less easily.

About six months after the mysterious disappearance of Seibert, my friend Böck, who had really been the closest to Seibert, telephoned to say he had received some surprising news. He went on to tell me, very excited and confused, that he had received a letter from the presumed-dead friend from Vienna. He had not been headed for the Königssee but for the land across the "great water"; for New York to be precise. He had made the journey to New York based on the sudden impulse to look for his wife who had run away many years ago. He had assumed that his estranged wife had turned her beauty to money, that she would support him in his professional advancement and that he would be in good hands with her loving care and attention. Above all, he wanted to earn money to be able to honour his obligations with his noble friends. He would not be able to return to Nuremberg, he added. His former bride-to-be had already forgiven him in a letter, and his goal was to stay in Munich where personal acquaintances and business friends were going to help him to start a new life.

Sharing this sensational news with my circle of friends did not have the effect that I had imagined. The majority were little moved, and others maintained that they had never believed the gruesome story of the Königssee. My friend Bloch and I, however, told him in the old friendly manner that we would be happy to support his plans with money, but what he asked for was so little that it could hardly be called a new sacrifice.

One day Seibert arrived in Nuremberg; we welcomed him warmly, and there was no mention of past events. We could see how hard the "old boy" had taken the embarrassing events he had suffered in the meantime. He did not talk about it much. Yet we found the tale of the meeting between him and his former wife very interesting indeed. In his head she had stayed young and beautiful, had loved him passionately despite all the trials and tribulations, and he had imagined their meeting to be a very romantic affair. With some effort he was able to track down her apartment in New York. He found an old, gnarled hag whose late husband had brought a lot of trouble, bother and worries into the marriage but had died without leaving any worldly goods. Old and sickly, she was forced to work to make a miserly living. Their meeting lasted only a few minutes. Despite his own looming hardship he gave her a few dollars, and his romantic dream was over.

He wandered criss-cross through this strange and eerie country to scrape a living, but he failed miserably. His money was almost all used up, and there was just enough left to pay for a third class ticket on a cargo ship to take him back to Munich. He died soon after, alone and abandoned, in a Munich hospital. None of us were there when he was laid to rest.

As mentioned before, we friends had chosen the wine tavern at the *Strauss* as our new meeting place after our exodus from *Hoffmann's*. *Strauss*, however, did not grant us asylum for long either. The noble hotel was sold and turned into a warehouse. So we relocated to the municipal wine tavern in the new townhouse on Fünferplatz, in whose hospitable halls the "Free Society" is feeling right at home to this day.

In the meantime we had sadly lost our dearest friend Karl Böck, who had been appointed to the supervisory board of our newly formed joint-stock company *Gebrüder Bing* . He had already been suffering when I left for a family trip to Wiesbaden. It was there that I received the news, in the most considerate manner as further proof of our intimate friendship, of the grievous loss from Herr Oberregierungsrat Gareis. My grief, and that of my family who all loved and revered the deceased friend, followed him beyond the grave.

The other members of the "Free Society", or rather its founding fathers, Fritz Tuchmann, Josef Merzbacher and I, still formed the core of club, which was joined by the dear friends Kommerzienrat Berolzheimer, councillor Gareis, councillor Michal, Oberstudienrat[59] Kellermann, Karl Dessauer, my brother Heinrich Bing and my highly-valued friend Jung, whose daughter Ida, a favourite of mine, went on to become the wife of my son Stefan. Herr Consul Lang and Herren Kommerzienräte Sachs and Metzger often joined us as guests, too. Another common guest was Herr Dr. Bernett, especially when the Natural History Society, whose director he was, needed money. I will talk more about that later. Herr Bankier Bloch, one of the oldest and normally keenest members of the union, he who had once done so much for the singer Kraus, was missing. He had deeply insulted me, for no reason in his passionate way, and furthermore had misunderstood a legal viewpoint on an occasion when I was trying to help him as a friend. He left our club, which under different circumstances would have been able to offer him many good things. The event that led to our falling out took place 30

[59] Formal title for a head of department at a grammar school.

years ago. We did not meet again. Bloch is now over 82 years old and still lives in full sprightliness in Nuremberg. I regretted that it came to the breakup with him, but the differences between us were unlikely to be bridged, at least not while Herr Bloch was still at the head of the bank. Even after I had to break off all personal relations with him, I still sought to keep up the important connection between my company and his firm. Again, however, it was his own fault that the final break was unavoidable. I have memories of many happy hours, though, that I have spent in his company, and I do not hold what he did to me against him at all.

Someone else who was to become a very dear friend to us was Herr Kommerzienrat Georg Dietz. I came to know and value him in Kissingen, where in subsequent years I used to spend a few weeks with my wife and my youngest daughter, Marie. We stayed at the same hotel. In Nuremberg our friendship grew more intimate and also involved my friend Tuchmann. We soon became an inseparable trio and were genuinely fond of each other. Dietz also joined the "Free Society" as a companion who comfortably and cheerfully took part in our conviviality, and who furthermore upheld friendly relations with me and Tuchmann, which grew increasingly stronger. Dietz, who owned a large grocery shop, was a very wealthy man, respected by all sections of the population, and he held many honorary positions. After the premature death of his wife, who by all accounts had been a woman after his own heart, he had to endure and suffer much. The health of this man, who normally had such a cheerful nature and who liked to enjoy the pleasures in life, has been subject to fluctuations in recent years. I am hopeful and convinced, however, that our dear and loyal friend will soon be completely well again and that we will walk together as contemporaries through this vale of tears for a long time to come.

Among the participants at our social evenings in the town hall tavern was also a Herr Dr Bernett, whom I have mentioned before; a young man who was officially employed as a sports physician by the Natural History Society and who, through his general abilities and lively participation in the society's efforts, had been appointed chairman of this institution. This explains and justifies my previously made comment, namely that Herr Dr. Bernett only appeared in order to advertise for the Natural History Society, or rather to raise some money for its purposes. "The venerable lady", as I jokingly used to call the society, was forever in financial crisis. Herr Dr. Bernett always tried to alleviate the situation to some degree by ordering us – I mean my friend Fritz and me, and especially Kommerzienrat Berolzheimer – some more or less painful bloodletting. Herr Kommerzienrat Berolzheimer and Dr. Bernett met under circumstances that are worth mentioning:

Dr. Bernett often visited the *Café Bristol* in the afternoons, usually at around the same time. He would play billiards with his friend Dünkelsbühler. Both were masters of the green baize, and I often joined them to watch their interesting, passionately played matches. I had got to know Dr Bernett well as a member of the Natural History Society, and after the billiard games were finished, he regularly walked back with me to our offices in Blumenstrasse. We usually talked about the adversities and hardships that afflicted the society under his leadership. It usually ended with him admitting that he could not steer the ship in times of financial difficulties, and our conversation would cost me several hundreds of marks. I helped him as much as I could. Sometimes more than I should. Often, however, I had to put him off by reminding him of the saying "When the need is greatest, God's help is nearest". He did not want to believe in it, and yet just such a miracle happened!

What Dr. Bernett considered a suitable means of boosting the society's finances was the purchase of a Zeiss projector (epidiascope). He explained that the apparatus would allow the most impressive presentation of all organic and non-organic creatures and things in such a way that any viewer would be most wonderfully impressed. He was certain that as a result the society would experience significantly increased membership numbers and thus revenues, which would see the society through some of its difficulties. The costs for such a machine were of course immense, requiring a sum of around 6,000 marks including installation.

One afternoon, on my way to the *Café Bristol*, I chanced upon Berolzheimer. As usual, Herr Dr. Bernett was there and just about to start the customary tournament with my friend Dünkelsbühler.

I called Herr Dr Bernett over to the side and quickly whispered to him that I wanted to introduce him to my friend Berolzheimer. This was an important moment, I said, and asked him to reply to my or Herr Berolzheimer's questions clearly and gallantly. The opportunity for Dr. Bernett to make a good impression on Berolzheimer was not to be missed. Then I introduced them to each other: I explained to my friend Berolzheimer that he was talking to the director of the Natural History Society, which was serving so many educational and scientific purposes. By the by, I mentioned the general issues the society was facing and then came to mention that Dr. Bernett had explained to me how the acquisition of an epidiascope would be of profound significance not only for science but that it would have an equally marked effect on the institute's financial situation. Sadly, however, it was impossible to even consider such a purchase since the necessary means were not available.

Herr Dr. Bernett then began to describe the advantages of such a device and added that there was no hope of such a purchase, since where were they to find a benefactor who would pay for such an investment!?

My friend Berolzheimer listened, it seemed, with interest, but said nothing. I then asked quite casually how much money we were talking about and whether such a sum could come under consideration. Bernett looked at me with surprise, since he had already told me this at an earlier occasion. It seemed as if he had not understood the purpose of our short conversation before I had introduced him to Berolzheimer, and it seemed that now he did not understand the intention behind my question. It was only when I grew impatient that he found the redeeming words. He explained that the price for such an epidiascope was around 6,000 marks, adding that the sum seemed so colossal that the acquisition surely would have to remain a dream. Now he had understood the situation well. My friend Berolzheimer still had not said anything, but suddenly he announced in his usual dry manner: "Herr Doctor, I will give you the money. Come and see me tomorrow."

I was richly rewarded by the look on Herr Dr. Bernett's face; he was beaming with joy and could not thank my friend enough for the magnanimous donation.

On the way home I told Berolzheimer that I was feeling a little guilty that I had helped provide him with such an expensive cup of coffee today. Berolzheimer replied, "Don't worry about it, and anyway, there was a bun with the coffee, too".

Fig. 30 Natural History Society meeting with new epidiascope, 1911. source: Natural History Society Nuremberg

I will give another story as a further example of how generous my friend could be: I arranged for Berolzheimer to be re-elected to the national board of the Bavarian Museum of Trade and Industry, to which he had once belonged a long time ago. I knew that he was touched by the honour, and I thought it appropriate for the interests of the museum to visit Berolzheimer in the company of Herr von Kramer. The two gentlemen obviously liked each other. Almost out of the blue, Herr Berolzheimer suddenly asked the meritorious museum's director if one or the other department of the institute was in need of a financial contribution. Herr von Kramer, who as I mentioned before deeply cared for the social well-being of his employees, replied that their pension fund was in urgent need of topping up. Berolzheimer immediately handed him a cheque made out to 20,000 marks, and what is more, sent a very valuable oil painting, a present intended for the director personally, to his house.

I could go on and tell many more such stories, only donations of this kind hardly count compared to the contributions he later made to charities and the arts. And yet this man wore a winter coat, a blue-grey fleece, which had been at its best over 20 years ago. And, just as in days gone by, he still tried to convince me to share a pot of tea at the *Phoenix* so that we both save 5 pfennigs. In this contrast there also lay a greatness which I will not attempt to explain.

Almost every year Berolzheimer came to visit me in Streitberg, once even in the company of his son, who lived in New York, the son's wife and their children, because he wanted us to meet his family. We were always delighted to have the dear guest stay with us, but he insisted that we did not go to any trouble on his account. He considered even our very simple lunch as too opulent. By contrast, his housekeeper could think of nothing better than to spend a few hours in our country residence, and she often brought us delicious gifts such as home-made cakes and Californian fruits.

Of course, Berolzheimer also visited the *Bing-Höhle*, whose wonderful features left him deeply impressed. He often talked about it. Once back in Nuremberg, he never forgot to thank us for our hospitality, but of course we always received him with delight. One such thank you note was in verse and arrived in Streitberg accompanied by a very beautiful oil painting. This is the poem he sent:

In a place where the Wiesent[60] calmly winds its way
Through flowery meadows with grace and allure,
There lie delightfully luscious slopes,
Famously known as the "Franconian Switzerland".

Mountains, valleys, heights and chasms,
Brought together as if by a miracle,
Lovingly fanned by herby airs,
Telling tales thought up by wizards.

This, Ignaz enjoys in gleeful bliss
And his delight, it tells it me straight,
That before the year is out he will again,
Flee the crowds of the city to this lovely place.

Now, by way of a thank you may he accept
With kindness this picture for his house,
Yet what Nature can give us in abundance,
Art can only return with imperfection.

(29th February 1902)

Berolzheimer had a great fondness for my youngest, and then still unmarried daughter Marie, and at various occasions, and usually

---

[60] The river Wiesent which flows through Streitberg.

upon his return from Marienbad where he went every year, she would receive presents such as valuable items of jewellery, embroideries etc.

I could tell much more about his extreme goodness directed at my house, and also about his unshakable sense of justice and his indignation about anything he did not consider fair or gentleman-like. For example, he donated the sum of 100,000 marks towards the creation of the municipal art studio, although at first he did not want to be named. At a large gathering organised to find further sponsors for the project, the chairman, Mayor von Schuh, opened the meeting with the remark that 150,000 marks had already been raised. This amount included the 100,000 marks donated by Berolzheimer while the remaining 50,000 was made up of several smaller donations. Since at the time my friend's generosity had received very little publicity, the audience believed that the whole amount, or at least the largest part, had been donated by a well-known gentleman who was present at the meeting, who strove for decorations and who was prepared to pay for them according to his means. He was often deemed to be the donor of the relatively large sum, and when asked about it directly he did not reply with a yes or a no, purporting that he was indeed the generous benefactor. He did nothing to divert the suspicion from himself. My far too modest friend was not present at the meeting, but when he heard what had happened it upset him very much, and he voiced his anger and indignation about this "false Dmitriy" in harsh words. These two men, to whom Nuremberg is greatly indebted, never came to an understanding; in contrast, they avoided each other.

That my friend's subsequent, generous donations dwarfed everything the Nuremberg of old or of today has ever seen in this respect, was a fact which the "unfair competition" eventually could not keep up with.

During my more than 20 years as a member of the administrative board of the Bavarian Museum of Trade and Industry I struck up a personal relationship with the director of the institute, Herr Oberbaurat[61] von Kramer, and of course with various other members of the board. I had a particular liking for Herr Kommerzienrat Ullmann, the Geheime Kommerzienräte Hornschuh and Winkler from Fürth, as well as Herr Director Füchtbauer of the industrial school in Nuremberg. Furthermore, I developed a real friendship with my colleagues from the board, Professor Hammer, director at the art school, and Kommerzienrat Heinrichsen. Among the senior officials at the museum I remember the curator of the collections, Herr Professor Stockbauer, as an especially dear friend. After his sudden death I was able to support his widow with help and advice, and she remains grateful to me to this day for the help I offered. This sorely tried, highly educated woman is still in correspondence with us.

With two gentlemen I esteem highly, Professor Dr. Paul Rée and Professor Stockmeier, who have always proven very loyal to me, I have kept personal relations until quite recently.

While I am on the subject I would like to point out the following: During my long life I have met so many outstanding individuals, be it in my business activities or while conducting important missions to which I had been called by the state, by corporations

[61] Head of the building and planning control office.

such as the chamber of commerce or the association for the protection of intellectual property, that it seems like a serious misconduct to quietly leave out so many related, interesting things. But how can I change that? I would be taking on a task that would go far beyond the scope of these simple recollections.

I also want to apologise to all those who have walked with me for a while in my life and to those members of my family whom I have not mentioned or mentioned only briefly in these unassuming pages. The aim of this book is really only to share that which is humanly touching, either because it is serious or because it is funny, and it does not claim in any way to be a literary work or a chronicle which could do justice to all the people, including relatives, who are dear and close to me.

I will come now to the two closer friends and colleagues from the trade museum, and firstly I want to introduce Herr Director Hammer to my readers. This kind and good-hearted individual sometimes played the part of the loner, but he really was nothing of the sort. He loved his art and a glass of good wine. If there was anything else he liked, I never found out. During the meetings at the museum, he would sometimes sit there as if it was no concern of his at all. More often than not, he would use the sheet of paper in front of him to sketch a portrait of one member of the society or another, or make a drawing of anything else that took his fancy. He would then leave these sketches deliberately, as if carelessly, by his seat, and yet it pleased him if I asked him to let me keep his improvised pieces of art. However, I have always found a way to express my gratitude in some shape or form, and there were plenty of opportunities for it.

I also often met the Professor at the official festivities honouring the Prince Regent's birthday etc. I would know then that we would not go without experiencing some funny episode involving him. Once the artist had had a few glasses of wine, he was like a changed man. Innocently he would come up to me, tenderly put his hand on my shoulder and passionately offer me the brotherly "Du". I could not help but happily accept it, and at the next meeting, after some initial shyness, we would go back to the formal "Sie".

It is a strange thing how a personal relationship is shaped or affected depending on the use of the intimate "Du" or the conventional "Sie". As far as I can remember I myself have never offered anyone the intimate form of address. I have been good friends with people throughout several stages of my life, without any reservations or restrictions on our mutual feelings, in an unfailing friendship, without ever using "Du". Of course, in such a friendship one observes more proprieties than amongst friends who consider the "Du" as a requirement for a close friendship. It has always been my sense that such a familiar relationship as it is created by using "Du" should only be entered into when one can assume that the friendship is not going to experience any kind of change over time.

Kommerzienrat Ernst Heinrichsen, second chairman of the administrative board of the Bavarian Museum for Trade and Industry, was a respectable personality and could count himself amongst the most influential citizens of Nuremberg. There was hardly a charity or a society that he was not a board member of. He held dozens of honorary positions. This came as no surprise, since Heinrichsen could be described as a brilliant speaker, a lovable conversationalist and – I did not think it wrong – a "drinkable" man who socialised with artists and had a notable artistic talent himself. His business, the manufacture of tin soldiers, suited him well in that respect. He avoided the mass production of the usual cheap tin soldiers; his artistic sense and his knowledge led him to a higher aim. If, for example, he wanted to recreate "Frederic the Great and his generals", "Wallenstein's Camp" or "The siege of Troy" etc., Heinrichsen spent years studying the details in preparation. He intended the resulting figurines to be true to history in their form as well as in their colours, and therefore it was totally justified that his products gained a reputation for their artistic and meticulous execution. And yet his competition, which produced for the everyday market, surpassed him by miles in revenue and profits. While he was sitting in his sunny, quiet garden in the suburb of Johannis, drawing up new sketches in a comfortable, paternalistic relationship with his workers, large factories with modern business operations were rising up in Fürth. These modern business operations were based largely on the Fürth manufacturers exporting their products very successfully to the four corners of the Earth; a system which Heinrichsen completely ignored while focussing his attention on maintaining direct relationships with his often quite fussy clientele. With all his talents, his education and his vast knowledge, Heinrichsen lacked one thing, and that was business sense. He could not adapt to the changing times and the resulting change in requirements.

Moreover, his kind of products were of little interest to the simpler toy shops. How could a brave craftsman or some other petit bourgeois be interested in the "Siege of Troy" when he wanted to buy tin soldiers for his little boy for Christmas? There was also another reason why Heinrichsen's business had not grown significantly despite the prestigious products. It was his versatility and his constant willingness to serve the *salus publica*, the common good, in one way or another. That cost him many precious working hours! Heinrichsen was obviously keen to get to know me better and be friends with me. On one occasion, he very jovially offered me the informal "Du". He was at least 15 years older than me, and confronted with this honour bestowed upon me, I was quite ill at ease. Due to this quickly-formed intimacy between us our conversations often revolved around his business. He complained that despite living in good circumstances, he was not making as much progress as he would expect, given the formidable reputation of his products. His revenues had not increased in three years but had remained more or less stagnant, while at the same time expenses for wages, living expenses for the family etc. were constantly on the rise. I frankly explained what I thought about the matter. I tried to get him to understand what causes I thought lay behind the lack of his success and pointed out that changing his production significantly was not really a solution since he had no competition in that respect. In my opinion he had to drastically change the sales part of his business, namely by dealing with exporting companies. He did not want to get involved in this at all; he believed that the exporters would only exploit him, push his prices down and steal his existing customers. Since I could not allay his concerns I suggested that I create a separate department in my company to sell his products. And not only would the products keep his E. H. trademark, but the company would also stress the fact that this special department would only be selling products from the renowned Ernst Heinrichsen company. We were even going to use his original selling prices, and my company was content with just a small commission.

This he agreed to, and from the moment his products were included in our toy pricelists his revenues increased significantly. He was very grateful, and the relationship between our families grew even closer. On the occasion of our silver wedding anniversary the Heinrichsens sent us a wonderfully artistic, even precious present, which I only recently gave to my daughter Bertha for reverent safe-keeping.

I could say a lot more about the originality of my friend, who certainly had his airs and vanity, but I will restrict myself to that which I consider necessary to complete the preceding notes.

When I said above that Heinrichsen could be described as "drinkable", the word was not coined by me. My friend told me that the famous poet Scheffel was a good friend of his. Every time he came to Nuremberg he would receive a note in advance telling him where the poet would be staying and when he would be expecting Heinrichsen. The note always included the instruction for Heinrichsen to organise a few "drinkable men". Now, Scheffel had announced his arrival again, and Heinrichsen invited me join him and the poet in the *Rote Hahn* the next day. I was an ardent fan of Scheffel's work, and I especially liked his delightful poetry in *Frau Aventiure.* My ardour was further intensified by the marvellous words in which the master impressively describes the scenic attractions, the land and the people of the Franconian Switzerland in his poem *Exodus Cantorum – excursion of the Bamberg Cathedral Choir boys through the Franconian Switzerland.* With a deliciously dry sense of humour he paints a picture of the quaint castle ruins of Streitburg and Neideck that are so characteristic of Streitberg:

> We continue our stroll up the valley
> where beyond bushes and meadows
> the castles of Schlüsselberg
> bravely guard the valley bend!
> They've been given evil names:
> On the left looms "Quarrel mountain"[62],
> and the rock face on the right
> proudly boasts "Envy corner"[63].
>
> At Streitberg the rock is sheer
> and white as if washed by the sea.
> The pilgrims' inn in the courtyard
> knows nothing about empty bottles.
> The bailiff of the castle, Christian,
> has a nose carbuncle red,
> and Frankincense, the castle's chaplain,
> dances round the glasses with him.
>
> In front of the Neideck over there
> we'll play the fiddle, too, and loudly,
> so that those by the gate, as it is custom there,
> will pay us our minstrel's pennies.
> Frau Wulfhild with the velvety hands
> appears wearing a garland of violets,
> "The men have come trotting from afar,
> well then, let's see you dance!"

---

62 Streit = quarrel, Berg = mountain

63 Neid = envy, Eck = corner. Scheffel used poetic licence to split the name like this; the origin of the name of the castle is quite different and has nothing to do with envy or corners.

I enjoyed reading these verses so much that I knew them off by heart, and I even used them in a propaganda pamphlet for the association for the beautification of Streitberg.

But now for the evening in the *Rote Hahn.* When we entered the inn, which was pretty busy, my companion swiftly walked over to a well-built gentleman who was inspecting his surroundings with keen, bespectacled eyes. He was sitting alone at a table, a glass of wine in front of him. My friend greeted the poet, who was the lone drinker, with his usual jovial manner, but the returned greeting seemed much cooler to me. When I was introduced with the most flattering words I only heard a weak mumble, and no handshake by the master followed.

We sat for a while in strained conversation which dragged on miserably, and the poet remained taciturn and gave only one-word answers. The situation was quite embarrassing and was not much improved either when his talkative friend did his best to further the conversation.

Fig. 31 Neideck castle ruins, 2008.

Then I remembered that Heinrichsen had told me the day before that the poet usually warmed up after a good bottle of Rhine wine; then he would turn into a rarely spirited and lovely conversationalist.

So I said, not directly to the poet but to my friend, that we should honour our famous guest by sacrificing an especially good wine to Bacchus. I ordered a real *Johannisberger,* which was of such good quality that it would loosen even a heavy tongue; its high price was a minor matter in this case. The first bottle was followed by a second. Scheffel was beginning to thaw, he praised the wine and in a sense us as his drinking companions. I had also warmed up with the unfamiliar drink, talked passionately about my deep adoration of the master and his works and recited from memory the above verses from *Frau Aventiure.* Scheffel raised his glass to me approvingly, but generally speaking our lively conversation did not raise above a certain banality. The master seemed tired, and I bid my farewells early in the evening. He cordially offered me his hand and added that he would send me a personally signed copy of his recently released new edition of *Ekkehard.* I never received a thing. "Farewell, it would have been so nice; farewell, it wasn't meant to be"[64].

My good relations, on a personal as well as a business level, with Kommerzienrat Heinrichsen continued unchanged for years, even if the fact that he and his wife moved to the neighbouring Wendelstein meant that we socialised together less often. One event disturbed our relationship, however, when one of my brother's sons bought a small manufacturing business for tin

---

[64] Quoting Scheffel's own poem (and later opera), *The Trumpeter of Säkkingen.*

figurines. Heinrichsen suspected wrongly that we had abetted this, and it came to arguments during which he, not knowing the facts, made a number of accusations that were most unjust. As a result, our friendship cooled considerably and for a relatively long time. Later, once he realised that the competition he had feared so much would not harm his business in any way, Heinrichsen seemed to regret his petty and most unjust actions and tried to make us forget the incident by being exaggeratingly kind and charming. He was not completely successful. The knowledge that he had thought me capable of such low actions was too painful to forget easily.

Then one day I heard that Heinrichsen was gravely ill and I invited him cordially to come to spend some time with us in Streitberg to convalesce. He accepted our invitation with joyful surprise, and we soon noted how well he was obviously doing with the rural quietude and the good food in our cosy country home. When he said his goodbyes, much healthier and fitter than when arrived, we both fervently rejoiced in the success of our invitation.

One day I read in an article in the *Kurier*, stressing the literary talent of the "esteemed gentleman", that Heinrichsen had published a book entitled *Moltke's War Horse.* The book, the article said, was not available in bookshops but was only given to friends and close acquaintances of the author. Only after several months did I receive a copy from Wendelstein. So he did still count me amongst his friends!

The tenor of the book was against a major byzantine trend at the time, and it condemned the greed for decorations and titles, the effort in every town and city to build monuments honouring the noble and the nobles, justifiably in a satirical manner. Yet the fact that it was a Jewish merchant striving to become Kommerzienrat, who tried to achieve this by hook or by crook by erecting a monument to Moltke's war horse in some small town, and mostly at his own expense, was not only meant to be funny but also, I presume, tendentious. This indeed quite liberal man, who in 1848 had bravely fought against any prejudice, especially religious ones, as some kind of Tribune of the Plebs[65], had now created in his Jewish Kommerzienrat not only a ridiculous but also a contemptible character. To make matters eminently worse, he included the Jewish Kommerzienrat's wife, "Rosalie with the voluptuous arms" in his seemingly lewd satire. That just seemed crude! In my letter of thanks I did not omit to praise that which was worthy of praise, but I did comment that otherwise the book had left me feeling embarrassed, especially his attack on the charms of the innocent Rosalie, and I added that in my opinion, and in all gentlemen's, "women were protected by a holy shield". He replied immediately, the tone of his letter was humble and wistful, and he admitted that his intelligent and well-meaning wife completely agreed with my verdict. He apologised.

We never saw each other again. Heinrichsen soon died after this incident. The work of this man, who was extraordinary in so many respects, left much less of a legacy than I had expected.

So as not to lose the thread I will have to return to what I still have to say about Berolzheimer and my other friends. At great expense, Berolzheimer had a generous educational institution, the

---

[65] During Germany's "failed revolution".

Berolzheimeranium, built in his home town of Fürth. He, who was so extremely frugal with himself, began to feel the tremendous joys that come with great wealth, when this wealth is put to the use of humanity, charity and science. My friend Fritz and I worked on the bold plan of persuading Berolzheimer to perform a similar feat in Nuremberg, namely for the building of a permanent home for the Natural History Society to guarantee its survival and development. This beautiful plan, inspired by many discussions at which Dr. Bernett was also often present, met with a certain positive response from Berolzheimer, yet it was not as simple as that. First a suitable site had to be found, which the council was to make available free of charge, and quite a few other things had to be organised which were not so obvious at first. What was strange was Herr Dr. Bernett's behaviour. This man, who used to be so modest, who was happy when he was given a small amount for his society, was now acting up as if he had every right to exploit us as he liked. He was no longer the pleading director of the Natural History Society, but now he was the director who wanted to have full control over our purses to do with as he wished. Any slight rebellion against it was answered with a lash of the whip aimed at the philistines that he certainly thought we were. And yet we – and that was Berolzheimer, Tuchmann and me – had donated generous amounts, even my brother Heinrich had contributed. As far as I remember we had made at least 20 to 25,000 marks available to the society to cover current or future projects. Curiously enough, Berolzheimer and my friend Tuchmann did not find the strange and arrogant behaviour of the doctor as odd as I did. They simply saw his insolence and greediness as enthusiasm for a good cause, and for which Berolzheimer had already been pretty much won over for further generous support. I do not want to go into too many details and will just say that the beautiful idea to build a proper home for the Natural History Society soon took shape, and the new building was also to serve as home for the Adult Education Association and for the Medical Association. Herr Dr. von Forster was to be champion for the Adult Education Association, probably due to the influence of his charming wife on Berolzheimer, and Herr Hofrat Dr. Goldschmidt, his nephew, champion for the Medical Association.

Berolzheimer, who had suddenly begun to experience symptoms of some strange disease, led the many prenegotiations and discussions regarding the project in the most patient and dedicated manner. A happy solution had been found regarding the location of the new Luitpold House, as it was going to be named in honour of the Prince Regent; the building was to be erected in the immediate vicinity of the Bavarian Institute for Trade and Industry. It was also decided now that apart from the Natural History Society, the Medical Association and the one for adult education were also to be housed in Luitpold House. With regard to its importance and purposes, the main part of the new building was designated for use by the Natural History Society. Before the plans were drawn up, however, Dr. Bernett caused some difficulties because certain facilities such as the auditorium, the reading room etc. were to be shared by the three societies. I did not blame Dr. Bernett in the slightest for wanting all of Luitpold House for his society alone; after all, that had been the original idea of the sponsor. The project, however, had grown far beyond the original plan; the Natural History Society was not being stunted, but it had to make arrangements with the other two associations.

The original budget for the building of Luitpold House now evidently had to be increased to allow for the accommodation of two further associations. Berolzheimer increased his contributions so that the available funds were now around 400,000 marks, including 40,000 marks donated by his two sons in New York. There was little anticipation to speak of. I often admired his abundance of patience when he was faced with new demands, often quite unreasonable ones, from all sides. There was also much debate about this in the townhouse tavern, and I often had to call a halt to it out of respect for my friend's diminishing health. It was usually the perpetually dissatisfied Dr. Bernett, who started these debates, and that may well have been the main reason why my request that he be more modest and spare our friend resulted in him becoming quite spiteful – and that is not too harsh a word – towards me. I tried to keep up the social aims of our little club in the old, familiar way, and I felt that cheerful conversation, stories, even those where it was hard to tell truth from fiction, were the best means to support our conviviality. Of course that did not preclude serious discussion of topics of the day.

Fig. 32 Luitpold House.
(c) Stadtarchiv Nürnberg A 38-C-122-9

Every member who was willing and able was encouraged to share events and happenings from their life journey, and the result of this was that our social evenings became enjoyable and interesting again. Every now and then we would also play the noble game of Tarock, only no player could, should they be so lucky, win for themselves. All winnings came into a joint kitty. Treasurer was Herr Oberregierungsrat Gareis, who was richly rewarded for his efforts and his delicious deliberations when he was reading out the accounts. He never said, "We have funds of 22 marks and 50", but "our cash assets amount to 2,250 pfennigs". We took out what we needed to cover the costs of our simple dinner, the remainder, and by far the larger part, would be transferred to Herr Oberregierungsrat Gareis for his children's homes etc.

At about the same time, a large, festive event was taking place in the Germanic Museum, which was going to be attended by the German Emperor and his wife, the Prince Regent, Reich-Chancellor von Bülow, the ministers and a number of other noteworthy personalities. I too received an invitation to this rare festivity, an honour recognising the modest contribution I had made towards the costs of the affair, just like other men of industry who had done the same. In addition, later on I donated the sum of 10,000 marks to the Museum for its purposes, and so I was generally considered one of its sponsors, even if not always with donations of that size.

The big day arrived. Its main purpose was the dedication of the new building of the Germanic Museum, but the courtly pomp suggested there may be other, ulterior motives too. Upon entering the festive room, I was blinded by the glittering assemblage that was crowding around the ladies and gentlemen of the highest orders. Without any decorations I felt so insignificant that I shyly retreated into a quiet corner. One of my "colleagues", a "Jewish Kommerzienrat" as Herr Heinrichsen had so aptly put it, happened to glance in my direction, but he was highly decorated and a close friend of the mayor's. He sheepishly looked the other way, he obviously did not want to see me, or rather he did not want to acknowledge me as his equal given the high society we were in. Then suddenly Herr Oberregierungsrat Gareis, dressed in his gala uniform with all his decorations, came away from the illustrious society. He walked up to me and affectionately led me by the arm out of my solitude and into the "light and glamour". Feeling right at home, I took a good look at the Emperor and the Empress and their entourage and enjoyed the healthy humour of a performance of some pieces by Sachs, and also the great hilarity with which the Emperor – the Empress less so – received this hearty fare. I probably would not have mentioned this story were it not for the fact that it was yet another example of how the sensitive and tactful nature of my friend Gareis always manifested itself in his thoughts and actions.

In our society, my friend Fritz was brilliant at telling old stories and anecdotes, which even the ancient Meidinger had received with the comment, "God, how old!" The stories did not become any newer by being repeated, which happened especially when a new guest joined us. Tuchmann himself joined the hearty laughter when I occasionally put on a parody and retold one or another of his "old chestnuts" with a face as if I had never heard the story before. At most he might painfully scold me for abusing his intellectual property. His descriptions of his journeys through Russia, Finland, Sweden and Norway, on the other hand, were quite interesting and vivid. An encounter with a wolf in

Finland featured heavily in one of them. This wolf was supposed to be a real, blood-thirsty and cruel wolf, the skin of which had sadly got lost over time.

In return, I often shared my many experiences in the Sudan, something a wolf could not compete with. Lions, tigers, elephants and buffalo lived there, and apart from the "terribly" venomous vermin there were tribes who liked nothing better than a bite of human flesh for their breakfast, lunch and dinner. I really did know the Sudan better than Lower Bavaria. This is why: I passionately loved reading travelogues, especially those from Africa. I knew everything important that had been written on the subject, no matter if it was by Livingstone, Stanley, Barth, Junker or Wissmann. I had particular sympathy for the fate of Emin Pasha, who was found and rescued by Stanley after a long and dangerous journey over the Congo and the Aruwimi rivers and Lake Albert. The rescue may have been somewhat ambiguous, in the typical English way, and the return journey to Zanzibar in Stanley's company may have provided Emin Pasha food for thought. I was fully informed about all things concerning this ever-changing story that was happening in the Sudan.

Every time I started talking about my commercial travels to Africa, which had the purpose of popularising tin spoons made by my company, people's ears pricked up. Starting in Triest I sailed to Alexandria, spent a few days in Cairo, where I visited a famous harem, and then I went up the Nile to Khartoum to ask for an introductory letter to Emin Pasha from Gordon Pasha, Governor General of the Sudan, to support the commendatory letter I had obtained from His Excellency Nubar Pasha, the Egyptian minister in Cairo. The expedition then took me down the White Nile, and after a long, perilous journey, which obviously also served business purposes, I arrived happily in the equatorial province and found Emin Pasha in Duffle on Lake Albert. He was in the middle of skinning rare birds in order to send their pretty feathers to the Ethnological Museum in Berlin, provided that the Mahdists, who were approaching his province, would not stop him from doing so. Within the sphere of influence of this great explorer and excellent administrator, I completed a massive deal in tin spoons and had the Pasha, who was quite favourably disposed towards me, send an express camel courier with my letters to Khartoum with the task of sending these letters on to Nuremberg most urgently. Speed was of the essence since it was necessary to build a large, second factory in order to be able to fulfil the considerable orders I had taken.

I did not accept interjections and disruptions during my stories, which meant that this yarn sometimes grew into a lecture which was interesting for the believers and amusing for the non-believers.

Very impressive were the stories which our dear friend Gareis shared from his career as a civil servant, from the early days until his important position as most senior administrator in the Nuremberg region. There were light and serious anecdotes, predominantly from a rural background, stories of what the forest told the forester, what the river told the fisherman, in short, the experiences of a man of maturity who had to deal with people from all backgrounds and who had an understanding of real life as it happened.

In the meantime I had also employed my friend Gareis' eldest daughter, Fräulein Marie Gareis. The young lady - and her siblings - had, under their parents' guidance (her late mother, who had died young, was a daughter of the Bavarian State Minister von Schlörs), received an excellent education and acquired a particularly good knowledge of foreign languages. She was fluent in French, English and Italian, and her conversational Russian was passable. She soon completed her commercial training; she put more into the business than she was able to take from it. This implies what important tasks she was being given. For over 15 years she went about her job in a most exemplary manner; it was a role in which she was able to be of outstanding service to the company.

Herr Oberregierungsrat Gareis began to suffer from poor health. It was a heart condition, which imposed the bitter necessity on this usually so healthy and untiring gentleman, to take a long holiday. During this time we saw even more of each other, since I could see the soothing and reassuring effect our friendly conversations about everything but his illness had on him, when we sat together, usually in the *Bristol,* of an afternoon. His physical appearance seemed to have improved much, too; I noticed this especially the last time I saw him, and I joked that I could picture him already returning to his role as governor of the district. I walked with him then to the museum where he wanted to attend an important meeting of the Red Cross. Later that evening and to my great sorrow I received the shocking news that my esteemed friend had suffered a stroke at the museum, which had, gently and painlessly, put an end to all his earthly pains and sorrows.

It was a black day, and it was going to rob me of another dear friend, Salomon Forchheimer. And still the trials were not over. Doctors had established what terrible illness had befallen my friend Berolzheimer; an ailment which was doomed to bring much pain and suffering to the afflicted and which was to lead to an imminent martyr's death. My friend had no idea of the fate that was to become him, especially since only rarely did he have cause to complain about some discomfort or a little pain. His features, which were still aesthetic and masculine even at his old age, showed no obvious signs of change either, and I often told myself that the doctors surely were too pessimistic, my friend would surely recover. However, fate knew no mercy. His death, which was a gentle one, left another great hole in our circle of friends, and of the old guard only Tuchmann and I were left.

The grief over our friend echoed through all circles in Nuremberg, the city which had made him an honorary citizen only a few years previously. A good man was lost, but to us he had been more than that.

When Berolzheimer left us friends behind, the plans for the new Luitpold House were already drawn up, and his heirs made the agreed funds available to the city. Our poor friend was not to experience the joy of seeing that which had been so dear to his heart completed.

The building rose up and was completed as the beautiful work of a generous benefactor who deserved special thanks and wider acknowledgement for many things that I will not mention. Many people, and especially those with influence, thought him too honest. On the occasion of the inauguration of the building, the mayor, Herr von Schuh, gave an impressive speech to the large crowd of friends of the deceased and the honorary guest, but I thought the speech too cold and not talking enough about the donor but too much about the details of the building, its costs etc. It was at the banquet that the unforgettable man finally received the honest and warm homage he so deserved. Only one person was missing, and that was Dr. Bernett. Apparently he was so piqued that against his expectations he was not, unlike his colleague Dr. Goldschmidt, awarded the title of Hofrat at the inauguration of Luitpold House. He had to be content with an honouring tribute, and the ungrateful, cold-hearted sycophant recompensed the late great man with this personal affront.

I did not get upset about it since I knew Dr. Bernett well enough; not just his virtues but also his great weaknesses, the origins of which were perhaps to be found in his childhood. Bernett's parents had been landlords at the *Zum Roten Kreuz* inn, a sleazy, third-rate hotel that went bust a long time ago. Whenever Bernett was pushing things too far, I would mention to my friends that if one were to scratch the thinly-applied varnish off Dr. Bernett, the *Son of the Rote Kreuz House* would always shine through. It also explained much of what made this otherwise talented man, who used to be so modest, so unpopular - not to use too strong an expression. His cantankerousness, insolence and intolerance, not mentioning the fact that he had not an inch of gratefulness in him, were all reasons why, after Berolzheimer's passing, he resigned from his role as director of the Natural History Society. His departure was not entirely voluntary; it was only a small group of supporters who tried to push him into a leadership role again by taking a general assembly by surprise. He was elected vice-chairman and would have been content with that role, only the other directors refused to work with him. Tuchmann and I also declared that we would resign from our posts as advisors to the board if Bernett was allowed anywhere near the rudder again.

I shall not forget to relate that Berolzheimer, Tuchmann, my brother Heinrich and I were made honorary members of the society while Bernett was its director. This event occurred at a time when the funds for the upkeep of the society were still wholly insufficient and Dr. Bernett regarded us as the best cash cows for the stocking of the society's coffers. But that was not his worst deed! We were richly rewarded with the knowledge that we had kept the society with all its splendid facilities afloat and that we cleared the ground for its future as a highly regarded institute to this day.

Some of my happiest memories, of the more humorous kind, are connected to my correspondence and personal contact with the multi-talented, modest secretary of the Natural History Society, Herr Hörmann[66]. Self-educated, he became extremely knowledgeable in many disciplines of the natural sciences, anthropology and prehistory and was of great service to the society. Despite our respect for real knowledge, we were both free of that scholar's arrogance that made us so often laugh out loud, for example when at an excavation a somewhat fragmented stone was called a "tool", or when a small piece of bone was labelled a "corpse". We would then say that the scientific label burdened the find with a mortgage[67] (which was meant to stand for

[66] A handwritten note in the manuscript says that he was made honorary doctor at the University of Erlangen at the age of 72 – in 1931.
[67] Mortgage = Hypothek in German, hence the word play with "hypothesis".

"hypothesis"). When I was successfully excavating at the Kummert's Hole, I dug up a large number of processed bear bones, which were undoubtedly used as tools (cf. Dr. Kellermann's paper *The Kummert's Hole near Streitberg*), a key anthropological expert argued that there was a possibility that these bones had been swallowed by hyenas and abraded by their stomach acid. Imagine first the kind of hyena who must have been able to swallow the bones, some of which were more than 20cm long! Once its stomach acid had done its business and shaped the incredibly hard bones as well as any prehistoric human would have done, the failed hyena would then have had to return to the Kummert's Hole and deliver the bones as if it was leaving a calling card.

I was allowed to laugh out loud at this learned nonsense; Hörmann, seeing that he was representing Science, could only smile!

During my excavations in Brunnstein, which I shall talk about more later, I found something that looked like the fossilised jaw of some animal. When I presented this strange object at the Natural History Society, the general consensus was to send the find to a famous professor of zoology at the University of Erlangen for identification and assessment. I thought the stone was, despite its indeed strange shape, nothing other than just that, a stone, but I did not dare to express my opinion. The scholar from Erlangen concluded that it was the fossilised jaw of some hoofed animal which did not, however, belong to one of the known local species.

The problem was not resolved by the professor, but an explanation was found by the society's assistant and non-academic member, H. Zippelius, who happened to be present at that moment. He said that he was convinced that the piece of bone was not at all from an animal's jaw but that it was a dripstone which could sometimes be found in caves. The assistant, who was well-versed in such things, was to be proved right.

The extent of what was permissible behaviour towards science was soon to be experienced personally by me and my feared competitor in snatching finds that were valuable to collectors. There was a note in the *Kurier* saying that while stubbing out the forest floor in the neighbouring village Birnthon, workers had found an incredibly large, well-preserved mammoth tooth. Anyone wishing to look at the find was to talk to the local innkeeper.

I was just thinking about how it might be possible to obtain such a fabulous piece for our society when the phone rang; it was Hörmann. If I had read the note, he asked, he was about to leave for Birnthon, and Prof. Dr. Bernett agreed. He was not sure what the quickest way was to get to this isolated place and was asking my advice. I knew how to interpret the request for advice and offered to provide a quick carriage and pair since I was quite interested in the mammoth tooth myself. We started the journey. En route we discussed how we might explain our trip to Birnthon without being too conspicuous. Our intention had to be kept as secret as possible if only to avoid us having to pay too high a price for the tooth. Herr Dr. Bernett entrusted me with the diplomatic mission, and what was more, he implied that if we were successful the tooth had to be purchased for the museum.

With my money of course. Typical Bernett! But then I knew that even before we set out on our journey.

We arrived in Birnthon and entered the small coffee room where we found the landlady alone. Having ordered a small snack, I asked in detail about the best route to the neighbouring village of Feucht, saying we had official business there. The pleasantly situated village was a popular tourist destination, and so it seemed that the landlady did not think our visit unusual. Our diplomatic strategy seemed to be working well. When I enquired, just by the by, about her absent husband's, she told me that he was in the woods, clearing the ground. So it was true! The forest floor was being cleared, and during the operation the mammoth tooth had been found!

At last I came to mention the excavations that had been carried out nearby, by asking if they sometimes found anything on the cleared forest floor. She had no idea, the landlady replied with such a calm and innocence that I was beginning to suspect that we had followed a red herring and walked straight into some prankster's trap. That was indeed the case. Even the landlord, when he arrived later, knew nothing of a find, and luckily he knew nothing of the notice in the paper either so that we were spared the humiliation and could return home with our disgrace intact.

On the way home, Hörmann was being careless and broke one of the carriage's windowpanes so that in addition to the bitter disappointment, the costs I had already incurred for the trip were increased even further, and quite significantly.

Later on we found signs as to who might have been the prankster who led us by the nose to our adventure. He had rightly speculated on the curator's zeal, and his instinct paid off. I was the one who paid for it, and my costs were painful and considerable.

I could tell many more of these funny tales, but I have to come to an end sometime, and so I have to restrict myself. One thing I shall add, and that is that my anthropological companion Hörmann often visited me in Streitberg. He was always welcomed with open arms and wined and dined accordingly. My collections there stirred his interest, which was so great that it would have filled his big rucksack if I had allowed it. To tell the truth, he mastered his great and easily comprehensible greediness even in that respect and remained modest and grateful. We kept up an amusing correspondence until recent times, and the testimonies of his loyalty towards me, documents of his delightful sense of humour, can still be found amongst my letters in Streitberg.

Due to my discovery and development of the *Bing-Höhle* in 1905 I was introduced to Herr Dr. Kellermann. I am much indebted to him and his publications about the cave, and I will talk about it more as I continue with this script. He is quite rightly called the godfather of this magical world which I developed in the Franconian mountains. It was not long until my highly esteemed friend – I think I may call him that – was counted among the regulars at our sociable club in the townhouse bar. His vast knowledge, his kindness and modesty meant that he became a respected and esteemed member of our society.

Herr Michal, a senior member of the district's administration who had been introduced by my friend Tuchmann, at first seemed a little shy towards his new acquaintances, but when the first, easily explained timidity subsided, this man who had vast knowledge, intelligence and warmth evidently felt comfortable in our midst. It had to be for a very good reason if he did not join us at the head of the table in the townhouse bar on a Saturday evening. He took part in the conversation in a cosily eager manner, no matter if at times we were telling funny anecdotes or discussing a serious, social problem that might have been linked to the heavy responsibilities of his high office. Herr Oberregierungsrat Michal was director at the local prison. I was later appointed a member of his charity for released prisoners so that I had even better opportunities to understand and appreciate his blessed work. Often my friend Fritz and I supported the efforts of this high-minded man more than he would expect in his great modesty.

So we had won two new members for our club, and we could not have asked for better or more suitable candidates.

Apart from my cousin Tuchmann and me, who had founded our little Saturday society, the following men could be regarded as the other close regulars of said club: our friend Georg Dietz, my brother Heinrich Bing, my dear friend Jung who had become related to me since the wedding of his daughter Ida to my son Stefan, as well as Herr Oberregierungsrat Michal, Herr Oberstudienrat Kellermann and Herr Karl Dessauer.

I would like to mention here that I first got to know and appreciate Heinrich Jung when we were both young men. His business knowledge was excellent, and yet he always sought to improve himself very successfully in other areas, too, particularly in literature. I could always tell that he had worked temporarily at the *Correspondenten von und für Deutschland* as he chose his words very carefully in order to do justice to not only the subject matter but also its style. Being in Jung's company was stimulating, and due to his great modesty he never let it show that he was usually at the giving end of things. One of his remarkable features was the touching simplicity of his standards which I often had the occasion to observe during his welcome visits in Streitberg. The simplest lunch seemed like a feast to him, and he would not accept even the most natural and most willingly provided gift or favour.

Fig. 33 Heinrich Jung.

My friend Jung passed away from his blessed life much too soon, in the year 1911. The great sorrow that filled his children was easily understood. He had been a loyal and caring father to his last day.

He was remembered with love and honour, even by those who had met him during his many years working in one of his numerous voluntary roles.

This painful event was followed in the same year, 1911, by a happy celebration in honour of my most loyal of friends, our "old Fritz"[68], as I often called him. We were celebrating his 70th birthday. That this event, celebrated within such a distinguished family, would not lack a certain glamour goes without saying. Yet this simple man did not hanker after pomp and glitz, and so all he received from his friends in honour of the great day was a simple present, an album with pictures of all those friends who had been, and were still, close to him over the course of many years. On the cover was a silver plaque that said "In memory of true friends". He was absolutely delighted by our simple gift, the nature of which he truly appreciated, and when we were celebrating his birthday in the townhouse inn he treated us to an exquisite dinner accompanied by fine wines that did the old connoisseur proud. Loving, touching and witty toasts were proposed to the old companion, who in return showed off his great sense of humour in his speeches welcoming and thanking his guests.

Fritz Tuchmann served our lovely little society like no other. He did not allow anyone to treat it with coolness or indifference, and he was for the cohesion of the Saturday evening society what the "whip" is for the British parliament.

For years I had been spending my summers in Streitberg, and he would often come and stay, either alone or in the company of the other friends. With all his simplicity, he appreciated the good things in life, and when his arrival was imminent, preparations were being made in the villa "for a hearty bowl of soup" and other things necessary for a sumptuous lunch. Once I was back

---

[68] The nickname "old Fritz", a term of endearment, usually refers to the Prussian King Frederic II (the Great).

in Nuremberg, usually around the end of September, it was not only the social evening in the townhouse inn that led us together but we would also meet on several other evenings in the week – our friend Dietz would usually join us – where we would feast on roast meats, baked fish or, the jewel of all Nuremberg delicacies, crisp hog roast.

A true passion of my friend's was the game of Tarock[69]. This was even stranger considering that even after years of playing the sport, and especially intensely so in recent times, he had still no idea how to play the simple game. (We, his co-players, would always say that Tuchmann had more cash than sense.) However, this was not always true, since sometimes our friend was incredibly lucky and won with even the worst of hands. He would then strike a winner's pose and take on an air of real superiority. A few marks won at cards gave him more joy than if he had won a hundred times that in the lottery.

I could tell many more such episodes, and of his other loveable idiosyncrasies I could also say much; yet I have to bid farewell to my friend. A final, sad farewell. My good companion, who had been a dear and loyal friend for over 65 years, found a sudden, and one can say ideal, totally painless death, which neither he or his family could foresee even a minute before. In the May of 1916 he was snatched from this life, and his children - whom I had always been very friendly with - lost the most loyal father. I need not explain what he had meant to me and our friends. Since his death I have not been able to bring myself to return to the townhouse inn, the place where we had spent so many cosy hours

[69] Traditional card game played with a tarot deck.

with our friend. Whether one day I will be able to go back, I cannot say.

I have not mentioned many, or any, family celebrations, engagements, weddings of my own children or of the large number of nieces and nephews, our silver wedding anniversary etc. in this book. Such events are usually shaped along the same template and pass more or less "wonderfully". I certainly won't deny that they were memorable times for my wife and me. Our offspring, however, are indifferent to such events and therefore I need not talk about them.

Yet there is one family celebration that I would like to recall, namely my second mother's 70th birthday (1892). She had looked after us four children from my father's first marriage well, and I am happy to pay my tribute to her here and again with heartfelt gratitude. The fresh and youthful-looking grandmother was surrounded by nine sons and daughters with their spouses and children, a large and cheerful circle which gathered in my parents' house in Fürtherstrasse to celebrate the occasion.

The special day was meant to honour the grandmother in a special way. My sister-in-law Sara, wife of my brother Adolf, had been appointed as director of events for the day. She had done a brilliant job rehearsing the well-known ballad opera "Little Song Bird" by Jacobsen with our daughters Berta, Frieda and Anna as well as her own daughter Lina, who had been justifiably given the lead character for song and play. With her performance of "Sing if you have the gift of song", or even more so with the natural charm with which she later performed as a "Barrison girl" at the *Phoenix*, my niece Lina won her future husband's heart. She is now happily married to our nephew Herr Dr. med Vidl Erlanger, a man highly esteemed by the whole family and our trusted family physician who exposes us as rarely as he can to the inconveniences of a serious illness. Hail his efforts!

The little actresses and singers made the "Little Song Bird" a great success. Grossmutter and the rest of the large audience were delighted, and my task, to supply lyrics celebrating the cause for the existing simple tunes, was also received with satisfaction. The day is sure to be remembered by all, and in particular by Grossmutter, who was very touched by the impressive homage.

The year 1906 saw the third great Bavarian National Exhibition in Nuremberg, this time on the grounds of the newly created Luitpold park. It was my opinion, and that of many others, that the exhibition was held too soon after the previous one in 1896. What progress could trade and industry show in the short span of ten years? The official line was that the exhibition would mark 100 years of Nuremberg's affiliation with Bavaria, which would occur in 1906. To me it seemed that the main purpose intended by our very energetic mayor Dr. von Schuh was to use the expected large influx of visitors to raise funds for the city of Nuremberg and its residents, which would enable him to realise his favourite idea of turning the grounds around the Dutzend pond into a large park with a zoo.

The expectation of many visitors and the implied boon for the city was not fulfilled. It was a washout, literally. It rained for days on end, for weeks even, and the huge exhibition grounds sometimes seemed deserted.

Under the masterful guidance by Herr von Kramer, director of the Bavarian Museum for Trade and Industry, a new world of glory and beauty was created. The unique landscape formed a delicious frame, but it required vast amounts of money to develop the barren land in such a way that it connected to the large, newly built exhibition halls in harmony.

I will briefly add that the main trade and industry show had nothing or only very little to offer that was new or worth exhibiting. Such could only be found in the magnificent exhibition in the machines hall, where many interesting exhibits illustrated technological progress. Our company, too, attracted the attention of the audience by demonstrating the then still new, fantastic invention by the Italian Marconi, a new apparatus for wireless telegraphy, built by us.

In the large industry hall our company was represented with a lavish booth. I could not warm to the style of the arrangement that was to display our samples. Massive columns supported and formed a relatively narrow room, on the right side of which dainty utensils for house and kitchen, silver-coated fashion accessories, brass and copper glistened and sparkled or appeared artistic in their pastel colours. On the left side was the realm of metal toys, represented with hundreds of different samples. All in all they were small items which could not and would not be in harmony with the gigantic columns of the space. An oriental bazaar, maybe the Court of the Lions in the Alhambra, even without the lions, would have been more suitable for our exhibits. The one good thing of the architecture was that you could not miss our stand! That may well have been the reason why I heard His Royal Highness Prince Ludwig, when he was touring the exhibition, calling from still quite far away, "Oh there is Bing, I have to have a look at once!" And so it was. We were prepared for the high-class visitors, and so directors, junior partners and department heads were paraded in front of the stand to await His Highness's arrival.

The Prince chatted very affably with me and then turned to the line of my employees as if expecting me to introduce them to him. I knew very well that the Prince would have liked to address

Fig. 34 Exhibition stand, 1906.

each and one of them with a few friendly, trivial words; yet I also realised how inappropriate it would have been to introduce so many men individually. Furthermore I had learned that the Prince was in a great hurry to proceed with his full programme. I therefore took the liberty to point out that the present gentlemen, in their entirety, were trusted and deserving employees of the

Bing company and that they were counting themselves fortunate to be able to show the prince their deep reverence. The prince smiled approvingly and said, while offering me his hand, that he "wished Bing and his Bingers well".

A few years later I was to receive him as an eminent guest in Streitberg, an event that shall be honoured with a special account.

The exhibition closed with a big minus which affected me and the company painfully since we had paid a large deposit as security. The sacrifices had not been made in vain though. The wonderful Luitpold park and its zoo are a lasting reminder of the year 1906, which must not be undervalued by the residents of Nuremberg.

I have finished the tales from my years of wandering and learning that inspired me to put them to paper. I bid farewell to the happy and painful memories that life has given me and I pray to God that he may soon let the sun of peace, which set two and a half years ago, shine over the people again. Today, on 22nd December 1916, the newspapers are reporting that there is a prospect that US President Wilson may try to arrange a conference for the warring factions with the aim of bringing about the much longed-for peace. Such promising news! May the weak hope that this man-murdering war may soon come to an end be strengthened and fulfilled.

"Amen!"

The feeling that peace is not a long way off now fills me with a confidence that will ring through these final chapters of my unassuming portrayals and depictions, even more so as all there is still left to write about is predominantly my beloved Streitberg and the times spent there. So off we go to Streitberg.

In 1899 I purchased the estate in Streitberg which had previously been held by the Fürsts[70]. To avoid any misunderstandings let me explain straightaway that the Fürst who left the little villa to his wife was not a real Fürst but a former alehouse keeper of that name. To do history justice I must explain the following details regarding the origins and the different owners of Villa Marie.

The country cottage was built in or around 1860 by the respected merchant Lehmann from Nuremberg who had made his fortune in South America. The plans for the building were drawn up by his son-in-law, the well-known painter and architect Professor Mayer from the Nuremberg art school. After Lehmann's death his daughter, who was ill and crippled, lived in the villa during the summer months. The country house then came into the hands of Colonel von Mohr, who sold it a few years later to postmaster Amm from Nuremberg before he relocated to Munich with his wife. Wisely, Herr Amm made many improvements where house and garden had been neglected in the past. The most important improvement it seemed, and not without good reason, was the transfer of the house to an old flame of his youth. The old flame had apparently married someone else in the meantime, yet an arrangement with the husband undid the tie, and the two lovers were united in belated matrimony for a happy ending. Their wedded bliss lasted for more than a decade until the husband died, seriously and deeply mourned by his wife.

[70] "Fürst" is a title of nobility which roughly corresponds to "Prince".

But what was a widow to do in and with a villa? Soon a new marriage tied the mourning widow to a Herr Fürst from Nuremberg, but his "so-called" educated wife did not really know what to do with him. He beavered away in house and garden, split the wood, brought in the coals, in short, he was only interested in the country house and everything that came with it. The most important thing to him seemed to be that he had something to do now that he was retired.

His wife did not enjoy this kind of country living, she missed the coffee mornings in town, and since the boredom grew more and more depressing, they offered me the house for sale. The first negotiations led to nothing since Herr Fürst's idea of a selling price was so excessive that there seemed to be no prospect of an agreement. Frau Fürst appeared to be more upset about this than I was.

I thought about building a house myself in Streitberg and began to investigate some interesting plots. But it was not meant to be! Herr Fürst succumbed to a severe pneumonia he had contracted while splitting firewood. The widow's grief about the sudden loss seemed lukewarm; the path had been cleared for her desire to move to Nuremberg. A few weeks after the death I was the new owner of the villa.

The initial joy was soon followed by the concerns that come with the possession of any property. Having taken a closer look I could see for myself that much still needed to be done to turn the delightful cottage in the style that was so typical for the area into a safe homestead. Only the gardens and the orchard were in top condition; Herr Fürst had been busy ensuring that.

Fig. 35 Villa Marie, ca. 1900.

At the time, the fact that our company was now a joint-stock organisation made little difference to my normal working hours and the demands it placed on me, compared to what they had been when we were still a large family business. Apart from the usual weeks of annual leave I did not have any more time than before. In order to supervise and fulfil the tasks which the purchase of the villa had put upon me I now travelled to Streitberg almost every Saturday, accompanied by my youngest daughter Marie, who was not yet married, and after whom the villa is named. I had to check on the necessary repair works or discuss with the craftsmen other new improvements that were due to commence etc. Above all, I wanted to remedy the greatest flaw of the estate, the lack of clean, potable water. It was a big task, despite the fact that Streitberg is blessed with a profuse number of sources which provide the most glorious water. There were long negotiations with the community about the joint use of such a source, but the question was resolved to everyone's satisfaction; of course not quite without some sacrifice. I was very respected all over Streitberg; due to my annual visits I was counted amongst the "iron stock" of the regular spa visitors and personally knew the residents well.

However, it was the typical rural way; the facts – their assurance that they were serving me selflessly while at the same time very selfishly insisting to be paid – stood in harmonious agreement. The charitable construction of a beautiful fountain for the village was my way of saying thanks to the community for letting me use the water from the source, which would otherwise just have run, unused, downhill from the Schauer valley.

Then followed the negotiations with the owners of the land, who had to give their permission for me to run thin, iron pipes through their fields or meadows etc. so that the source water could be carried to my villa. These problems were also solved through the granting of vast compensation payments for absolutely meaningless favours. Yet, some of the farmers were still being difficult. One of them, an otherwise good neighbour of mine, did not want compensation, but he expected me to divert some of my water through pipes to his house where I was to install not only a well in his courtyard but also water pipes to his kitchen and stables, all at my expense of course. To that I could not agree, if only for technical reasons, and so my supply had to be diverted a long way around his property.

Even my closest neighbour, an innkeeper who was as such already benefiting from my purchase of the villa, wanted compensation for granting me the favour of allowing a few metres of pipes to be buried on his property: In memory of his generous act I had to donate a little fountain.

Another of my new fellow citizens went so far as to send me a letter saying that he thought I was like the "Maiden from afar"[71]. I appeared to have a gift for everyone, only he went empty-handed. My well-read friend received a blue banknote – I was very generous at the time – since I enjoyed his brazenness and the classic quotation, and he enjoyed the money. Today we are good friends, and he still tries to prove to me sometimes that his demand for a little "douceur" or "baksheesh" had not been totally unfounded.

At last all difficulties had been overcome, and the glorious water was available in the villa in abundance. A fountain installed in the garden, crowned by a figure depicting the "little man with the geese"[72], a present from my friend Tuchmann, spewed the glistening water out of the geese's beaks into a basin enveloped in ivy. Finally, my donation of the village fountain was inaugurated to the joy of the assembled residents, and I received a grateful telegraph from the local government.

Even before the purchase of my estate, however, I had already had a disagreement with the local government, or rather its head, the master butcher Nützel. Nützel was a good and honest man whom I had known well for 30 years before I bought the house. When I first came to Streitberg he was the manservant in the inn *Zur Post* where his wife, who is still alive today, worked as a maid. Nützel was a man of good sense and a good judge of the rural

71 "Das Mädchen aus der Fremde" - a poem by Friedrich Schiller.
72 "Gänsemännchen", a famous fountain in Nuremberg.

Fig. 36 Villa Marie, 2011.

conditions, so it was no surprise that he presided over the village regiment as mayor for over 25 years until he died in office.

I have mentioned previously just how very much I was interested in and attracted by excavation work, and so while I was roaming through the meadows in and around Streitberg I was always eagerly looking for a prehistoric burial mound that could be sacrificed to my passion. This hope was never realised, but I did come across a number of accessible grottos and small caves which did not look too difficult to explore, and which in addition offered the advantage that any excavations could be carried out in intervals. Any possible finds could be kept safe underground. Obviously, I did not have the time to carry out a systematic, uninterrupted excavation over several weeks.

So I was granted permission by the local forester Baltheiser, a well-educated man who was amenable to such undertakings, to dig up the very romantically located Brunnstein cave in the national forest. Every time I had a day off and could free myself from any commitments I went to Streitberg to dig. I do not want to digress too much because I will come back to this later anyway. I only want to explain the events that lead to the threat of a rift between me and Mayor Nützel. When we were digging at the Brunnstein cave and at the end of the day my people carried their loot-filled bags back to Streitberg, we walked past the Villa Hildebrandt. The owner of this villa must have put a bee in the mayor's bonnet, as the saying goes. He described the valuable treasures that we were unearthing and how suitable they would be for the establishment of a new museum in Streitberg.

The mayor put in an official complaint at the forestry commission in Gössweinstein as the superior authority against the forester from Streitberg because he had given me the permission to excavate the Brunnstein cave. The result of this complaint was an inquiry by the forestry commission and a temporary suspension of my digging work. I was furious, and things were not helped by a half-hearted letter of apology by the mayor. It appears that in the meantime, he had been overcome by a certain morning-after feeling regarding his denunciative proceedings against me, which was boosted even further by the dressing down he received from his intelligent wife, who had always had great affection for me.

What he actually wrote regarding the whole affair was funny enough. He said that he had to do his duty since the architect Hildebrandt had explained to him that the finds dug up in the

Brunnstein cave were enough to fill an entire "aquarium", and other such nonsense. He invited me to return to the cave, adding that he was sure the matter could be resolved and that he did not want to lose my friendship.

Apart from the fact that he was sincere in what he said, the rogue had heard meanwhile that the forestry commission in Gössweinstein had granted me the unrestricted permission to continue my excavation work. Nevertheless, I made peace with the mayor, even though I could not stop myself from asking him the next time we met whether, if I had had to abandon the excavations at his instigation, I could have been of any use as an attendant when he went to buy his pigs for slaughter.

Fig. 37 Ignaz with his daughter-in-law Ida and her children Lilli and Franz.

The new property caused me more trouble than I had anticipated. True, there was now an abundance of marvellous fresh water in both the house and the garden. Not only the little man with the geese, but a picturesque fountain for the house also bestowed the blessing of the refreshing drink, which some people prefer even to champagne.

On the other hand, the water falling from the sky seeped straight through a more than slightly leaky roof and entered the sleeping and living quarters of the house. On one instance it got so bad that one night my daughter Marie was almost swept away in the floods. The complete re-roofing of the house resolved the issue for the future.

Even worse was an accident that my wife and I almost experienced first-hand. Immediately after we left Streitberg following a short stay, a large piece of the massive 5 to 6-metre-high wall, which formed the edge of our terrace in the garden, collapsed. Under different circumstances it could have been a disaster. It took many weeks and large amounts of money to rebuild the terrace wall, and my dear fellow citizens who really could have been brought in to share the costs (the collapsed wall also formed the border to the large cellars of the local brewery) knew how to weasel themselves out of it. Surely the new owner of the villa would not risk his friendly relations with the other residents in a lawsuit? I often thought wistfully of a comedy that had amused me in previous times. It was called "Two happy days". The first happy day related to the purchase of a villa, the second to the sale of it.

When my wife and I came to see the country house for the first time, invited by the Fürsts, it was a beautiful summer's day, and the place oozed peace and cosiness. Herr Fürst was busy in the orchard, Frau Fürst, in a flowery Turkish dressing gown, welcomed us in the summer house, a smartly dressed servant girl in a white apron opened the door, in short, it seemed "so-to-speak" (Frau Fürst's catchphrase) as if there was not a hair out of place. And yet, where there are flowers there are snakes!

As lovely as the property appeared to be, there was a lot of rot, and many things were behind the times. Nothing that could not be fixed with money and good words, however, and so after only a few years of owning the villa we thought that no other house in the world was prettier or more befitting to its beautiful surroundings nor was there one that gave a family a cosier or better-ordered little home.

We were already looking forward with great joy to the time when it would be possible to spend a whole spring or summer in our little house. For the moment that idea was out of the question, since I still had a number of duties that bound me tightly to the business and its tasks. Yet it was a blissful feeling when during my occasional trips to Streitberg – usually related to the excavations at the Brunnstein cave – I was able to sleep in my own house.

My liking for cave exploration was only increased by my first success, and soon the nucleus of a collection of finds that were of interest to science had come together. I think I may be permitted to describe such a cave day as it happened at the excavations in Brunnstein: The evening before the dig the required number of people were engaged to arrive at the site on time. During the summer that time was 6 o'clock in the morning. There were usually six to seven people of which everyone had to do the kinds of jobs they were most suited for. Two men, the brightest and most experienced ones, had to dig the ground up and out. They had to conscientiously ensure that they did not miss or damage any findings. Two other men carried the excavated soil and stones towards the entrance of the cave, while the rest had to check very carefully for any objects amongst the rubble that might have been missed by the others.

I would usually sit on a canvas chair near the entrance to the cave on a terrace that had been formed by the dug up earth and stones. If a particularly noteworthy object was unearthed in the cave, it had to remain in its original position until I had inspected it. This happened quite often. The Brunnstein cave was roomy but not blocked off. We were sure it was somehow connected to the very large, adjacent Schönstein cave. It was an absolute delight to look out over the wonderful landscape with its scattered, embedded boulders from my terrace. The backdrop was formed by the mighty rock faces of the Schönstein.

At lunchtime my team gathered on the terrace to have a very simple yet extraordinarily generous meal of cheese, bread and beer that I provided. The hour-long rest would usually be spent chatting happily with the men. They were all from Streitberg, the people I brought in to work on the cave explorations, people I had known for years and who all had enthusiasm and devotion towards, some even an excellent understanding of, the fairly easy work. First in line in that respect was the foreman, Konrad Arndt, who is the warden of the *Bing-Höhle* today, closely followed by Ulrich Merkel. Moreover, he had acquired a great technical knowledge of the geological conditions around Streitberg while working hard in his own quarry at the entrance to the Lange valley.

During one lunch break I decided to test the intelligence of my crew by asking them an unusual question. To answer this question they had to not think about what is possible or impossible, but instead they had to decide what in their opinion would happen next if the event had really happened. So I began:

Imagine, we are all working in the cave. Friedmann is furthest into the cave slaving away at a 3m-high earth wall (Friedmann, by the way, was the least likely of all of us to be slaving away at anything). Suddenly, above this earth wall, there appears a terrible, larger than life figure with a flaming red beard, who with an abominable voice and a wide-open mouth shouts out the words "Earthlings, out with you!" Fearing for our lives, we rush out of the cave and just see how the giant seizes Friedmann on the terrace and throws him high into the air towards Streitberg. Then the beast grabs a massive pine, pulls it out of the ground and swings the gigantic tree threateningly towards us. Confused, breathless and scared out of our wits we reach Streitberg. In front of Scheumann's inn a large crowd has gathered. They are standing around Friedmann's body which landed there when the giant threw him into the air. Now the people are questioning us as to what happened. The Unbelievable, the Incomprehensible has happened. Friedmann's body is refutable evidence of the fact. Our statements, made under oath, are recorded by the authorities. The Lange valley lies abandoned – only dread and horror live there now.

So then I asked the question: "What impact will this terrible event, which we swear is true, have on the world?" – Silence. At last one or two men said: "But it's not real!" I explained to them that I knew that of course, but that was just a side issue. We had to assume as fact that this dreadful event really happened as we had seen it and sworn under oath, and I was expecting my question to be answered under this assumption. Again silence. At last Friedmann replied, "If that story was true, the world would just go dumb again." I thought that was an appropriate reply.

Then came the time where the popular saying "What you wish for in your youth, you will have in abundance in old age" came true for me. I had never really understood what these words meant, considering how few wishes from one's youth are fulfilled in one's old age. In my case, however, the saying was applicable. My business duties were slowly being reduced until only those were left that I had taken on voluntarily as a member of the supervisory board. The company directors had sorted themselves out in such a way that I could spend the entire spring and summer in Streitberg, and autumn and winter too if I wanted. Endless possibilities opened up to indulge my passion for digging. There was no lack of suitable test objects, nor of time or money for the arising costs, which by the way were high enough. In order to be successful one has to be willing to make sacrifices to the Goddess "Anthropology".

One of my nieces who lived in Streitberg, Olga Hirsch, one of my sister Marie's daughters, was a dear companion to me for such expeditions. Her stamina, her insight and her love for the matter in hand made her a good fellow who happily accepted the ups and downs and the troubles of our shared labour.

After many more or less successful excavations I now come to the most important success I ever enjoyed in my efforts to be of practical service to science. I must start by saying that with increasing age I found the often hour-long walks to the distant excavation sites somewhat difficult, and that we had run out of suitable sites in the surrounding area that seemed worth investigating; the only exception being a fantastic find which was discovered by me and my niece Olga with Merkel's help in his quarry in the Lange valley. The find consisted of some mighty mammoth thigh and joint bones, which now are kept safe and secure as the crowning glory of my collection.

I was now longing to find something in the close vicinity of my villa that would give my urge to explore a purpose. I was in luck! During a ride with farmer Braungart, who also ran a hackney carriage service, he happened to mention that there was a small cave in his woods in the Peterswald which I could excavate if I wanted to. So I asked a forester who knew the woods and especially the small grottos and caves very well to lead me to the suggested site. We found an insignificant fox or badger hole – surely that was not it? And yet the descriptions by my informant seemed very different. He suggested that surely I had not found the right spot. To my joy, and his great benefit, I eventually found the right place.

The circumstances under which I discovered and developed this cave, the *Bing-Höhle*, are public knowledge. Everything is explained in the leaflet given to each visitor of the cave, and a number of papers were also published to describe the facts. I can therefore skip the multiple incidents connected with the development of the cave. What I would consider worth saying, or rather describing, is the first time, this solemn, unforgettable hour, when in the company of Olga Hirsch, my loyal companion and faithful Eckart[73] of the *Bing-Höhle*, Herr Kellermann (and I believe my brother Edmund and his wife), I set foot in this land which had lain dormant in a majestical, magical beauty for thousands of years and had now risen to a new life. Naming two of the most beautiful rooms "Olga's Grotto" and "Dr. Kellermann's Grotto" was my way of expressing the gratitude I felt towards the two people for their sharing in the hard work and in my success. The report published by Dr. Kellermann in the *Fränkische Kurier* after his first visit to the by then fully developed *Bing-Höhle* is so interesting and impressive in all its parts, be it the scientific contents or the description of the actual cave itself, that I think I can justifiably say that he has adopted this youngest and probably most beautiful fairy princess in Franconia as his own. I reprint his report here. It will forever form an important and substantial document in the archives of the *Bing-Höhle.*

A visit to the newly developed Bing-Höhle *near Streitberg*

> *A new addition has been made to the long list of known caves which further enhance the enjoyment of nature for the visitor rambling through the Franconian Switzerland, a new cave which lies in a touristically superbly convenient spot, right at the entrance to the Franconian Switzerland. Herr Kommerzienrat Bing from Nuremberg has the great merit to have developed this cave, which is distinguished by its numerous dripstones of unusual variety and beauty. Following a friendly invite by the explorer himself, the author of these words visited the cave and can now report on his impressions.*

[73] A mythical figure in medieval German literature.

In order to get to the cave, one has to leave Streitberg by the signpost pointing to the Prince Rupprecht cave and climb the south-westerly face of the Schauer valley. To the right of Prince Rupprecht way, a newly installed path leads through a beech forest up to the entrance of the cave, situated at the foot of a small rocky knoll. After only a ten-minute climb one has reached one's goal. The cave entrance is a curved vault of low height and narrow width; a wall and a solid wooden door seal the entrance. The rock on the eastern side of the entrance is non-layered dolomite into which thick layers of white chalk protrude on its western side. The cave itself lies in layered limestone.

Its discovery is strange enough, and its development required a massive effort of work and purposeful energy. Herr Kommerzienrat Bing arranged for excavations looking for prehistoric objects at the cave entrance, which was almost entirely buried. While emptying the cave of earth and mud, unmistakable traces of inhabitation by humans were found; humans who were still in the very early stages of cultural development. Shards of earthenware with very rough ornaments, traces of fire as well as animal and human bones were brought to light. After about 30 metres these finds stopped, and ceasing the operation here was considered. Then, signs were discovered that indicated the cave might extend further into the mountain. It was also known that foxes and badgers often used the narrow passage, and an experienced hunter had advised that dachshunds sometimes spent days in the subterranean cavities.

Fig. 38 The Candle Hall.
© Michael Diefenbach

They decided to proceed and soon discovered a passage rich in stalagmites (dripstone columns that grow from the bottom up), but it was so low that one could only crawl through it.

The cave floor was solid calc-sinter. This sinter layer, which had an average thickness of one meter, was broken up, and the clay and mud from underneath was dug out in order to create the space needed to walk comfortably through the cave. Because of the great hardness of the calc-sinter, this was a very onerous and time-consuming task, which took 90 dayshifts. The further forwards they proceeded, the more magnificent the cave turned out to be. In one place they found a cove of immense height filled with dripstones; the "Holy of Holies". After advancing 90 horizontal metres deep into the mountain, it appeared that they had reached the end of the cave. They did not come across any forks in the cave apart from one single, narrow, and therefore impassable, corridor which runs in parallel with the cave for a while.

Since it was unlikely that such a massive channel would stop suddenly without branching out somewhere, they kept looking until they found an opening, but it was so narrow though that no adult could slip through it. A thirteen-year old boy, the son of one of the men working at the cave, agreed to squeeze through it. He returned with the news that the cave continued on the other side and that a man could comfortably walk through it. When sent through the opening again, the boy stayed over three quarters of an hour and the men waiting behind began to worry. The courageous little explorer, however, returned with such good news regarding the course of the cave that the workers vigorously returned to their work. Following the course of the mud-filled crevice, they burrowed underneath the sinter layer. Soon they had cleared a relatively wide extension of the cave that was accessible almost everywhere by walking upright, which was rich in all kinds of dripstone formations and whose ceiling rose at times, like the vaulted ceiling of a church, to a considerable height. The total length of the cave from its south-easterly entrance to its north-westerly end was around 300 metres, i.e. roughly the distance between the King's gate and the Kasematten gate[74].

The whole thing presents itself as one of those caves which were described by the meritorious explorer of caves in the Franconian

[74] Two of Nuremberg's city gates.

Switzerland, Major Dr. Neischl, as a fissure cave. The rain-water of times gone by ran through long, parallel fissures which crisscrossed the chalk layer resting on top of the shell limestone until it reached the impermeable layer where, following the path of least resistance, some of these fissures expanded into channels. One of these channels created at the bottom of the fissure is our cave. Once, a mighty source of water would have sprung from the - now dry - mouth of the cave, not unlike the ones we still find here and there in the Franconian Switzerland, e.g. near Behring mill. Over millennia, the continuing erosion of the mountain through water draining off either above or below ground decreased the drainage area of the source until at last it ran dry. As the remains found at its entrance show, the dried-out mouth of the cave served animals and humans as a home. Since no remains of cave bears, otherwise so commonly found in the Franconian Switzerland, were discovered, the source must have dried up after the time when these animals populated the area. On the inside, delicate dripstones were now beginning to form, decking and embellishing the cave, a process that is still continuing. Mud washed into the cave slowly closed up the entrance, until only small animals such as foxes and badgers were able to get in. This sealing of the cave ensured the undisturbed growth of the dripstones and, by collecting the water and preventing any sudden air exchanges, impacted their formation.

After walking through the first 30 metres of the cave, the visitor is then accompanied on both sides by a vast number of stalagmites; short but strong little columns. It is like walking through a picture gallery since one finds oneself in the passage-way that was dug through the mud and sinter layers which is about chest-high. The one-metre thick sinter layer of white, coarse crystalline calcite, sometimes interveined by yellowish layers, is a good indicator that the loam washed in by the rain dammed up the seeping water that collected on the cave floor. Yet there was another consequence to this subsequent collection of water, into which the feet of the already existing stalagmites were steeped. On the edge of this cave lake, which evidently existed for a long period of time, a flood mark formed in the shape of a delicate ledge of calc-sinter protruding several centimetres from the wall. Always at the same height, it runs along all sides of the cave and along all the stalagmites inside it, and it gives evidence of the depth of the pool of water that was here thousands of years ago. This pool must have disappeared suddenly, since there is not a trace of a second, parallel ledge.

The stalagmites in the front area of the cave are of a yellowish colour and not translucent; they are made up of dense or very fine crystalline calcite. An abundance of dripstones can be found here, even where the cave rises to a greater height, and this is also where we find the "frozen waterfalls" as seen in other caves, next to rag or drape-like formations hanging from the ceiling, and numerous little stalagmites at the tips of which water droplets twinkle in the light of the miner's lamps.

Having walked through the first 90 metres of the cave, one descends a few steps down a wooden staircase to reach the even more interesting part of the cave that was discovered later. Here the passageway gains noticeably in height and width. In some parts the walls are devoid of dripstones, and then the thick strata of the adjoining, layered rocks, like cyclopean masonry, become visible. In one such place, where the rectangular cross-section of the wall is so regular that it appears to be man-made, a single, giant stalagmite rises up in the middle of the cave like a monument, almost touching the ceiling which is around three metres high at this point. Like most stalagmites of this cave, this one is slim and cone-shaped; its surface is not smooth but strangely stepped, not unlike the shaft of a palm tree where the remains of withered leaves are still visible. One would almost think that a wise master builder had banned any other dripstones here in order to present the beauty of this ONE *formation in the proper light.*

We continue onwards, when suddenly the cave opens up into a kind of hall; we are in the Candle Hall. Here we find slender, several-metre high, non-tapered candle-like stalagmites, some of a blinding white colour; they are made of translucent calcite. If one knocks these columns with a bent finger, they ring, and if ones touches such a ringing column with the hand, one can distinctly feel it oscillating.

Every section of this cave greets us with a new and wonderful view. Next we arrive at a room where the floor and the walls twinkle with innumerable little crystal mirrors. With every movement of the body or the lights, different areas flash up. In a sinter basin filled with crystal-clear water we find crystal geodes made up of thousands of little calcite rhomboedrons, fully formed on all sides and not attached to the ground, whose surfaces shimmer through the water. We are in the presence of one of nature's secret laboratories where crystals grow; a spectacle rarely witnessed by the human eye. If we still believed in mountain spirits we would have to consider this crystal palace - or Floor of Diamonds as Bing calls it - to be the royal palace of the underground souls. But alas, used as we are to admitting more mundane considerations when observing natural phenomena, we inquire after the correlation of the facts. We know that crystals form most beautifully and most regularly when solidification occurs extremely slowly, in a consistently saturated solution and under consistent temperature conditions. Such conditions obviously exist in the rear part of the cave, maybe 40 to 50 metres below ground level, where events such as air exchange, water evaporation and the escape of the carbon dioxide dissolved in the limestone occur extremely slowly.

At another place in the cave we come across a number of splendid stalagmites, broken off at the bottom and leaning with

Fig. 39 Translucent stalagmite.
© Michael Diefenbach

their tips against the cave wall. A smaller column of these broken ones is still resting on its base and has reattached itself to it, albeit at a crooked angle, through the continuous growth of the dripstone. The destruction in this cave - until recently inaccessible - evidently resulted from strong tremors such as can be caused by large rockslides.

Further along we come to a fragile, vertically developed stalactite which is suspended on one side from the ceiling like an elegantly curved curtain. Since this structure also rings when knocked, it was not inappropriately called the Harp. In another place, a short stalagmite curtain runs through the centre of the cave, hanging from the ceiling like a teaser above a stage. Its hem is studded with very thin, colourless calcite crystals that make the curtain look as if it was adorned with expensive lace. A large sinter pool is still filled with water; some dry sinter basins contain cauliflower-like formations. Another sinter basin is almost entirely covered by a flat sinter layer except for a small opening in the middle, the edges of which are also covered with these cauliflower-like formations. There are also some stalagmites where we find these granular or cauliflower-like formations on their bottom halves. This is how the stalagmites show the high-water mark in a different manner compared to the one we saw in the gallery cave. Sometimes one hesitates to put the foot down out of fear of breaking the fragile, sometimes only paper-thin edges of the sinter basins. Finally the floor rises a little, we walk across a slanting rock face through which trickle-water has gouged narrow, parallel grooves, until we reach the last sinter basin, the Ice Sea. Its flat sinter cover is cracked in many places as if the water draining from a frozen pond had robbed the icy blanket of its support. Thus we have reached the end of the cave; for the time being, I should say, as the cave itself probably continues somewhere.

These descriptions of the strange formations are in no way exhaustive; even a second visit would not be enough to do them justice.

At the moment various areas of the second part of the cave can only be reached by crawling and dressed in overalls, which is no easy task for people with a certain embonpoint, but once access to the cave has been improved, that will no longer be necessary. Any obstacles are being removed in the same practical yet gentle manner as in the first part.

Around all this magnificence, almost everywhere, there still rests the magical air of something pristine and unspoilt. Deep

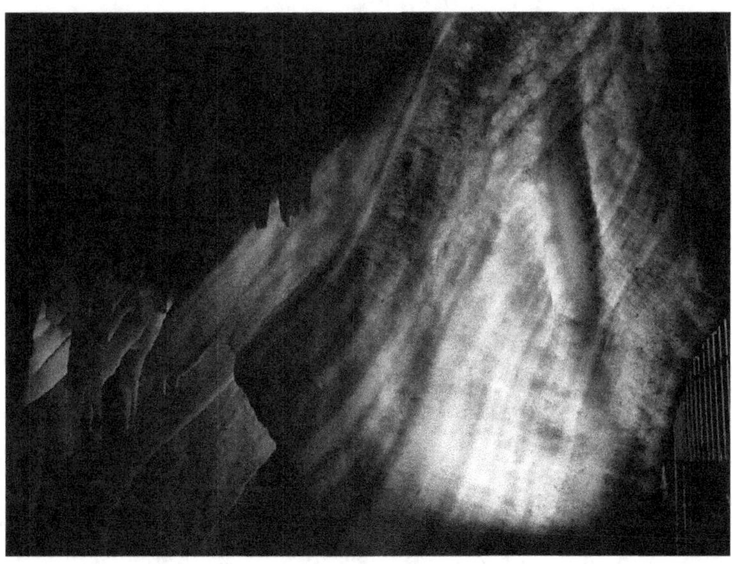

Fig. 40 The Harp.
© Michael Diefenbach

inside the cave the white walls are still shining like new, no rough hands have yet damaged the fragile shapes as they have elsewhere. Other caves may surpass the Bing-Höhle *in size and extent of their halls; their corridors may be longer and more labyrinth-like (although the second part of our cave also contains a short, accessible parallel corridor), but no other known cave in the Franconian Switzerland matches ours even closely in the diversity and beauty of its dripstone structures, which here are so close you could almost touch them. No other offers us such splendid crystal formations and such delicate, translucent stalagmites of pure calcite, nowhere else do we find such manifold sinter basins. One would have to travel very far indeed to find a worthy match to the* Bing-Höhle. *There may well be more, and possibly equally magnificent caves in the Franconian Switzerland, as Major Neischl justly assumes, but where is the lucky knight who will wake a second sleeping beauty from her thousand year-long slumber?*

We can only wholeheartedly congratulate the purposeful discoverer and developer of the cave on his wonderful success, as well as the charming Streitberg which has gained an "unearned added value" through the development of the cave.

May this newly discovered shrine of nature, which tells us of the quiet, continual and therefore powerful workings of the natural powers that are so unnoticeable to us in the short time of our human lifespan, be protected from thieving and uncaring hands.

8th November 1905

In the line of those who dedicated enthusiastic spoken and written homages to the young beauty in Streitberg I would have to mention my brother Edmund in first place. If I have called Herr Oberstudienrat Kellermann the cave's Godfather, I would have to ask my silver-penned brother Edmund, who so adored beauty and truth, to give the bride away. Thousands of visitors have become loyal and admiring friends of the *Bing-Höhle* thanks to his solicitations. How serious his enthusiasm for the new cave was is shown by the following poem which he dedicated to me at some occasion.

Stalactite and -mite salute!

I approach thee as your humble servant,
Oh Prince of Caves, you King of Tinware.
Allow me to present to you
The stalactites and –mites salute.
Eternal sleep seemed out lot,
Lost forever in the womb of the earth.
Our only wish day in day out
Was for a Kommerzienrat to dig us out.
Who would discover us to his honour,
But our tears just kept on dripping.

Then we heard a knocking and a banging
From far away at first, then nearer,
Sounds from outside, were we going mad?
But then we heard the babble of voices,
"Friedemann, mate, reckon it's a cave?"
To which same grunted back:
"Dunno, maybe, it could be one,
But's just as likely that it's none."

Soon after that, the bright light of day
Reflected in a thousand crystals.
Like diamond-studded mats

A-twinkling the "Sinners' slabs".
People are flowing in like rivers
Mouths wide open, eyes all agog,
Delighted, moved, dumbfounded,
When Arndt the guide masters the harp.

And if the rush is much too pressing,
Arndt only needs to hoot for help.
Rumour has it that this kind of music
Is all that's needed to be happy.
In times to come you will be praised
And hailed as Streitberg's benefactor,
Pointed out to child and grandchild,
And every goat boy will know you well.

As long as the Wiesent continues to flow
And the trout dashes through its waters,
As long as eels still wriggle through the Wehrmühl,
And there are glow worms in the night,
As long as the Muschel source bubbles,
And the flowers blossom in the Lange valley,
As long as in the sunny weather
Rocky ruins tower high
The ruins that shelter your villa
Where you're happy and in good spirits,
As long as one stalactite is still standing,
The flame of your fame will continue to burn!

I cannot possible list all those by name who as sincerely enthusiastic admirers of the *Bing-Höhle* did everything in their power to recruit friends for her. I do not think that there was a single newspaper of importance in Bavaria that did not publish an original article about the new discovery. From all sides I received splendid essays about the *Bing-Höhle*. *Das Bayernland* published a particularly beautiful description of the cave, and as a result of which its witty editor Leher and I became closer. And the local head teacher, Herr Grimm, incorporated a wonderful description of the cave into his widely used schoolbook, which could not have been more poetic or impressive.

Special thanks goes to my esteemed benefactress Frau Dr. Else Dormitzer (pen name Else Dorn). Not only did she publish delightful portrayals of the cave in the Nuremberg papers, but she also arranged for an impressive show of pictures from the cave in a prestigious cinema in Nuremberg. The understanding woman even brought a first-class newspaper man from Frankfurt, the editor Ziedler, to Nuremberg by car. Subsequently, the *Frankfurter General Anzeiger* published a superbly written article about the cave, the effect of which showed itself in a notable increase in visitors from Frankfurt.

Thousands made the pilgrimage to Streitberg to behold the new miracle; in a sense every single visitor with an understanding for and an appreciation of the works of an ever-naturing nature, which he would have witnessed inside the cave, could be regarded as a herald of this magical world.

A poem from the visitors' book, which acts as an extremely effective reminder to the visitor not to damage the wonderful and fragile structures in the cave with a "rough hand" and not to disturb the solemn atmosphere of a visit was justly adopted as some form of preface to the little flyer which every visitor to the cave was given as a memento. Its author, a warm-hearted, understanding nature lover who, despite the prose imposed upon him by his important office in the company, had retained his sense for beauty, was Herr F. H. Huber. He has spoken to thousands through his atmospheric verses, for the leaflet had seen a circulation of around 50,000 even before the war. It goes like this:

Naturae Monumentum

Here, where nature in her omnipotent workings
Has created an opus of majestical proportions
In rocky stones and thousand-year old crevices
Which man is left admiring wide-eyed,
Enter, stranger, into this magical kingdom
Where a century is like one hour!
Behold these natural formations with awe
In this magical realm's splendid palace!

Beware the rough hand, that it may damage
Nothing in these underground treasures.
And when you've finished your dreamlike wander
And step into the daylight, tell others
That you have here, deep in the mountain night,
Seen the splendour of a magical tale,
Far from the sun-drenched meadows,
A monument to naturing Nature!

I shall add here and now that in the war year of 1915 the famous painter Professor Matthiesen from Copenhagen sent me a letter to ask my permission to use certain settings in the famous *Bing-Höhle* as subjects for his paintings. He had been assigned by his government to decorate the new national museum in Copenhagen, and his intention was to use motifs from the *Bing-Höhle* for the rooms dedicated to geology and mineralogy etc. I refused since I did not think that during these times of war Streitberg was a suitable place for a foreigner. Matthiesen, however, still achieved his goal. The Danish embassy in Berlin intervened in his favour, and the district authority in Ebermannstadt officially supported Matthiesen's request. The artist and his lovely young wife came to Streitberg. An interesting and pleasant couple! They were enchanted by the cave, no less than we were by their visit, for the artist had created some marvellous pictures. In a sense, today the *Bing-Höhle* can be seen, immortalised, in Copenhagen.

Then a great day for Streitberg came into view. Prince Ludwig of Bavaria, the current King, was going to attend a meeting of the Canal Association in Bamberg. After the meeting, according to his schedule, he was to go for a ride through the Franconian Switzerland, and he was going to come and visit the *Bing-Höhle* while he was there. There was also the prospect of having tea in his honour at the villa. A sounding had been taken as to how I felt about this idea, and of course I declared that I would do everything necessary to prove myself worthy of the great honour bestowed upon my house. Firstly, a large commission arrived in Streitberg, headed by His Excellency Freiherr von Roman, district president of Upper Franconia. They wanted to visit the cave, if only to convince themselves that such a visit did not present any dangers for any of the noblemen. His Excellency, an extraordinarily "weighty" person in every way, struggled to walk up the steep hill that leads to the cave entrance. However, when my young and pretty niece, Fräulein Olga, offered her arm as support to His Excellency, he seemed to gain new strength, and the young, attentive lady heard many a flattering, thankful word from him.

At the visit, the cave made a big impression and was found worthy of a visit by a royal prince. Then the villa was inspected, from top to bottom right into the cellar. Everything was considered to be fine and dandy, and a highly-decorated agriculturist from the party evidently provided the eminent president with reassuring information regarding the contents of the wine cellar.

There were about 15 gentlemen who gathered around the table in the large living room in order to discuss the details of the coming royal visit. The conversation went very peacefully and in high spirits. Babette, our sterling cook who was always ready to be of service and who would, upon occasions such as this, exhibit even greater levels of competency had - with Olga's help, my wife was not in Streitberg - prepared a snack for the important gentlemen. The dining table displayed an abundant feast for the eyes and the stomach. Lean ham, finest cheeses, fresh butter, smoked salmon and tender tongue as well as cold roast; everything was presented in the most appetising manner and reassured the gentlemen that we would look after His Royal Highness very well. All this was accompanied by fine wines, which, like the delicacies from the table, the gentlemen were not shy to partake of. The atmosphere rose, the speeches began. Everyone was feeling very chatty, especially His Excellency, and the host talked freely and naturally too. After coffee they left. A heavy head, and a deep sigh of relief!

The day before the arrival of the Prince in Streitberg brought a heavy rainstorm with thunder and lightning, and for us it meant the worry of "What if it's like this tomorrow?" How lovely it would have been to have breakfast in the garden, it would have framed the rare occasion so beautifully. And yet it was raining cats and dogs, with no end in sight! But the heavens relented.

The next morning the sun was shining brightly, bathing the glorious landscape, resplendent in spring blossom, in warm, golden light. Weather truly fit for a prince!

The arrival of His Royal Highness was planned for 10 o'clock in the morning. His schedule allowed for a one and half hour visit of Streitberg. It was very little time for the intended programme: reception, walk to the cave and visit of same, breakfast at the villa. Thanks to my prudent and far-seeing tactics everything went pretty smoothly. The Prince arrived on time. He climbed out of his car, walked up to me and also greeted Herr Oberstudienrat Kellermann, whom he had personally known and respected for a long time. I had asked Herr Kellermann to be on hand in case the Prince had any scientific questions during his visit that might have embarrassed me. In the Prince's entourage were many distinguished gentlemen, amongst them of course His Excellence von Roman. The vicar of Streitberg, Pastor Weiss, had also come to the reception, though I had asked him in advance to keep his speech short with respect to the circumstances. It would have been better if he had said nothing at all. He already went shy when His Royal Excellency touched him by the sleeve and pulled him into the shade. "The sun is too good to us over there, vicar. Now we can start." And he started. The vicar could not remember the beginning of the speech he had prepared. He wanted to say that according to the church's records, the Prince's grandfather, King Ludwig I, had once visited Streitberg, but in his confusion he talked about King Ludwig II, the Prince's father, whom he put in the grandfather's place. He called the Prince "His Majesty" and in a banal manner wished him a good time in Streitberg, where he hoped to see him again at the villa. In short, it was a shambles that made me angry and impatient. I winked at him to remind the completely confused speaker of our agreement, and at last, after painful minutes, we were released. Just like the last time in Nuremberg, when the speaker I had dedicated to deliver the homage to the Prince had his mishap, the Prince again had me understand that he "was used to these things, the main thing was always their good intention."

Then, without further delay, we went straight to the cave. The fire fighters we had placed in certain positions as posts looked very impressive. The Prince's entourage counted over 30 people, especially many members of the country gentry with aristocratic-sounding names. The whole party was meant to attend the breakfast, and we were well prepared in that respect. The cave had exactly the kind of delicious effect on the Prince and his guests as I had expected, and I myself conducted the tour. I kept my explanations factual and avoided any exuberance. At the end of the cave, when we arrived in the most beautiful and unusual chamber, the crystal grotto, I asked permission to say a few words. My speech ended with the announcement that this wonderful grotto was going to be called "Prince Ludwig Grotto" from now on. The prince seemed to have liked my speech; he shook my hand and thanked me for the honour, which he was glad to accept.

Now back home again. At the entrance to the villa, which in honour of the day had been decorated simply but effectively, I was horrified to see the veterans' association lined up in rank and file with flying colours. Not another speech! Already more than one hour of the time dedicated for the visit had passed. The chairman of the association, a respectable weaver fellow, spoke succinctly without crippling any of his words, and the Prince seemed very satisfied when the patriotic cheer rang out.

Up the decorated stairs we went, onto the garden terrace where the table, adorned without any special splendour except plenty of flowers, was awaiting the guests. But there was to be another reception! My ten-year-old granddaughter Dora, a bright and very pretty little girl, was to present the Prince with flowers and recite a little verse that I had composed for the occasion.

> Oh Prince, allow these little hands to present
> you with these sweet-smelling flowers.

But, oh dear! The child could not get beyond the words "Oh Prince", and her honest eyes were brimming with tears. I prompted her the few words, but she could not say them. The Prince could not have been more touched by the failed reverence even if she had spoken the words perfectly. He put his hand on my granddaughter's head, took the flowers out of her hands and said comfortingly, "It's alright, my dear child."

One thing to add is that during the official visit to the cave, His Excellency von Roman, who had already become acquainted with the effort involved in climbing up to the cave once, chose to retire to a comfortable sofa in the villa for a little nap.

Now everyone sat down at the table. At the top end sat the Prince, the adjutant general Freiherr von Leonrod on his right and me on his left. The other guests sat down wherever they fancied. The breakfast was opulent; it had been carefully selected and supervised in all its details by the owner of the grand hotel, Herr Lotz. It was a happy, cheerful affair, and the noble visitor thought it was excellent. The only annoyance was that the adjutant general constantly pulled out his pocket watch to indicate that the allocated time had passed and that the meal had to come to an end.

At the time, my son-in-law Benario and his family were staying with us. Unfortunately there had been no seat left at the table for him. Misled by Benario's black suit, a guest called out to him, "Waiter, we need some cutlery over here!" Nevertheless, I was able to introduce the alleged waiter to His Highness, by his profession as editor of the *Frankfurter Zeitung*. The prince was unprejudiced enough to acknowledge the democratic publication in front of my son-in-law as a very good newspaper.

After the allotted time had been exceeded by almost an hour and the luncheon was already being prepared in the neighbouring Muggendorf, the Prince indicated that it was time to leave by lighting his cigar. He bid me a very affectionate farewell. It was not until they had left that I realised to my horror that the special cigars - with the picture of the Prince and his noble consort which I had ordered from Hamburg especially for this day - had not been offered.

It was very easy to be in the company of the Prince, who was so affable and so well-versed even in the things regarding the lives of ordinary people. All one had to do was start a conversation with "Your Royal Highness", and then one was free to talk about anything and to reply frankly to any questions he might ask.

For those of you who enjoy good food I shall list the tasty dishes which were offered to the noble visitors, according to the original order of courses.

Breakfast

celebrating the visit of

His Royal Highness

Prince Ludwig of Bavaria

Beluga caviar "Malossol"

Ostend lobster in jelly

Oder crab timbale

Gull eggs

Cold Rhine salmon with mayonnaise sauce

Jellied Altmühl eels

Roast saddle of veal Hamburg-style, garnished

Roast beef, rare, with side dishes

Tender loin with fresh bean salad

Glazed Coburg ham

Ox tongue with frozen horseradish

Pheasant breasts on toast,

with Cumberland sauce

Strasbourg liver pâté

Hazel grouse in jelly
Chicken Metz-style, with ravigote sauce

Salads

Compotes

Cheeses

Wines:
1904 Kallgartener Schönhell, Auslese
Crescant Fürst von Löwenstein
1865 Castanienbuscher Traminer
Ruinart père & fils, Carte blanche sec.

Villa Marie, Streitberg, 3rd June 1908.

The reader must not conclude from this, however, that such extravagances would ever have been served at the villa again in any shape or form, either on a weekday or on a holiday. Our many guests, including those of high rank, would always be well, even abundantly, catered for, but we served plain and simple food; never did we allow gluttony or overindulgence, or anything else that smacked of ostentatiousness, to settle in our simple country home. On the evening of the princely visit, a rather large number of gentlemen from Bamberg appeared on our doorstep, led by my brother Edmund. They had attended the lunch in Muggendorf, and my brother had raised their hopes that there might be sufficient delicacies left over from the royal breakfast for them to expect a particularly delicious evening meal at the villa as a kind of post-visit celebration. My brother Edmund, who had a good nose for such things, was right. There were plenty of good things left, and the improvised dinner not only provided entertaining company but also food and drink that even Lucullus, God rest his soul, would have been proud of.

Life in Streitberg was business as usual. "Guests came and went." Sometimes I said that our house was the most-visited in the whole of the Franconian Switzerland. But it was no wonder, since the large Bing mishpocha often besieged the little town for weeks, almost leading people to believe that every sunny summer's day was another family gathering of the Bing kinship. During the main season, i.e. in the holidays, we would regularly have ten to twelve guests for lunch, who would also stay at the villa overnight. Other relatives and friends came and went as they pleased, coffee and cake were served on almost every sunny day, and friends from Nuremberg dropped by, whose visits I always appreciated very much.

When the members of our Saturday evening circle came to visit, I would usually send the car to fetch them and later to take them back to Nuremberg again. Our family life, the idyll of Streitberg, did not suffer in any way from this hospitality which we provided with joy and gladness. Why should we not be happy when sons and daughters filled the house and grandchildren made their presence known with their merry games in the garden. I often said, and not without good reason I think, that a country home without guests will soon bring boredom and even resentment, and those who came to see us knew perfectly well that they could be sure of a heartfelt welcome.

In addition, the friends of my son Dr. Siegmund Bing, among them the painters Kremer and Grassman, the highly gifted brothers Professor Dr. Jakob and Dr. Fritz Jakob were always welcome guests. So was our neighbour, the artist Lamm from Muggendorf, who had won so many admirers for the Jura mountains with his delightful landscapes and accomplished etchings, and we have spent many animated hours in the presence of this brilliantly witty painter.

We gained a new neighbour in my cousin Kommerzienrat Max Philipp Tuchmann when he left Nuremberg and moved to Streitberg. He built his house on the tennis court which I had previously installed below the *Bing-Höhle*. It has sweeping views of Streitberg and of the picturesque castle ruins.

Villa Marie and Villa Waldhaus maintain good relations, which are deepened by the unifying game of skat, although I have to admit that my cousin, Frau Kommerzienrat Klara, far outclasses her husband and me in this ingenious game. The vigorous lady achieves anything she puts her mind to.

It was always an extraordinary pleasure when my nephew, Herr Elkan, a dentist from Düsseldorf who had married our niece Aennie, came to stay with us for a while. The couple were not only happily united in a harmonious marriage but they were also equally harmonious in music. My niece masterfully accompanied her husband on the piano when he used to sing old and new melodies with his powerful baritone voice, to the delight of his audience. We often held these concerts in the villa, too, and the kind and highly gifted singer did not tire of living up to my fondness for Wagner with a great willingness. I would like to express my deep sense of gratitude to a good man and true artist.

Of the societies that came to see the cave and also my by now considerably extended collections I should name the Society for Prehistoric Bavaria. It was Dr. Forster again, with his wife, who brought the learned party with their ladies to us. Following the visit of the cave everyone gathered jovially at the villa where guests and hosts alike would be animated and delighted by many a kind word. Of course these get-togethers did not pass without treats; again the food provided was simple, but good and plentiful. The guests parted, grateful and satisfied in every respect.

In the meantime I had initiated another dig which was going to keep me busy for over a year, with interruptions of course. When I started at the Brunnstein, I was probably the first person in Bavaria to dig in caves in order to investigate what tools, weapons or jewellery prehistoric humans had left behind. This was to enable us to draw conclusions regarding the living conditions of prehistoric humans and to find out about how they lead their primitive lives. My thesis was this: Prehistoric humans could live much more comfortably and safer in one of the many accessible caves and grottos as we find them in great numbers, especially in the Jura mountains, than if they had had to rely on building their own artificial homes with the miserable tools they had at their disposal. This also justified us to conclude that numerous traces of troglodytes of one kind or another could be detected while searching through these caves that had been accessible since time immemorial. Through all the excavations I carried out, this hypothesis was more or less confirmed.

The finds at Kummert's Hole - the dig in question - clearly proved that the caves in the Franconian Jura mountains were not only lived in, but also that these caves often served certain social purposes. I recommend Dr. Kellermann's essay *Kummert's Hole near Streitberg* to anyone interested in further information on this subject. A few copies are kept at the villa in Streitberg.

Another place of discovery is the tuff quarry near the Lange valley. Nearly all the treasures that were found there have been incorporated into my collection, and most of them had either been unearthed by myself or my friend Uller (in other words, Ulrich Merkel), who had already made many finds at the Brunnstein..

By the way, I have written a guidebook about my collection, which enables even the layman to navigate through it. My niece Olga, who is very familiar with so much of it due to her working with me, has agreed to take on the role of curator after my death.

The general meeting of the German Anthropologists Convention was due to take place in Nuremberg. Again it was Herr Hofrat von Forster who, as chairman of the committee and supported by his witty and learned wife, was to prepare this highly regarded, scholarly convention. His mission was not only to enable the scholars and scientists to plan their work, but also to offer them rest and animation in the old town of Nuremberg. I had also been assigned a role - on the finance committee of course! As you will see, my task there turned out to be more important than merely the provision of filthy mammon. It was agreed that an excursion to the Franconian Switzerland should be part of the programme. The destination was Muggendorf, with a stopover of several hours in Streitberg for the purpose of visiting the *Bing-Höhle* and my collections, particularly the finds from Kummert's Hole. Dr. Kellermann's exhaustive article about the scientific results of this excavation had been included as a special edition in the commemorative programme which the Natural History Society had published on the occasion of the Anthropologists' convention.

Herr Dr. von Forster explained to me that even the most famous explorers were aloof and unamenable to caves and bones unless there was a certain degree of hospitality involved. I understood the hint and offered a fine, cold breakfast. This reminds me of an incident that happened in a noble family in Nuremberg where famous artists used to go in and out. One day I heard the lady of the house make the following comment: "At Barnay's we had hot food, at Possart's we had cold; so Possart was offended that we had had hot fare at Barnay's." Herr von Forster was of the opinion that, especially with view to the time of day, "only hot" would be good enough. He refused to accept any objections with regard to the kitchen, much too small for such a purpose, insufficient crockery and cutlery etc. He insisted that hot food - that he was sure of, he said - would be the highlight of the day. The wonderful cave itself seemed to be of little importance.

Having conceded to serve hot food - after consultation with my wife, whom I must commend on her willingness to always help out at these events despite the effort it involved - we began negotiations about the number of guests. Apart from Herr and Frau Dr. Forster, councillor Stucky representing the district government, and of course my highly esteemed friend Herr Dr. Kellermann, only out-of-town guests came into consideration, and preferably those bearing a famous name. We set the number of invitees at 25, and Herr Dr. Forster was to present the invitations in my name to the guests of his choice. Even Princess Therese of Bavaria, the King's sister, received a request for a royal appearance which was kindly submitted in person by Herr Dr. Forster; however, she was unavailable to take part in the excursion to Streitberg. I received a letter of thanks from her.

I myself had been denied any influence on the question of who to invite to our house since the Forsters themselves had already trouble enough choosing only 25 from the shortlist. Not even the director of the leading Natural History Society, or my best friends such as Fritz Tuchmann etc, could be considered. Only one of my acquaintances, about whom I will say a few extra words, was in luck. It was Herr R. I had known him for over 50 years. We both used to take part in the lunches at the *Adler Hotel*, from which I broke off at the time because the landlord considered us to be some kind of "vultures". Herr R. was more thick-skinned than me. When he visited the villa, the best fare was always just good enough for him. Often, he would even try to fleece my collections, with little or no success. The latter can be explained as follows.

After a long career as a manufacturer who successfully turned pigs bristles into brushes of all sorts, he was now able to enjoy life as a rentier. He educated himself and became a private scholar. The fresh horses he harnessed for his new life were Anthropology and Prehistory. He travelled far, and through his skilful manner he became acquainted with celebrities of the anthropological field. But life being life, despite his not insignificant collections and his contact to the experts, he remained an amateur of science. As for so many others, the poet's words applied to him:

> "Set wigs of a million curls upon thy head, to raise thee,
> Wear shoes an ell in height,—the truth betrays thee,
> And thou remainest—what thou art."[75]

An amateur after all, who longed to be more. Only the scientific airs were real. Once he let me have a "silex", or a flint, a small shard which he had apparently found in a cave in the Vézières valley in the Dordogne in France. In his view it was a scraper, and he estimated that this questionable artefact was 74,500 years old. I did not check!

There is a reason why I inserted this little episode here, it serves a certain, explanatory purpose for what follows later.

---

[75] Misquoted from Goethe's Faust. Translation of the original provided by www.gutenberg.org.

Thus, the Princes of Science - Klatsch-Breslau, Geheimrat von Luschan and other famous men whose names I do not recall - arrived with their wives, escorted by Herr and Frau Dr. Von Forster and presented themselves at the villa.

Off we went to the cave where preparations had been made such that these guests of honour as invited by myself were given the tour first and then returned to the villa for lunch. Everything worked out fine. The table was laid with the best crockery, the copious amounts of food were ready, and my daughters Frieda and Anna, my nieces Olga and Aennie and a lady friend of ours, Frau Hachenburger from Berlin, had been designated to wait on the guests. It only added to the conviviality of the special occasion that the waitresses were dressed in the very pretty traditional costumes of the Franconian Switzerland.

Now lunch was being served! In order to answer any questions regarding dress code, the printed invites included a special note to advise guests that ordinary day or travelling suits would be adequate for the reception at the villa. In addition, everyone was free to choose where to sit at the table, and next to whom. As a true historian, I will note the order of courses at the meal: We had consommé, trout from the Wiesent, fresh and cured ox tongue with vegetables, stuffed roast venison with side dishes, desserts, cheese boards, followed by coffee. It goes without saying that it was all accompanied by good wine.

Before lunch I noticed that there was a spare seat and asked Herr Dr. von Forster to send for my friend R., who was in Streitberg at the time, to join us at the table. He came, sat and ate. The food, served in the garden, tasted delicious, and one could tell by looking at the guests how at ease they were in my house. I gave a speech, some words of welcome which were received with applause and in which I explained how in this same place we had entertained the Prince, who was to go on to wear the royal crown, and how today it was my great honour to welcome so many Princes of Science as highly esteemed guests to my house. And yet I felt closer to these noble guests because of my practical activities in the scientific field; while at the same time I knew very well, and I assumed my dear friend R. did too, that our connection with science could only be regarded as superficial. We both could not live down the fact that we were merchants by trade, that I had processed the notorious tin, my friend pigs' bristles, even if with quite satisfying success. Real science was intolerant, I added, and did not forgive dilettantism. If one tries to approach her as a layman, one hears the voice of the Earth Spirit:

> "Thou'rt like the Spirit which thou comprehendest,
> Not me!"[76]

Poor amateurs!

My humorous speech unleashed a flood of equally funny and witty toasts. Only my amateur-colleague R. made a gloomy face. Of course I did not mean to offend him with my speech, yet the spiteful little remark had its place for more than one reason and could only be to his benefit.

---

[76] Translation of the original (from Goethe's *Faust*) provided by www.gutenberg.org.

I also raised a very warm, and enthusiastically received, toast to my highly esteemed friend Herr Kellermann, which reflected our personal relationship and his importance as a man of science.

The inspection of my collections, particularly the one from Kummert's Hole, concluded the meeting. The guests left with the highest and most heartfelt praise and gratitude for the reception, the meal and the conviviality of the get-together. Even my friend R. was in a good mood again.

One more time I was to have the great honour of meeting with His Royal Highness, the Prince Regent Ludwig, now King of Bavaria. The course of his tour of honour through his country saw the Prince Regent come to Nuremberg for a stay of several days' duration. He was accompanied by Her Royal Highness, the royal consort Princess Ludwig, and a number of their daughters. A large dinner reception at the castle was announced, and I received an invitation. To attend such a reception is quite a relaxing affair. One sits sufficiently far away from the noblest guests in order to be uninhibited in one's conversation with one's neighbour whilst enjoying the wonderful delicacies offered on the table. On the other hand, the subsequent meeting held by the noble guests after the meal is trickier. There is always the chance of being addressed or ordered to present oneself. At the meeting, I kept a respectful distance, but the Prince Regent came up to me anyway, looked at me through his sharp spectacles somewhat unsure, shook my hand and asked how the cave was doing. I quickly replied that the cave, unlike all other transient things, grew more beautiful with age. The noble man apparently remembered what had been said in Streitberg about the constant reforming and growing of the dripstones; he smiled approvingly and seemed to think that my answer was very appropriate.

Since the Prince Regent seemed to hesitate in dismissing me, I dared to mention that the memory of his royal visit to Streitberg remained unforgettable, but that ever since I had had the good fortune of welcoming His Royal Highness to my house I had been racked with the guilt of an incomprehensible omission. The Prince looked at me questioningly, which I interpreted as his gracious permission to continue. I explained that I had considered it proper for the great favour which His Royal Highness had bestowed upon me with a visit to my house to have cigars made especially, in Hamburg, from the finest Havana tobacco and adorned with a picture of His Royal Highness and his wife. It was a great misfortune that we had neglected to offer His Royal Highness the exquisite leaves at the appropriate time; an ineptness for which I could still not forgive myself for today. The Prince laughed and said kindly: "I am sure you found a good use for those fine cigars; I wish for my fellow men to enjoy the good things in life, too."

We are approaching the end of this narrative. As a joke I asked my brother Edmund, since he had given me the inspiration to write this book, to pen a foreword to these pages. He mounted the Pegasus, masterfully tamed and guided him, and subsequently surprised me with a celebratory poem the content of which is far too flattering for me to be able to use it as a foreword or even to publish in its entirety. Nonetheless, I cannot deny myself repeating a couple of verses, and I ask the reader to understand that they were not influenced by me, even if these lines still contain too much appreciation and praise for me.

Whenever in a cosy circle, Ignaz would
Share colourful tales from the richness of his life,
How from an early age he worked so hard,
And the bubble of many an illusion burst,
How the stunted little form grew to a mighty tree,
When he, without rose-tinted glasses,
Knew how to describe friend and foe
In vivid pictures, with humour and with wit,
Then I urged my brother:
So much that is worth so little,
Is written with high gestures and import.
Pray, give us YOUR story now.
After much dithering he finally succumbed,
Dipping into his lasting memories,
Until at last, dedicated to your children,
We have a book, the story of your life.

If I were to list all the important guests, dear acquaintances, friends and relatives who had visited us here in Streitberg over the past fifteen years, it would surely turn into a visitors' book (like the one at the *Bing-Höhle*). "Who knows the nation, who the name, Of all who there together came?"[77] seems to have been coined especially for our country home. Yet all were welcome, without regard for rank or confession, learned or not. For us it has always been the individual that counts. To this day the villa has been the centre of our cosy family circle; friends and acquaintances have always felt at home and at ease there, and the residents of Streitberg honestly respect and revere its honorary citizen and his family.

[77] Quote from Schiller's *Kraniche des Ibykus - The Cranes of Ibycus.* Translation by www.has.vcu.edu.

I have finished. The purpose of this record will, I hope, have been achieved. I want my grandchildren to see that the serious side of life, the loyal performance of one's duties in our chosen profession, the battle with adverse circumstances and everyday life with its strict duties should not stop us from enjoying the pleasures of life. We are to walk through fields and forests, over mountains and through valleys, take part in all things human, good and beautiful, and to build an altar in our homes to cheerful, decent conviviality.

I am closing with the words that a wise soul mounted above the entrance to the villa in Streitberg, a long time before I bought the house.

Enter cheerfully,
Leave us joyfully,
If you're only passing,
May God bless your path.

May it always be like that. The house extends its greetings to all good people; may it be blessed with peace and joyfulness in return!

Nuremberg, Christmas 1916

Ignaz Bing
Geheimer Kommerzienrat

My Travels

In the war year of 1915, I committed the memories from my childhood and my young adulthood to paper; the stories I recorded pertained mainly to my commercial career and my part in the development of the *Gebrüder Bing* company. I called them *Tales From A Merchant's Life.* Even if the account was meant only for my nearest and dearest and did not make any claims of being any more than that, I did feel that because of the unfavourable times and my gloomy mood, this brief sketch of my life would give my descendants only an incomplete picture of me. There was little in the book that even hinted at what it was that had led and guided me through the tough trials of life, and through the pains and sorrows of a difficult job. The times spent with intimate and loyal friends, the warm-hearted humour that filled so many happy hours, cheery and harmless events that young people are interested in, were only touched upon fleetingly.

This explains why I felt the urge to write a sequel to my memories, and in 1916 the book *Family and Friends* was born.

I want my children and grandchildren, who, God willing, will soon be walking in a peaceful world again, to learn from it that their father and grandfather did not only spend his daily life striving for earthly possessions, but that apart from the most loyal and blessed performance of his professional duties, he never neglected or rejected that which points us humans to a higher goal, which ennobles us and puts us above the mere obsession of becoming rich. If and how I achieved this with my book is for my descendants to decide.

And now, in the third year of the war, I am taking on a further sequel, a description of my experiences during my travels, whether they were business-related or, even more so, undertaken in order to recover from work or to see the world. So here we go, *My Travels.*

To begin, I have to look back to my earliest youth. The first journey I remember happened when I was two or three years old. I can still remember very clearly being pushed forwards and backwards in a basket pram in the kitchen at home in Memmelsdorf, crying for a type of regional cake called "Bubela" (etymologically "Bubele").

My second, real journey was our move from Memmelsdorf to Gunzenhausen. I had nearly reached the age of 15 at the time; apart from us four older siblings and my parents, the latest arrival, my youngest brother Heinrich, all of nine months old, was also packed into the carriage which was to take us emigrants from Memmelsdorf to our first stop at Bamberg. One kilometre out of Memmelsdorf my parents realised that the changing mat for the youngest offspring had been left behind. It fell to me to walk back to fetch said mat. I could have thrashed the boy for the hassle he caused me, but there was no point - all I could do was run as fast as I could out of fear that the carriage might continue without me. The ins and outs of our arrival in Gunzenhausen are explained in detail in *Tales From A Merchant's Life.*

My third and this time totally independent journey is worth repeating here because of its purpose and because of what happened: When the year dedicated to my commercial education in Ansbach was over, my parents' concern with finding a suitable apprenticeship for me was very much in line with my own desire to go out and see the world. In Gunzenhausen, no such apprenticeship could be found, so I had to look around to see if I could find a position for myself. A tour of our numerous relatives was considered suitable for this purpose, not least because the customary "ten pennies" from the members of the extended family would help with the journey costs. My journey kit was quickly assembled, and everything fit into a small gripsack. It was very little indeed that was supposed to serve as support for a man's exterior during his great journey into the big wide world.

My first stop was Fürth where two of my uncles lived, brothers of my late mother, rich and highly esteemed hop traders. Naturally I paid them a visit to explain my wish to find a position as a commercial apprentice. I was received coolly; they said they would see what they could do, and I understood their gift of a *sechsbätzner* (= 24 kreutzers = 70 pfennings) from one of the kind aunts as the unmistakable hint that they had seen enough of me. The other aunt gave me some apples and nuts and a thick slice of rye bread as provisions for my journey. I was happy to move on since my wanderlust was greater than my pride, hurt though it was by the modesty of the offered gifts.

I made my way to the *Three Kings Inn* from where the horse-drawn omnibus was to leave in the evening for Neustadt on Aisch, the next stop on my journey. From there, more of my relatives were to be subjected to contribution. At the *Three Kings*, certain of good company, I had to wait for an hour for the omnibus, which even then was not in a hurry. The beer I had ordered did not seem to instil the landlord with any kind of respect for my admittedly rather small person. He addressed me with "Du", wanted to know what I was doing in Neustadt, etc. I thought I would gain more respect if I asked for a cigar. The landlord handed me one and said laughingly: "Boy, if you are going to smoke, tie up your trouser legs." I sensed what he meant. Oh, if only I had remained that innocent angel! Instead of pleasure the cigar brought me nothing but pain!

So I arrived in Neustadt on Aisch at around nine o'clock in the evening. The inn, where I was to spend the night, was hosting a ball. The young traveller asked modestly for something to eat and received, without being asked, an enormous omelette. He felt like some important gentleman: a pancake that he did not have to share with anyone was quite an event in his life!

Then I was shown to a poorly furnished room. But what a fairy tale-like dream! I listened to the music from the ball through half the night until I succumbed to sleep. In the morning I was able to stay in bed for as long as I liked since the day's task was only a one and a half hour's walk. After breakfast - one cup of coffee with sadly only *one* bread roll - I used the sechsbätzner that I had received in Fürth to pay my bill. Then I counted my money. I had two guilders = 3 marks 40 left, a respectable sum given that I was only visiting relatives who apart from free board and lodging usually gave me a few coins to get rid of me again.

Actually, the last bit is not quite right. Only twice did I get the sense that I had better not stay for long, and in both cases I knew that it was the circumstances and not a lack of hospitality that were to blame.

And so I took the walking staff to hike to Pares, the birthplace of my second mother, where one of her brothers and my grandmother lived. I was welcomed with open arms, and into such a plain little house that I asked myself where I was supposed to sleep at night. "A big heart makes a big house!" There was a guest bed in the attic; a wooden chair with an earthenware bowl and a matching water jug served as my washstand. But what else does a young boy need who slips into bed, is soon fast asleep and does not wake again until it is almost morning? I thought the food in the little house was quite excellent. After 62 years I can still picture the wonderful plum cake of which I could eat as much as I liked. But I did not stay here long. The little place did not have much to offer apart from a terribly swampy village road, and the little house seemed to be faring very well without me, too.

So I left the next morning, with a parting gift from grandmother of 30 kreutzers = 80 pfennings in my pocket. Furthermore, a young man my age was to be my free guide, and he walked with me from Pares to Markt Scheinfeld, my next destination. It was a long way - over three hours' march - and we had a nice chat along the way. When my mother first came to Memmelsdorf, his sister had been her maid. It was the same maid who had once upset my father with some silly clumsiness so much that he had called her "You imperial cow!" She took it as some kind of flattery and replied naively: "I wish I was an imperial cow!"

In the region of the Steiger Forest we came to a mountain crowned by a large, old castle and a church. It was Schwarzenberg castle, which belonged to an Austrian magnate, and in the valley below sat the town of Scheinfeld. This was a view I was familiar with since six years previously I had spent several weeks with my grandmother in Scheinfeld, when we had also hiked up to the castle.

Fig. 41 Schwarzenberg Castle, Scheinfeld.

I bid my loyal guide farewell - I forgot to pay him - and loped down the hill towards my grandmother's house. I was welcomed warmly, but the good woman had grown old and hence more impassive. I went to some lengths to explain to her that the intention of my travelling through the world was to find an apprenticeship. I was hopeful that my uncle Bernhard, who lived in the same house, would be able to help me on my quest.

My grandfather Baer Bing came to Scheinfeld from Würzburg, where his father[78] had held the influential post of Chief Rabbi, to marry the only daughter of a small business owner. Later he took over the shop and, lacking any real business sense, eked out a living running the drapery business.

My grandmother, an exceptionally good, bright and beautiful woman, managed the shop in Scheinfeld, while grandfather walked to the neighbouring Markt Bibart every day to sell the goods he had brought along in some sort of subsidiary business. I think I may have mentioned already in *Tales From A Merchant's Life* what an amazingly talented writer my grandfather was. He lived quietly as a true philosopher and left the daily chores and his little business in the care of his wife in order to study good books and write some himself, too. That was his world! It appears that my grandparents had actually been quite wealthy as that is the only explanation as to how the considerable number of children that came out of their marriage were able to receive a good education and later on, when they set up their own households, substantial financial support from their parents. There were six sons and one daughter, all married and living in good, middle-class circumstances. I never met my grandfather, he did not live to an old age.

I can see grandfather and grandmother in front of me, immortalised in an oil painting, the colours as fresh as if the pictures were only painted a year ago, and yet they are over 100 years old. They are dear, invaluable objects of mine, which ended up in my possession by some lucky coincidence.

---

78 Abraham Bing.

So I was in Scheinfeld, and as I mentioned before, my uncle Bernhard, a well-educated and well-spoken merchant, lived there too, as well as my uncle Moritz, the cloth-maker, and uncle Alexander, the hosier. Both had gone from being craftsmen to being merchants, and they managed very well. And even uncle David, the youngest of the six brothers, who had married and moved to Giebelstadt near Würzburg, was staying with my grandmother on a visit. I had not met this uncle beforehand and was quite charmed by his kindness towards me. And it was to get even better! When my uncle Bernhard declared that he could not accommodate my wish of working in his employment, adding that I was far too gifted to work as a shop assistant, and he was about to give up his little spice shop anyway, that option was ruled out. I canvassed the relatives with the result that my capital increased by one guilder, i.e. 1 mark 70 pfennings, including the travelling costs I had already incurred.

My uncle David invited me to accompany him to Giebelstadt and spend some time in his house. I gladly accepted. It was not like I was missing out on anything in the meantime, and I enjoyed the idea of going for a long hike with the prospect of guaranteed, free board at the end. So, farewell to grandmother and the relatives!

From Scheinfeld we were going to walk to Ochsenfurt and then take a stage-coach to Giebelstadt, in the middle of nowhere. My uncle had settled there as a purse-maker and married a local girl. The long walk to Ochsenfurt took more than six hours, but I enjoyed it. The uncle had much to say that was of interest to me; first about his wanderings as a young apprentice, then about the circumstances leading to his settling as a master craftsman in Giebelstadt. I was also very interested in what he told me about his family, about the hop trade, which he had started and which had led him far into France. He added that his financial situation had improved and that he was seriously considering moving to Strasbourg. I listened intently to this kind and amiable man and asked him lots of questions, and thus gained his trust and goodwill.

In Giebelstadt I had a wild time. My cousins, four boys and two pretty girls, gave me plenty of opportunity to play in the woods and the fields, in the streets and on the frozen river, and to enjoy the pleasures of a real life in winter to the fullest. I also found that my aunt, a very simple woman, took a liking to me, and nothing disturbed my free boy's life apart from the thought of what my parents might say. Two weeks had passed since my departure, and I had not sent a single note home. How was I to look for or even find an apprenticeship on these journeys criss-crossing the land? But a young man of my age at the time does not worry for long, and so I continued to live for the day. Everything comes to an end eventually, and so one day I had to say adieu to the family I had come to love. My aunt and uncle took me the nearby Würzburg in a coach. They had business to do there and knew of an opportunity for me to get a ride to Dettelbach where my uncle Leopold was a doctor. In Würzburg I received my parting gift; not in cash but in form of a pair of rubber shoes, which were to bring me little joy. The sleigh ride from Würzburg to Dettelbach, however, was wonderful. It came about because a rich wine dealer from Würzburg, who was good friends with my uncle Leopold, offered to drop me off in Dettelbach. I sat in the tight sleigh somewhat squashed between the wine dealer's extremely beautiful and graceful daughters, and I was overcome by a blissful cosiness. I only wished the ride could have continued for longer. Once we arrived in Dettelbach, I was not taken directly to my relatives as I had expected but was to stay with the wine dealer's family for supper. The hospitable home and its inhabitants had something so elegant about it, the likes of which I had never seen before, and I felt like I was living in some beautiful fairy tale. This feeling was not disturbed either when the food was served. It consisted, as my aunt later explained, of chicken ragout with mushrooms. And yet this ending of the fairy tale was not quite to my taste. How to approach this dish? It did not seem proper to hold the chicken leg with my fingers, and I was not experienced enough to tackle it with a knife and fork. I was very grateful, but hungry, when I left my noble hosts. They were the Feldheim family, and I would see them many more times when I was older.

My uncle's house now was a welcoming place. I did not know him or any member of his family personally. It was a strange household: My uncle, a high-minded and warm-hearted man whose large country practice kept him busy from morning 'till late, had patience and understanding for everything concerning his close family and the larger mishpocha. However, his devotedness to the suffering humanity was equally great. His wife, too, was good-hearted and took the upbringing of their many children off his hands. Sadly some of these children were not very able, which may well have been caused by the fact the parents were closely related. And yet the parents were so full of love that they did not seem to notice the poor, deficient faculties in their children. They considered them all kind, intellectually advanced and physically attractive. The parents smothered their offspring with equal amounts of love, and it was touching to see how they completely overlooked the many obvious weaknesses and did not regard them as a cause for worry for the future. One example: My uncle often said that his oldest daughter blossomed like a rose. Once, he said, an omnibus driver was so astonished and blinded by her beauty when he saw her that he stopped the vehicle in the middle of the road. The fact was that the ungainly young lady had not moved out of the way in time, and the omnibus had to stop to avoid hitting her.

I could tell dozens of such stories that I heard then or later on.

My aunt and uncle had wonderful things to say about each of their children, only it all sprang from their parental love, which sees nothing but the good and the lovely, even where an otherwise uncritical eye would perceive the danger of such an overestimation.

I, too, felt surrounded by this warm, overflowing and forgiving love by aunt, uncle and the children. I felt happy and cheerful in their midst. My dear uncle also took a great worry off my shoulders when I confessed to him that I had not sent a single word home during my pilgrimage or received from them. I asked him to send a letter to my parents in an attempt to lessen and apologise for my neglect, and that is what he did.

He praised my demeanour, my intelligence, my obvious maturity beyond my years etc. to the skies. A letter from home soon arrived and with it the permission that I might stay another eight days in Dettelbach.

I also made myself useful in the house by writing the annual invoices for medical treatment, with assistance from my aunt. The area around Dettelbach is densely populated, and, when the wine turns out well, the people have good incomes. Yet my uncle's invoices were less than average. The billing was particularly strange in some cases, and part payments in kind, e.g. wine, potatoes, fruit, oats, etc, had to be taken into consideration. My uncle was also the doctor for the local Franciscan friary, which had a large community in Dettelbach. When the experienced and extremely well-meaning doctor fell ill, they prayed for his recovery in the monastery.

His consideration for the feelings of others was also remarkable. When a patient was nearing their death, he would immediately go to the friars so that the patient would receive the consolations of their religion in time.

I would see my dear uncle many times in my life, right up into his old age. He was over 80 years old when I saw him at the funeral of my uncle Moritz, his second oldest brother, in Scheinfeld. Two years later I paid my last respects to the noble man himself. The hearse, which was to take his body to the distant Jewish cemetery, stood in the middle of the market square in Dettelbach. The Father Guardian from the friary made a very moving speech dedicated not only to the doctor but to his friend and counsellor, too, and afterwards he and all the other Fathers and Brothers from the friary joined the cortège. My uncle served the people of Dettelbach for over 50 years. Despite his oversized, exhausting practice he accumulated no remarkable worldly goods or riches. Yet, the gratitude and respect of the thousands who knew him as a friend and helper will remain with him beyond the grave.

I have included this episode here because I omitted to mention this exceedingly highly respected man in my book *Family and*

Friends; not due to a lack of piety of course but because I could and would not write a family chronicle. I might well have written many good and interesting things about the lives and fortunes of my relatives on both sides of the family - there were seven uncles and one aunt on my father's side and three uncles and four aunts on my mother's side; my quill, however, would have been too weak for such a task, and I also had to consider how such detailed family portrayals would be without context for my descendants.

So I have to travel back to where I left off 62 years ago to pick up the thread. My eight-day holiday in Dettelbach was nearing its end. The days were passing far too quickly, uninterrupted by any remarkable events. But, lest I forget, the rubber shoes I had received as a present turned out to be a real hindrance. My wading through the snow caused first the one, then the other sole to come off the top leather, or rather rubber. Not even Hans Sachs[79] could help! The cleverest of all the cobblers in Dettelbach tried to repair them with pitched thread: the rubber slit open. Even glue and pitch were no good, and the delicate pitch-maker, moved by my doleful face, consoled me with the assurance that I would find a more experienced colleague in Bamberg, which he knew to be my next destination, who would be able to help me.

Then came the day of my departure. Hugs and displays of affections, something which I did not know from home, made leaving even harder than it already was. Adieu, you good people.

[79] Hans Sachs (1494-1576); famous cobbler turned Nuremberg master singer.

Once I arrived in Bamberg, I was full of hope and certainty that my odyssey of finding an apprenticeship would come to a peaceful end. After all, it was a big city with much doings and dealings, and influential relatives would be able to assist me in reaching my aspired goal.

I stayed with my dear aunt Reitzenberger[80], who was loyally looking after her late sister's children. There were no unnecessary luxuries, just Puritan simplicity. No maid either; those tasks were carried out by the two adolescent daughters. These cousins were by no means pretty, quite the opposite, but they were warm-hearted and kind. Since no other room was available, I had to spend the nights on a sofa in my uncle's bedroom, which he was already sharing with his grown-up son. This alone made it necessary for me to move on soon, which reminded me of the unfortunate rubber shoes. I asked my cousins for advice - they had no comfort for me. Talking of the cobbler, however, reminded the elder sister, Emilie, that my boots needed cleaning. She asked me if she should blacken or polish (grease) them. I answered: "Emilie, you can blacken one boot and Hedwig can grease the other one, then you'll both have a memento of me."

The next day my uncle, a very simple, well-respected businessman, took me to see a Herr Eger, a merchant he was friends with. It was his wife, however, who seemed to be the controlling authority as far as I was concerned. The company dealt with draperies, retail and wholesale, and also dabbled in a small banking business. My uncle put forth my request, praised my intelligence and everything else as is customary in these situations.

---

[80] Jette Reizenberger, sister of Ignaz's mother.

He asked them to take me on as an apprentice. The merchant remained silent; his wife looked at me more closely and said abruptly that I was too small for an apprentice, I would not be able to lift the heavy cloths onto the shelves. I realised that persuasion would be useless so I replied brazenly that I was much stronger than I looked; that like Samson my long hair gave me great strength, and as long as it was not cut off I would dare to lift the merchant's wife off the floor. She answered flippantly that I should have my long curls cut off anyway, I looked like a Galician. So onwards again, leaving this Bavarian "City of the seven hills" for Gunzenhausen.

Despite the forgiving letter I received in Dettelbach I was a little afraid of what my parents would say about my tour which had failed to produce the desired outcome, and wondered how I could justify the experiences *ut mine Stromtid*[81]. Shyly I entered my parental home. The reception seemed very cool, and I was sure that no fattened calf was going to be slaughtered to celebrate the return of the lost son. After a strict questioning my father asked if I had borrowed any money, and how much. Now came the moment of my triumph. I laid the seven shining guilders that I had scrounged on the table. Everything was forgiven and forgotten!

Now I can jump ahead many years. My commercial career began. I entered a firm in Fürth as an apprentice, and where my years of wandering took me once I had finished my apprenticeship is

---

[81] *Ut mine Stromtid*, meaning "Tales from my time as a farm manager", a novel in Low German dialect by F. Reuter, published 1862-4; Reuter refers to his years on the land after his release from prison. *(source: http://www.answers.com/topic/ut-mine-stromtid.)*

described in *Tales From A Merchant's Life*. True, during these wandering years I was often tasked with representing the companies I was working for on business visits, and I could tell many stories, even interesting ones, from those days. On the other hand, this "travelling uncle's" pilgrimages have already been described so often and in so many ways that I doubt I could add anything new. The people that make up the milieu of the travelling representatives are usually cheerful, good-humoured folk who are always up for some banter or a practical joke. During my many encounters with colleagues I have often had opportunity to see for myself what self-sacrificing and loyal companionship there is between business colleagues. In no way does this preclude the rivals from engaging in a fiercely competitive battle which is fought with all the ruses, cunning and deceit at their disposal. Once the battle is lost and won, however, winners and losers will treat each other with decency and in a friendly manner, and neither party will have forfeited their swagger, which is always bigger than the next man's.

Then I became an independent merchant myself, the owner of a haberdashery wholesale business. The gold-plated company sign, which I have talked about previously, gleamed in all its beauty. I was not spared the joys and sorrows of a travelling salesman - at my own expense this time. But I do not want to talk about these travels either, nor about the favour or disfavour of the customers, nor my coachman and his purebred horses which led my ark through the land, nor of any of the other things which give a certain character to business travels. On the other hand, I shall not entirely pass over my journeys undertaken for the purposes of buying.

There is a big difference between buying and selling. The former, i.e. buying, is of a much more personal nature; it is influenced by many things which the salesman who remains tied to a certain job can hardly ever conquer. I think I may say without arrogance that my talent for buying, my nearly unfailing intuition for what the company could successfully offer its customers as well as the respect and the trust which I earned from our suppliers, had the most outstanding effect on the development of the company. The significance of this was not only the advantage of my close personal relationships with the main suppliers to our company, whether they were located in Berlin, Vienna, Dresden, Solingen, Lüdenscheid, Ruhla or anywhere else, but also the fact that I was training my companions on these travels so that they could represent me in the future should that become necessary. This precaution, however, became irrelevant later on when the company started to manufacture our own products and the annual buying trips became less important.

The first time I went to Berlin was on the occasion of a journey to Hamburg when I had the mission to dispatch my brother Berthold to America (see *Tales From A Merchant's Life*).

It was a dull winter morning when I arrived in Berlin on my return journey from Hamburg. I had the whole day free since my train to Nuremberg was not due to leave until late in the evening. Business duties I had none. Our young company would only endeavour to make connections with manufacturers in Berlin when our working capital had increased sufficiently, and furthermore, when we were able to assess which foreign products might serve to complement the industry in Nuremberg. A winter's day spent aimlessly in Berlin in those days was boring and melancholic. I was already considering taking an earlier train home when I remembered that six months earlier I had made an acquaintance from Berlin during a long summer stay in Streitberg. When I met him, Herr Teubner was a tired, sickly man with a very healthy and buoyant daughter. He was staying a in a small, uncomfortable flat and seemed to be struggling to get by. I encountered them often, which gave rise to the opportunity to get to know each other better. This in turn obliged me to introduce Emma - that was the young girl's name - to the social circle that met at the *Post* at Häffner's. Emma was extremely grateful for the distraction from the monotony of her life in Streitberg, and the old man also seemed to be glad of it. As these things go, we enjoyed each other's company, and if the young lady had no education to speak of, at least her Berlin accent helped to tide her over it. Furthermore, she was very modest and was delighted about any small gallantries, including mine. The father became increasingly worse, and the two Berliners had to depart. As was my custom, I gave Emma a parting poem which may have served this purpose on previous occasions. I asked for one as a return present. That evening, Emma pushed a note into my hands which I read back in my room. On a torn page ripped from a notebook she had scrawled in a child-like, awkward handwriting a little rhyme that I had known since my childhood:

> Think of me far, think of me near,
> Think of me often, think of me dear,
> Think of me when you breathe your last,
> And remember how I loved you in the past.

In order to reinforce the evocative rhyme she had attached a few forget-me-nots with black sewing thread. I had no occasion to thank her personally for such a warmly expressed friendship of the soul, since Emma and her father left in the early hours of the next morning.

So I decided to visit my acquaintances. I knew that their flat and shop were in Alte Jakobstrasse, and I spent rather a long time there looking for a haberdashery shop. At last I found the metre-long shop sign which displayed - like an obituary - in white letters on a black background the name Teubner and also a whole list of goods available in the little shop. I entered. Behind the desk stood a portly woman, whose good looks had an unmistakeable similarity to Emma's. The mother. I introduced myself and asked how Herr Teubner was. She called out in her Berlin dialect

Fig. 42 Petristrasse; a typical street in Berlin, 1880.

and grammar: "Oh dear, oh dear, my dear Otto died three months ago. He talked me so good of you!" I was glad to hear it. "And our little Emmeken, she won't believe her eyes when she sees her boyfriend in Berlin", etc, etc.

I first expressed my sadness at the news of Herr Teubner's passing, and then I asked where Emma was. "Oh dear", she replied, "did I forget to mention that Emmeken has a fiancé? He is foreman at Barthel's album factory, not handsome but quite good. My son-in-law to be wants to set up his own bookbinding business. Emmeken has gone with him, they are having a look at a shop in Dresdner Strasse."

Somewhat surprised by the engagement story I looked quite sheepish, but the jovial woman's manner meant that I did not feel shy for long. She urged me to come for coffee in the afternoon, she wanted to introduce me to the family, and Emmeken would not forgive me if I departed without seeing her.

I promised half-heartedly to come; yet the promise was not kept. I sent a note to say I was not going to come. Incidentally, later on I often visited Emmeken as a well-established bookbinder in her little shop in Dresdner Strasse. I always bought a notebook from her, which always cost me one mark more than anywhere else, but I am not complaining.

Not counting the above-mentioned disappointment, my first visit to Berlin did turn out to be an important one for the development of my business.

After the offered coffee afternoon in Alte Jakobstrasse had fallen through, I managed to visit a sample room of a large commission business. I was amazed by the many industrial products made in Berlin, a large number of which would be suitable for selling to our existing customers. I drew my own conclusions for the future and departed that evening quite satisfied.

Now I will turn to describe a journey I made 48 years ago, one which had a great, and I can say happy, influence on the rest of my life. I am talking about the honeymoon I undertook with my young wife in the wonderful month of May. The destination had been dictated by the young couple's financial situation. Paris, London, the Riviera were out of the question for a week-long trip. After careful consideration, Frankfurt on Main was chosen as their destination. From there, excursions to Homburg, Wiesbaden, maybe even Rüdesheim could be made without adding significantly to the expenses. The young couple had not seen any of the towns and cities in mind and were most delighted by everything they were offered on their significant trip. The wonderful days passed too quickly, and yet we were keen to return to the simple home that had been prepared for us in the meantime by loving and caring hands.

Now the daily routine demanded its rights. Apart from at lunchtime, I was at the office from early morning until late in the evening. Yet we were healthy and happy, and Goethe's words "Bitter weeks, merry parties; Work at day, guests in the evenings" also came into their own every now and then.

Alas, I want to write about my travels, and these take me back to Berlin. I wanted to turn the thoughts formed during my first, accidental visit to Berlin into actions, i.e. assess if I could, without much money but with plenty of good words, win profitable connections. My touting means consisted of 300 thalers = 900 marks. In Nuremberg I had asked my cousin Heinrich Iglauer, who spoke fluent North-German and knew Berlin very well, to recommend a good but simple hotel. He pointed me in the direction of the *Deutsche Haus*[82] in Klostergasse, where many "business people" stayed, he added. I arrived after a long journey and frozen to the bone.

My cheap hotel bore all the hallmarks that characterised Berlin at that time, such as its open sewers and third-class hackneys. The entrance hall looked no different from any ordinary house entrance, which led straight into a steep set of stairs without carpet or other covering. A porter, a cross between a concierge and doorman, led me to the first floor and then criss-crossed the corridors, to a dingy little room. Its only window overlooked the courtyard. It was filled with a musty, stale smell that reminded me of sausages, so I immediately opened the windows wide to let in the cold winter air. I proceeded to the dining room. In the long room, a large number of guests were seated at the tables. The guests were remarkable in that most of them had not taken off their round head coverings - round felt caps or black silken kippot. Seeing this in context with their long sidelocks, it dawned on me that the *Deutsche Haus* provided lodgings for the kind of noble Poles of which at the time there were many roaming through the German countryside as beggars and peddlers. Let me add this; my Poles did not appear dirty; on the contrary, many striking characters stood out from the crowd.

---

[82] Lit. "German House"

I sat down at a table and was going to order my dinner. An old man, his crown also adorned with a silken kippah, approached me and introduced himself as the owner of the inn. He also asked me if I wanted to have a kosher meal or was I planning to go out for dinner. In that case he could recommend a good restaurant in the neighbourhood. By then I knew where I stood, in other words, the whole *Deutsche Haus* really should have been called the *Jüdische Deutsche Haus*[83]. I inwardly cursed my cousin in Nuremberg for recommending this promised land of my fellow Jews. And yet, to be truthful I really ought to have thanked him for it. Apart from the delicious dinner which tasted wonderful, the nature of the hotel also proved to be rather useful for my business purposes. Once I had eaten my fill and was enjoying a cigar in the warm and comfortable bar, my host asked me what it was that I was looking to buy in Berlin. I made it very clear to him that it was none of his business and demanded to know what he was after with such a question. He looked at me in surprise and I realised that he thought me a novice, or a "greenhorn" as they say so fittingly in America, at least as far as business in Berlin was concerned. He went away and returned with a large number of letters from Berlin-based companies. I read through some of these letters and discovered the solution to the puzzle: They were offering remainders, junk and damaged goods at a cheap price. Most of the guests at the inn were focusing on this kind of trade in Berlin.

Now I understood my host, the head coverings and the sidelocks of the guests. Even the musty smell in my room. Yet I would

---

[83] Lit. "Jewish German House"

not want to be without the memory because of it, since in a way the *Deutsche Haus* was the first stage to my advancement.

Amongst the offer letters that had arrived at the *Deutsche Haus* was an offer of slightly damaged photo frames, from one of the top companies in the industry. I came, saw and bought. The company was most interested, though, in how I was going to pay for the goods. They would not agree to three months' payment terms. The agreed deal was, as they say in English, "half and half": 100 thalers cash then and the remainder in three months' time.

In this way I managed to broker compromising terms for the payment of further batches of goods I was to acquire. I exploited my feat of paying the frame manufacturers the 100 thalers in cash by always giving their name as a reference. The reputable house, however, brought a sudden halt to this gambit by sending a strongly worded letter demanding I stop my shenanigans. In years to come, I will say this now, they welcomed me as a highly respected business friend and even invited me for lunch when I came to visit the company. These beginnings were hard and humiliating, but I had done good work in Berlin. All those who had put their faith in me had nothing to regret.

It went on like this for some years. However, when I came to Berlin between Christmas and New Year, the situation had changed immensely; not just for me, but also for the capital of the German Reich herself, which had grown immensely.

The Berlin of the early 1860's with its almost provincial facilities had disappeared, or at least it had been so transformed that it was now in no way inferior to any of the other European capitals, and in many things it was even far ahead of them. And I myself no longer arrived as the "knight-errant of the order of the *Deutsche Haus*", but as the owner of a highly regarded business whose reputation and renown was growing year on year. One can say that at the time the company was regarded as an important factor in the dealings between trade and industry.

On my subsequent trips to Berlin I was almost always accompanied by a diligent colleague who acted as some form of escort. Usually it was Herr Dietz, whom my readers might remember from *Family and Friends*. He was the hero of the episode that we experienced at the forester's house at Altenhof.

Let me describe a journey as it would have occurred under the improved circumstances. On Boxing Day we would take the fast train to Berlin. My conscientious and always precautionary wife provided me and my travelling companion with all kinds of good and useful things for the long trip. There would be wonderfully delicious pieces of tongue, foie gras, wine and liqueur, in short, everything was of the best quality. At 4 o'clock in the afternoon the train pulled into the station at Hof, which was intended as our coffee stop. An hour before Leipzig, the delicacies of the picnic basket

Fig. 43 Barracks in Lichterfelde, ca. 1900.

from Nuremberg would be most thoroughly examined. (They did not have dining cars then.) After an opulent, cold supper we would take tea in Leipzig and smoke our evening cigar. Usually, a little chat with the conductor would bring about the very welcome "coincidence" of having a compartment for ourselves, and we would try to enjoy a little nap between Leipzig and Berlin. The train rattled along, interrupted by only a very few stops, through the wide Nordic plains; the characteristic pine forests of the large surrounding area of Berlin appeared like passing silhouettes. At last we saw a piece of pale red sky, which could only be the reflection of the thousands upon thousands of lamps that light up Berlin at night.

Then came Lichterfelde with its imposing barracks for the Prussian cadets, which appeared magnificent in this light, and at last the train pulled into Anhalter station. No longer was there a foul-smelling, third-class hackney half-filled with straw for me as it had been in former times; now a dashing, elegant cab drove us through the generous Wilhelmstrasse via *Unter den Linden* to the *Zentral-Hotel.* Since I had told them that I was coming, I was greeted like a little prince by the head porter, the maître d' and the page, who was holding the hand luggage, in short, I was received and accommodated with all the ceremonies that befit a guest of rank.

True, I also received a number of letters here too, but they were of a different character to the ones at the *Deutsche Haus.* The letters, polite and heartfelt, were from local top-ranking companies who were inviting me or asking for the honour of being allowed to introduce themselves to me at the hotel, and indicating large business transactions; in short, implying that here, the merchant from Nuremberg stood not only on solid ground but also that the new Berlin was keen to find and prepare a way, not only to support the company with their varied products for sale, but also for the time that would come when the company from Nuremberg would be successfully offering their own products for sale to the people of Berlin.

Visits to Berlin's major industrial enterprises were no longer conducted by trotting through the long streets of the city's business quarters on foot; instead I now rode comfortably in elegant carriages hired for the day. Unlike in the earlier years, I no longer frequented *Gratweil's Beerhalls* in Dresdner Strasse, where I would have lunch, preferably the traditional udder schnitzel with spinach, for 90 pfennigs; instead I now dined in fine restaurants. In the evenings we would go to one of the better theatres, which reminds me of the following episode:

The Meiningen Ensemble were guesting in Berlin. It was at the time when this company were making guest performances on all the main stages in Germany with great financial as well as artistic success. The Meiningers were performing *The Maid of Orleans* in some theatre (I cannot remember exactly which one it was). Herr Dietz and I went to see the show together. The general circumstances of the Meiningers' guest performances, their artistic aspirations and intentions are well known and have been acknowledged. It is not my place to comment on them; I can only say that the performance of *The Maid* was a harmonious interaction in a setting that was always stylish and as historically correct as possible. The leading parts were played by top-ranking actors, and I remember that the *Bastard* was played by Kainz, who subsequently rose to great frame, and Joan by Amanda Lindner.

I was deeply moved by the play, and I noticed that the eyes of my somewhat sensitive companion welled up occasionally, too.

Then came the scene where the coronation procession gathers outside the cathedral in Reims. It was an unforgettable picture of pomp and circumstance the likes of which no other German theatre could stage. Then suddenly, my companion burst out laughing with the effect that the members of the audience nearest to us expressed their displeasure in no uncertain terms, and I was most painfully embarrassed. There was no way to suppress this inexplicable, incomprehensible laughter. Dietz must have noticed himself the awkward situation he had thus put us both in, but he had no power to get his hysteric laughing fit under control. We started our disruptive retreat accompanied by hissing and booing from the audience, with me whispering that the man was ill, and I thanked God when we had left the theatre behind us.

I was more worried than angry about my companion's strange behaviour. I knew him too well not to think immediately that this awkward incident might be connected to some mental trauma. At last the laughing fit subsided. I asked him sincerely what I was to make of this episode. Then he explained. He, Dietz, had seen a production of *The Maid* performed by a wandering theatrical company in the Lower Bavarian village of Dingolfing. He had suddenly remembered how the coronation procession was acted out in Dingolfing. The realisation of the tremendous, inconceivable difference between that performance compared to the one by the Meiningers had caused his rudimentary laughter. Nothing in the world could have stopped it.

Another time Dietz succumbed to a similar hysteria when he was with me and he saw Cologne Cathedral for the first time. Then, it had been a crying fit.

I have travelled to Berlin many, many times, and all the trips passed in a more or less similar fashion. Several funny episodes happened on those trips. Nevertheless, I want to refrain from describing my excursions to Berlin. The trip would merely be the framework for experiences from my life as a merchant. Like a snail that carries its house, a merchant, an industrialist, drags his profession wherever he goes. If I were to describe all my journeys of a business nature then I would not only fill one book but several volumes with these memories. Maybe it would have been better if I had dedicated my weak pen to such a project; it certainly would have made a didactic book for young business people which I could have had printed and "milked" for my benefit.

So no more, or at least not much, about business, and on to the travels that had nothing to do with it! Although the working businessman can never be switched off entirely.

In 1873, i.e. two years after the Franco-Prussian war, I decided to go to Paris. I was excited to see the metropolis, especially at a time when the events of the war were still fresh in everyone's memory and Paris could therefore, potentially, have been a dangerous place for a German to be. What made matters worse was that I could only just about make myself understood in French, but I was not able to hold a conversation.

I was accompanied by my young brother-in-law Albert Ottenstein and a merchant from Nuremberg, who had run a small export business in Paris before the war. The journey went via Strasbourg where my uncle David Bing had moved to from Giebelstadt. He was the same uncle with whom I had walked from Scheinfeld to Giebelstadt as a fourteen-year old. We had not seen each other since.

We stopped at the *Maison Rouge*, and in the evening we went to see the relatives. We were welcomed with the same warmth that is inherent in all the members of this family, and sat together in friendly conversation until dinnertime. We refreshed our memories of our days in Giebelstadt, and I told my relatives the ending of my adventurous journey and also mentioned the demise of my rubber shoes soon afterwards, which caused great hilarity all round. We also talked about more serious issues, however, such as the siege of Strasbourg with all the horrors it entailed for my relatives, or the heroic resistance of the city, and my uncle warned me sternly against making careless comments in Paris, since its residents still regarded all Germans, even Alsatians, with mistrust and cold hostility. I told him calmly that I had not expected circumstances to be any different and that he could be assured of my tact and my caution. I was glad that my youthful brother-in-law also heard these warnings, and that he thus received confirmation of what I had told him before the start of our journey regarding our stay in Paris and the strict restraint it implied.

The next morning we took a tour of the sights in Strasbourg, especially the wondrous cathedral. We departed around midday. We approached the French border a little nervously, but crossing the border from the Reich to France was a quick affair. We were not even asked to show our passports; it sufficed to hand over our business cards.

Then we were crammed into French carriages, which were far behind German ones in terms of comfort and cleanliness. We rode through the romantic valleys of the Vosges mountains and drank the customary glass of champagne in Epernay, which tasted like cider to me. At about ten o'clock in the evening we happily reached the capital city of "belle France". A cabby took us to the *Pavillion Hotel,* which was under German management and had been recommended to me in Nuremberg and also in Strasbourg. The house was frequented mainly by Alsatians who were allowed to feel French and speak German there. The next morning our fellow Nuremberger took the lead. Here follows another business interlude:

We went to see his French business acquaintances, mostly small manufacturers for toys and hundreds of other articles which the French collectively call "quincaillerie". Everywhere we went, we were treated politely, sometimes even jovially, but then we did come as buyers. I also met another fellow countryman, the owner of C. F. Eckhardt, whose brothers were friends of mine and ran an important export business in Nuremberg under the same name. He was our guide when we visited another group of Paris companies, and on this occasion I again found the French amiable and willing to make entering into business relations with them as easy as possible. They laughed benignly at my attempts to talk with them in their language and about the funny sounding results those attempts produced, too. This concluded the business part of the trip.

We saw everything that forms part of the usual programme of a trip to Paris: the great collections at the Louvre, the Les Invalides, Notre Dame and Madelaine, the fabulous gardens of the Parc des Buttes Chaumont, the Bois de Boulogne, the Parc Monceau, the opera etc. Lastly, we visited the famous cemetery Père Lachaise; we rode the long journey there on the top deck of an omnibus. Next to us sat an old woman with a market basket on her lap. Once the very simple-looking woman had realised that I was speaking German with my brother-in-law, she addressed us in German with a strong French accent: "Ah, the gentlemen speak German". She said that she lived with her married daughter in Paris; she had come from Lorraine 20 years ago and could still not speak a word of French. Those words sounded so homely and familiar that I was quite touched. I squeezed her hand to confirm the connection we had as compatriots and, justified by her poor appearance, said that I could spare a few francs. She declined politely, adding that she was not lacking any essentials, and we parted like old friends.

Our stay in Paris was coming to an end. We were often recognised as Germans, but we did not encounter a single hostile face, let alone a word or an act that could have been interpreted as such. We felt quite at home and praised the politeness of the people who not so long ago had suffered a bitter defeat in the war with Germany. Had that been forgotten already? Well, one must not count one's chickens before they are hatched. Here is an example why:

On our last day we wanted to go out for a special meal and eat proper French cuisine. We were recommended the famous restaurant *Riche* near our hotel. On almost every other day we had been more than satisfied with the food and drink offered at the *Maison Nuval*, the whole arrangement was very homely. But it had nothing of the famous Paris about it. So this time we set off to the fine dining house *Riche*!

When we entered the elegant restaurant, almost every table was occupied. The head waiter noticed our hesitation caused by the situation and helpfully led us to a little side table, which happened to be free. He handed us the menu, which was written in such a flowery script that neither I nor my brother-in-law were able to decipher what it said. We wanted to have a special meal, however, and did not just want to choose something willy-nilly. The waiter grew slightly impatient with our indecision; he had certainly noticed that we were German. He took the menu and passed it to a very elegant looking gentleman who was in conversation with another man at a table next to us. I thought I understood that the waiter was looking for his mediation in order to find out what we wanted. Indeed, the distinguished gentleman turned to us and asked in perfect German "The waiter does not understand you, would you please let me know what you would like." I judged the situation perfectly; he only wanted to help the waiter out, but apart from that he wanted nothing to do with us.

Under those circumstances I did not hesitate long and ordered a chateaubriand and a bottle of red wine and thanked him very politely but tersely for his translation.

My brother-in-law did not grasp the situation as well as I did. He thought the elegant gentleman was a German with whom one could have a cosy conversation from which one could learn something interesting. He started telling him for how long we had been in Paris, how much we liked the big city, and when we were going to return home. Stony silence! The gentleman, decorated with the medal of the Légion d'Honneur, pretended that he had not heard these unsolicited comments and pointedly turned his back on us. Humiliation! My brother-in-law was very embarrassed, but I thought the lesson was well deserved.

We returned to Germany via Belgium, with the feeling that Paris was a magnificent city. But what can compare with home, with Germany?

In 1897, I attended the wedding of a relative, which was celebrated on a grand scale in an old-standing inn in Bamberg. After the festivities, the animated partaking of which had left me with an upset stomach, I immediately departed for Hamburg, accompanied by the often-mentioned Herr Dietz. From there we were going to go to Amsterdam via Cologne. I wanted to see what novelties the amazing world fair had produced. I had been looking forward to this trip, but whether it was this bout of indigestion or something else that inhibited my capacity for travel impressions; either way, I brought nothing back but the vast impression that the sea and the beach at Scheveningen had had on me. I was glad when we arrived back in Cologne late at night.

The next morning we saw the mighty cathedral right next to our hotel, and this was the moment when my companion Dietz, a Catholic zealot, was so moved that, as I mentioned previously, he broke into a crying fit.

Fig. 44 Cologne Cathedral, ca. 1900.

Later that day, the train took us along the sunny Rhine, and we agreed that our fatherland was the most blessed and most beautiful of all the countries in the world.

In my book *Family and Friends*, I had already mentioned that the *Rote Oechslein* in Nuremberg was a regular meeting place for my friends and me, and that its landlord, Herr Segitz, was widely regarded as a highly educated man. He knew how to retain his dignity despite his trade, which brought him into contact with all the different levels of society. I gladly agreed when he suggested one day that I accompany him on a trip to Switzerland. It was in May, and the plan was that I left for Constance a few days before Segitz to see if the famous *Insel Hotel* had rooms available, with a view of the lake obviously, for the two of us. Then I was to telegraph home.

So I went. Once arrived in Constance, I could not get to the *Insel Hotel* quickly enough. I asked a cabby to take me there. He gave me a funny look, which I interpreted to mean that the hotel was probably full and the cabby was concerned that it was a wasted journey. To my surprise I saw the hotel in front of me before I had even made myself comfortable in the cab. But everything was eerily quiet; the huge hotel seemed deserted. A sleepy-looking man took my luggage and I asked him if rooms with a lake view were available. This was affirmed sleepily, too. No bell sounded, no porter or garçon were to be seen. On the other hand, I had the greatest choice of rooms with a view of the lake. I could easily have had the whole enormous floor to myself, just like during my autumn trips to Streitberg.

At last the sleepy man enlightened me: The hotel did not normally open until June, at the moment he was the only guardian of the hotel, but if I chose to stay, his wife could make me an omelette. I was quite dumbfounded by this explanation and longingly looked out of the window across the vast, wonderful lake to Friedrichshafen, my soul still looking for the land of the Swabians[84]. That was where we had arranged that I should wait for Segitz if the *Insel Hotel* should be full.

I could not have borne the ghastly loneliness in a house that could accommodate more than 400 guests. With a few marks' gratuity I bought back my freedom and the sleepy man took my

---

[84] Play on words on an often-quoted phrase from Goethe's *Iphigenia in Tauris*, where the main character is looking for the "land of the Greeks".

luggage to the harbour, since I wanted to catch a boat to Friedrichshafen in a couple of hours. Earlier I had wired a telegram to Nuremberg: "*Insel Hotel* full, going to Friedrichshafen *Deutsches Haus.* Awaiting you. Reply." Then I had a quick look around Constance. This town, rich in memories, appeared delightful to me, but I wanted no more of the *Insel Hotel.*

Arrival at the *Deutsche Haus* in Friedrichshafen: It was the same hotel that in recent times has gained a certain fame by being Count Zeppelin's home for several years; real Swabian *gemütlichkeit*, and guests who do not mince their words were already customary when I visited. A telegram from my future travelling companion was waiting for me, announcing his arrival in a few days' time. So I stayed another two days on my own in this comfortable house and enjoyed my time very much. Opposite the inn, and belonging to the house, was a large barn on the lake shore which provided me with the perfect location for my favourite pastime: fishing. In Lake Constance there lives a kind of small fish (redfin perch), their numbers in the millions, and at certain times they show themselves in huge numbers right by the shore. I was lucky - it was the best time for fishing. I only had to dip my line into the water and immediately a fish would be thrashing around on the hook. Some morning or evening hour spent fishing resulted in over 100 fish caught. The hotel turned some of them into a tasty dish for me, the remainder ended up in the pots of the hotel kitchen.

I went to the Royal Gardens and found a suitable place that was as if it had been designed for some quiet reading; sometimes I would take the steamboat to the Swiss shore, preferably to

Rorschach, where the station terrace offers a magnificent view of the entire Lake Constance.

Once Segitz had arrived, we immediately continued our journey, destination Zurich where we stayed at the hotel *Baur au Lac.* Nothing special happened during our stay in Zurich, and all that I remember is that my companion praised the excellent wine at the hotel, especially with regard to its low price. He was the connoisseur, he should know. Besides, he praised the impeccable conditions in Swiss hotels generally, and given that he had been a director of a large establishment in Germany for many years, he was a competent judge. Usually taciturn and reticent, he was like a changed man. The golden freedom and the feeling of having been relieved of the burden of his profitable yet small business had brought about a complete transformation of his character.

Cheerful, up to all kinds of fun, generously tipping (he managed the funds), joking with a Swiss *maidli* in a café - I had not imagined my travelling companion to be so entertaining.

Then on to Ragaz, from there to Chur, pressing forward all the way to Via Mala. We left our luggage at the station in Ragaz. On the return journey we stepped off the train at Ragaz to collect this luggage, making sure that we left some items on our seats to reserve them for us, as it is common to do in Germany.

Meanwhile, a large group - some kind of singing club, it seemed - had boarded our car and taken all the seats, including the ones reserved by us. The items we had left on our seats had been thrown aside. We politely asked that the seats which we had had since Chur be vacated for us, pointing out that we had reserved them with our bags before we had left the carriage. What followed was a lecture delivered in Swiss-German, claiming that it was none of our business where a free Swiss took his seat, and we should not stick our noses into things that did not concern us. We took our case to the conductor, but he evidently had little interest in this affair that irked us so. He only mentioned that we were free to look for another seat in the next car. There was little else left for us to do. We gathered our luggage, and faced with their jeering looks and mocking laughter I could not stop myself from commenting that we had now experienced a good dose of that famous Swiss courtesy.

Then all hell broke loose. Clenched fists were punched threateningly into the air, abuses like "you idiot!" filled the car, and indeed the conductor had to come and cover our backs as we were retreating. The risk of a punch-up, where we would have been at the receiving end of most of the punches, had come very close. Greatly agitated, we took to our new seats. I would have given much to punish these brutal and drunken louts harshly, yet what use is it wishing for something when you have no power to make it happen? A higher power was to deliver our longed-for revenge:

The destination of our trip was Rorschach. In Sargans the line splits in two, the other way leading to Zurich. We had heard that the group had wanted to go to Zurich, and indeed in Sargans they got off the train and boarded the train to Zurich waiting at the platform. Not only were our previous seats free again now, the whole car had emptied. That was when we spotted a number of rucksacks on a bench; they had been left behind by the drunken sinners. I indicated to Segitz with the wave of a hand to help me bring them to the window, opposite the group who were now wildly gesticulating towards us. When the Zurich train started moving, we tauntingly lifted up the forgotten bags. Our friends were waving madly, beckoning us to throw the said bags out of the compartment window so that they could be sent after them as stranded goods. Obviously, we would not think of it! We tossed the rucksacks to the floor, kicked them with our feet and then pushed them deep into a dark corner where they would probably stay for a long time. It appeared that wine bottles in the rucksacks had also suffered from our boot treatment, as we could see a large puddle forming when we went to witness the burial site of Swiss courtesy before leaving the car. Judgement of God! This was the only adventure of our six-day long trip which we were able to share with our friends in Nuremberg as genuine and true.

In later years I often returned to Ragaz, and every time I passed Sargans, I could not help but think of this episode.

Since my role in the business did not allow me to take longer holidays, my excursions never lasted for more than a week, and even then it always needed a friend to make the first move.

My friend Merzbacher was an enthusiastic lover of the alpine world, even if not to the same extent as his brother, Professor Merzbacher, the famous explorer and traveller who left none of the most difficult mountain tops in the Bavarian, Tyrolean or Swiss Alps unconquered. My friend was holidaying in Jenbach (Tyrol) and asked me to join him on a week-long trip together. After many letters to and fro, I left for Jenbach and arrived there in the evening. The trip started with a good omen: the Kaiserjägers[85] were carrying out an exercise, and the jaunty hymns of the military band and the atmospheric folksongs of a very capable group of singers - belonging to a choral society from Innsbruck - rang out in turn. Furthermore, it was a wonderful moonlit night, which bathed the mountains and valleys in a magical light. My friend was usually quite monosyllabic and would only warm up when he talked about the nature of the mountains that he had climbed on his alpine tours. His thorough knowledge of German literature, past and present, also provided me with many stimulating hours, and his talks about the subject were lively and instructing for me. The morning after my arrival we went down the valley to Wörgl station. From there we took the mail coach via the Turn pass to Kitzbühel, Mittersill and Zell am See, where we wanted to spend a few days.

In the first little town of Kitzbühel, where we were going to spend the night, we were not very well received. My friend seemed to have an inkling of something, for he warned me that the guest-house would only provide shelter for pure Aryans, and he was not sure whether we would be able to work around this difficulty. The comfortable inn was managed by a portly woman who welcomed us not unkindly. She did not scrutinise us too closely either. The house was indeed quite full, so when we were told that they would be happy to offer us food and drink, only there were no beds available, we did not take offense. Frau Tiefenbrunner, that was the landlady's name, pointed us in the direction of a bookbinder who lived very near and who would be pleased to offer us his well equipped guestrooms. That was indeed the case! The question of whether we had been recog-

85 Tyrolean Mountain Riflemen

nised for what we were, and had thus been forced to lodge with Meister Paster, remained unanswered.

The next day we continued our journey deeper into these wonderful mountains, and we arrived in the beautifully-situated and much-visited Zell am See with enough time to find lodgings that would provide refuge to us tired ramblers. The guest-house *Zur Post* received us warmly. Our plan was to proceed from there, via Fusch, to Ferleitern, a terrace on the ascent to Mount Grossglockner.

Yet the next day brought terrible rain, and there was nothing else to do but to curse said rain and to sit around in the uncomfortable lounge. Then the businessman in me woke up, for opposite the guest-house there was a grocery shop, *Kastner (deceased) and Heirs*. Why should I not ask this firm to add Bing's products to their range of goods? I took my price lists with me and went touting for business. My friend was going to have some coffee, but it was hours until we were to meet again. When I returned, I held a contract worth over 400 guilders from the promptly-paying company in my hand. The newly made business friend remained a good customer for many years and once even came to visit our company in Nuremberg.

This is how in some cases business and leisure can come together quite harmoniously, provided, of course, one has a Bing price list on hand and a good understanding for what to offer ones' customers.

The next day was another dull and rainy one. My companion, who knew the area well, said that there was nothing else to do but to go on a little tour which we had not originally planned to go on. So back to Mittersill we went on the omnibus, from where we had to look for a way to get to Krimml in order to see the most important waterfall in the high Alps. As luck would have it, the innkeeper from Neukirchen, which is exactly half-way between Mittersill and Krimml, happened to be in Mittersill when we arrived, and he offered to take us on to Neukirchen for just a small charge. His means of transport was a small cart normally used for pigs.

We left in the pouring rain and reached Neukirchen three to four hours later, wet, tired and hungry. We found lodgings in a small wooden house where the rain hitting the roof made an incredible noise. At first I thought the waterfall from Krimml had something to do with it as well. After a very simple but tasty dinner we asked our landlord if he had something to read for us, a newspaper or similar. He replied in the negative, but having given it some thought he mentioned that the vicar of Neukirchen had died recently and that he had acquired some books from his estate which he wanted to show us. And so he lugged over three massive tomes. It was a strange, and in its way great opus, which had been started around 50 years ago and had now been left unfinished due to the vicar's death. The albums included thousands of pictures, collected from all over the world, cut out of fashion journals, satirical magazines, fairytale books, some holy, some profane, and every picture had been annotated with a caption in beautiful, clear handwriting. One clipping, for example, showed an elegant young lady in a low-cut dress, and the caption read: "See here the image of a worldling, it will find its place in hell, where the path of vanity will always lead to". Or of a train: "There they go, the defiant ones. The pious pilgrim's rod has rotted, and those who charge at God's fortress shall rot, too!" I had copied several of such comments from the books, but they have gone missing over the years. The tomes went under the heading *The Pyramid in the Wilderness*, which was a very apt title for the vicar's gigantic opus and the oppressive isolation of his parish.

Fig. 45 Krimml Waterfalls, Austria. © Manuel Heinrich Emha.

The landlord would have let me have the tomes for a small sum, but I was worried about the burden of carrying them with me, but I have often and deeply regretted not taking *The Pyramid in the Wilderness* back with me to Nuremberg.

The next day, with good weather, the landlord took us to Krimml in his rural vehicle. One hour before our arrival in Krimml we started to hear a dull roar, which increased in intensity the closer we approached our destination, and which at last reached its crescendo: an immense thundering boom. It was the waterfall, where the wild Ache, a forceful mountain stream, plunges, in three stages, down a 300m drop into the valley below. The spray of the mass of water gushing down, shimmering in all the colours of the rainbow, was a magnificent sight. We climbed up the mountain along a specially created path to the place where the Ache flows over the top and stopped to take in the awe-inspiring views of the immense torrent on our way up and down.

When we arrived back in the valley, still deeply moved by the immensity of what we had just witnessed, we had to realise that the sublime and the bizarre are not necessarily miles apart. We were looking at the back of the simple but quite large hotel where we saw, lined up neatly in a row on a balcony, no fewer than 18 of those porcelain bowls that are normally kept discreetly hidden in bedside tables.

Back in Zell, we were at last setting off on our excursion to Ferleiten. We walked through the long, romantic Fusch valley and spent the night in a kind of hotel, which in terms of comfort and especially its excellent food towered high above anything else that we had encountered on this trip. I even found it to be so comfortable that I chose to abandon the idea of going to Ferleiten, a journey that was going to be quite difficult anyway, and let my friend go by himself. The next day he returned, excited by all the things that he had seen. I, on the other hand, could tell him how very much I had enjoyed the magnificent walks along the river Fusch, and how the food and service at the hotel had been nothing less than magnificent either.

Our tour was nearing its end. We took the mail coach via Lofer to Reichenhall, all the way through wonderful mountains; it took us a whole day. From Reichenhall we went straight home to Nuremberg without stopping.

A lot of work was waiting for me, but the pure air of the mountains had awakened new energies in me, and the very low expense of the trip was easily made up for by the order from Kastner's heirs' grocery shop in Zell.

A year had passed, and I chose a good companion to help me spend another week in the mountains, this time walking in the Salzburg Alps. I had business to do in Vienna, and my travelling companion was to meet me in Salzburg on the way back. It was a very strangely turned out, young and unmarried merchant who wanted to join me for the trip. He was a slim, elegant character with wonderfully pure features, black curly hair, a dreamy expression, almost an ideal figure, and if I had to make a comparison to someone it would be that he bore an uncanny resemblance to the late, unhappy King Ludwig II. In addition, he had a rather select dress sense. He usually wore a black, corded coat, and in my opinion the young man looked like a young, noble Pole, like they are sometimes described in novels. Furthermore, he had a genteel, confident demeanour which he had perfected during a long sojourn in Paris; in short, he was an interesting person who, without intending to do so, attracted attention to himself wherever he went.

And yet there was something about him that worried me sometimes. He often showed an abstraction, or even absentmindedness, to the extent that he completely lacked what is commonly referred to as reliability.

When I arrived in Salzburg on a cold day, Franken - I will call him that - had not yet arrived at the hotel, even though the arrangement could not have been any clearer or more binding.

Instead, a letter arrived, which began - I remember it exactly - something like this: "Shall I travel? My conscience says 'yes'! My teeth are chattering, 'no'!" It was his way of saying that the chilly weather was making him reconsider his travel plans. The fact that we had an engagement, that we had made plans together, that I was waiting for him in Salzburg - all that meant nothing to him. I telegraphed him: "Say yes or no, immediately!" He replied that he would arrive in Salzburg the next day. I went to meet him at the station. When he stepped off the train, he was carrying a small suitcase that would hardly hold even the most essential items for a week-long trip in one hand and a red folder in the other. It was the weekly newspaper published by his friend Rochefort in Paris, from which he wanted to read me certain passages on the way to the hotel. I did not let it come to that but instead asked him how he was going to manage with such an unsecured suitcase, and such a tiny one at that. His striking corduroy coat was also totally unsuitable, in its place he was lacking a decent winter coat to keep him warm and dry in case the weather changed, which is known to happen quite suddenly in the mountains. He had no answers to that. I was very upset, and things were not made better by the fact that my young friend looked like a Polish Prince or like an affected actor. Anyway, my lecture did not make an impact on him, and the facts could not be changed.

At the hotel he caused further annoyance. I had booked a room for my companion which he did not like. He asked the maître d' how much it cost and thought it was too much. Like a proud Pole, however, he said nothing but complained - completely unfoundedly, of course - that the smells coming from the kitchen were finding their way into this room. He said that he would prefer a small, cheap room on the fourth floor, the view over Salzburg would no doubt be wonderful from there.

When we entered the busy dining room, he refused to sit at the table d'hôte, explaining that a simple dish would suffice him. I told Franken curtly that that was not acceptable; I had already reserved the seats, and today he was to be my guest. He accepted gladly, and he thought the food was exquisite.

The reader must not assume that my companion had been tactless or selfish in this. He was neither one nor the other. It was simply that he had a certain naïve misunderstanding of the real world. The world and its beliefs meant nothing to him, not even what people thought or talked about him. He lived as he thought best, and accepted all other opinions too.

At the table there were also many travelling women, and some real ladies of a very elegant appearance among them. Many beautiful eyes were focusing on my friend; he did not even notice. What I noticed, however, was painful: I remained completely unnoticed.

We bid farewell to Salzburg and continued our journey to Gmunden, an elegant town frequented predominantly by rich Viennese families.

On the lake promenade, my friend again attracted many probing looks, and he did again on the boat that carried us across the lake to Ischl, where we arrived at midday. All the hotels were full. One hotel offered us two small rooms in the attic, and even in those tiny lodgings we could only stay for one night. They had already been reserved in advance by someone else. I was quite put off by all this and was about to suggest that we leave when I realised that my companion had gone missing. After lunch I had wanted to rest a while in my room, while Franken had decided to take a look around town. He had wanted to be back for coffee. Hour after hour passed. I was not worried, since I knew his dreamy, erratic manner, but the whole business made me angry. I had to stay in the hotel since there was the risk that if he did not find me there he would do something that would split us up entirely. Late in the evening, when I was about to retire to my room for the night, he came back to the hotel. I greeted him less than coolly and was about to declare that from now on we had better go separate ways when he started telling me how he had been approached by an elegant, pretty lady on the promenade. The lady had invited him back to her villa for tea. He had gone to her very elegant house, where he also accepted an invitation for dinner. She, in other words the lady, and he had sat in her garden for a long time and talked almost exclusively about Paris, which the elegant lady knew very well. He did not know her name and had not been asked his.

There was no doubt that this romantic episode had happened exactly as Franken had told it. Lies were alien to this "pure fool"[86], and I could conceive of this adventure quite well. At the

86 The lead character in Richard Wagner's opera *Parsifal.*

time, Ischl was teeming with real ladies and those of the demi-monde; it looked as if an enterprising woman had taken a shine to the beautiful young man and was sufficiently free from prejudice not to take exception to spending some time with him.

The next morning he wanted to show me the mysterious villa, yet I declined. From Ischl we took the famous trip to Hallstadt and its lake. Before we went, we negotiated with the concierge that he should reserve a room for us as we would be back in the evening. I gave him a good tip, and so it was possible for him to hold an acceptable chamber with two beds for us. I was not very comfortable with the idea of "two beds", but needs must.

When we arrived in Hallstadt from across the lake in glorious weather - it was Sunday - the whole lakeshore was busy with big and small boats and barges, with and without sails. A wonderfully tempting sight! I have always enjoyed boats. I had acquired a remarkable skill in rowing and steering on the river Altmühl in Gunzenhausen and on the Dutzend pond in Nuremberg. Given such an opportunity, it was only natural that I should want to offer my companion a taste of my skills. He himself knew nothing of rowing. So we hired a light rowing boat, I told Franken what to do, and, with more emphasis, what not to do. These trips are not dangerous, but nevertheless one has to be extremely cautious.

Off we went, rowing to our hearts' content, always keeping the boat in shallow waters near the shore. When we had had enough we went ashore and looked around the very old, highly interesting little town with the aim of visiting the massive waterfall, which hurtles from Dachstein towards the lake. A good-looking young lad of around 18 years was our guide.

In my usual manner I asked the boy about his trade, what he had seen of the world etc. He was a logger, and from Monday to Saturday he worked in the high forest felling trees. He slept in a wooden hut with his fellow workers, was as fit as a fiddle, and had no worries that plagued his innocent and cheerful disposition. When I asked him what he had seen of the world, he replied that he had never left Hallstadt; even Ischl, which was only a few hours away, he knew only from hearsay. When I asked him if he was not interested in going out to see the world, and why he was living in such a confined existence, the lad replied that he could not care less about the world, he knew and loved only the forest, it was all very merry there.

Fig. 46 Lake Hallstatt, 1899.

In the meantime, the little town of Hallstadt has achieved a certain fame for the recently discovered, great prehistoric burial sites. Hundreds of these prehistoric burial mounds have been excavated and innumerable finds have been unearthed. They are predominantly tools and pieces of jewellery made of bronze, in multiple forms and types. The assumption in scientific circles is that these sites were created about 500 years BC. The over-abundant finds brought to light in Hallstadt now represent the most important material for comparison with all other finds from any other country.

We crossed the lake in order to catch a coach that would leave for Ischl from the pier. We wanted to visit the well-renowned theatre there in the evening. When we arrived, Herr Franken noticed that he had forgotten his binoculars as well as some other items in Hallstadt. I could not stop him from taking the steamboat back to Hallstadt, but he assured me that he would return in time for the theatre.

My travelling companion, who had already caused me so much anxiety, did not turn up; I went to the theatre by myself. Even if I was not seriously concerned about my absent friend, thinking about what he might be up to did have an impact on my enjoyment of the delightful Viennese operetta. I told myself that if he had arrived in Ischl, he would have come to the theatre, even if it was late.

When I arrived at the hotel at 11 o'clock in the evening, Franken was not there, nor had he sent a message. I went to bed, having informed the porter about my missing companion and his potential return at a late hour. Around 3 o'clock in the morning I woke up. Bright moonshine was filling the room - the other bed was empty. I made my decision: The conditions of this trip were unbearable, I had to take flight. Early the next morning I secured a seat in the mail coach to Berchtesgaden. I left a letter in the hotel telling my former travelling companion briefly that I was going to spend three days in Berchtesgaden and it was up to him if he wanted to follow me there or not. He did not come, nor did he send a message. Upon my arrival in Nuremberg I heard that Franken had returned. I would have preferred not to see him, but it could not be avoided. He approached me quite unself-consciously, began to talk about all kinds of things, and it was as if our joint trip had completely escaped his memory. When I asked him why he did not return to Ischl from Hallstadt - as agreed - or why he did not at least send a message to Berchtes-gaden, he could not really give me an answer. He stammered something about an adventure in Hallstadt, not unlike the episode with the lady in Ischl. I sensed that a dark fate was lying in store for the young man who stood before me in all the beauty of his youth. And so it was. A year later this radical free spirit, a friend of Rochefort's, had gone mad and subsequently been locked up in a lunatic asylum. When he died at an early age it came as a relief from his incurable mental derangement.

The fact that my travel recollections mostly refer to short trips, usually of no more than a week's duration, is explained by the circumstances under which I had to carry out my business activities in the early years. Just as my wife would not leave our band of children for even a day, I found it difficult to entrust another skipper with the helm of my ship for several weeks. My partner, my brother Adolf, spent nearly nine months a year travelling on business for the company. Sure, I had trained up diligent colleagues, but my sense of responsibility would not allow me to be absent from the business for more than a week.

The following account describes another week-long excursion. This time my usual travelling companion Dietz and I wanted to visit the Royal Bavarian castles, which had been opened to the public after the tragic death of King Ludwig II.

My dear friend Böck had prepared for this expedition a - what he surely considered - pleasant surprise. Dietz and I were standing on the platform, waiting for the fast train that was to take us to Munich, when our friend Böck appeared, accompanied by two pillars of our social club - Herr Seibert, the skilful singer, and "brother-in-law" Gugler, who were going to join us on our trip. Both men have been introduced to my willing readers in *Family and Friends*. Böck was beaming with joy over the successful surprise. Obviously I welcomed the gentlemen as companions for the promising tour, yet I had the feeling that the restful holiday I had imagined had all of a sudden become more complicated. I do not want to give away what happened. We were only half way to Munich when opinions divided over the hotel where we were going to stay and the manner in which the evening was to be spent. My suggestion of staying in a guest-house which I knew to be solid and not too expensive was not well-received. Both men could not doubt my unbiased recommendation, but they had been told in Nuremberg that the only place suitable for a short stay was *Hotel Grünwald* located near the station. I acquiesced; after all, it was only for one night. The hotel was very busy and my companions did their utmost to turn the maître d' against us so that he treated us in a rather offhanded way. They clumsily asked for the price, thought it too high, wanted to know if there were any cheaper rooms available, in short they did not miss anything that would have the concierge and the room waiter know for certain that they were dealing with mean-spirited travellers. I let them do it and kept thinking: "It's only for one night!" I took the maître d' to one side and asked him politely to assign the best possible rooms to me and Herr Dietz and emphasised that the price was irrelevant. He replied that everything would be in order when we came back from our evening outing.

The discussion of how and where we should spend the evening began already in the foyer of the hotel. I pointed out that we could answer this important question during a short walk through the town. I was concerned about an argument in front of the staff. We finally agreed that we would visit the Hofbräuhaus, where the democratic company and excellent beer was known to further enhance the *gemütlichkeit,* the conviviality.

That was indeed the case. Not so much for Dietz and me, who took our leave at 11 o'clock, but certainly for our friends, who had been so lovingly entrusted into my care by my old pal Böck at our departure from Nuremberg. The next morning I heard that the gentlemen had not returned home until around 3 o'clock and that they had to be urged to be quiet and not to disturb the other, sleeping guests. Oh the glamour of travel! I myself was about to face a very unsettled night. The well-meaning porter had arranged for a bed to be put in a large room which was intended as an extension to the adjoining dining hall. It goes without saying that such a room was everything but cosy. But what could I do? I thought woefully about the warm reception at the inn where I normally stayed, and the eagerness of the staff to arrange everything according to my wishes. And here - this cold, enormous room with six doors! And it was going to get worse! After I had been in bed for a little while I thought that gas was escaping from somewhere in my room. I could detect a penetrating odour, just like gas. I got out of bed in order to at least open a window. Yet that was not possible since I could not open the external shutters, which were locked - it was a ground floor room. Of the six doors, I could only open the one that lead to the dining hall. What to do? Everything was dark. I did not dare turn on a light because of the risk of explosion; the simplest thing would have been to pull the bell, but - maybe because I was too agitated - I could not find one in the room. I gathered my clothes and got dressed in the pitch-dark dining hall before looking for the night porter. Then the lights came on. A waiter who evidently still had some work to do in the dining room, was my saviour. I quickly told him what I thought was putting my young life in peril, but he reassured me. He explained that the gas-like smell came from the many stuffed birds which adorned the room. In order to protect their bodies from decay, they are soaked in a solution which emits this particular odour. He assured me that I could go back to sleep safely. I gave the waiter a good tip for his satisfying answer and asked him to wake me up at 7 o'clock in the morning.

Our train to Herrenchiemsee[87], our next destination, was due to leave at half past nine. The next morning, when I was having breakfast with Dietz, who had, as usual, arrived on time, our travelling companions came down the stairs looking very bleary-

[87] An island (Herren-insel - "gentlemen's island") in the Chiemsee, a large lake in Bavaria, also known as the "Bavarian Sea".

eyed. They did not want to take their breakfast at the hotel but in a coffeehouse. I quietly pointed out that that was not usually done, yet they stuck to their plan because firstly, one did not have to care about what the hotel thought; secondly, because a morning walk would do them good; and thirdly, because a breakfast in a coffeehouse was much cheaper than at the hotel. I could not argue with that.

I urged the gentlemen that they be at the station no later than 9 o'clock since the train to Herrenchiemsee is known to be crowded, and it was advisable to find a seat as early as possible. They promised they would and then agreed with the concierge that he would ensure their hand luggage was sent to the station in time. They abstained from the custom of tipping the concierge and the room waiter.

Dietz and I arrived on time, and our luggage was also delivered promptly. No sight of our companions. At last, ten minutes before departure, they came running. Nonetheless, we were unable to take the train we had envisaged. The porter had, with or without bad intentions - who knows? - omitted to send the luggage of the frugal travellers, and the knowing valet did not show the tip-less gentlemen any understanding either. The best train was missed; the next would not leave for another three hours.

There followed a thundering tirade against the slovenly guesthouse; the two men insisted that I come with them to give the "lazy rabble" a piece of their mind. I rejected that firmly and said instead: "Dear gentlemen and friends! You rejected the hotel I suggested on the journey here yesterday, despite my recommendation. How could I now vilify the one that yesterday you praised so highly? You alone are to blame for what you are complaining about. I know you as honourable citizens who stand their ground, but about travelling - excuse the harsh words - you know nothing. You don't know the malice that is borne by hotel staff towards guests who don't leave tips. But even lodging a complaint with the head waiter, or even with the hotel owner, would be a fruitless endeavour. The head waiter, rightly or not, demands his obolus, too, and the fact that you even avoided breakfast at the hotel against my advice moves you into the category of the ever-wronged traveller, because you don't respect certain, if unwritten rules of the hotel business. Leave these remarks unanswered, you cannot teach me better or different. Make sure that your luggage is at the station on time for the next train, and I will ask for the honour of your company for a hearty lunch at twelve o'clock." The restaurant I had chosen was a well-known wine tavern in Burgstrasse.

They accepted my invitation most amiably, and the thunder of their anger rolled off into the distance. We had a very enjoyable lunch together. The food and drink were excellent and the atmosphere most congenial. This encouraged me to go ahead with a diplomatic plot which I had already hatched that morning. This course of action seemed vital to me lest the little holiday be spoiled for me. Yet I had to proceed with caution! I did not want to hurt the valiant friends' feelings. So I began:

"We are sitting here as friends; let us raise our glasses of this noble grape juice and drink a toast to our friends in Nuremberg. Three cheers for friends! But we shall be honest with each other, the first condition of a true friendship. While you gentlemen both have been, and are still, highly respected members of our old, social club in Nuremberg, a trip undertaken in each other's company brings to light certain issues which can jeopardise the harmony between otherwise gallant men. One can and must not patronise another. Yet what can be done if one party does not want to give up their usual habits and opinions in favour of the opinions of another? Differences in opinions on otherwise minor matters are accentuated on the road; one is no longer on home soil where everything takes place according to a familiar routine. Herr Dietz and I have travelled the world far and wide; we have gained our experiences and know what to do and what not to do when travelling. You, my friends Gugler and Seibert, have not travelled beyond the city gates of Nuremberg in years; you are still lacking the understanding of many inherently small matters, but matters which determine whether a trip turns out to be an ordeal or a delightful pleasure.

I can and will not talk you into changing your view, but I am afraid that if we go on as travelling companions we will run into differences which will be equally uncomfortable for both parties. I therefore suggest that we proceed as planned with our excursion to Herrenchiemsee and have a lovely day out. In order to prove my loyalty to you I had given up my original plan of going to Reichenhall and was going to follow you to Salzburg. Now I think it will be better if we part ways in Chiemsee so that each of us can continue with their preferred programme. We could then meet again in Berchtesgaden where Herr Dietz and I will spend several days after our visit to Reichenhall."

My calm speech was received with full appreciation. I ordered some very good cigars, which served as a substitute for a peace pipe. Having visited the Royal Palace in Chiemsee, we went our separate ways in a merry mood and on the best of terms.

It is rare that two people will find each other who, irrespective of how close they might be as friends, will get on well on a joint journey. The reasons behind this are so obvious that I do not need to go into much detail in this regard. It makes a big difference whether one spends a few social hours with a friend or if one spends whole days together.

Due to the disappointments I had suffered on many a journey where I was tied to some companion, I decided to embark on my next excursion alone. I had often heard of a particularly delightful tour which led into the heart of the Bavarian High Alps, to Garmisch, and from then on to Innsbruck, the capital of Tyrol.

It was May, and it was enticing me to travel. Well-equipped, I bid my farewells to my wife and children. Off I went on my ride to the old, romantic country!

My first stop after Munich was Weilheim. I wanted to overnight there and reserve a carriage to take me on the beautiful journey to and the through the High Alps. I arrived in Weilheim in the evening. The walls of the High Alps stood menacingly before me like towering heavy, massive, black clouds.

A local cabby who was waiting at the station with a good-looking coach immediately saw that something was bothering me that was somehow connected to his vehicle. He asked me if I would like to take a trip into the mountains, maybe to Tyrol via Garmisch, up to Innsbruck etc. He seemed to be a straight, reliable man. I asked him in a roundabout way how much such a trip would cost.

He named a price which I considered fair, but I was not in the mood to commit myself to a binding agreement. I told him that I would let him now later that same evening since I was going to spend the night in Weilheim. What was I to do? I felt so lonely and abandoned. Over there was the menacing, black mass of mountains, through which I was supposed to make the long journey all on my own. Suddenly, in the midst of my doubts, there arose a vision in front of my mind's eye of my beloved Streitberg in all its spring glory. Furthermore, I could see as clear as day the deep meaning and truth of the words that Goethe has Mephistopheles say in *Faust*: "The worst society thou find'st will show thee, Thou art a man among the rest." Back to Munich! The next day I arrived in Nuremberg and greeted my wife, to whom I did not need to explain much. She understood my flight from solitude, and she knew where I would find relief.

That same evening I found myself in Streitberg, looking out from my usual, familiar window at my beloved valley, at the familiar heights, and I felt happy and contented.

The best holidays are always the ones that take parents and their children out into the beautiful, open countryside. I, too, was granted that pleasure. Those trips often took us to Neumarkt, but mainly we went to Streitberg or Muggendorf. As our four daughters and two sons grew older, the children's desire to discover new places on our holidays grew stronger. I was not opposed to their wish, but the question was, where to go instead? With my daughters Frieda and Anna I went out into the world to discover new lands. As our base we chose the inn *Zum Schwan*, which I knew as a comfortable and well managed guesthouse, in Würzburg, and from there we were going to go on expeditions to find a suitable holiday home. I had always been fond of Würzburg with its formidable location, its churches and old streets, its exceptionally beautiful palace and its friendly, sociable population. This was in addition to the excellent food at the hotel, good, comfortable rooms and a large terrace with a view over the Main river and the imposing Fortress Marienberg on the opposite bank. What a wonderful place to have a freshly brewed coffee with my much-loved breakfast cigar!

We chose three consecutive days for our expeditions. In the evenings we wanted to return to our dear and much-appreciated *Schwan.*

On our first trip we headed to Kissingen[88], where my daughters had not been before. We stopped for lunch in the *Wittelsbacher Hof*, a simple but good restaurant which was usually patronised by tourists and unmarried civil servants who were in service in Kissingen. Lunch was already being served when we arrived, and we were seated and served at a side table. The group at the main table were involved in a lively discussion about a matter which - after listening carefully - I recognised as the "Jewish question". At the head of the table, like a Praeses, sat a very distinguished gentleman with a snow-white beard who did not seem to care about the debate. The main roisterer was a scrawny, canny-looking Saxon who tried to establish in a loud voice that the fact that there were so many Jews amongst the spa guests in Kissingen implied that soon no decent man would be able to visit this spa town. The admission of Jews should be disallowed or at least be made very difficult; no decent hotel should be accepting

[88] A popular spa town in Bavaria, renamed Bad ("spa") Kissingen by King Ludwig II of Bavaria in 1883.

Fig. 47 Fortress Marienberg, Würzburg.

them as guests, he asserted. Then he turned to the gentleman at the head of the table and asked: "What does the Geheimrat think of this matter?" The questioned man looked the Saxon in the eye and replied in a tone that could not have been more contemptuous: "I don't think anything of it; I find this antisemitic company too filthy!"

Then another gentleman rose from the table and said to the surprised and very embarrassed Saxon: "Just so you know it, now and for all the future, I share the views of the Herr Geheimrat." He left, soon to be followed by the plain, Saxon Jew-hater. The unprejudiced men were, as I later found out, a world-renowned professor from the university of Würzburg and a high-level civil servant in Kissingen.

After this, which was for us a very delectable interlude, my daughters and I visited the beautiful sights of this spa town, which I had always held in high regard and given the nickname "little jewellery box". We walked along the stunning, shady path that leads through delightful meadows to the *Saline* palace and looked at all the other sights. In the evening we returned to Würzburg highly satisfied. Nonetheless, it was perfectly clear to me that, despite its many attractions, Kissingen was an unsuitable destination for a holiday with the whole family. Especially from mid-July, i.e. during the holiday period, the town is overcrowded with spa guests, it is impossible to find a quiet place, and most importantly, during the peak of summer the air there is particularly humid and oppressive.

In contrast, I had very fond memories of the little town of Mergentheim in Württemberg. I used to go there quite regularly on my business travels, and I remembered especially the hotel *Zum Hirschen* as a plain, solid guesthouse. I remember for example one little episode that happened during one of my earlier visits to Mergentheim. The first time I visited the little town on business, I was seated next to an elderly, portly man for lunch. He immediately started a conversation with me, asked what I did for a living, what I was selling etc. The way he was asking these questions made it clear that he was an educated man, and of course I answered all questions politely. The soup was brought in and the elderly gentleman was served first. Later, when the meat was served up, I could not believe my ears when the waiter, serving him first again, addressed the man as "Your Royal Highness". And there was I, sitting right next to His Royal Highness, favoured even more by his conversation with me, which he continued, too, during the course of the meal. How was I to square the simple guest table which comprised of travelling salesmen and local, low-level civil servants with the presence of His Royal Highness? When the lunch was over, several Mergentheim citizens arrived for coffee. They sat down at the table without any ceremony, greeted His Royal Highness with a little bow, who in turn immediately started to chat affably with them.

One part of this conversation, which - judging by the subject matter - was with a wine merchant, made the whole affair even more peculiar. Wine merchants are not known for wanting to avoid a business deal, even less so one that involves a member of the royal family, and yet it seemed that this was the case here. The Prince, and given the formal address he could hardly be less than that, asked the merchant why he had not yet delivered the order he had placed months ago. He said he had not a single bottle of that wholesome and very drinkable *Leidesheimer* left in the house. "Well, Your Royal Highness", replied the vintner with the same clever smile that I had seen with the other guests, "we had a poor harvest this year. I need to keep back a few reserves. Maybe I can be of service to His Royal Highness in the future again."

The Prince took this obvious excuse calmly, bowed to me, shook hands with the others and left. As I found out later, the man was Prince Paul von Württemberg, who had spent all of his sizable fortune on extensive travels and a lavish life-style at Court and who now lived in some kind of exile, far from the official residence, in the royal palace at Mergentheim. His servant was an old spinster and his courtly banquet was a very modest lunch and dinner at the *Hirsch*, paid for monthly by the Court. The tradesmen, including the inn's landlord, were strictly forbidden to lend the Prince any money. Whoever disregarded the ban would be left standing, which did not trouble the Prince too much.

After this digression let me return to our trip to Mergentheim! Apart from the inn *Zum Hirschen* I also remembered the very beautiful location of this little town and its healing spring with its excellent reputation. It is to this spring that Mergentheim owes the building of an extensive bath house in the last century. Would we not find a quiet, pretty place for our holidays here?

I had already written to the local spa doctor who had sent me a printed leaflet detailing the illnesses with which the spa could help. Strangely, he left my question as to whether one could overnight at the bath house unanswered[89]. Upon our arrival in Mergentheim we went straight to the baths. A long corridor stretched all the way through the fairly long building from one end to the other. There were bathing cells to the left and to the right, complete with wooden tubs and furnished, or rather cluttered, with old junk. Some of the cells contained potatoes or coals, some household goods, and the whole place looked so miserable, dejected and disorderly as if the intention was to frighten off any potential guests. At the entrance to the bath house we found a door with a sign saying "Dr. N." So in we went to at least find out the meaning behind this complete and utter mess in the bath house and its evident decay.

We found a totally shrivelled, ancient-looking couple in tatty clothing - Herr Doctor and his wife. Our visit did not seem

---

[89] In Germany, bath houses traditionally included hotel rooms to allow for easy access to the baths.

welcome; neither the doctor or his wife changed their posture when I introduced myself as the Kommerzienrat from Nuremberg who had asked for a prospectus. The doctor explained that one could not overnight at the baths. The relevant rooms were no longer furnished; one had to find accommodation in the town. Of the bath cells, only three were in use before the beginning of July, and even that was too much given that apart from the citizens of Mergentheim, who could use the baths virtually for free, only two or three guests from out of town had used the baths last year.

He, the doctor, had not paid rent in years, and the council had not only waived the rent but even paid him a small sum for the administration. Once their finances improved, the council would modernise the baths and run them itself. And that was the end of the audience.

My daughters turned up their noses at what they had seen and heard, but I comforted them with the promise of the inn *Zum Hirschen*, where we would be received magnificently and whose cuisine alone would be worth the journey.

I had forgotten to account for the fact that it had been 25 years since I had had the pleasure of sharing an excellent meal with His Royal Highness. When we entered the dining room, all the tables were taken, the room overcrowded. Just like at the bath house, everything had an air of neglect about it, no trace was left of what it had once been.

Some agricultural convention was holding a meeting in Mergentheim, which explained the current overcrowding. With some difficulty we found a table, but our desire to eat was overlooked by the waitress as well as by the landlord and landlady. At last, when some of the guests had left, I managed to stop the landlord. I told him who I was, explained the memories I had of his establishment and asked him to please bring us some food and drink at last. The landlord grew palpably more polite, brought us some roast pork or similar, not bad, but not good either, and then led us to the first floor to show us the rooms. Everything could still have turned for the better, yet it was not meant to be. Torn bedside rugs, stained and greasy tablecloths, grey floors, dubious bed linen etc. painted a wretched picture compared to how I had described the hotel. I did not beat about the bush when I explained how badly I was disappointed by the baths and the hotel and how, given these circumstances, I preferred to leave the beautiful town of Mergentheim that same day. The landlord looked crestfallen. I almost felt sorry for him, yet the *Schwan* was calling us up the Tauber river back to Würzburg.

Before we left we sent a telegram to Nuremberg:

> Mergentheim - the end of time!
> Here we could never stay,
> Muggendorf, we're on our way!

The destination of our third excursion was Bad Brückenau, about which I had heard many good things. The journey there was pleasant too. First we went to Gmünden station, prettily located in the Main valley, surrounded by the picturesque heights of the Spessart mountains and overlooked by the old castle ruins from a wooded height. Then, onwards through the lovely meads of the Sinn river to Jossa, and from there to the royal baths of Brückenau. We were in raptures at the view from the station, positioned high on a hill, over the town which itself was situated in a delightful meadow with the Sinn river flowing through. Old King Ludwig of Bavaria loved staying in Brückenau. The fresh air from the Rhön mountains, the endless mountain forests lining the valley, and the little manor houses, built in the style of the Trianon palaces[90], which served as residences for the King and his entourage - including the King's mistress Lola Montez - made the whole place appear worthy of a noble royal residence. The King did much for Brückenau. When a disease-riddled harvest caused a famine in these rough Rhön mountains, the King ordered the building of a *kursaal*[91] which looks like a Greek temple with its mighty columns, and which cost, according to the present files, more than seven million guilders = 12 million marks. The baths had not yet opened when we visited, but the manager had already arrived in Brückenau. He received us very kindly, and on his suggestion we rented a sufficiently large flat in the Langbau, a former *maison de plaisance* of the archbishop of Würzburg. The main attraction of the flat was an enormous stone balcony, adorned with the bishop's coat of arms, on which the whole family could be seated very comfortably. We liked everything well enough, including the food we ate at a solid guesthouse whose plush bedrooms far exceeded our expectations based on the simple exterior of the house.

In a cheerful mood we continued our journey to Würzburg, and from there we returned home. We had found what we were looking for. The following trip to Brückenau dutifully lived up to our promises. Clean, well furnished rooms with plenty of space for Father, Mother, six children and a maid, good food, curative

[90] In Versailles.
[91] Main building in a spa town, mainly used for entertainment purposes.

baths, fine company, beautiful excursions including to the town of Brückenau etc. Everything we needed to make us feel happy and contented.

Yet when comparing this beautiful area with Streitberg, there was something missing in the landscape that I could not quite explain. I used to say that Brückenau was like a beautiful woman without a soul. It was this soul that I found in my dear Streitberg, with its towering cliffs and ancient castles, its sweet valleys and clear, babbling brooks.

Fig. 48 Kursaal Bad Brückenau, 19th century.

The massive Kursaal building, which, if put in the right place, could be likened to a magnificent temple, did not seem to fit into the rural area either. However, it would be ungrateful to underestimate how much we enjoyed our stay, and in our hearts we remained very grateful for the fine hospitality.

The fact that I had not seen much of the world until I was in my fifties kept my *wanderlust* alive, and I wanted to catch up on what I had missed. Apart from the fact that my circumstances, including my financial situation, now allowed me to go on travels for which in the past I would have had neither the time nor the money, my daughters had grown up enough to accompany me as willing and keen companions, receptive to the beauty of the world. We began discussing plans for our spring trip already in the winter. My wife would not be talked into joining us on our travels; she said she had to look after the house and the other family members who stayed behind. The only excursions she would take part in and enjoyed where the ones where, like a mother hen, she could keep all her loved ones under her wing.

Another May approached. We decided to go on a several week-long tour to the South, with the final destination of Venice. I had chosen my daughters Frieda and Anna as well as my niece Lina, now Frau Dr. Erlanger, as my companions. My eldest daughter Berta had married by then.

At the end of our first day, we arrived in Zurich, well-equipped and in a happy mood, via Friedrichshafen. En route we had met an interesting, highly educated gentleman. He was the legation secretary at the German General Consulate in Smyrna. He had many stories to tell, and we stayed in correspondence for a good number of years, mostly discussing the trade relations which we had introduced in the Greek-Oriental regions.

In Zurich we stayed in the small hotel *Zum Storchen*[92], for this was the place where our representatives stayed when they were doing business in Switzerland. Experience had taught me that one could usually expect a comfortable stay in a hotel preferred by travelling salesmen. In Zurich, however, the stork - a zoologically speaking fairly harmless bird which contents itself exclusively with the catching of frogs etc - turned into a bird of prey which dug its claws deep into my purse. And this is how it happened:

92 "The Stork".

Fig. 49 Berta Hirschmann with her children Ernst, Trude and Paul.

The owner of the small guesthouse also ran a considerable warehouse and was as such an important customer of ours, which is why our representatives etc. always stayed at *Zum Storchen.* He was also renting out the hotel to a tenant. Now to my surprise I found that the tenant was a Nuremberger, from a family who was well-known but who had not progressed much. We were welcomed with open arms. I immediately realised that they were planning on making a bountiful haul on the bank of the Limmat - the river which ran behind the hotel. We were given the best rooms, the food was good and plentiful, and the landlord had reason to bill us accordingly. Yet what the *Storch* considered appropriate in this respect was excessive! A third of the requested amount would have accommodated us comfortably at the fine *Hotel Baur au Lac*, with change to spare. My clever fellow countryman, who knew very well that he could not justify his bill in detail, simply put: "Board and lodgings for Herr Kommerzienrat Bing Esq., his daughters and niece, etc." I will keep shtumm about the exact amount the *Stork* robbed me of.

Then off we went to Lucerne. In the past I used to stay at the *Gotthardt Hotel*, a simple guest-house near the station. This time we were planning on doing the same; only the old *Gotthardt* no longer existed. In its place stood a massive new building with a palatial vestibule; in short a Swiss hotel on a grand scale. Everything had turned lordly stiff, even the owner, who used to be an agreeable, talkative host, but this time he only offered me a formal bow. We took part at the evening meal which is celebrated in Switzerland with a special formality. Attendance was poor however, and the large dining hall stood in stark contrast to the small group of no more than 12 people who had gathered there. Behind almost every chair stood a waitress dressed in black with a white apron. The girls looked like nuns and served with an unshakable austerity. One single gentleman who sat next to us dared to make a joke. No-one laughed. I thought the whole arrangement far too bizarre and could not refrain myself from supporting my neighbour by asking if this was in fact a funeral meal. This improved the atmosphere at the table markedly; even the nuns smiled discreetly. Otherwise everything in the hotel was impeccable and the prices modest. I telephoned the *Hotel Splendid* in Lugano to ask if they had a room for us. In the meantime, we had a good look around Lucerne, took a steam-boat across the whole wonderful lake and returned cheerfully to the *Gotthardt* hotel. The response from Lugano had arrived - the hotel was already full and could not accommodate us as guests. We did not worry about it too much in the certain knowledge that once in Lugano we would be able to make do, and left.

We were looking forward to the journey, since we were expecting to see so many beautiful and impressive things on the way! First the train journey along Lake Zug, with the Rigi, the two myths etc. on the one side and the impressive Uri-Rothastock on the other, and then finally at the Southern tip of the lake, near Fluelen, we saw the giant pyramid of the Bristenstock rise up, its top covered in snow. We had already had a good look at these mountains from the steamer, but the light had not been very good, and now this bright and fresh May day bathed these sights in a new, impressive and enchanting light.

In Altdorf the railway began its ascent, and the foothills of Mount Gotthard no longer showed signs of spring. Higher and higher the train climbed. Even the layman can recognise and admire the amazing achievements of the engineers who built this track, which leads the way for all the people-uniting railways. With every new gradient the train climbed, the landscape grew more wintery, and just before Göschenen, the station where the Gotthard Tunnel begins, the snow was several metres deep.

Fig. 50 Lago di Lugano, ca. 1900.

The large waiting room at the station was well prepared for the arrival of this many travellers on their way to the Italian Switzerland and beyond. All one had to do was sit down at one of the many laid up tables, and the food was served immediately. Soup, roast meat with side dishes, as much cheap Italian red wine as one wanted - and the whole meal was 2 Francs. Very cheap and good. Still, no need to feel sorry for the restaurant owner, for he made good money. It is all in the quantity.

After an hour's break the train continued. As was predictable, the journey through the tunnel offered nothing much of interest. But when the train leaves the dark burrow behind, half an hour later, how interesting would it be to observe the snow fields receding to make way for green meadows and to see the Italian sun at last plunge the vernal, flowery landscape into a warm light. That was

Lugano. Now all you have to do is imagine the wonderful Lago di Lugano to complete the picture.

Our first task was to find accommodation. We wanted to spend a few days in Lugano. At the station, which was quite high above this town with a very Italian feel, several omnibuses from the larger hotels were preparing to depart. I could tell by the arrogant faces of their drivers that the carriages had taken departing guests to the station but that there was no space left for newly arrived strangers. We also saw a number of loitering hotel servants. I asked which of them could tell us of a decent house where we would find a room. Only a small, starved-looking young boy with a bound cap stepped forward. He said he was from the *Gotthard*, a small but very nice house, very close to the station. We had just come from the "big Gotthard", and so we were going to give the little one a try! As promised by the servant, the hotel was indeed tiny, even smaller than we had assumed. The patron arrived with a bow, continually chatting, now in German, now in French. The lady of the house also appeared to make our reception even more memorable and greeted us warmly. Indeed, our accommodation was much better than I had expected. The three girls had a suitably large room, and I, a single traveller, was given a small room, very simply furnished but clean.

We were quite contented, especially since lunch was adequate, too. In fact, we were quite comfortable in "*Lilliput House*". Besides, we were planning on making excursions from Lugano so that in the end we did not worry too much about whether we were staying in a very good hotel or not. Admittedly, the night did not turn out too well for me since the bed was very hard and my body ached the next morning. The young ladies, however, in their deep sound sleep were not affected by the uncomfortable circumstances in the slightest, and I did not let it spoil the little *Gotthard* for me either.

The next morning I asked the patron of the house to exchange 50 German marks in gold for Swiss francs. Due to the higher exchange rate of the German mark, he should have given me an amount of francs worth 51 marks 50. The Italian, too clever by half, tried to cheat me and instead of giving me more, he gave me 6 francs too few. I was not deceived by his rambling and emphatically demanded my 50 marks in gold back. While incessantly gushing a stream of words, half in Italian, half in German, he kept adding mark by mark until finally the exchange was concluded with only a minor loss on my side. The lesson I learned was quite useful insofar as from then on, contrary to my usual habit, I scrutinised every bill and rejected any direct or hidden extra charges. Once on Italian ground this caution was necessary not only in small hotels such as the one in Lugano, but at every single instance involving payment or the exchange of money. How often I found that I had been lumped with money that was either fake or of a lesser value!

Lugano itself offers many charming sights; not only because of its wonderful viewpoints which are reached by electric or cable railways, but even more so because of the magnificent lake with its bays on whose banks the town of Lugano is situated. The town itself displays the colourful picture that comes with an Italian population. One only needs to stand near the quay where the steamers are moored, or visit the fish market or one of the many *osterias* in the narrow roads, and one feels as if in Italy. And how suitable Lugano is for further excursions, and the main temptations would be the near lakes, Lago di Como and Lago Maggiore. Nonetheless, we could not stray too far since the days passed quickly; we wanted to see many more sights on our journey, and we did not want to exceed the agreed duration of our trip of three weeks.

We decided on a trip to Lago di Como as it was easier to get to than Lago Maggiore. The steamer took us to the picturesque little town of Porlezza, situated nearly at the Northern end of the lake from where we took a kind of land train to the station of Menaggio on Lago di Como. The journey with the land train took around half an hour. We then followed the stream of tourists, and a little steamer took us across the lake in 15 minutes to Bellagio, a town visited by an extremely large number of tourists and summer anglers. From there one has a wonderful view of the massive mountain, which in turn is towered over by Monte Rosa. We took coffee in a beautifully situated coffee-house on the beach. Oh little *Gotthard*, how honest you were compared to what the pirates of Bellagio considered permissible. Four cups of less than mediocre coffee and a little bit of cake - 12 francs 40, not including a tip! Things like these can spoil even the most magnificent scenery! Hence we did not stay long and sought to reach Porlezza on Lago di Lugano as quickly as possible, from where we took the steamer to return to our little *Gotthard*. The journey, which took about three hours, was very interesting. It was a glorious evening, and sitting on deck was a delectation. Even the magical searchlights, intended to dissuade smugglers, on the Swiss as well as on the Italian banks of the lake, added to the particular charm of the trip. Then the sky turned pitch-black. Dazzling lightning bolts competed with the searchlights, and the lake and its banks where often plunged into blinding light. Then we heard the deep, rumbling thunder, and at last the drenching rain came lashing down and drove us into the cabin. When we arrived in Lugano, a brilliant starlit sky looked down upon us.

The next morning we commenced our journey to Milan. Lodgings in the *Spatz*[93] hotel (owned by an emigrated Nuremberger) had already been reserved in advance.

Leaving the little *Gotthard*, another funny episode was in store for us: As was my usual habit, I rewarded everyone who deserved it with a generous tip. As we were leaving, the patron caught me by the arm and screamed in my face that his douceur had been forgotten. It was he, he shouted, who was not only the loyally caring host for his guests but also the porter, the man who could give information about anything, and it was he who had to make sure that the luggage was sent on properly since his driver was not reliable. He whinged and whined enough to make a stone cry. Yet I was impervious to his cheap lament and could only reply that I had never come across a begging hotelier. And thus we parted never to meet again. We set off to Milan.

I was not particularly impressed by Milan. The town was lacking the original style of Genoa, Florence and other Italian cities. The *Spatz* hotel received us warmly, and its director, who also played the part of the omnipotent "maître d'", gave us some nice rooms. I noticed straight away that the shrewd man with his impressive, black sideburns had a fine nose for "good or stingy" guests. He seemed to count me among the "good" ones. Whoever goes tra-

[93] English: sparrow

velling to Italy with three young ladies must have the necessary money and cannot be miserly. He would have known that from the way I looked after my companions. I, on the other hand, had already heard in Nuremberg that a bird of prey had made himself a nest in the *Spatz* and was mercilessly plucking everyone who stopped at the inn. So I was on my guard. I demanded to pay for everything we ate and drank at the hotel straight away, in other words daily bills. And yet after our departure from Milan I came to realise that I had been duped after all. With remarkable cunning, indirect taxes, or rather robbery, had been calculated into the daily bills. Had I discovered this while still in Milan, it would surely have been an "easily forgivable mistake".

I do not have to describe here what we saw and admired in Milan. Every guidebook will tell you what a traveller must or might see in the city. We were content with the main sights and the most unusual ones. Despite the odd, beautiful gravestone I was left cold by the much vaunted Campo Santo. By contrast, what poetry lies in our own St. Johannis cemetery in Nuremberg? Largely unimpressed we left the big city, the last stopover that stood between us and the hotly awaited Venice.

Having telegraphed the hotel *Bauer-Grünwald* in Venice we received the reply that rooms had been reserved. The journey from Milan to Venice is not very scenic. Only every now and then one catches a glimpse of the silhouette of the Maritime Alps. At last we reached Mestre station, the last one before Venice. From there onwards the train continues along a high dam, flanked on both sides by the waters of the lagoon.

And then the station, the only one in Venice! And yet neither the interior nor the exterior of the entrance hall were in any way extraordinary, indeed it was so characterless that I cannot remember for the life of me what the building actually looked like! All I can remember is that an attendant, some form of porter, said to me in German that we should find and reserve one of the gondolas, which were moored on the canal right by the station. Our luggage would then follow. That is what we did. While we were waiting for the luggage, the *gondoliere* took the girls up and down the canal, and I stayed on the quayside until everything was sorted.

By then, night had descended on the lagoons and the faintly lit Venice. It was a little eerie on the boat to the hotel. We left the wide canal and turned into very narrow, very dark side canals, where voices called out warning us to move to the side or to be careful, and the gondolas passed each other like ghosts. At last we could see some lights ahead, and the vestibule of the *Bauer-Grünwald* appeared in front of us. We were welcomed as usual, but also by the director himself. To my surprise he told us that the rooms we had reserved were no longer available due to some force majeure. These rooms now had to be kept free for His Royal Highness, the Duke of the Abruzzi, who was to arrive the next day in order to open an art exhibition. The director therefore offered us comparable rooms in an annexe, which was located far away from the main hotel. As Royal Bavarian Kommerzienrat I could not put up with such an affront! I declared resolutely that I was not going to accept this imposition, bearing in mind that the young ladies needed to be considered too. If necessary, I said, I would find a different hotel, and on my return to Germany I would not hold back on making public what the *Grünwald Hotel* considered acceptable behaviour towards German guests. There had been no need for me to get so wound up in my moral outrage, as the rest of the story will show: The director asked me to calm down. He could see very well, he added, that my indignation was justified and suggested the following: His Royal Highness was not expected until the following afternoon, and he would let us have the rooms destined for the Duke for the night. The next morning he was sure that a solution would be found. We agreed to that. We were then shown to an indeed princely, or at least very superior parlour, which had doors leading to three very small and very simply furnished bedrooms. For a moment I thought that the parlour was like smoke and mirrors to make the puny rooms we were given more palatable. On the other hand I was very glad to be so relatively comfortable. Of course, when in Venice one does not spend one's time in a salon, yet it was a good feeling to have such a superior, neutral room for our use until the next morning.

As we were leaving the hotel the next day, I told the chambermaid, who spoke very good German, that according to the director we had to move to other rooms within the hotel, adding that we were being ousted by the Duke of the Abruzzi. I reminded her not to leave any of our belongings behind during the move. The maid did not seem to take my message seriously; she only said that the director had not mentioned anything to her.

After breakfast we asked the porter to find us a reliable guide for the day. He had already arrived. A decent looking, older gentleman introduced himself and explained an extensive programme. I told him, however, that the route and the order of the programme were too complicated for me, we just wanted to see what we were interested in and had time for.

First we went to get a good overview of Venice, which included the Piazza San Marco, the Doge's Palace, St. Mark's Basilica, the Rialto Bridge and the Campanile as well as lunch in a real *osteria* etc. If you do not know Venice and will probably never go there, then I advise you to buy a good travelogue. As such I can recommend the Italian journey by a certain author and poet by the name of Goethe, who also held the post of Geheimer Rat and Secretary of State and lived more than 100 years ago in Weimar. (I jest, of course, and I expect that this little joke about Goethe as a travel writer will not be misunderstood by my readers.) The fact is, having read Goethe's *Italian Journey* more than 50 times, I

Fig. 51 Ignaz with (possibly) his daughters Marie and Frieda, Val Sinestre, 1908.

was well prepared for Venice. Many of the things that Häring - our guide - explained I knew already, and he looked surprised when I added to his lecture in one way or another. Judging by his pronunciation rather than by his looks I could tell that our guide was a member of the Jewish faith. First, he led us to St. Mark's Basilica where he eagerly told us the legends of the various saints whose statues are on display in this magnificent, unique house of God. I listened to him for a little while, and then I remembered a funny anecdote about a banker from Frankfurt who was baptised years ago. When a stock exchange speculator later told him something that he thought unlikely, he interrupted the speaker with the words: "Don't even try it, you can tell that to a goy!" I repeated the words of the banker from Frankfurt, and Herr Häring looked at me ecstatically. "I seeee", he said, "this is all unnecessary then." He then became very intimate, in fact more so than I liked. He told us that he was from Saaz in Bohemia, the famous hops town. I will not bore you with retelling the story of how he ended up in Venice through marriage. His business, trading with mussels and other marine products such as urchins, corals etc. was not bringing in enough money, especially since his daughter lived an extravagant lifestyle, and his wife, in her vanity, supported the extravagance. A gloomy family picture, yet we felt sympathy for him.

When we left the amazing Doge's palace after our visit, it was already long past midday, and we had planned for Häring to take us to a real *osteria*. The girls, too, showed a keen interest. We wanted to get to know the country and its people, yet our guide did not agree. He claimed that an *osteria* was not a comfortable place, adding that polenta and fish fried in cheap oil were everything but appetising, and the company there was not suitable for young ladies. I insisted on my plan, however, and so, shaking his head, Herr Häring led us to a small restaurant near the Piazza di Marco which was nothing like an *osteria.* A sweaty waiter in tails, Austrian no doubt, formerly white tablecloths stained with wine, a Viennese menu listing goulash, traditional Austrian salted and smoked meat, wienerwurst - all these things pointed to the fact that this was without a doubt a Viennese restaurant with which Herr Häring was, I am sure, in an agreement when his foreigners wanted to visit an *osteria.* The price for our curiosity: poor food, served with the typical "Bitt' schön, gnädiger Herr"[94], a rather large bill including no doubt a commission for our Herr Häring.

We did not want to see anything else that day so we said goodbye to Herr Häring by paying him generously for his troubles and drove to the wonderful Lido in order to rid ourselves of the onion smells from the fake *osteria* in its clean air.

The next morning Häring was back. Under his guidance we visited the palaces along the *Canale Grande*, with their glorious architecture and interiors, the richly stocked and highly interesting museum and famous churches, and we even climbed the Campanile, a building that seemed constructed for eternity, and at the time nothing indicated that several years later it would collapse and lie in ruins. The fact that attempts were made to drag us into one of the shops selling products from the Venetian glass industry on the piazza represents a customary business practice many foreigners fall prey to.

---

[94] "Gnädiger Herr", literally "gracious gentleman": polite Austrian form of address.

For the evening we had hired a box in the large *Fenice* theatre, quite an expensive affair. Nonetheless, we did not regret a single penny of it. Quite apart from the charming view of the elegant, richly decorated ladies from Venice's aristocratic circles, we were completely enthralled by Massenet's great opera *Werther*, which to my knowledge has never been performed in Germany. Given the simplified story the text itself is not corrupted as badly as the libretto to Gounod's *Faust*. The mostly lyrical music by the famous French composer is equally moving and touching. The stage direction was masterful, despite the fact that some arrangements were not derived from the original as written by Goethe but determined by the free approach of the libretto writer. For example, at the beginning of the last act, after Lotte hands over the guns requested by Werther to the messenger, the backdrop is the illuminated old town of Wetzlar. Snow is falling, and Lotte, full of fear for Werther, is walking fast towards the town. She is accompanied by atmospheric music on her way. The fact that the dying Werther recognises his ardently beloved and that the scene ends in a brilliant, passionate duet is merely the style of French opera.

I completely forgot to mention what happened to the Duke of the Abruzzi, and I will tell it now. By the second day of our stay in the hotel, the chambermaid had still not announced the arrival of the Duke, and it appeared that we did not have to give up our rooms. Was the whole story just a trick in order to push up the bill? I approached the director to find out more. He told me that His Royal Highness had not arrived in Venice and that we could keep the rooms. Since the Court had already paid a deposit, he would be able to reduce the price for the apartment for us. In response to my question how much I would have to pay the director told me a sum which still seemed quite high to me, but I did not say anything about it.

On our last day we strolled around Venice without Häring. We bought little souvenirs as *mitbrings* for Nuremberg. I would like to add that we had received only good news from home and that we sent messages back daily. We chose picture postcards for our messages, which were very popular even then. Every postcard sent by us was signed off with the same words: "Love to Schladitz; and tell the boys to be good." *Schladitz* was the nick-name we had given our little daughter Marie, who was only ten years old at the time and who was always asking for a *Schladitz* bike. The boys were my sons Siegmund and Stefan, who were still attending school.

While strolling through Venice we also happened across the fish market, which was offering a wide, but unappetising choice of seafood, or *frutti del mare.* There were large vats, the contents of which men were working on with wooden clubs. They were making polenta, the selling and buying of which was a rather clamorous and boisterous affair.

Life in the narrow streets is very noisy, especially where people are offering something for sale. If someone has a scrawny old chicken for sale, they announce it to the world so loudly and aggressively that it cannot be overlooked, or rather it cannot be over-*heard.*

Before we left Venice we went to the Lido once again. We were quite taken with the wild sea; we went there to get some respite from Venice. On the last evening we went to a different theatre, the name of which escapes me, and saw a faultless performance of Puccini's *Bohème*.

We had made good use of our time in Venice and seen much that we will remember forever, and yet we were filled with a calm joy when we began our journey home; which is what our departure from Venice signified. Besides, the journey home was to be very enjoyable in itself. We were not going to return via the same route we had come, but our next destination was Bolzano, where we were going to stop over for a few days. In Milan we were joined by a young, very agreeable clergyman who was on his way to a seminary in Innsbruck where he was going to finish his degree. He was talkative and kind. The longer he stayed with us, the more he confided in us, though his talk was directed mostly at the young ladies. He seemed reluctant to leave us, even the girls' innocent teasing did not change that. After a long journey from the Italian border along the Adige valley through the magnificent alpine landscape we were finally approaching Bolzano. I knew this outstanding South Tyrolean tourist attraction from previous visits, as well as the highly acclaimed, and deservedly so, guesthouse *Zum Greif* where we had booked lodgings. In Bolzano we said a warm goodbye to our travelling companion. Later I found out that the playful girls had slipped him a note saying, "Change direction".

Off we went to the *Greif*, where a welcoming statue of Walther von der Vogelweide[95] was standing guard at the entrance. The proprietress of the house, who managed and supervised the many tasks involved in running the hotel, welcomed us warmly; we

[95] Walther von der Vogelweide; a celebrated 12th century lyric poet.

were shown simple but nice rooms, and a short time later we were sitting at the table in anticipation of a tasty and plentiful dinner, feeling more comfortable and at home than anywhere else on our trip so far. It was no surprise, for the *Greif* offered everything one could ask for. Friendly and attentive service by neat waitresses, a wide choice of dishes, excellent - and not too expensive - local wines, a dining room always filled with cheerful tourists and interesting company, and finally very modest prices. All this together gave the hotel a very individual, lovable character. The *Greif* is a place one enjoys coming back to again and again, and as I am writing this down, in the freezing cold, while there is a war on, I think longingly back to those days which I will never be able to relive again.

We wandered through the lavish scenery, resplendent in its spring blossom, sometimes along the river Talfer, sometimes along the Eisack or Adige; in the afternoons we drank coffee in the old romantic Runkelstein Castle. Nothing reminded us of the stiff, unwelcoming hotels in Switzerland or the trickeries we had experienced in Italy. Everything was properly German, in the best sense of the word. The evening before our last in Bolzano, the military band played at the *Greif*. Not just the many hotel guests but also the Bolzano society, including foremost the officers of the garrison, filled the dining room. The elegant officers sat near our table, and it goes without saying that young ladies who feel watched will not leave the opposite side unobserved either. That is what they call coquetry!

When Bolzano, the *Greif* and the late King Laurin[96] lay behind us, and the train started rolling towards Innsbruck, a naval lieutenant commander joined us who, skilfully and tactfully, engaged us in a conversation primarily about the various beauty spots in the countryside that we were passing through. Yet he also had a good strategy for slipping in a few personal remarks indicating that he had noticed the young ladies at the *Greif*, etc. My daughter Anna appeared to be suffering from travel sickness - he offered a migraine stick; in short it was obvious that the young officer was keen to become acquainted with me and my family. In Innsbruck he said his goodbyes very politely and graciously, stood outside our compartment until the departure of our train and then took his leave in a very amiable manner. Naturally, this interlude was much talked about for the next while.

In Munich, our usual hotel did not have any rooms for us. I thought about the *Bamberger Hof*, which I still remembered fondly from my days as *commis voyageur*, a travelling salesman. When we arrived there, we saw my brother-in-law Mohrenwitz from Bamberg standing in the entrance. That was a good omen! This travelling uncle always knew exactly how to judge the assets of a good hotel. Persuaded by him, we took lodgings in the recommended hotel. And by itself it was no mistake. Rooms, service and food were good, only there was a lively busyness about the place. Male and female figures were darting over the stairs and along the corridors, disappearing into the rambling building, then others followed, and at last my young companions, too, though it was odd that when they were standing by the window, they were

---

[96] King Laurin - a mystical figure said to have lived in the Rosengarten, a mountain group in the Dolomites. There is a statue depicting the death of King Laurin in Bolzano.

often looked at and waved at from the street. The accommodation did not seem entirely suitable, and it was too late when I found out that there was a kind of musical hall and that other events for gentlemen were taking place at the hotel. We came to no harm, but I gave my brother-in-law a proper ticking-off afterwards.

To everyone's great joy we arrived back in Nuremberg. The boys and Schladitz (Marie) received a cute souvenir, and the former were promised that I would take them on a trip during the next holidays. That promise would indeed be fulfilled.

Fig. 52 Ludwig Brüll.

Our trip did have an epilogue: I received a letter from the lieutenant commander we had met on the journey from Bolzano to Innsbruck. He wrote, very tactfully and elegantly, that one of my daughters, namely the tallest of the three ladies, had already made a deep impression on him in Bolzano, and he asked if he be permitted to become acquainted with my family. He said he lived in orderly circumstances as senior lieutenant commander in Riva. I answered him politely that the young lady he described was my brother's daughter, i.e. my niece Lina (now Frau Dr. Erlanger), and I did not think that, as far as I could tell, she was considering leaving her country. He was free, I added, to discuss this directly with my brother. Then another letter arrived from Riva, which I liked a lot less than the first one. Herr Lieutenant Commander made it clear, and very unequivocally so, that he also felt warmly towards my two daughters and remained persistent in his desire to get to know my family. By way of reply I sent him a card announcing the engagement of our daughter Frieda with Herr Ludwig Brüll.

A short note with congratulations arrived, and that was the end of this funny and much laughed-about episode.

The school year was over. The boys had come home with good school reports and had not seen much of the world. I was therefore planning on taking the two of them on a pleasure trip which I thought would be very enjoyable. Via Eisenach we were to go to Hamburg and from there to Westerland on Sylt[97]. Cheerfully we set out on our journey and arrived at Eisenach in the evening. I noticed on our journey to Thuringia already that my boys showed very little appreciation for the beautiful countryside. They would laugh about every little incident during a stopover at a station, about a waiter calling out "Cognac" with a singing voice, but as I said, they were seemingly little moved by the scenic attractions of the magnificent Thuringian woodlands. Even the appreciation of nature must be learned!

Therefore I had no high hopes that a visit of the Wartburg would make much of an impression, and I was not wrong. My eldest son, Siegmund, whose decent grammar school education had at

---

97 Part of the North Frisian islands, Sylt is the northernmost island of Germany in the North Sea; Westerland was then and still is a very popular and fashionable resort.

least heightened his interest in the history of his Fatherland, joined me in visiting this star of the German castles, this seat of legendary memories[98], while the admittedly much younger Stefan preferred to await our return in the restaurant.[99]

Fig. 53 The Wartburg, ca. 1900

That concluded our visit to Eisenach and the Wartburg. We took the midday train to arrive in Hamburg at the *Belvedere Hotel*, right on the Alsterplatz, at around half past nine in the evening. We stayed in the hotel, and the concierge showed us a program which indicated that the next day there was a tour of the city starting from the Alster pavilion, followed by a visit round the harbour. I thought this was the perfect way to familiarise ourselves with the large, impressive city of Hamburg, by land and by water. Furthermore, the price was very modest - the tickets were only three marks each. We bought the tickets from the concierge, and

[98] Amongst its many claims to fame, the Wartburg is best known for the fact that Martin Luther stayed at the castle following his excommunication by Pope Leo X and translated the Bible into German there.

[99] Stefan was only about 14 months younger than Siegmund; at the time of this trip, probably in the summer of either 1895 or 1896, Siegmund would have been 16 or 17, Stefan 14 or 15.

the next morning we appeared on time at the point of departure where two or three mail coaches were taking in the ticketholders. Now the boys were wide-eyed! This was something different from the Thuringian forest, the Harz mountains or the Lüneburg Heath! The trip lived up to the promises made by the programme. We visited the nicest parts of Hamburg by carriage, and the summer morning was crisp and invigorating. At the port, a small steam sloop was waiting for the guests, and the harbour visit was about to begin. There were around 60 to 70 passengers who were supposed to board the peculiar little boat. I was beginning to have second thoughts, but then I said to myself that the harbour police would not have licensed such a boat if it put the lives of its passengers at risk. Once on board the swinging cockleshell, and it was standing room only, it was very crowded, and I was pushed right to the front of the boat towards the bulwark, and I had to hold onto the barrier for support. I was so uncomfortable that I felt very uneasy during the tour of the port, with all its noise and hooting by the criss-crossing ships. It was to get even more uncomfortable! Suddenly a large coal barge appeared from out of a side canal which our little steamer was unable to avoid; our boat scraped the side of the barge with the effect that the first digits of two of my fingers on the right hand, which had been holding on to the railing, were completely squeezed off. Oy vey, the stock for our trip to Sylt was low! The boat interrupted its tour and took us back to land to some kind of lifeboat station, which in my opinion was hopelessly under-equipped for cases like mine. A ship's doctor, a certain Dr. Durlacher, happened to come by and administered first aid. Judging by the quickly applied emergency dressing, he thought that three fingers had been crushed. However, with careful movements I could establish that this was not the case, and that the accident was not as bad as that. Later on, thanks to Dr. Durlacher's intervention, the very capable Professor Kümmel from the Eppendorf hospital came to see me at the hotel. He operated on what was left to be operated on and consoled me with the fact that I had been quite lucky under the circumstances. He was right of course. The accident could have easily cost me a hand or an arm. When the injuries were covered with a dressing which, according to the doctor I did not have to change for weeks, I had the boys sent up to my room. I was smoking my cigar and told them the news that the accident did not spell the end of the trip, and that after a few days' stay in Hamburg we would continue our journey to Sylt.

Even so, I was not feeling too well; severe pain, nights spent in an armchair, sleep induced by morphine and finally the messages sent home, at first only to the sons-in-law in Nuremberg, made the whole affair awkward. I was in this kind of mood when I asked the visiting Herr Professor Kümmel if I ran the risk of blood poisoning with such a bad injury. He replied gruffly: "What are you talking about? Go to St. Pauli[100] tonight and drink a good bottle of red wine, that is the right kind of blood poisoning!" And that's what I did. Three or four days after the disastrous harbour tour my son-in-law Brüll arrived to take me back to Nuremberg. Nonetheless, I would not agree to that under any circumstances; quite apart from the fact that I did not want to rob my sons of their pleasure of the trip, according to the professor the sea air could only be beneficial to my nerves. The

---

100 Hamburg's famous red light district, although its reputation may have been less seedy at the time of Ignaz's visit to Hamburg.

fact that I did not return home but was going to Westerland also convinced my extremely worried wife how little the accident really meant. Reassuring letters were sent home, and after a six-day stay in Hamburg we reassumed our journey to Westerland.

My son-in-law Brüll was a good travel marshal, experienced in all things that would make such a journey as agreeable as possible even under these aggravated circumstances. We chose a mail train for the journey to Hoyer Lock, from where the ship left for Westerland. The mail train departed from Hamburg two hours earlier than the tourist train coming from Berlin, but it offered the distinct advantage that we would be able to have a compartment to ourselves; in the ever-overcrowded tourist train that would have been out of the question. There was another reason why I preferred the mail train, namely that it offered the opportunity for me to get to know the land and its people. The journey was extremely comfortable. We stopped several times for coffee, I was given a certain overview of the beautiful land, and finally we arrived half an hour before the

Fig. 54 Ludwig Brüll with the family car.

tourist train in Hoyer Lock. I had hoped that we would therefore also have the opportunity to arrange ourselves comfortably on the boat before the large crowds of tourists would stop us. Sadly that was a delusion! The ship that was to take us to Westerland was indeed no more than 100 metres away from the station, but not in water but literally stuck in mud, or - put more drastically - in the muck. The reason was that there is a canal from Hoyer Lock to the mudflats which are only navigable for the steamer at high tide. The same goes for the canal itself. The ship had entered the canal on a rising tide, and at low tide it spent a certain time lying in a waterless ditch. Only when the waters had risen high enough to float the ship can departure even be considered.

We had arrived at Hoyer Lock at about six o'clock in the evening; it was not until 9 o'clock that we were expected to depart. Three hours' wait! It was a long stopover, and the frugal dinner and the many cups of tea did not help much to pass the time.

At last the time of our departure approached. My loyal, caring son-in-law had organised a comfortable chair for me on deck, which I did not leave for the entire crossing. It was a wonderful summer's evening, the air moved slightly by a gentle breeze, and for the first time since the accident in Hamburg I felt free from the usual near-constant pain in my injured hand for several hours.

And how magical my first trip at sea seemed to me! Once we left the canal behind us we were on the open sea, i.e. the mudflats, which at low tide are a slimy sludge, streaked by draining water and smelling anything but sweet. In the night, however, with a rising tide, the trip had a mystical air about it.

At the bow of the ship stood a sailor with a long rod who was taking regular soundings and then shouted the depth of the water in English to the machinist via a speaking tube: four, five, six... After a little while it seemed that the risk of shoals had disappeared and we were heading, without soundings, towards a well-lit beach. Soon after that we reached Munkmarsch port on Sylt.

I have to mention that even before he had left Nuremberg, my son-in-law Brüll had asked a business acquaintance of the company's, who had a branch in Westerland, to arrange for suitable accommodation for us. In a few minutes, the little train took us from Munkmarsch to Westerland. Several members of the Wünschmanns, our host family (including a young lady whom we immediately nicknamed "Wünschmaid[101]") were waiting for us at the station and welcomed us with open arms. They had already been informed about my accident. Accompanied by this train of family members we arrived at a simple little house, where on the upper floor rooms had been prepared for us. The rooms were very clean and despite their simplicity, not without comfort. Anything that we thought was missing was made available immediately.

The next morning we were served coffee in a kind of summer cottage and found out a bit more about our hosts. Father Wünschmann had come to Westerland with his exceedingly beautiful wife and made a lot of money as a shipping agent, forwarding passenger goods and freight cargo from Westerland to Munkmarsch port and vice versa. When the introduction of the railway made this kind of freight traffic obsolete, he had

101 "Maid of dreams"; Ignaz is playing with the family name Wünschmann, which literally means "Dream-man".

Fig. 55 Westerland, Sylt, 1890s.

already accumulated enough money to build two small guesthouses which yielded good rents, and he speculated with land which I am sure worked out in favour for the shrewd and prudent businessman. Some of the numerous members of his family, seven sons and three daughters, had already been taken care of. The eldest daughter was managing the second guest house; the youngest, a true Frisian beauty, was looking after us and was not just met with wholehearted applause by my sons, but she also aroused the admiration of my nephew Max Ottenstein from Nuremberg, who was on a business trip in Holstein and had come to see us for a few days. He would have loved to carry the enchanting island girl off with him back to Nuremberg.

My son-in-law had now left again, we had had only good news from home, and so we arranged our daily routine as is customary in Westerland. The two poles of our days were the beach and the heath, and I can say that despite the occasional severe pain in my fingers, I grew very fond of Westerland. At the end of our stay I had become so familiar with the island's particular beauty, life on the beach and the heath in bloom that I declared Westerland to be my "Streitberg of the North", and it was to remain as such for the future.

Twice more I would return, but I will write more about that later. We said our heartfelt goodbyes to the Wünschmanns, hoisted the anchor, and after a night spent in Tondern we travelled via Hamburg to Berlin. On this trip, too, my son-in-law Brüll was our "loyal Eckart[102]" again and organised everything.

At the station in Hamburg, my son Stefan had eaten a tough piece of meat which left him with an upset stomach. He was in terrible pain, and under those circumstances I wanted to go back home as quickly as possible. Once we arrived in Berlin, however, and had found comfortable lodgings at the *Zentralhotel*, my son was beginning to feel better, and indeed after a couple of hours the pain died down completely. Consequently, we could have followed our original programme and stayed a few days in Berlin to give my sons the opportunity to get to know the capital of the German Reich. Yet I was filled with a certain trepidation and unease and was longing to be back at home. In the early hours of the morning, Stefan - who had made a full recovery by then - and I took a cab to Anhalter station, taking a detour via *Unter den Linden*, the *Tiergarten*, etc and seeing a good part of Berlin on the way. In the evening we arrived back in Nuremberg, having been away for about four weeks. A journey, begun with the best intentions, had come to an end. Even if the accident in Hamburg

102 A brave hero of German legends.

meant that some hopes had not been fulfilled, we still remembered many good times, too.

With spring drawing near, I felt a pressing urge to travel, and there was no lack of willing company to join me. I had heard much good being said about the Austrian Riviera, of which Abbazia[103] is considered the centre, and I imagined that a journey there via Vienna, the Semmering and the magnificent Styria would be exceptionally delightful. My daughters Anna and Marie were to come with me. It did not take long for the preparations to be made, and so we started our journey to the Adriatic in early May. We could easily have reached our first destination, i.e. Vienna, in style by using the express train, which travels through the night and is equipped with dining and sleeping cars. Yet I preferred to take the simple fast train, which, once on Austrian soil, turned into a stopping train. Apart from saving 50 marks in total, I also believed that the trip through such a beautiful part of the Danube Monarchy in the daytime would be very interesting for my daughters. In how far this was true, I cannot remember, yet I was not under the impression that my companions had a particular enthusiasm for the beauties of nature. They were much more interested in being comfortable, which I personally can often do without, but when comfort is being offered as standard I also know how to appreciate it.

Having arrived at Vienna Westbahnhof after a long journey, we took a speedy Fiaker[104] to the *Kummer Hotel* in Mariahilferstrasse. I had good memories of the *Kummer* from my business trips. I remembered the excellent food and drink with particular

---

103 Now better known under its Croatian name, Opatija.
104 Typical Viennese horse-drawn buggy.

fondness, especially the juicy beef with peeled giant cucumbers, their apple strudel and other Viennese specialities. The rooms, too, I thought were extremely elegant for my circumstances at the time, and on the way there I was already praising the cosy home waiting for us in Vienna to the skies.

Well, we were about to come back down to earth with a bump! I had forgotten that my last visit to Vienna was over 20 years ago. The hotel with its sparse lighting was barely recognisable. The dining rooms with their public bar customary to Vienna were already closed, and our allotted rooms appeared not to have been aired for some time. The room waiter was barely able to persuade the kitchen to make some scrambled eggs for us. In short, the *Kummer* was an all-round disappointment.

By contrast, Vienna had grown considerably, and what I was going to show my little daughters was overwhelming. We visited Schönbrunn Palace, the Prater, the city park, the Ringstrasse, the old, elegant Vienna with St. Stephen's Cathedral, the castle, the Imperial Crypt at the Capuchin Church, the Court Opera[105] and many other sights, while also rigorously sampling the still excellent cuisine in elegant restaurants. And yet the effect that large cities have - on me at least - soon became apparent: before long one has had one's fill of them. We were longing to get away from the crowds, the noise, the hustle and bustle of city life, longing to go out into the countryside, to follow the call of the mountains and to see the blue Adriatic Sea. That was our destination, and it made our departure from the beautiful city of Vienna all the easier.

---

105 Now the Vienna State Opera.

Early the next morning we went to the Süd-Bahnhof. I handed our hand luggage to a porter to carry into our carriage. We had been sitting in our reserved compartment for a while, but there was no sign of our porter. So I gave one of his colleagues some small change and asked him to find the missing man (after all, the train was due to depart in a few minutes) all the while loudly cursing the Austrian lack of work ethic, of course. At last I could see the man coming towards us rather unhurriedly, and I only just heard his colleague, whom we had sent to find him, shout after him in the broadest Austrian accent: "Hurry up, his Lordship is already fuming!"

We had already forgotten the annoying little incident before we had reached the limits of the imperial city. In two hours, the express train raced across the rich, blessed plains in front of the Semmering with their many large houses, flowering gardens and picturesque settlements of stately homes, villages and little towns. Then the train climbs up the steep and winding tracks along the mountain until it reaches a plateau covered deep in snow, where the famous, luxurious hotels of the Semmering are gathered. The clean, crisp morning air refreshed our minds, in spite of the uncomfortable demi-compartment coaches that were commonly used on the Südbahn. We were delighted by the glorious scenery and the wonderful weather. As the sun climbed higher in the sky, the narrow compartment, plain and not quite clean, with its hard leather seats, grew more and more uncomfortable in the increasing heat. My daughters grew sleepy, saw relatively little of the magnificent - and yet lovely - high mountain ranges and seemed to be very glad when we reached our destination of the day, the beautiful city of Graz. The famous town on the river Mur received us warmly; we chose to stay at the same inn where our employees stayed when they travelled to Austria on business. We strolled through the city's streets and parks; everything was very pretty but did not leave a lasting impression. I cannot even remember the name of the operetta we saw that evening in the delightful theatre in Graz. A rare case, since my memory is normally very good!! It must be testimony to how tired and jaded we were after the long journey.

Fig. 56 Graz; river Mur and castle, 1912.

The next day we resumed our journey to Fiume[106] under the same, or even worse, conditions that the Südbahn asks their passengers to put up with. Green Styria lay behind us, now replaced by rough, dark karst. The journey was by no means uninteresting, since we were new to the mix of peoples - Croats, Dalmatians, Italians, Slovenians, Bosnians, etc - at the stations

---

106 Nowadays better known under its Croatian name, Rijeka.

and we enjoyed this opportunity to get to know these different types of peoples by their physiognomy.

Again it was late, around 10 o'clock in the evening, when we arrived in Fiume. The hotel was a severe disappointment, much worse than the *Kummer* in Vienna. Quite literally, the hotel seemed to be a combination of grime coupled with poverty. We were barely served any food, and I will keep quiet about the rooms and the beds. In the morning, when we demanded breakfast, we were shown to a room which doubled up as a public café full of dirty men and women. The floor looked as if it had never been cleaned and was being used as a general spittoon; in short, it was a scandalous affair, which we could not leave quickly enough. We had our hand luggage taken to the port a full three hours before the departure of our boat to Abbazia, then strolled through the unattractive Italo-Hungarian town to see the blue waves of the Adriatic. Soon the misery of the hotel was forgotten. A soft, refreshing breeze was blowing over Kvaerner Bay, which carried us on our steamer to Abbazia. It was a different world! A wonderful, tropical landscape, wonderfully kept parks and white country houses shimmering through laurel hedges seemed to tell us that the long, hard journey was to conclude here in very agreeable harmony. The large *Stephani Hotel* offered us friendly bedrooms, comfortable areas for meal and leisure times, and at last a restaurant - a mix of Viennese cuisine with seafood delicacies - that exceeded our hopes and expectations.

We were out and about every day, went on daytrips on the steamer, hired a rowing boat for the day, and we did not tire of spending time in the port and on the beach where we enjoyed new, vibrant images and distractions.

Since then I have often longed to return to Abbazia, yet my old age prevents me from fulfilling my dream. The memories, completely untarnished, will remain with me for as long as I live.

When at last it was time to return home, we decided to go via the Tyrol. We followed the way back to Laibach, where we were going to stop for the night and continue our homeward journey from there through the Puster Valley.

It is always awkward to arrive in a foreign city by night. In Laibach we felt this to be particularly painfully so. At the station, the political situation and the edgy mood between the small German minority and the Croat-Slovenian majority of the population of Laibach was palpable. To make matters worse I had forgotten to bring the address of the German-run guesthouse that had been recommended to us in Nuremberg. My inquiries for a good hotel were, since I had asked the question in German, either ignored or answered in such a way that it was meaningless to me. We left our luggage at the station and found a cabby outside whose driver spoke German. He took us to a hotel that did not look too bad. Our reception was not unfriendly, but we did notice that the owner was not a German. We were given everything we asked for, if not in a dismissive way but not exactly with a smile either. When I asked at what time the first morning train to Villach left Laibach, I could not get a proper answer. There was a quiet defiance about these people which one could not help but be infuriated by.

We had no other choice but to go back to the station through the badly lit streets to obtain the necessary information. On the way, we had to ask for directions several times, but we either received no answer at all or a reluctant reply in Slovenian. At last we found the station. I introduced myself to the railway official with a packet of cigarettes, and little by little I was told the exact departure time of the best train to take us away from the unwelcoming town of Laibach.

The next morning we arrived at the station one hour early. We had to buy our tickets and check in our luggage. When at last the counter opened, I asked for three tickets to Bruneck, one of the largest places in the Puster Valley. The official looked at me blankly and replied curtly that there was no Bruneck station on the Villach-Franzensfeste line. I insisted politely but sternly that Bruneck station did not only indeed exist, but that it was one of the most important ones along the entire line. A shake of the head! At last a station officer who had overheard the conversation said something to the official behind the desk in Slovenian. After a repeated shake of the head he took up a printed directory: Bruneck was found, and we received our tickets[107].

We breathed a sigh of relief once we were aboard the train, which travelled at a snail's pace to the station of Villach, where we had a three-hour stopover. First we went to the guesthouse near the station where - according to my directory - our company's representatives would stay. We wanted to take our lunch there. They had a different reception for us than in Laibach! German hospitality from the host and the hostess, an excellent meal and

107 It is likely that the officials knew Bruneck under its Italian name of Brunico.

exhilarating as well as enlightening conversation made the hours pass quickly. Back to the station! Our train through the Puster Valley was ready. Given the few passengers on the train we could spread out in our carriage and get comfortable for the almost eight-hour long journey that lay ahead of us. If the journey from Laibach, Tarvis-Villach had already been very enjoyable because of its magnificent views of the mountain range of the Kvaerner Alps, expectations were even higher for the narrow Puster Valley, flanked on both sides by the Tyrolean Alps. Yet it was not meant to be! After an hour's journey a snowstorm descended on us, mixed with rain and hail, which denied us those views almost until the end of our trip. The fact that an Austrian senior civil servant joined us at some point was welcome insofar as his company led to some engaging conversation which was to everyone's benefit.

Had we continued for an hour longer we could have reached the central station of Franzensfeste[108], where the Puster Valley line terminates. I wanted to stay over in Bruneck, however, since our longstanding representative Herr Dietz, whom I have already mentioned as my travelling companion several times, had previously told me that the Bruneck guesthouse was quite excellent. Reception and fare justified the praise completely. The hosts took a real delight in their guests from Nuremberg, and we had to promise that we would come back and stay for longer. We also realised how good it feels to hear the true German greetings "Grüss Gott" and "B'hüt Gott"[109].

---

[108] Nowadays more commonly known as Fortezza.

[109] Meaning "hello" and "goodbye", the phrases translate roughly as "God welcomes you" and "God bless you".

The next day we arrived in Innsbruck, where another excellent hotel welcomed us. We visited every corner of this lovely, beautiful city where so many sights commemorate the Tyrolean military hero Andreas Hofer, but the most beautiful feature of the Tyrolean capital will always be its unparalleled location.

Then on we went at a fast pace. Upon our arrival in Kufstein we greeted the national colours of Bavaria, all the while our hearts were full of gratitude for the wonderful holiday we had had. One more stopover in Munich, and then a ceremonial reception in Nuremberg, where we found all our loved ones in good health.

In Muggendorf, a neighbouring village to Streitberg, a Herr Dr. Sommer was working as a general practitioner. I met and learned to respect him even before we bought the villa. Once my family and I were spending an increasing amount of time in the Streitberg region during the summer months, our relationship grew even more affectionate. By then Herr Dr. Sommer had set up his own home by marrying the love of his youth, and due to the fact that the families spent much time together, our relationship with the young, lovely couple turned into a lasting, friendly neighbourliness which brought great joy and excitement to both parties. It goes without saying that this diligent doctor who was highly respected by all professions also became our family physician.

The afore-mentioned journey to the Adriatic Sea rekindled my longing to see Westerland again, which I had visited some years previously under such difficult circumstances. I could not discuss this with my wife; she always became frightened when she heard the word "Sylt". And yet I could not stop thinking about how lovely it would be to experience a second North Sea tour, only this time in full health and in a happy mood, in other words, under a lucky star. What I longed for eventually became true!

The first question was, who was to come with me? No-one from the family was available. The year was well advanced, the school holidays were over, and yet I found a better companion than I could have hoped for, someone who completely reassured my wife. It was Herr Dr. Sommer, the hard-working doctor who had not left Muggendorf in years, and he accepted my invitation to come and see the world as my good friend and personal doctor with great joy. Thus we set off, light-hearted and in beautiful sunshine, sometime around mid-September.

Our first destination was Leipzig. I had an important business matter to prepare there, and talking about it with Herr Dr. Sommer, I was able to see that he had a great understanding of commercial issues, too. The business matter was concerning the rental agreement for the business localities which are still being used by our company today. Once the work was done, we visited the municipal theatre. The piece and its performance were bland; the only thing I remember about it was how plainly many of the ladies were dressed - not just in the stalls but even those on the dress circle. In my opinion, the theatre is no place for every day clothes, nor for the display of evident and exaggerated luxury.

The next day we went to Berlin. We had both seen the city's tourist sights on previous visits, and therefore I have nothing of importance to add. By contrast, Hamburg was a new world to both of us, and for Herr Dr. Sommer even a completely new world. We were glad to be spending a few days in the magnificent Hanseatic city, and I was eager to see what my friend the doctor would make of this unique, extensive place. We found lodgings at a well-reputed hotel situated by the Alster dock. The "*Pain Hotel*" where I had lived many years earlier when I had had that severe accident, had been pulled down and replaced by a sizeable office block.

The first sight that any stranger goes to visit in Hamburg is the harbour, and no-one can defy the effect the magnificent view has on the observer. To me, the sight was nothing new, and yet, seeing the massive river with its many hundreds of ships and boats that were arriving, preparing for their voyages or being anchored in Hamburg, I was gripped by a mood that can only be experienced but not explained. Herr Dr. Sommer would be so amazed, I thought! I was moved by the same anticipation that

Fig. 57 St. Pauli Landing Bridges, Hamburg, ca. 1900.

always grips me when, back at the *Bing-Höhle*, I assume the role of the tour guide for a particularly important guest who has not been to the cave in Streitberg before. I am always delighted by the visitor's surprise and admiration at what they are being shown.

The solemn moment did not fulfil my expectations entirely. It was in the good doctor's nature. He did not like admitting when he was surprised. He took everything for granted, whether it was something small and meaningless or something great and sublime. Having arrived at St. Pauli Landing Bridges, he had barely taken in the full view of the harbour when his interest turned mainly to the technical installations, which he had explained to him by a sailor who happened to be there. His demeanour was similar when he visited the *Bing-Höhle* for the first time. It is not that he was unimpressed by the many beauties, only a certain detachment did not allow his emotions, his opinion of what was great and beautiful, to go beyond a certain point. For example, during his first visit to the *Bing-Höhle* - a cave which no nature lover can visit without being deeply moved by the wonders before him - he bet me that he could find his way from the end of the cave back to its entrance without the need for a light. I can only remember one single incident on our trip when Herr Dr. Sommer could not find enough words of enthusiasm. We travelled down the Elbe river to have lunch at the famous *Park Hotel* restaurant. I remembered their excellent food from my previous visit. Dr. Sommer was no gourmet; after all, the rural conditions of Muggendorf are hardly the right breeding ground for gourmets. However, he did have a good understanding of what fine dining was. The amount and quality of the food presented at the *Park Hotel* was unsurpassable. This was a lunch he would never forget, and years later he and I would still talk about those culinary delights.

When we wanted to leave the *Park Hotel* and return to Hamburg with the scheduled steamer, we were unsure about the exact arrival and departure time of the ship. On the pier, a solitary man overheard us talking. He turned to us without being asked and said that he was equally uncertain and that his sister was just now consulting the timetable. He pointed over his shoulder to a lady who was indeed looking at the timetable mounted on the pier. The lady joined us, and we greeted and informed her politely. She was a beautiful woman in her twenties with elegant yet simple looks, who, as much as we could tell, had regular, beautiful features behind her veil. We had a half-hour wait, and this time was sufficient to get to know these people as if we had been socialising with them for months. This, however, was thanks only to the exceedingly forthcoming gentleman, who talked relentlessly about this and that, and in such a confident, or rather, complacent manner that his seemingly very tactful sister was quite embarrassed. We remained quite reserved ourselves; none-theless, we could not hide our hilarity about the brashness of the gentleman who was continually asking questions and answering them himself. We found the situation amusing rather than annoying, especially since the lady's elegant reserve stood in such refreshing contrast to the well-meaning, but somewhat intrusive manner of her companion.

At last the steamer arrived. We took our seats next to the two siblings, for that is indeed what they were. During the trip, the young man explained that he was studying in Berlin, was just about to take his exams, and that he was spending his holidays with relatives in Hamburg. His sister had accompanied him on the excursion to the *Park Hotel* as a favour. Now he wanted to know if we were from the South, since he thought that our accent indicated that that was the case. I glanced at the sister to reassure her that we found her brother's prying entertaining and that she need not worry that we might hold his inquisitiveness against them. She smiled back at us, indicating clearly that she was not to be held responsible for her brother's strange manners.

I decided to teach the endless questioner a lesson, which was also to be met with the sister's approval. When Herr Scholar repeated his question about our nationality, stressing that we were certainly not from Berlin, I admitted the latter. I said that we thanked God every day that we were not Prussians, whose national characteristics were much laughed at and less admired where we were from. I added that I could not be certain yet that he, as a Hamburger, had already acquired these characteristics during his stay in Berlin, but he seemed to exhibit a certain predisposition to that effect.

Herr Dr. Sommer was even more to the point and declared that some of the famous Berlin blabbermouth was indeed shining through. The lady laughed out loud and shot her brother a mocking glance. He did not drop his equally brazen and funny way for a second and started to rant about the cumbersome, South German manner, in particular about beer-drinking Bavarians and other things which the North Germans, rightly or wrongly, attribute to their fellow Germans from the South. "And now at last", he continued, "tell us where you are from, what you are doing in Hamburg, where you are going, and what you do for a living". Of course, he was only asking these questions in jest, he was only exaggerating the Berlinesque style and thus seemed to have the last laugh.

"You want to know where we hail from?" I asked the flippant youngster. "We make no secret of it, since our names have already been published in the *Hamburger Fremdenblatt*[110]. We come from Bavaria, and we are Bavarians. Our mission is something which we accomplished very successfully today at the *Park Hotel*, namely a comprehensive review of Hamburg's restaurants. We can disclose who we are without blushing. Here, you shall have it in black and white." And with that I handed him my business card. "My companion is regarded as an excellent medicine man who is accompanying me as my friend and personal doctor. If you are feeling unwell in body or in mind, my esteemed doctor will be glad to advise you."

We were all in a very jolly mood, and the pretty sister in particular seemed to enjoy the humour with which we were responding to her nosy brother's questions.

The young man's eyes opened wide when he read the business card I had given him. He lifted his hat and said in a loud voice, without regard to anyone else around us, "But why didn't you say that you are a *Kommerzienrat* and the other gentleman a doctor; I would have behaved myself! Please excuse my behaviour, gentlemen." Following that he introduced himself and his sister properly.

---

110 One of Hamburg's most important newspapers during the 19th century, the *Fremdenblatt* (literally: "paper of foreigners") had started out in 1828 as a list of foreigners arriving in Hamburg.

What followed is not worth recalling; only one thing I will mention, namely that we were asked to continue our cosy, cheery conversation that evening at the *Alster Café*. Since that suggestion was also warmly supported by the very jovial young lady, we promised to join them after the play. I cannot remember which theatre we went to, but the performance was not finished until after 11 o'clock.

When we arrived at the *Alster Café*, our acquaintances had left already. I learned that the brother and sister were from a highly respected family. The connection had been established; the relationship was to develop further in the future.

The next day we left for Westerland-Sylt. I had already made that journey, but this time it was something quite different. The jolly doctor, who recognised and judged everything he encountered, even if it was for the first time, who had seen all kinds of human behaviour, and I, with my great capacity for new impressions and my interest in the foreign country, enjoyed ourselves immensely. Before we knew it, the near-empty train pulled into Hoyer Lock. We had to wait a long time until the boat went, just as long as a traveller coming from Streitberg has to wait in Forchheim before he can catch the train that will take him to Nuremberg. The steamer for Westerland was still stuck on the muddy bottom of the canal, and I was able to explain to the doctor exactly what needed to happen before we could set sail.

At last the incoming tide was so high that our ship, like a patient who had fully recovered, was rocking gently on the water with billowing sails, ready to hurry unhindered towards her element, the open sea. (This is of course merely poetic licence, since the ship did not actually have any sails.) The weather was pretty inclement that evening. This time there was to be no sitting in cosy armchairs on deck, no view of the sea at night, no starry skies. We and about a dozen other people took our seats in the dank cabin and drank - Herr Dr. Sommer will swear under oath that this is the truth - no less than three or four cups of black coffee, maybe a couple of *schnapps* too, until we arrived in Munkmarsch from where the little train took us to Westerland in just a few minutes.

At the station we found an envoy from the Wünschmann family. We had very elegant lodgings in the little house; and Herr Doctor was missing only one thing: even at this late hour, it was nearly midnight when we were drinking our tea, he would have liked to be introduced to the "dream maid". No chance - it was too late for that!

Having spent a good night, I noticed at breakfast that the doctor was missing. He had gone to the beach without me, he had taken his bearings around Westerland, and upon his return he talked about the place as if he had been a regular visitor to this sea resort for twenty years. Everything went very quickly with him. He had even found out already that as general practitioner he was entitled to use the baths etc. for free. He was one of those people whom the motto *nil admirari*[111] seemed to have been coined for. Anything wonderful or special one showed him was immediately turned into a "thing", which he looked at and judged in his own way, no matter if it was the glowing seas or Cologne Cathedral. Apart from that we wandered peacefully across the

111 Latin for "to admire nothing".

heath and through the island's marshes, visited the picturesque Frisian villages with their old-fashioned, and often very valuable installations, walked for hours over the dunes along the beach, and this busy idleness was made even more enjoyable by the good provisions and by the fact that my companion had now also made the acquaintance of Wünschmann, Wünschfrau and Wünschmaid. The Wünschmann family were the epitome of a family solidly united in their aim to protect anything that might be beneficial to the family and the advancement of its individual members. There were the parents, a handsome, sprightly couple, seven sons, four of which were serving with the Guards Regiments in Berlin, and three charming daughters. All the siblings were endowed with the same beautiful, Frisian looks as their mother, and all had the good, Saxon business sense of their father. One son was employed with his aunt, who owned a large hotel in Bordighera[112], and was expected to run the hotel himself one day. Another son was the tenant of the eminent new *kurhaus* in Westerland, and for the third son, Wünschmann senior had built a large guesthouse in a top location in the town which was very busy with overnight guests during the season. The second eldest daughter was married to the owner of a large confectionary shop and elegant café. The eldest daughter independently led a busy guesthouse, which was also owned by the family, and the idea was that after her marriage she would take it over as her own. The youngest daughter, the original "Wünschmaid", could be described as an extraordinarily beautiful girl and was engaged to a respected merchant in Westerland, who had business relations with our company amongst others. The family had a high level of activity, harmony and strong will when they were

[112] Italian resort on the Riviera near Sanremo.

supporting a member of the family and when they were striving towards consolidating or growing their wealth. Wünschmann had, for example, predicted the development of Westerland's property market early on. He had acquired premium sites for little money and made large profits when he sold them or developed them himself. There was just one business deal, with his son-in-law confectioner Wiedemann, that brought him great unhappiness. What had happened was this: Next to his son-in-law's property was a large plot facing the very busy promenade. The site was ideal for erecting a large building, and with space for a sizeable garden. Wünschmann talked his son-in-law into buying the plot, and indeed we saw that a part of the site had already been developed into a beer garden or café. In my opinion the confectioner had made an excellent bargain; the beer garden was already bringing in more than enough money to cover the interest payments on the purchase. Yet it seemed to me that the man was somewhat ill-humoured by nature, and at the time he took the greatest pleasure in accusing his well-meaning father-in-law at every opportunity of having badgered him into such a bad deal. It was no good that Wünschmann offered to buy the property from him; Wiedemann would only claim that it was all idle talk etc. The relationship between the Wünschmanns and their son-in-law was very strained and uneasy during my second stay in Westerland. I could not bring Wünschmann to come with us for a chat in Wiedemann's café, as he used to love to do. I saw an opportunity that would bring the family dispute to an end and see the unappreciated father-in-law immensely gratified.

I could estimate fairly well how cheaply Wünschmann had sold this plot, the prime location in all of Westerland, to his son-in-law, and I calculated that I would make a very good deal if I bought the property myself for a few thousand marks more. I told Wünschmann that I was not looking for a property at the moment, but that I would like to buy one in Westerland, my Streitberg of the North, should the opportunity arise. Wiedemann's site, which was causing him such unhappiness, would suit me very well. I said that I was going to have a serious chat with him, adding that I would of course, if I were able to buy the property, pay for it in cash, and that I was not planning on paying any less than his son-in-law had paid for it. I had the same conversation with Wiedemann, explaining to him that this was a great opportunity to rid himself of the property that was causing him so much grief, and that it would also put an end to the looming family discord.

Wünschmann was only partly pleased by my suggestion. On the one hand he would appreciate it very much if the accusations stopped, on the other hand he was sorry that such a valuable property should not remain in the family.

My offer was received unenthusiastically by Wiedemann; he said he had got used to the whole thing now and was going to consider selling the property carefully. Now I had brought the matter to maturity and was about to make the final blow. I persuaded my host to accompany me to his son-in-law's, explaining that the moment had come to compensate him for all the grievances he had suffered regarding this property. He came with me, but he was very worried about this meeting with his son-in-law and what it might hold. We sat down, ordered some coffee, and I bid Herr Wiedemann to join us for a talk. He arrived a little flustered and greeted his father-in-law self-consciously; I immediately launched into business. I asked if he was willing to let me have the garden plot to the conditions I had advised him of, adding that I did not mind paying a few thousand marks more if that would speed up the affair. Wünschmann shifted uncomfortably about in his chair; he was evidently afraid that his son-in-law might agree. Wiedemann, however, was quite phlegmatic and said that he did not like selling what he now owned, and with that my host began to look freer and more cheerful. I replied that I had heard from many people how Herr Wiedemann thought the new property was a cause for bother and concern, and now I had to assume that it was all just a game. To put an end to this, I explained, I was increasing my offer by 10,000 marks so that he would end up with a nice bit of profit on a piece of land that had caused him to reproach his father-in-law, here present at this table, so often and so bitterly. Now came the retreat. Wiedemann admitted unreservedly that his father-in-law had not only advised him well but also extremely selflessly, that he was grateful for it, and that he would not sell the plot even if he were offered 20,000 marks above the original purchasing price. This was a wonderful gratification for my clever Saxon, this good family man who was looking after his loved ones so loyally, and the whole family remained deeply grateful to me that I had worked so hard to bring it about.

Our days in Westerland were coming to an end. We had greatly exceeded the time we had planned to stay there. Our hosts and their families saw us off affectionately, and we started our return journey via Kiel, whose significance as the most important naval base for the German Reich I do not need to underline.[113] We

[113] Kiel was declared a "Reichskriegshafen" (Imperial War Harbour) by Kaiser Wilhelm I during the Franco-Prussian War in 1871.

stayed most comfortably at the hotel *Germania*, and the doctor was particularly impressed with the food they served. The fact that the hotel had an efficient way of arranging the strict separation of guests and the many marine officers frequenting the hotel was something I noticed with displeasure. A separate entrance had been secured for the marines from the street, there were closed doors and a glass wall cutting the dining hall in two, in short creating an unapproachable world for the mere traveller. These examples of an often-hurtful caste spirit have not made us Germans popular in the world.

We strolled around the port, took a motorboat trip to where the Kiel canal flows into Kiel bay and marvelled at the enormous battleships anchored at the port. Next to one of those giant ships lay the *Hohenzollern*, which carries the Kaiser over the seas when he is taking a break from his worries and affairs. The doctor wanted to visit a battleship, which I had heard was meant to be arduous. I therefore let him go by himself, and I spent the midday hour in the famous Kieler beer cellar. At the agreed hour we met at the hotel, each highly satisfied with our day's work, and very late that evening we arrived in Hamburg. We set up quarters in a good hotel near the Dammtor, since we were planning on taking the first train to Frankfurt in the morning. From there our next destination was Wiesbaden. I was looking forward to being in the city that I loved, and I was going to stay there for a few days to partake of a *Traubenkur*[114]. The beautiful landscape, the nearby Rhine, the wonderful parks and the elegant city - everything comes together to make leaving Wiesbaden a sad affair. And yet I, and the doctor too, I think, was overcome by a

114 "Course of grapes" - a health diet based on grapes and grape juice.

longing for homeliness, and so we set off home, grateful for the weeks we had spent together as good, cheery travelling companions.

A few weeks later I received a card from Hamburg with the words: "We are still sitting in the *Alster Café* waiting for you. Dyrenfurth and sister." Our acquaintances from the *Park Hotel.* From our chance meeting there developed a friendly communication, and a few years later Fräulein Dyrenfurth came to be our guest in Streitberg. The magical veil had disappeared, and with it the illusion of the lady's extraordinary beauty. What was left was still sufficient. The lady, of elegant appearance and of tactful and straight demeanour, cheerful and easy-going, won the full affection of the whole family, and whenever the opportunity arose we kept up our correspondence.

When I described Westerland as my "Streitberg of the North", I should rightfully call Bolzano my "Streitberg of the South". A comparison with Streitberg always indicates that no other place will ever be as dear to me as this little village in Franconia and my little house there. I have been to Bolzano many times in my life, and under varying circumstances, and every time I notice anew just how at home I feel there and how good and comfortable a hotel the *Greif* is.

The pleasures of the journey to Bolzano itself must not be under-estimated either. Who does not like to turn their step towards the beautiful Munich, a lovely city that offers so much to the visitor? Is it not a wonderful thought in itself to know that you are going to spend a few days in Munich, and then to be riding a speedy train across the Brenner Pass into the Tyrolean mountains towards the sunny South before arriving in the hospitable Bolzano? Admittedly, the short trip to Bolzano, where the days usually all pass in the same manner, does not give rise to any special, noteworthy incidents, which in fact may be a blessing in disguise, in particular for the traveller looking for some peace and quiet.

The only tour to Bolzano I will include in these travel stories is one that I made with my two nieces Olga and Aennie Hirsch. I wanted to combine business with pleasure. The "business" in this case was that I wanted to show my niece Olga, who was disinclined to marry, that there were still men who might bring an aloof maiden's heart to reason.

Once we had arrived in Munich, my nieces went their own way while I waited for the knight St. George to come and slay the dragon of indifference to the male sex. St. George arrived: A very tall, handsome man who in my opinion looked as if he was destined to be a dragon slayer. We had a very nice chat; he turned out to be a giant with the heart of a child, and we arranged a meeting for the next day where my ladies were to be present. When my nieces arrived back at the hotel, I told them about the arrangements and was true to my honest feelings full of praise for my, as I was hoping, future nephew-in-law. In the evening, we went to the theatre, which was renowned for its exquisite performances of comedies. During the interval, we happened across - I will stick with the name - St. George in the foyer, and I had no choice but to introduce the two parties to each other in the customary way. The gentleman was quite shy, it seemed partly because my nieces were all dressed up and looking adorable.

The introduction ceremony had to be extended to include my hero's parents, who were also present. Truth be told, I was quite pleased about the chance meeting, since I told myself that it would lessen the certain awkwardness of the meeting planned for the next day.

After we said our goodbyes and we had not moved far away from the other party, my two nieces burst into uncontrollable laughter. The hilarity was aimed at St. George. Apart from his massive figure, both girls claimed that he had fish-eyes, and all my reasoning counted for nothing. The story was finished before it had begun. Late that night I wrote him a convoluted note saying that the planned meeting had to be cancelled due to unforeseen circumstances. I received no reply. It is an unthankful business, playing cupid.

We went on to Bolzano. It was around the middle of March, and there was a thin layer of snow on the plateau around Munich, which grew thicker as we approached the mountains. The Inn valley was completely covered in snow, and there were massive snowdrifts along both sides of the tracks all the way up the height of the Brenner. Now we were eager to see the effect the sun's kindness would have had south of the Brenner. We even expressed our expectation of finding blossoming shrubs and green meadows. Yet the snow did not want to yield, and it was only just before our destination that the black or brown earth of this fertile land was freed of its white blanket.

At the *Greif* we were received with the usual, warm welcome and a certain grandeur by the manageress of the hotel. That night the excellent military band played in the hotel dining room. Thanks to my previous stays, Fanny, the attentive waitress, remembered me well and gave me my usual table. I was also still in favour with the diligent maître d', who had taken on some of the director's roles, so that we were feeling completely at home. The director was a handsome man and looked remarkably like my brother Heinrich. We tried, in jest of course, to find out where the resemblance stemmed from. Questions about origins, mother and father etc. were asked and answered, and the equally eloquent and kind man displayed a great sense of humour; he pretended not to understand the questions or tried to make them even funnier by the way he answered.

The sun in Bolzano had grown stronger. The days were getting warmer so that on some days the music at the *Greif* was played outside. A crowd would gather then on the large square, consisting mainly of very good looking Austrian officers. In how far this fact was appreciated by my nieces I cannot say; yet they did not seem to be bothered by it in any way.

We did what everyone does in Bolzano in spring time: We went on long and short excursions, and we decided to take a trip to Soprabolzano. The electric train climbed the 1400 metres and delivered us there. As it happened, our trio had turned into a quartet by the time we arrived at our destination. A not bad-looking young man had introduced himself as the aristocratic manufacturer of loden material, Herr von Brunneck, and asked for permission to join us. He had already made the acquaintance of my young ladies in Bolzano and was blushingly following in their tracks - with what hopes or intentions, however, I was unable to find out. The view from Soprabolzano towards the Seiser Alm, the Schlern and the Rosengarten is so immensely beautiful that we arrived back in Bolzano highly satisfied, and so did our loden youth. I never saw him again - if my nieces did, I was never told.

It was nearly the end of March, and we were eagerly looking for signs of spring and its effect on Bolzano's vegetation. There was little to see in that respect; by contrast we were convinced that in the valleys of the Franconian mountains the first flowers of spring would already have dared to show themselves. We decided to leave Bolzano for a few days to find real spring with flowers and trees in blossom, and what is more, we wanted to wander amongst palm trees.

"*Knowst thou the land where the lemon trees bloom*[115], and thieving Italians to your pockets bring doom?" So off to Riva, to the exceptionally beautiful Lake Garda, most of which now unfortunately belongs to the Brigands, whom we protected for over 30 years only to find ourselves betrayed by this gang in this current war.

In Riva, we stopped at the *Hotel Lido Palace*. From its terrace one has a view of a considerable part of the mighty lake surrounded by proud heights. An avenue lined with real palm trees leads up to the hotel, which itself is situated in extensive gardens where spring had indeed arrived. We had thus found what we had been looking and hoping for.

We were offered good rooms, though they were not quite as comfortable as the pretentious reception hall and the whole affair with doorman, page boys and uniformed attendants had led us to

---

115 J. W. von Goethe in "Wilhelm Meister's Apprenticeship".

expect. We had a look around the town and returned to the hotel for dinner. The general table d'hôte was finished, and we wanted to choose something nice à la carte. The menu featured four to five dishes; a sparse selection for a hotel of such high rank. Our waiter seemed to still be suffering from the shock of the catastrophe of Messina[116], which, he told us, he had experienced. Every time we chose a dish he first went to the kitchen and then returned with the message that that which we had chosen was already sold out. In fact, the only thing they had to offer was an omelette with far too little ham on the side. There is a price to pay even for walking under palm trees! We were, however, more bemused than annoyed by the oddities of our proud inn, and our Ganymede, who was familiar with the weaknesses and deficiencies of the business, joined us in our hilarity.

Fig. 58 Palace Hotel Lido, Riva.

[116] Presumably the 1908 earthquake.

The next day we went on a tour of Lake Garda. As a consequence of the early departure time of the ship we were unable to eat at the table d'hôte. We did not worry about it though, since the tour of the lake only lasted a few hours, and if necessary something could be had on the ship. More than that! We had barely entrusted the Italian steamer with our lives before a garçon in greasy tails invited the passengers to lunch - cover three francs. My nieces were not in the mood to follow the call. The deck smelled so intrusively of onions and oil that it was enough to make you feel full already. I ventured to sit down at the table anyway. I have always strived to familiarise myself with the customs and traditions of foreign countries, and that includes the people's food and drink.

In the cabin, maybe a dozen people were sat at a narrow table. The table was laid with an undoubtedly dirty, formerly white cloth; the knives and forks had greasy wooden handles. In short, it was a very unappetising affair. The first course arrived: an indefinable dark broth with what I assumed were pieces of lamb. After the first spoonful I had had enough. This was followed by chicken and rice, a not unusual dish which at home is one of my favourites. The rice was soaked in yellow oil that had a peculiar smell and taste which took some getting used to. The chicken meat was tough and bland. I did like the cheese which was served afterwards and of which I consumed a rather large amount, and I very much enjoyed the oranges served at the end.

The food did not agree with me. Immediately after the meal I developed severe stomach pains, which spoiled my enjoyment of the boat trip and the landscape. Only when we arrived in Gardone did I begin to feel better. Yet I did enjoy Lake Garda.

We experienced not a just a green-tinted winter, but a real spring and pleasant, warming sunshine. Our time was up, we returned to Bolzano, and a few days later we were back home.

One does not always need to go abroad to find beauty, since the German spring with all its poetry and splendour stood knocking at the door demanding to be let in.

I visited Bolzano one more time. Westerland, too, was visited a third time, accompanied by my daughter Marie and my niece Olga, but I have the feeling that the descriptions of the places revisited, even if at different times, are falling into a certain monotony, especially when there is no personal touch to the events, or when there are no more encounters with interesting people. I can only say that every journey that is undertaken in good physical and mental constitution is enjoyable, provided that one does not spoil the magic of travelling by and for oneself. Whoever takes to heart every bit of discomfort, be it on the journey or in the accommodation, whoever makes dictatorial demands when restraint and a proper assessment of the situation is needed, had better stay at home. I have had many acquaintances, even friends, whom I enjoyed spending my time with, but given their idea of what and what not to do when travelling, I knew better than to invite them as my travelling companions or to join them as theirs.

I feel the need to make these comments now because I was planning to make an important journey, the telling of which shall conclude this book. For this journey it was particularly important to find the right company, since I could not count on family members to accompany me. The daughters were married, the sons in business, and my wife did not want to leave her snail shell.

Every year at the beginning of February, I heard one or another of my friends at the club say that they were about to go on a trip to Italy, usually with the destination of Nice[117]. Very often I was invited to join them, with reference to the fact that an experienced companion was invaluable for any traveller to the wonderland of Italy.

For a long time I had no inclination to follow their siren call. I would have loved to travel to Italy like Goethe did, or at least guided by an art historian who would be able to explain the abundant art treasures in Italy's galleries to me, yet there was no opportunity for it, and what is more, I had grown too old for a journey of this kind to Rome by now.

What the other gentlemen amongst my acquaintances were looking for in their annual spring holidays to the South was to escape the German winter, to wait in a good hotel under the mild Italian sun - be it in Nice, Montone etc. - until a real spring, not just a green-tinted winter, had returned to Germany. What more did I want?

Among my acquaintances there was one Charles Haas from Nuremberg who explained to me emphatically what he was seeking and expecting during his annual spring holiday in the South. It was neither the casino in Monte-Carlo nor the German Tarrock in Nice, but merely the effect the Italian spring had on

---

117 Although part of various Italian and Sardinian empires and kingdoms for much of its history, the city of Nice has actually been French since 1859.

his mood and on his health, and the escape from the misty, cold German winter.

Herr Haas was unmarried, and his business obligations - shared with his younger brother - did not cause him any concerns either. He had spent a long time in America, had seen much of the world, and his clear, level-headed views enabled him particularly well to properly assess that which comes into question when travelling in general and when spending time in a foreign country in particular.

If for example Herr Haas recommended a hotel, one could rest assured that it was justified. And he certainly included the aspect of cost in his assessment. Doing the right thing was very important to him, i.e. he did not fail to do what travellers are morally obliged to do, but at the same time he strictly insisted that he received a return service. Moreover, spending time with this always-friendly man was not without its uses for me either. It was in my nature to go beyond merely exploring the place where fate had planted me. I may well say that in my business I have fought back anything that might have damaged or harmed it in any way. But I was more than "just a businessman", and it seemed to me that a journey to Italy was inextricably linked with not only the travel impressions of the beautiful landscape, but also with the search for the opportunity to visit a few Italian cities where a great past had left its mark, and where the immortal pieces of Italian art could still be seen in galleries, museums and architecture.

For this purpose, Herr Haas was not a suitable guide or companion. What he was looking for in the main was a good hotel, a few acquaintances and, at most, a watchable theatre performance. This completely sufficed him, and he had no interest in that which I was longing for and which remained alien to him. He was a completely unemotional man, whose knowledge of the banking business was generally acknowledged to be excellent, and I did not mind listening to him talk about an important economic matter, which often helped me understand an issue better than if I had read the fat volumes written by some national economist. I also valued his practical advice regarding certain financial questions in my business. However, in a way, we complemented each other quite well, and I decided to join him as his travelling companion for a several week-long stay in Nice. I was hoping that once there I might have the opportunity to visit Florence and Rome.

Herr Haas was in charge of procuring the tickets, which were valid only on the specified date, and which were required for the use of the Berlin-Nice luxury train. We met up in Munich, took an express train to Bolzano, and a few enjoyable days later we were awaiting the luxury train which was to take us south.

Everything worked beautifully. The train driver had already been informed that he was going to pick up two more guests in Bolzano, a compartment had been reserved for us, and we sat down on our seats with contentment. It was an elegant room that was going to be our home, intended for only two people, and equipped with a basin and all kinds of other comforts. It was not called a "luxury train" for nothing!

The train departed Bolzano at around 3 o'clock in the afternoon. The snow masses of the Brenner lay behind us, but there was no sign of spring. The landscape looked bleak and frosty. Herr Haas warned me not to expect a fast rise in temperature and a thus related increase in vegetation. At this time of year - mid-February - even Italy was still cold, sometimes even very inhospitable. There were, however, a few surprises waiting for the first-time visitor, especially on the Riviera.

Having whiled away the time with light conversation, we arrived at Verona at around 8 o'clock in the evening. We were called to the dining car. Herr Haas, who in my opinion was excessively careful with regard to his stomach, had brought a thin slice of roast veal with him from Bolzano, while I enjoyed going to the dining car. The meal there was abundant and good. When I returned to our compartment, our beds had already been prepared for the night. Herr Haas chose the lower bunk while I was given the top one, which was reached by some sort of Jacob's Ladder. Then we were bidden to be quiet.

I spent a not uncomfortable night in some kind of half-sleep. Through the windows in the roof I saw the stars twinkle; the muffled rolling of the wheels seemed elegant compared to the clattering of the night trains I was more used to. The whole business was focussed on the passengers' comfort.

Upon our arrival at the station in Milan I did not hear any loud voices, nor did I notice a noisy stopping or departing of the train. Gently and without interruption, the travellers were led into the land where lemon trees bloom.

After a few hours of deep sleep I was awakened by a thundering noise which was repeated at certain intervals. I had no idea what it was. Suddenly, I thought that the rolling thunder might actually be the sound of waves breaking on the beach; and that's indeed what it was. The train came to a halt in Genoa. Slowly, dawn was turning into day. I wanted to get up, but Herr Haas, who was now also wide-awake, would not allow it. I was to wait another hour. At last, having restored my personal appearance with a thorough wash, I was permitted to go to the dining car to have breakfast.

Now I saw the surprise, or I may say the wonder, that Herr Haas had hinted at. A few days ago we had been surrounded by snow and ice, and now there lay before my astonished eyes a landscape bathed in sunny morning light revealing fruit-bearing trees, blooming roses and other splendid flowers. A world of wonders for the traveller from the North who approaches this region for the first time.

There were still another two hours to go until we reached Nice, and I remained glued to the window for the rest of the journey. And yet I noticed a certain monotony, or better still, undifferentiated beauty about the landscape passing by. In the foreground the blue, shimmering sea, crashing violently onto the rocky coast, then a narrow strip of cultivated land in abundant fertility, pebbled with white houses and picturesque old towns, while the background was bordered by olive groves and vineyards on steep hills, towered over by grey rocks which seemed devoid of any vegetation.

Over breakfast, I had met a fellow countryman and his wife who had made the journey to Nice several times before, and we agreed that the valleys of our native Franconian Switzerland, with their ancient castles on wooded heights, had a quieter and really more impressive effect on the senses and the soul than this sea glazing in the sunlight, the narrow piece of land and the treeless mountains.

This is not to say that the classic beauty of the passing landscape was alien to me, or that I did not appreciate it. After all, it was like a beautiful dream to me, as if I had been picked up from the bleak and snow-covered North and put down in the wonder-world of this southern landscape.

We arrived in Nice and found good accommodation in the *Hotel Des Anglais.* The hotel is right on the *Promenade des Anglais*, had an excellent restaurant and seemed to be frequented predominantly by fellow Germans. The owners, too, were Germans. I met more people from Nuremberg whom I knew more or less well and was greeted warmly by all. If I want to be honest, however, I must say that the company was not great, and that any holiday in a German spa town, be it in Kissingen, Wiesbaden or elsewhere, was more pleasurable and had more suitable, engaging company to offer than gleaming Nice.

My travel guide had a strict timetable, which I naturally adopted, and which made the days pass with a certain regularity. The programme included a morning stroll from 10 'till noon on the promenade, where we came across many acquaintances with whom we made meaningless conversation. Then, from noon 'till one, preparations for lunch; after the table d'hôte came a somewhat extensive nap. At 4 o'clock, coffee and concert or theatre in the vast municipal establishment of the *Casino de la Jetée*, which had the added benefit of being across the road from the hotel, and which hosted concerts, plays and roulette games. At 6 o'clock in the evening one had dinner, an abundant 6 or 7-course meal; dress code was black or white tie.

After dinner one sat down in a basket chair in the reception area, watched the other - generally speaking not very interesting - people, until at last, at a time when in Nuremberg one would retire for the night, we would go to the *Cercle.* In order to gain

Fig. 59 Hotel des Anglais, Public Gardens and Casino, 1890.
© Snapshots of the Past.

access to this casino, one had to be introduced by someone known to the management and purchase a ticket which was valid for the duration of one's stay in Nice. The entrance fee was 30 francs, and the doorman expected an additional tip. The stakes at the *Cercle* were high, if not quite as high as in Monte Carlo. Excited men and women, the latter often in striking dresses, were sitting at the gambling tables with greedy eyes, and, depending on the flow of the game, one could observe their expressions of greed, distorted and frozen faces, in short, all the changing effects brought on by the devil of the game.

Needless to say that there was no shortage of painted women with more or less real or fake diamonds either. The *Cercle* also had a large restaurant, where I regularly met with other gentlemen from Nuremberg. We usually sat together at a table, and that was all I could bear, since the casino and its people disgusted me. Amongst my closer acquaintances was a man from Nuremberg who was consul for one of the northern states, and as far as I could tell he was doing a pretty good job. He wore a number of decorations on his chest, which appeared to bear testimony to his diplomatic talents. He had a very high opinion of himself, his capabilities, the position he had been entrusted with and everything that concerned his person in general. It would be difficult to give an accurate account of the combination of self-assurance and self-importance he embodied. I would not even have mentioned it, had my meeting with Herr Consul in Nice not had a further important consequence, to which I will come back later.

When our group from Nuremberg sat together in the *Cercle* restaurant of an evening, it was always Herr Consul who shared some of his quirks with us and thus caused general amusement, though often unintentionally so. One evening, for example, the waiter passed some cigars round and offered some to the consul. Our friend shook his head and asked the waiter: "Savez-vous, qu'est ce que-c'est un schlemiel?"[118] The garçon clearly under-

[118] "Do you know what a schlemiel is?"

Fig. 60 Casino and public gardens, Nice, 1899.
© trialsanderrors (flickr)

stood and was quick to reply: "Un schlemiel, c'est un homme, qui ne fume pas."[119] We gave a round of applause.

Another time it happened that a lady had sat down at our table. She was known to one of the gentlemen at our table but did not know our Nuremberg diplomat, nor did he know her. When Herr Consul arrived and noticed the elegant, beautiful lady he did not wait for an introduction but introduced himself by saying that personally, he had a passion for wine, women and song, and that he had only given up on the latter, i.e. song. He would later repeat this joke in Nuremberg many times. He evidently thought that this lady was one of the kind of women most commonly

[119] "A schlemiel is a man who does not smoke."

found in Nice. I could not help drawing his attention to how inappropriate his comments were, and the lady reinforced the lesson by asking if "this gentleman" belonged to us, adding that his manners were not indicative of it.

Our consul sought to improve the uncomfortable situation that he had got himself into in his own way. He apologised and requested that he be permitted to buy a few bottles of champagne to atone for his sin. We laughed and accepted the offered champagne.

In fact, several funny episodes happened, and I will recount some which I still remember.

One day, I came across the factory owner from Nuremberg, whom I had met in the dining car on the train to Nice and whose pretty and elegant wife I mentioned, in the *Jetée*. Despite his great wealth, my fellow countryman was known as a penny-pincher. He was also henpecked by his wife, who - in this regard at least, driven by her own thriftiness - completely agreed with her husband. The only items they would spend their money on in abundance were those that would add glamour and status to one's outer appearance, i.e. hers, such as jewellery and fine clothes. The wife wanted to play roulette, cheaply, with a bet of only 5 francs. The husband grumbled, saying it was a waste of money, and it almost came to a row between the two. I sought to improve the situation and asked the wife to place a bet for me, seeing that it was just about the thrill of the game, and handed her 50 francs. She hurried joyfully to the gaming table and returned, after a little while, beaming. My money had brought her luck, she claimed, she had won over 100 francs.

It goes without saying that I expected her at the very least to give me back the 50 francs I had handed her to placate her gambling obsession. I was obviously going to be magnanimous and let her keep the winnings. Yet the "lady" did not even consider it worth going into the details of the circumstances that had enabled her good fortune. She kept my money and the winnings. Typical for the women at the *Cercle*.

Another time an acquaintance invited me on an excursion by car to a very pretty resort not far from Nice. We were going to have lunch there. The lady who had been so informally insulted by the Consul as I mentioned earlier was also one of the party. It was a really lovely and entertaining excursion, but it was to come with a big bill. I had settled the rather large bill at the elegant restaurant, and the cost for the car. We had agreed that all participants would share these costs equally; it was a sum of at least 100 francs. Only one single gentleman offered to pay for his part; the others remained significantly quiet. Evidently I could not claim the sums I was entitled to as forcefully as a bailiff. Yet I learned my lesson from this incident and emphatically rejected any further attempts to have me be cashier general for such extra pleasures. Nonetheless, I thought it was extraordinary how quickly a German gentleman could change under the influence of the Niçois surroundings.

Apart from the fact that we lived next door to each other at the hotel and ate together at the same table, I obviously spent a lot of time with Herr Haas, who had so faithfully and safely brought me to Nice in the first place. Herr Haas had a large circle of acquaintances with whom he had been spending his time in Nice for years. He had many interesting stories to tell about the

Fig. 61 Promenade and Palais de la Jetée, Nice, ca. 1880.

individual people. One day an old man joined us on the promenade, whom Haas greeted warmly. We were introduced, and I had the sense that I had met the friendly-looking man before. That was indeed the case: Herr David Mayer, a banker from London, previously Paris, was friendly with the Bierer family in Fürth, which was how the *Gebrüder Bing* company had come into business with his establishment. He had granted our company a small credit, which he increased significantly after we paid back this loan quickly, despite all the adverse conditions, when the Franco-Prussian war broke out in 1870. I have described this event in great detail in my first book *Tales From A Merchant's Life*. Herr Mayer remembered the episode well and also knew how much our business had grown in the meantime and how the times of such exotic lending deals were over. He made a few very flattering comments about it to me. I was able to truthfully reply to this modest man that the credit he so faithfully granted my company in its early stages had been more significant than he appreciated, and that I would therefore be eternally grateful to him.

We met several more times, and I was very pleased when I was able to render him a small service just before our departure from Nice. A year later, the lonely man - he never married - died in London.

Herr Haas and I also took a trip to Monte Carlo and visited the casinos. The images were the same as in the *Cercle* in Nice, only more so, increased by the splendour of the multiple gaming halls, the size of the bets waged and by the altogether international character of the players. Apart from the professional con artists, glamorous members of the aristocracy and high finance were also represented. In contrast to the show in Monte Carlo, the *Cercle* in Nice seemed almost middle-class.

By now the weather had turned dull and cold, which made spending time outside uncomfortable. Herr Haas had already warned me that even in Nice there was no such thing as eternal sunshine; nevertheless I was still surprised by the sudden change in the tableau: grey sea, grey skies, cold rain and glum people in winter clothes on the promenades. The flowerbeds were covered with blankets to protect them from the frost, the rooms were cold and uncomfortable; in short, I thought longingly about the warming fires of my northern home, and also how in a few weeks the German spring would be in no way inferior to his southern brother. I was tired of Nice and wanted either to go home or, if possible, see a bit more of Italy in the company of a good friend.

I knew exactly where I wanted to go, but where to find a companion who would join me with zeal and understanding?

Then something unexpected happened: when I told the consul from Nuremberg about my plans, he was very enthusiastic and immediately proposed himself as my loyal companion. He pointed out, not in jest, that if we were to be robbed or even captured by robbers, the state he so expertly represented as a diplomat would deploy all instruments of power to come to our rescue. Given that the forthcoming journey would take us near Abruzzo, I thought the argument quite valid. Furthermore, I was of the opinion that my fellow Nuremberger countryman's well-known peculiarities could not pose a considerable risk to my itinerary. After all, I could and would not undertake a purely educational trip but wanted to get a general impression and over-view of the things a tourist on a flying visit to Genoa, Florence, Rome and finally Naples would see. I had prepared myself well for the most important sights by reading the best specialist books on the subject, and in any case one also has one's Baedeker to hand. The union between the consul and me was formed, and we were to depart as early as the next day.

Several members from our Nuremberg acquaintances had come to the station to see us off, and a few jokes - some good, some bad - were made about our travel alliance, which they thought would not survive the duration of our several week-long trip. Those pessimists were wrong. As soon as we were on our way to Genoa, I described to my companion in fine detail what I was expecting from our joint tour. He agreed to everything whole-heartedly.

By then, the sky had cleared, and we were enjoying the wonderful views of the sea and the beautiful countryside. After all, on my way to Nice I had travelled through the largest and most beautiful part of the Riviera at night-time, and now I could see and hang on to this wonder-world to the fullest.

Wonderful Genoa, where we were going to spend a few days, was coming into view. I can keep the description of our visit there short. The sights the city has to offer, and that is mainly the *Camposanto*[120], have already been extensively and accurately described in hundreds of travel guides. How the landscape, the city and the sea come together to form a harmonious, singularly beautiful picture can hardly be described, it can only be experienced with the soul. We departed Genoa only reluctantly; moreover, my companion had considered our excellent hotel there as *standesgemäss*[121]. Since we were on the subject, we had a long discussion about the term *standesgemäss*: The consul insinuated that his title was superior to mine of a Kommerzienrat. I did not accept that. I explained that in case of some diplomatic or personal matter, his title of Consul could be withdrawn quite quickly and unceremoniously. A Royal Bavarian Kommerzienrat would only run that risk if he were to steal the silver crockery and would be stupid enough to get caught red-handed. He had to admit that I was right. Furthermore, in hotels Herr Consul knew how to act like a worldly-wise gentleman. Even in Genoa I had noticed that he generously rewarded the attendants with their customary tips, a fact which reassured me in an area which is of

[120] Cemetery in Genoa, Camposanto monumentale di Staglieno.
[121] Lit: befitting his social status

great importance when travelling, and which made my companion more personable.

We made the best use of our two days in Genoa, and then we went off to Florence. I was looking forward to this famous city of the Medici with great expectations, a city whose infinite art treasures are a world of their own, and one that no immortal being is ever likely to embrace in its entirety. And I could not spend more than four or five days in Florence, which is not even enough time to pay a fleeting visit to the masterpieces in the Uffizi and Pitti Galleries alone.

I decided to part company with Haas in Florence and to visit the city's abundant art collections with a good guide instead. I was sure that a programme could be compiled for Herr Consul, which would be more to his taste than visiting museums.

When we arrived at the hotel, I was able to immediately satisfy myself that my companion knew how to look after himself. The hotel was busy and had only two rooms left. One was a dungeon, with a window into a dark, narrow alley, the other one roomy, well furnished overlooking a large square with the incredibly magnificent Cathedral and the tall bell tower in the background. Without a word the Consul seized the incomparably better room and left me with the dark chamber. Did a consul rank higher than a Royal Kommerzienrat after all? I hid my annoyance about his inconsideration, or rather his insolence; yet it did reinforce my plan to use the days in Florence as I thought fit. My companion could go and see how he got on by himself; after all, he had his elegant room! I briefly explained to him that I thought it best if we made our own arrangements for Florence as we pleased, since our interests in art and other things were too disparate, while we could join up again later on for an overview of Florence and its surroundings.

Without much further ado I told him that on the first day I was only going to visit the Pitti and Uffizi Galleries and that I would not come back to the hotel until the evening. By voluntarily paying a little extra, I had secured myself a really well-informed guide, and I left the astonished consul standing.

Having seen some pictures and having read expert literature, I was already familiar with most of the masterpieces I saw that day. Yet how different an experience it is to see the originals of such immortal creations, such as the ones by Titian, Botticelli and so many other masters whose art remains unparalleled to this day.

My knowledgeable guide also understood how to prevent me from becoming fatigued, and so my visit to the galleries turned into an unrivalled feast day which I will never forget. Just when we, i.e. the guide and I, were standing before one of Titian's paintings which can be regarded as the epitome of female beauty, Herr Consul suddenly appeared. He said he could no longer bear the loneliness and that he, too, wanted to do more in Florence than just eat and drink, and that he wanted to look at the famous paintings, too. He had come to the right place! He was enraptured by Titian's *Venus of Urbino*, for which I think the Duchess of Urbino sat - or rather lay - as a model, but it was not clear whether the rapture was directed at the artist or at the woman's bare private parts. He would have liked to see more of such paintings, but it was late, and so we went to dinner together at a renowned beer bar where they had real *Münchner* on tap.

Strange though it seems, Germans abroad tend to prefer visiting bars which are supplied by German breweries, even if they drink little or no beer at home. I could not deny myself this pleasure either, regardless of whether I was in Paris, Brussels, Venice etc. The reason behind this may well be a certain pride in our national drink, and also the feeling of homeliness which has us hoping to find a *Münchener Hofbräuhaus* in every bar abroad.

Well, in that respect, Florence was a disappointment! The guests were sitting unsmilingly over their *schoppen*[122] of *Münchner Spaten*, and the majority of the guests were drinking a good light Italian table wine, which was cheaper than the beer.

The next day Herr Consul wanted to join me to, as he put it, get a healthy dose of art. He had been taken by Titian's *Venus* in the Uffizi Gallery. I did tell him that while it was true that the Palazzo Pitti held some of Titian's grandest works, I could not guarantee that he would see another little or even un-clothed *Venus*. He was not to be put off, however; he wanted to come with me and see and admire the same things as me, despite the fact that he did not know much about art. One had to have something to tell back home, he said, and I did not mind: in for a penny, in for a pound.

The next morning after breakfast we went to an evidently well-run barber shop near the hotel. Upon entering the shop, my travelling companion belied his claim in Nice (at an occasion that he does not care to remember) that from the famous saying "Wine, Women and Song", he had only given up the song part. Without a care for anyone present, he burst into a famous aria

[122] Schoppen: about half a pint.

from the *Barber of Seville*, and in Italian, too. At first astonished faces all around, then half a dozen of Figaro's followers joined in the song with understanding and cheer. The incident was very funny, and I took great pleasure in it, too.

Then our loyal guide arrived, and we resumed our walking tour of the galleries, the cathedral, the crypt where the princes of the House of Medici have been laid to rest as well as the Battistero di San Giovanni. With the latter, the bronze doors in particular are regarded as an unequalled piece of art, and Michelangelo is alleged to have said that he imagined doors like these at the gates of heaven.

The amount of what we saw that day might be regarded as an insurmountable task, and yet there remained so many things of importance and grandeur to see and admire. We only paid a fleeting visit to some of the unique Renaissance buildings dotted all over Florence. I realised that I could not cope with the excess of epic impressions exerted by Florence, and that my capacity to absorb was being confused and limited by the sheer boundlessness of sights. Moreover, we had already spent more time in Genoa and Florence than we had originally planned, and so we decided to dedicate our fourth day in Florence to visiting natural beauties. The best view over the city and the surrounding countryside can be had from the famous terrace, which - either the area or the terrace itself - is called "Fiesole". The view from a respectable height over the city with its many towers and large monumental buildings, is an awesome sight, made even more impressive by the scenic hillsides and the great silver river winding through the sunlit valley. The effect of this total image will remain unforgettable to the viewer. And yet I have to say that the view from the castle down over our dear old Nuremberg with its medieval towers and city walls, over the wide plains with the dark forests in the background, bordered by the blue mountains of the Franconian Jura, is no less impressive.

Afterwards we took a speedy cab and went on a daytrip to the various sights in the vicinity of Florence, accompanied by our guide whose precise knowledge of everything necessary for his profession came in very useful, and who knew how to combine modesty with gentlemanly ways. We sent "sweet greetings" with a basket of exquisite fruit back home and readied ourselves for the journey to Rome.

I did not want to leave Florence, partly because our German-owned hotel was very comfortable. The journey to Rome is not very interesting from a scenic point of view, and so it offered us the time to talk about the passing landscape or to study the guidebook in reference to what lay behind us and in front of us, whichever we fancied.

At a station in I cannot remember where, a chance meeting with the daughter of a Nuremberg lawyer I knew (Justizrat Hahn) offered a welcome distraction. She was on honeymoon with her husband from Berlin. The very pretty girl had become a very beautiful woman who did not have to shy away from a comparison with the Italian Signorinas. Greetings from home!

When we had only a few hours' journey ahead of us, I was gripped by a certain impatience. I was excited to see what would indicate our arrival in the vicinity of the eternal city first - the Roman *Campagna*, the Tiber, the Alban Hills or the dome of St. Peter's. Alas, in the end it was none of these. Black clouds were gathering on the horizon and it started to rain, but not in the usual sense of the word. In fact, the commonly used phrase, "the Heavens opened", was very apt, and we pulled into the station in Rome during a torrential downpour.

From Florence, we had telegraphed the *Grand Hotel* to reserve rooms, and we had sent the name of this hotel home as our postal address for Rome. We were very disappointed when the driver from the *Grand Hotel* told us at the station that his hotel was full and that they had, in order to help us, reserved two pretty rooms for us in the *Continental Hotel*, another first-class hotel, opposite the station. It was a kind service, which despite my disappointment I appreciated very much, and given the endlessly pouring rain it seemed advantageous to find lodgings so quickly and in such close proximity.

However, Herr Consul was of a different opinion. He said he knew of a second hotel that would be worthy of having us as guests, namely the *Quirinal*, as he had been told by a reliable source.

I remonstrated that the *Continental* was a first-class hotel, we should give it a try for one night and if necessary have a look around for something else tomorrow, when the weather might be better. My remarks fell on deaf ears. The Herr Consul insisted we drive to the *Quirinal*, in spite of the lashing rain and in spite of the driver's repeated reassurance that the recommended hotel really was top-class. I had to acquiesce.

When we arrived at the *Quirinal* dripping wet, the reception area was bustling with an elegant crowd, and the director faced us rather coolly, as if to say that our presence was not required. The consul told him our names and titles and began to explain how we had in fact reserved rooms at the *Grand Hotel* only to be told upon our arrival at the station that it was full. This piece of cunning spurred the director on to return an even more effective one; he said that he did not wish his hotel to be used as a stopgap. He explained that he only had one very large, elegant room with an adjoining alcove available, and that all the other rooms were taken. We could have these rooms for a minimum stay of five days at fifty francs per day.

My diplomat friend made a long face. He pulled me to the side and said that we should head straight back to the *Continental*, the hotel previously so vehemently rejected by him. He complained that 25 francs per night for each of us was sheer insolence. I declared firmly that I was going to stay where I was, adding that he had got us into this situation, and now he had to stay and face the music. He had nothing to say to that.

The maître d' took us up three flights of stairs to the rooms which the director had described quite accurately. A very large, elegant room and a small alcove with a bed in each. The consul started immediately to settle in the lounge-like large room, praised the furnishings and evidently did not even consider the fact that I might have the same right to claim the lounge for myself. I looked at him sharply, and he seemed to get the hint that this time I would not take it as quietly as I did in Florence if he chose to live better and more elegantly than me at my expense. He therefore asked me what we should do about the rooms. I replied that a compromise was the only option, and that in this critical case we had to toss a coin. A ten-franc coin, heads or tails was to decide: heads the alcove, tails the large room. Alas, Lady Luck was not on my side, I had to retire to the alcove.

So there we were in the Eternal City! I rose early and looked out of my window. I wanted to see a bit of Rome. I saw a very wide road leading from the station to the city centre, quite uncharacteristic, fairly busy, a cab stand near the hotel. The cab drivers were wearing round hats made of oilcloth; in short, a picture I could have seen in any larger city. Nothing pointed to the fact that I had spent the night in Rome, yet one incident sparked my curiosity:

Opposite the hotel there stood a large, four-storied building, and on a balcony on the fourth floor, in the bright morning sun, a young couple were holding hands and blissfully looking up to the sky, seemingly indifferent to the rest of the world, high above mankind. Who were the happy couple, I wondered?

After breakfast the question arose of how to spend the day? The best option is always, at least for the kind of tourist we were, to take a guide, of which there are always a number mulling about in the hotel. The receptionist will usually recommend a man who is an expert in his field, particularly if he sees the prospect of a nice reward as was the case with us. Rome was no exception. We hired a cab in order to familiarise ourselves with the main sights on the outskirts of Rome. Above all, my consul friend wanted to see the Pope. That was essential in Rome, he said. I did not bother to reply; I left it to our guide. He explained that "seeing the Pope" was not so easy. It was necessary to obtain a letter of recommendation from the German embassy which might possibly enable one to attend one of those mass audiences which were held at the Vatican at certain intervals. In his opinion, the guide added, the main attraction that pulled the educated classes from all over the world to Rome were the signs that indicated Rome's great past or the immense art treasures displayed in the collections, whereas the possibility of seeing the Pope was just of minor importance.

I was very pleased about these appropriate comments, and they made me realise that we had the right cicerone for our visit to Rome.

We went to the Forum Romanum. With its gigantic ruins, its individual columns and broken temples, this world of destruction and decay gives evidence on a grand scale of a lost world which celebrated a culture of god worship and of commemorating its worthy leaders and remarkable citizens. These ruins have puzzled many an archaeologist. My fellow countryman did not know what to make of this field of rubble and seemed to hold the view that the municipal authority would be wise to clean up the area and use it to enlarge and beautify the city, just as Emperor Napoleon III had improved and beautified Paris with the construction of new boulevards.

Our guide, who was still a little agitated about the previous Pope question, was about to answer, but I stopped him with a wave of my hand. He continued with his narration, described one formation of columns as the Temple of Saturn, another as the Arch of Septimius Severus, albeit accompanied by extensive, not entirely comprehensible explanations for which, it seemed to me, a guidebook would have been the better option.

The consul made a long, impatient face and turned away from the classical ruins almost indignantly. I felt that it was required to prop up his confidence in the many eternally beautiful sights Rome has to offer and to let rise before his senses an image of overwhelming greatness. So off we went to St. Peter's Church!

The square in front of the largest basilica in the world - I am not sure if St. Peter's, in its totality, is not in fact the largest building in the world - is vast, and the image is reinforced by the magnificent, crescent-shaped colonnades leading up to the church. In the centre of this place full of ornate flowerbeds stands a massive obelisk in a straight line with the main entrance to St. Peter's, which, with its cupola towering over everything, is regarded as the main landmark of the Rome of today.

I was less impressed by the front of the cathedral. Then we stood inside the largest, and greatest, shrine of the Catholic world, speechless and awestruck by what lay before our eyes. The enormous, magically lit room seemed like a revelation from a different world. One is seized by a feeling of peace and harmony, and one understands what is meant by the only redeeming Church. We moved on. In a hushed voice our guide explained the marvels produced by immortal artists for the adornment of

Fig. 62 St. Peter's Square, Rome, 1909.

the cathedral. I was only listening with half an ear, since the whole picture of this noble temple had such an immense effect on me that I found the comments only distracting.

My fellow countryman had also fallen silent; proof that he was not unmoved by the greatness and the sublime all around us. This spoke to him differently than the ruins of the Forum Romanum.

At last we stepped outside again, into the blinding light, but we had had enough for the first day of our visit. We yearned for fresh air, green meadows and shady trees. Our guide appreciated that, too, and took us to the Pincio Gardens. They are the green vein of life in the elegant, Roman world; there are beautiful gardens, teeming with locals and tourists, and elegant cabs complete the metropolitan picture. This, in my opinion however, lags far behind that of the Corso of the Prater in Vienna or the area of the *Tiergarten* in Berlin. But that is just by the by. Looking out from the terrace, with its sweeping view of the dome of St. Peter's and over the city, we take in the Eternal City of Rome, with all the evidence of its unrivalled thousand year-old history. It is a great task that Rome sets for those who come to visit, and who come not just as globetrotters, but to sink themselves into a cultural epoch which came thousands of years before ours. By contrast, how quickly one has seen the sights of Vienna, which after all can boast a memorable past itself. A few days of seeing the historical and other sights, and one is free to spend one's time at will in the midst of the magnificent countryside or amongst its pleasant residents.

The realisation that one can only grasp and understand so relatively little of the immense art treasures, of the invaluable surviving remainders of the old Rome, causes almost physical pain. The Vatican and its 13,000 rooms epitomises Rome. Who can visit all 13,000 rooms? Who is able to see all that Rome has to offer the art lover, the historian, the archaeologist, during a short stay of just a few days, let alone study it so well that it could be of any benefit? It takes a universal mind like Goethe, and a Goethe who, free of any professional obligations, educated in year-long study, supported by brilliant teachers such as Winkelmann etc. and surrounded by artists and art followers, can afford to spend a long time in Rome, nearly forgetting his cold, northern home in the arms of a Roman beauty.

We had already spent a few days here, and yet apart from a few strolls through the city where we visited the Pantheon, the Trevi Fountain and many other things, the only sights I had studied more closely, supported by our knowledgeable guide, were the Forum Romanum and St. Peter's.

What should we do during the remaining two days we had planned for Rome? Even our guide was unsure what programme to suggest, even more so since my companion was more interested in food and drink than in art or in that which had been preserved of Rome's past. He was perfectly happy when he could see the Castel Sant' Angelo, the Colosseum, Trajan's column etc. from the cab, and truth be told, he had a point. We did not have the time to study or learn about anything as much as the world surrounding us required, and so there was nothing else to do but arrange with our guide what we were going to see during the remaining two days. We agreed that we were going to visit the

Vatican Museums including the library and the Villa Borghese with its art collections. Furthermore, in passing we were going to stop at St. Peter's again for a quick visit, and take a cab for an afternoon's tour along the Via Appia.

I can easily omit a detailed description of what happened during those two days. Herr Consul enjoyed in particular the excursion with a good, Roman vehicle, out into the *campagna.* He felt at home there, and the ruins on both sides of the road, the most impressive indicators of Rome's former greatness, well, in his bourgeois conception of order he would have preferred to see them cleared away!

He was not even impressed by the collections in the Vatican; he found the pictures too holy, the sculptures too incomprehensible. Something reminded me of a shop in Florence selling very pretty marble items for 50 marks and more including packaging. Oh holy simplicity! I wanted to have some fun, and so I told my companion, before we arrived at the Vatican, that amongst all the collections I was mainly interested in a funerary monument which a Roman artist had created for a friend of mine, who had died a tragic death along with his two sons. This friend, I said, who was originally from Greece but had owned a large business in Rome and was as such engaged in an active business relationship with my company, was called Laocoön. He often came to see us in Nuremberg, I added. One Summer's evening he was swimming in the Tiber with his two sons when an extraordinarily large snake, which had accidentally swum up the river, wrapped itself around him and his sons so tightly that neither he or they were able to extract themselves from the deadly embrace. The Roman artist, I claimed, had captured the moment of their terrifying

Fig. 63 The Laocoön Group.

death and the expression of their faces so skilfully that this artistic masterpiece was now on display in the Vatican.

When we stood in front of the statue of *Laocoön and His Sons*[123], Herr Consul did not like it; he said it was inappropriate for a cemetery. I replied that his judgement stood in stark contrast with the poet and art historian Lessing's opinion, yet he was just as unfamiliar with this Herr Lessing[124] as he was with my business friend Laocoön!

Anyway, the main thing is that one is happy within oneself. My fellow countryman took his lack of understanding of what is holy and sublime to thousands of people with such contentment and so little discomfort that I, in the embarrassed sense of inadequacy with which I faced art, almost envied him. Nonetheless, I still

---

123 A marble sculpture depicting the Trojan priest Laocoön and his sons being strangled by sea serpents.

124 Gotthold E. Lessing (1729 –1781); German writer, philosopher, dramatist, publicist and one of the most outstanding representatives of the Enlightenment era. Also famous for his friendship with the German-Jewish philosopher Moses Mendelssohn.

had Goethe's *Italian Journey*[125], and, combined with what I had gleaned from this book, I was able to get a deeper understanding of the beauty and significance of what I had seen, even if only fleetingly or superficially.

Our days in Rome were coming to an end, and we were about to depart for Naples. Before we left Rome, however, Herr Consul and I paid a visit to a large shop, the owner of which I knew well. Every year he came to Nuremberg and made significant purchases with our company. We wanted to buy small gifts as souvenirs of our trip for our loved ones at home, i.e. Roman or Italian arts and crafts or products of the local industry; however, of the latter there was nothing original or suitable available in the otherwise very well-stocked shop. In addition to the familiar Italian glass wares and majolica[126] we were offered German, French, English and even American goods, and in the end it was a rather large box that we sent to Nuremberg after all. Yet it cannot have contained many characteristic items since I do not remember ever seeing my daughters with any of them. Only my two boys took pleasure in their cheap American pocket watches, though not for long. The "Americans" failed, and no German watchmaker of character wanted to try and repair this "rubbish".

Our journey to Naples had nothing noteworthy to offer: an area of little scenic interest, its population often plagued by malaria. Only the Royal Palace of Caserta, a very impressive edifice, attracted the passing traveller's eye. Moreover, it started to rain heavily, and just like in Rome we were to expect a wet and uncomfortable reception in Naples. Nonetheless I was full of ex-

[125] Goethe's report on his travels to Italy.
[126] Italian glazed earthenware.

pectations and exaltations! What magic lies in the word "Naples"! I was prepared to see innumerable immensely beautiful and interesting things in the following days, yet all that took second place to my anticipation of seeing a world lost over 1900 years ago and now largely brought back to light. Pompeii! How delighted I was when back home a prehistoric burial mound was opened and I was able to take part in the work. What joy we felt when a fibula, an armlet or even a Celt (a bronze weapon) was found. Now, however, the goal was to communicate with the cab driver who was to take us to the hotel where we had reserved rooms. It probably would have sufficed to say "Grand Hotel", but in order to reinforce the effect Herr Consul emphasised it as "Grande Hotelo", while I maintained that it was not even Italian. In order to avoid complicating the communication further, we left our luggage at the station.

With the rain lashing down we drove through narrow, poorly lit streets which seemed to be paved with shining black marble. I explained this phenomenon to my friend: the roads were in fact paved with lava, and since the nearby "Vesuvius company" provided more than sufficient supply, it made perfect sense that it was put to good use.

When we came out of the warren of narrow streets we saw a wide promenade along the seafront, somewhat brighter, and lined on one side with respectable buildings, mostly hotels as it seemed. Before we reached our destination, however, we were to have a little fright. Out of the darkness, a badly dressed individual inspiring little confidence suddenly jumped into our cab, sat down on the front seat and gesticulated madly towards us. We tried to make the cab driver remove the unwelcomed guest from the carriage, but he did not or would not understand us, and the whole incident would have been very frightening indeed had the vicinity of the hotels and relatively bright street lights not revealed that the attack had a harmless explanation. And so it did! Just before we arrived at the hotel, the bandit, as the terrified consul called him, jumped out of the cab. The concierge had a natural explanation for our unwelcome and frightening surprise: it was the Naples way of pointing out sights, mainly attractions such as entertainment bars etc. to newly arrived strangers, who were assumed to speak Italian. It was merely harmless intrusiveness, which is why the cab driver had not intervened. Other places, other manners.

The very hospitable hotel - its owner was German - seemed well run and was busy with many international guests. We joined the evening table d'hôte, and I was not a little surprised to see that the consul was not content with just a ribbon in the button hole, as he had been so far on our journey, but that he appeared in black tie radiating with the pomp of his three medals. It was obvious that it was causing quite a stir, while I cursed his bad taste and voiced my indignation. He remained quite cool, however, and said that this was the only way to maintain social status in Southern Italy, and he could not care less what others made of it. I asked him what his intentions were for such a masquerade other than inflating our hotel bill. He replied that could not be of importance, and after all we were sharing the bill. I had nothing to retort to that logic!

Early the next morning we arranged for a capable guide. This useful and not uncommonly well-educated kind of hired servant can regularly be found in the large hotels and is associated with the concierge, who will take a certain percentage of commission from the earnings. In accordance with my discussions with the concierge regarding what I was expecting from a guide, adding that I did not mind spending 10 francs extra, we were introduced to a trustworthy and not unintelligent man. He reminded me of my cicerone Häring in Venice, not only because they shared the same nationality and confession. I told him straight away that we did not care to see everything that the Baedeker considered worth seeing; we did not have the time for that anyway. Our stay was just long enough to visit the *Museo Nationale* and the site where all these wonderful, abundant treasures of the vast collection were found. And the aquarium. We would only be able to exchange calling cards with Mount Vesuvius, the island of Capri, the churches and all the other things a tourist would normally go to admire in Naples. We would return at a later date and spend weeks in Naples to study the city's art treasures, its magnificent surroundings and its particular national life that distinguish it as so unique. I do not think that our clever guide believed me, but he completely understood and quickly gleaned that this curtailment of the programme he had had in view did not entail a curtailment of his fee.

I must add here that the rooms we had been given at the hotel had a magnificent view of the sea with the distant island of Capri, of the smoking Mount Vesuvius and of the picturesque city of Naples; a picture that needed no explanation from our guide.

We started by visiting the *Museo Nationale.* I could have spent days there. This was the spirit which I comprehended, to which I felt so near[127]. Treasures from a distant time, from the buried ruins of an art-loving city, with its temples dedicated to the gods and its magnificent buildings, lifted from the site which was discovered and revealed only recently.

Pompeii! The sheer number of things to see! I will not even attempt to explain the individual items which could fill all the museums of the world while still leaving enough to excite and satisfy archaeologists and art lovers alike. There is just one treasure, singled out by the guide, which I will mention: a centre-piece, found completely intact, consisting of three tiered glass bowls. These bowls had been engraved in wonderful detail and with unparalleled skill with hundreds of scenes and figures, all depicting the twelve tasks of Hercules. I am unable to describe the art and the technique used to create this object, all I can say is that the Kensington Museum in London offered the Italian government the sum of 20 million francs to buy it. If Italy were to sell off her art treasures, this essentially poor country would rise to become one of the world's richest.

After more than six hours in the museum, I was still reluctant to leave it. My travelling companion had tired of it, but I have to admit that he found great pleasure in many objects which testified how elegantly Pompeii's citizens had furnished and decorated their homes. He was particularly surprised by the well preserved, richly decorated iron money chests, which could be seen as evidence for the fact that the merchant class can look back over a long history going back many thousands of years and is likely to

[127] Expression loosely based on a sentence from Goethe's *Faust*.

have done more for civilisation and culture than the robber barons who are ancestors to most of our aristocratic families today.

We had a delicious lunch in a not very large but beautifully situated dining hall on the seafront, which was something between a simple restaurant and an *osteria.* We asked for coffee to be served on the terrace, where the guide and I out-smoked even Mount Vesuvius! Herr Consul could not share in our comfortable pleasure, and I remembered the poignant remark made by the waiter in Nice: "Un schlemiel, c'est un homme qui ne fume pas."

Opposite us lay Capri like an "Island of the Blessed"; longingly I looked over to it. Yet the path of duty pointed to Nuremberg; the magic of Italy had already kept me away from the business tasks awaiting me there for too long. A few more days, and we had to commence our homeward journey.

We discussed with our guide what we might visit in the short space of time available. We had agreed to see Pompeii on the last day before our departure. Our guide commented that it was regrettable if the only other thing we were going to visit was the aquarium, while Naples still had so many other sights to offer. At most we would be able visit the higher parts of the city from where one had an unmatched view of Naples and its surroundings near and far. Given that we already had a very similar view from our hotel room windows on the fourth floor, I preferred to see more of the street life of the big city, especially where the famous *Lazzaroni*[128] lived. Our guide was opposed to such a plan; he said it was an area we could not visit, even if guided by him, without running the risk of experiencing disagreeable incidents.

---

128 Generic term referring to the members of the lower class of Naples.

The tourists were partly to blame themselves, he added; they wandered through the streets teeming with poverty, dirt and vice with an intrusive curiosity that provoked the already volatile population, all of which had already led to a number of rather unpleasant and embarrassing scenes. Even if one was careful and tactful, one would still be harassed beyond all measure by beggars. If one did not give them anything, one might be physically abused; if one did, one would fall victim to the vermin prowling about the streets. Either way, no-one worthy would benefit.

On the trip to Pompeii, for which he recommended we use a hotel cab, he said we could safely take a route that would take us through some of the narrow, dirty streets where the poorest parts of the population lived. Even then, he advised us not to look much to the left or to the right, since the mob would hurl abusive language as well as dirt and filth at the cab.

Our guide made this statement so convincingly that we kept away from the areas in question which were linked to the "darkest part" of Naples.

Our visit to the aquarium was worth our while. I had imagined the institute, for whose restoration and upkeep the German Reich was providing significant sums, to be much bigger, but what there is to see, explained by experts - usually young German scientists - is indescribably interesting and engaging. It filled us with pride that even here, in a faraway land, German scientists have been given such ambitious goals, and I could not refrain from sharing this with our erudite guide. He seemed quite touched by my comments and gladly accepted my heartfelt invitation to join us for dinner in an elegant restaurant near the Galleria Umberto[129]. Our meeting was very enjoyable, not only because of the exquisite meal, complemented by a fiery, noble local wine, but also because of the extremely interesting information he shared with us about his scientific assignment, about the land and its people, and about the history of Pompeii, which we were going to visit the next day. It was not until late at night that we parted from our amiable compatriot, who was so full of hope for the future.

Fig. 64 Spaghetti drying in Naples, ca. 1900.

Very early the next morning, in bright sunshine, a swift horse and carriage took us out of the city boundaries of Naples; the azure blue sea on our side, and Mt. Vesuvius covered in gloomy clouds of smoke in front of us. We passed through a number of picturesquely situated but squalid-looking little towns. I thought it was strange to see ropes strung across the width of the streets on which spaghetti, the national dish, were hung up to dry despite the dust from the roads and the swarms of flies, just as it is commonly done with laundry. Italians probably do not think twice about it, but it would be a while before I would partake of spaghetti again!

129 Main shopping street in Naples.

We also came through Herculaneum, which in ancient times had suffered a similar fate to that of Pompeii. Here, however, it is impossible to carry out systematic excavations such as the ones in Pompeii because a new, sizeable town has risen on the site of the ruined Herculaneum in the meantime.

At last we were approaching Pompeii. My eyes were used to finding prehistoric burial mounds in woods and meadows, since I often do it at home. To our guides' great surprise, and even more so of Herr Consul's, I announced that a long, 12 to 15 metre high hill rising from the plain indicated those parts of Pompeii that had yet to be unearthed. That was indeed the case. At last we stood on the ground, shuddering with the thought that once there had been a flourishing, heavily populated city here, brought to a gruesome end by the dark, mysterious, subterranean forces of nature.

We stepped through an excavated gateway, which had had a roof added to its top floor, and entered the "dead city". Nonetheless, our wistful and anxious mood did not last long, since a colourful, international crowd of people, noisy and wildly gesticulating men and women with bad taste brandishing red Baedekers seemed almost funny, and certainly incredibly contradictory to the tragedy of these ruins.

It would be pointless to even try to describe what a guide will show and highlight as particularly noteworthy to a stranger on a fleeting visit to this only partly excavated city. The forum, the relatively large baths for a city of around 30,000 inhabitants, some individual elegant houses which still contain the original furnishings as they were discovered, and at last, for a little tip, a house recognisable from the outside as once having been in the service of *Venus vulgaris.*

In Italy, "tipping" is a very important factor, equally effective as the baksheesh is in the Orient, and by promising a large reward I wanted the guide (not just a tourist guide, but one employed in Pompeii by the government) to take me to one of the many excavations which are being carried out on a daily basis. He was agreeable to my offer, but he pointed out that it had to be done quite inconspicuously, in other words I had to pretend that the works did not interest me. He added that it was strictly forbidden to take tourists to the excavation sites, but that he had a good friend who would risk it.

Soon I was taken to a place where more than 20 people were busy digging up the earth alongside a house already laid free. They were carefully inspecting the rubble before it was being taken away by little donkey carts. Apart from a few broken fragments, which were carefully secured, nothing was found.

A little disappointed, I thought about the wasted 10 francs and said to myself that my excavations at the Brunnstein cave were certainly no less interesting.

After that, as agreed, I went to find my companion the consul and our Naples tour guide in a tavern where we were to have refreshments. The simple dining room was crowded with tourists, and to cap it all, male and female mandolin players were showing off their musical talents. Thankfully, there was no space for the tarantella dancer, an old, jaded wench, to unfurl her charms. In Italy, at every occasion, everyone and their mother wants to make money and exploit the tourists, with the result that it often spoils the atmosphere, be it on a visit to a *campo santo*, on a gondola in Venice or on the island of Capri. This may also be true for other countries, but surely nowhere is it so obtrusive and undignified as in Italy. What's more, the prices charged in shops where tourists might want to buy something are exorbitant. Naples is the main market for coral jewellery. We wanted to buy a few items, and the concierge recommended a shop which he said was fair and fit. Carefully he added that there were shops selling at much lower prices, but they were usually selling fake goods. Trustingly we visited the recommended business. I was surprised at the high prices, but after the previous experiences I had become shrewd and I was not to be duped. They demanded 60 francs for a fairly pretty necklace of white coral. I offered a third and still paid 10 francs more than the thing was worth. And to top it all, they still give you fake or short change; such little tricks are customary and not considered reprehensible.

It would be presumptuous to claim that all Italian merchants were liberally taking advantage of their customers, but, as I have said before, I have never been cheated on my travels as much as I have in the country of "holy egotism".

After this digression I have nothing left to say about the beautiful city of Napoli. The consul and I had both had enough of our endless holiday, and we were missing our families, our work and the beautiful forests of Germany. In our minds we found the *Schmausenbuck*[130] more delectable than the pine groves or the grey-leafed olive trees in Naples. So we said goodbye!

---

130 A hill on the edge of Nuremberg.

I always find the departure from a large hotel rather embarrassing. I am happy to give everyone what they expect and do not fret about whether the recipient deserves their tip or not. But this pantomime of walking past a long row of claimants is repulsive, or at least very unpleasant. There was the director, the room service waiter, the maître d', the waiter, the day and the night concierge, the first and the second valet, the apprentice waiter, the liftboy, and last but not least the pretty chambermaid Zerline. That episode passed, too, and we arrived at the station over half an hour before the departure of our train. Our luggage had arrived much earlier but had not been checked in yet. The conductor explained that the clerk refused to deal with the luggage because it had arrived half an hour after the cut-off time. I noticed this was a trick, since other people were involved in this charade who had nothing to do with the matter. The stage direction was brilliant. First the cab driver from the hotel: he talked vehemently to the officer, who kept shaking his head. Then some kind of concierge arrived, who announced that the train was about to depart, at which point a porter started pointing to our suitcases still standing in the luggage room, all the while madly gesticulating. Since the story had to come to an end, I had the officer know that we wanted our luggage checked in and that we did not mind if we paid 10 francs for the officer's special effort. That worked! We received our luggage slip, which said that our bags weighed 150 pounds more than they actually did, and we therefore paid at least 40 francs more than would have been fair.

What's more, we later found out that we had been given 10 fake Lira. Yet how little did all that mean to us when, once inside our luxury compartment, we were back on German soil. German punctuality, not servile but reliable, seemed a more delightful possession than oranges and macaroni. We were as happy as children to be able to turn our backs on a spewing Mount Vesuvius and the dead Pompeii. We shouted "Eviva" when the stately train, which in its parts is a massive testimonial to German industry, pulled out of the station.

The journey home offered nothing of note. We left Naples at around 9 o'clock in the morning and went via Rome, Florence, Genoa, Milan and Innsbruck to arrive in Munich the next day at about 11 o'clock in the morning. Refreshed by a typical breakfast - veal sausages and *Hofbräu* beer - we celebrated our homecoming with a festive reception in the evening. Everyone was well and glad to be reunited.

The blue mountains of the Franconian Jura rose before my eyes, and I said to myself, the next trip is to Streitberg!

The reader of these pages must understand that the man behind them wrote this his third book not because he presumes himself to be a writer, but because he wished to create, in these anxious times, a few hours of distraction from the oppressive worries of this terrible war, now in its third year, by remembering the good times of the past.

Streitberg, May 1917

Ignaz Bing
Geheimer Kommerzienrat

Statt besonderer Anzeige.

Am Sonntag Abend ist im 79. Lebensjahr, doch zu früh für unsere Liebe und Verehrung, der

Geheime Kommerzienrat **Ignaz Bing**

Ehrenbürger der Stadt Grünhain i. S. und der Gemeinde Streitberg sanft entschlafen. Er blieb bis zum Ende ein ganzer Mann, starkgeistig und gütig.

Nürnberg, den 25. März 1918.

Im Namen der in tiefer Trauer Zurückgebliebenen:

Ida Bing, geb. Ottenstein.

Die Trauerfeier findet Mittwoch den 27. März vormittags 10 Uhr auf dem neuen israelitischen Friedhof vor der Überführung in das hiesige Krematorium statt.

Von Beileidsbesuchen und Blumenspenden wolle man Abstand nehmen.

166404

Resources

The following sources were used as references throughout the book, and they provide fascinating further reading on the history of the family of Ignaz Bing, Jews in Germany in general, and of course of the *Gebrüder Bing* company.

Websites

cjh.org
Centre for Jewish History

en.wikipedia.org/wiki/Abraham_Bing

hdbg.de/juedische-friedhoefe/index.php
List of Jewish cemeteries in Bavaria (in German)

jewishencyclopedia.com/articles/2677-bavaria
History of the Jews in Bavaria

jewishencyclopedia.com/articles/3308-bing-abraham

rijo.homepage.t-online.de/index_int.html, and in particular:

rijo.homepage.t-online.de/pdf/EN_NU_GA_hopstrade.pdf
About the hop trade in Nuremberg

rijo.homepage.t-online.de/pdf/EN_FU_JU_barbeck.pdf
History of the Jews in Nuremberg and Fürth

traditional-tin-toys.co.uk/tin_toy_manufacturers.shtml
Excellent information about *Gebrüder Bing* and other tin toy manufacturers

wikipedia.org

wikipedia.org/wiki/Bing_(company)

zinnfiguren-bleifiguren.com/
Extensive history and lots of pictures of factories etc. (in German)

Books:

Elon, Amos: *The Pity of it All: A Portrait of Jews in Germany* 1743-1933, (Penguin Books, 2002)

Highly recommended for detailed information on the life of Jews in 19th century Germany, including the influence of Heinrich Heine.

Articles:

Loewengart, Stefan: *From the History of my Family, The Bing Family of Nuremberg*, Kiriath Bialik 1980

Index

Most people and places are only listed where relevant, ie. usually where they are first introduced at the beginning of a story or episode.

www.ingramcontent.com/pod-product-compliance
Lightning Source LLC
La Vergne TN
LVHW010048170826
845678LV00012B/2086

9780956337016